01 - 096

W9-CHR-191

TAKING CARE of BUSINESS

The Dictionary of Contemporary Business Terms

Donald L. Caruth • Steven Austin Stovall

Printed on recyclable paper

NTC *Publishing Group*

Lincolnwood, Illinois USA

14.95

Library of Congress Cataloging-in-Publication Data
Caruth, Donald L.
    Taking care of business : the dictionary of contemporary business
terms / Donald L. Caruth, Steven Austin Stovall.
        p. cm. — (Artful Wordsmith series)
    Rev. ed. of: NTC's American business terms dictionary.
    ISBN 0-8442-0902-3 (pbk.)
    1. Business—Dictionaries. 2. United States—Commerce–
–Dictionaries. I. Stovall, Steven Austin. II. Caruth Donald L.
NTC's American business terms dictionary. III. Title. IV. Series.
HF1001.C33   1996
650'.03—dc20   96-26184
                                                  CIP

Manufactured in the United States of America.

6 7 8 9 0 VP 9 8 7 6 5 4 3 2 1

Introduction

The free enterprise system was nurtured, shaped, and developed in this country. In the process, the many fields of business developed unique words and expressions that now follow American business practices into the other nations of the world. Unfortunately, the special vocabularies of business are not always easy to understand, especially for those whose native tongue is not English.

This volume offers over 4,000 basic and essential words and phrases used in American business. The most common and useful vocabulary items have been selected from the following business disciplines or fields: accounting, banking, data processing, economics, finance, government, human resources management, international trade, industrial engineering, labor relations, law, management, management science, marketing, production, operations management, statistics, and transportation.

To make this dictionary more helpful, each entry contains an example, illustration, or clarifying note—whichever seems appropriate for the entry. The organization of the entries is quite simple and includes considerable cross-referencing. The definitions and explanatory material have been presented in language that is as simple as possible. Explanatory material and cross-referencing notes appear in parentheses immediately after the definition.

Words or expressions that are entries appear in **bold type** when they occur as entry heads and *slanted roman type* when they are cited elsewhere in their own entries or other entries in the dictionary. Words that are cited but are not entries appear in *italics*. The examples and illustrations appear in *italics*. An arrowhead (▶) appears before each example, illustration, or clarifying note.

The American business system is a fascinating field of study—and an increasingly important one in this age of globalization. This dictionary will make the basic vocabulary of business available to students and businesspeople around the world.

A

AAP See *Affirmative Action Plan.*

ABA See *American Bankers Association; American Bar Association.*

abatement the termination of a lawsuit for want of proper parties. ▶ *Since the plaintiff is now deceased, the case is in abatement.*

ABC method a method of classification and prioritization whereby items are sorted into three groups based on their importance, dollar value, or size, with A being the most important and C being the least important. ▶ *The ABC method is a widely used time management technique, with items labeled A receiving the highest priority.*

ability 1. the power or capacity to do or perform. ▶ *The shipping department has the ability to deliver merchandise within two days.* 2. the competence (to do something). ▶ *Larry has a special ability when it comes to understanding mechanical drawings.* 3. a talent. ▶ *Not everyone has the ability to play a musical instrument.*

above par at a premium or above face value. ▶ *The company's bonds are now selling at $2.00 above par.*

above the line pertaining to the customary balance sheet, revenue, or expense items as opposed to unusual items. (The opposite of *below the line.*) ▶ *All normal expenses for the period are shown above the line on the income statement.*

abrogate to cancel, void, annul, repeal, or abolish summarily. ▶ *Companies sometimes use bankruptcy to abrogate their labor agreements.*

absentee one who is not present. ▶ *Absentees may have their salary docked.*

absentee ownership a condition that exists when the owner of an income-producing property resides in a location geographically removed from that property, or when the owner of a business does not take an active role in the day-to-day management of that business. ▶ *Absentee ownership is common in retailing.*

absenteeism a condition that exists when workers fail to report to work at their scheduled time. ▶ *Absenteeism is usually higher on Fridays than it is on Thursdays.*

absenteeism rate the ratio of days lost due to worker absences to the total number of workdays available. ▶ *The company's absenteeism rate was higher this month than it was for the same month a year ago.*

absolute advantage the condition that exists when one producer can produce a given good more efficiently or at a lower cost than another producer. ▶ *This company has an absolute advantage over its competitors when it comes to manufacturing ball bearings.*

absolute sale a sale in which the buyer and seller reach agreement with no conditions or restrictions imposed by either. ▶ *It was an absolute sale and no changes in the agreement could be made.*

absorbed cost **1.** an added cost, such as freight, that has been expensed rather than passed on to the customer. ▶ *An absorbed cost is considered to be a cost of doing business.* **2.** an expenditure recognized as an operating cost, either at the time it is incurred or at some subsequent time, and transferred to a profit and loss account at the end of the period in which it is designated as an expense. ▶ *An absorbed cost appears as an operating expense in the profit and loss statement.*

absorption costing AND **full costing** the assignment of both fixed and variable costs to goods and services. ▶ *When absorption costing is used, all expenses are allocated to the products a company manufactures.*

abstract of title a document containing the history of a parcel of land. (The abstract summarizes all transactions, such as claims, lawsuits, liens, mortgages, deeds, etc., that affect the property.) ▶ *A purchaser of land always insists on an abstract of title.*

accelerated cost recovery system a technique by which fixed assets put into service after 1980 may be depreciated more rapidly than was previously allowed under Federal tax laws. ▶ *The accelerated cost recovery system is a provision in the Economic Recovery and Tax Act of 1981.*

accelerated depreciation a method used to depreciate capital equipment at a more rapid rate than the customary straight-line method of depreciation. ▶ *Accelerated depreciation is used to bring about certain tax advantages by lowering taxable income.*

accelerating premium pay an incentive wage payment plan whereby workers being paid on a piecework basis receive a higher rate per unit as they produce more units. ▶ *Accelerating premium pay encourages efficiency and productivity.*

acceleration clause   a provision, often found in a negotiable instrument, such as a note, that hastens the instrument's date of maturity upon the occurrence of some event. ▶ *Because payment has not been made on this note for three months, in accordance with the acceleration clause the entire amount of the note is now due.*

accelerator principle   the idea that changes in demand for consumer goods give rise to greater changes in demand for producer goods. ▶ *The accelerator principle suggests that increased demand for consumer goods results in greater investment in plant and equipment.*

acceptable quality level   a predetermined level of quality that is considered to be adequate in a statistical quality control system. ▶ *In an order processing system, an accuracy rate of 99.99% is sometimes an acceptable quality level.*

acceptance   a time draft (bill of exchange) on the face of which the drawee has written the word "accepted" over the drawee's signature, and has indicated the date the draft is payable and, frequently, the place where it is payable. (See also *bank acceptance* and *trade acceptance.*) ▶ *Roger indicated his acceptance of the draft by signing it and writing [accepted] above his signature.*

acceptance sampling   the use of statistical sampling to determine the acceptability of lots of manu-

factured goods. ▶ *Carlson Manufacturing Company is using acceptance sampling to control its quality levels.*

acceptance theory of authority   the concept that the real source of personal authority in an organization is not the organization, which ostensibly confers authority on someone, but is rather in the acceptance by subordinates of the power that a superior holds over them. ▶ *According to the acceptance theory of authority, a supervisor has authority over subordinates only to the extent that those subordinates accept the supervisor's authority.*

access time   **1.** the time interval between the instant when data is called from a computer storage device and the instant it is available for processing. ▶ *Access time is incredibly fast today.* **2.** the time interval between the instant when data is ready to be stored and the instant the storage is completed. ▶ *As improvements are made in computers, access time decreases.*

accident frequency rate   the number of lost-time accidents per million man-hours worked in an organization. ▶ *The accident frequency rate is computed by multiplying the number of lost-time accidents by one million and dividing the resulting number by the total man-hours worked during the period.*

accommodation endorsement   the signing or endorsing of a note or draft by a second party solely for the purpose of inducing a financial institution to lend money to a borrower whose credit alone is not substantial enough to warrant such a loan. (The endorser is legally liable to repay the loan in full, but does not expect to do so.) ▶ *The bank was unwilling to grant Tom the loan without an accommodation endorsement.*

accommodation paper a note or similar obligation, the payment of which is guaranteed by some party other than the one receiving the benefit. ▶ *Accommodation paper is executed to assist the drawer of the paper.*

account 1. a detailed statement of purchases and payments representing a contractual relationship between a buyer and a seller. ▶ *Our account with Fuller Furniture has been paid in full.* 2. a detailed statement of debits and credits made to assets, liabilities, income, and expenses to reflect changes in values. ▶ *These items should be credited to the travel expense account.* 3. the depository relationship between a bank and a particular customer. ▶ *Tom has an account with the First National Bank.*

account reconciliation plan AND **ARP** a service offered by commercial banks whereby the bank, for a fee, furnishes high-volume depositors with a list and total of paid checks in numerical order, and an identification of outstanding checks in order to facilitate reconciling or balancing the customer's check register with the bank's statement. ▶ *An account reconciliation plan simplifies record keeping for a depositor.*

accountability responsibility for one's actions. ▶ *Joan has total accountability to her boss.*

accountancy the theory and practice of accounting. ▶ *Many top executives are well-versed in accountancy.*

accountant a person who practices accounting. ▶ *Our accountant suggests that we update our record-keeping system.*

accounting period the period of time for which the operating statements of an organization are prepared. ▶ *The most common accounting period is one month.*

accounting practice 1. the professional work of a Certified Public Accountant. ▶ *My CPA's accounting practice is strictly limited to tax work.* 2. the customs and methods of accountants as expressed in or revealed by their daily activities. ▶ *Accounting practice has evolved over a long period of time.*

accounts payable 1. the amounts owed by an organization to trade creditors for the purchase of goods and services. ▶ *Accounts payable are open accounts not evidenced or supported by promissory notes.* 2. the department in an organization that maintains records of amounts owed to trade creditors for the purchase of goods and services. ▶ *We need to hire two more people for accounts payable.*

accounts receivable 1. amounts owed to an organization by its customers for goods and services. ▶ *Accounts receivable are open accounts not evidenced or supported by promissory notes.* 2. the department in an organization responsible for maintaining records of amounts owed by customers for the purchase of goods and services.

▶ *According to accounts receivable, we have not received a payment on your account for the past two months.*

accounts receivable turnover the ratio obtained by dividing total credit sales during a given period by accounts receivable. ▶ *Accounts receivable turnover is a measure of how long it takes a firm to collect its credit sales.*

accretion the increase in economic value of assets brought about by any cause; for example, the aging of whiskey or the increase of flocks and herds. ▶ *Accretion is not experienced by all assets since the majority of assets decrease in value over time rather than increase.*

accrual the recognition, in accounting, of events as they occur. ▶ *An accrual accounting system estimates and accounts for expenses on a daily basis.*

accrual basis a method of accounting in which income is recognized in the period in which it is earned whether it is received or not, and expenses are recognized in the period in which they are incurred whether they are paid for or not. (Contrast with *cash basis*.) ▶ *The accrual basis provides a more realistic view of income and expenses than the cash basis does.*

accrued expense an expense that has been incurred, but is payable at a future date. ▶ *The cost of electricity is an example of an accrued expense.*

accrued income income earned, but not yet received. ▶ *Accrued income will be received at some point in the future.*

accrued interest interest earned, but not yet received. ▶ *Accrued interest will be received at some future date.*

accumulated dividend See *dividend in arrears.*

acid test the rigorous testing of a product, concept, theory, etc., especially in an informal manner. ▶ *Let's put this new wrench to the acid test by asking some actual plumbers to use it.*

acid test ratio AND **quick ratio; liquidity ratio** the ratio of cash, trade receivables, and marketable securities of an enterprise to its current liabilities. ▶ *The acid test ratio is a measure of a firm's liquidity.*

acquired surplus the surplus of one enterprise existing at the time of its acquisition by another firm. ▶ *The acquired surplus is equal to $2.00 per share.*

acquittance a document giving written evidence of the discharge of, or freedom from, a financial or other type of obligation. ▶ *The court granted an acquittance in the matter of Harold's financial obligation to Irving.*

acronym a word formed from the initial letters of the words in a name or phrase. (An *acronym* is a form of verbal shorthand that makes it easier to refer to an item or concept. They are frequently encountered in business and government.) ▶ *PERT from Program Evaluation and Review Technique is an acronym.*

across the board **1.** applied to all areas equally. ▶ *Expenses will have to be cut across the board.*

2. a flat percentage increase or decrease in wages or a fixed amount per hour increase or decrease applied to all jobs in an organization. ▶ *The new union contract calls for an across the board increase of 5 percent next year and 10 percent the following year.* **3.** an increase or decrease in prices covering the entire line of goods produced or handled. ▶ *We will need to increase our prices on dresses by 5 percent across the board.*

act of God　a natural force such as a flood, lightning, an earthquake, or a hurricane that causes a loss of property. ▶ *Damages from an act of God are not usually covered under an insurance policy.*

active market　a market in which there is a substantial amount of buying and selling. ▶ *There is a very active market for steel stocks today.*

active partner　a partner who has contributed to the capital of a partnership and who is involved in management decisions. ▶ *Any partner is considered to be an active partner unless otherwise indicated in the partnership agreement.*

activity charge　a service charge imposed on a demand deposit account where the average balance maintained is not large enough to compensate for the financial institution's cost of handling the checks drawn on the account. ▶ *This bank has a minimum activity charge of $5.00 per month.*

activity ratio　a financial statement ratio that measures how effectively a firm is in using its resources. (Any of the following is a commonly used *activity ratio*: inventory turnover ratio, total assets turnover, fixed assets turnover, and average collection period.) ▶ *All of the activity ratios point to a general downturn in profits for the Acme Corporation.*

actual cost　the amount paid for an item, including freight and installation, but not including any interest on the debt used to acquire the item. ▶ *The actual cost of an asset may be greater or less than its market value.*

actual damages　the losses that have actually been sustained by an injured party. ▶ *An injured party, as a matter of right, should be compensated for all actual damages.*

actuary　a person who calculates insurance risk on the basis of experience tables. ▶ *Bob is majoring in mathematics because he wants to be an actuary when he graduates from college.*

ad hoc　for this special purpose. ▶ *We need to appoint an ad hoc committee to investigate the alleged embezzlement of funds from the Dean's office.*

ad hoc committee　a committee established to deal with a single problem, usually of a nonrecurring nature. ▶ *We have appointed an ad hoc committee to determine the cause of the accident.*

ad hoc policy　a policy established for a special, one-time use. ▶ *An ad hoc policy addresses a situation that could not be anticipated.*

ad valorem　a property tax computed on the value of the property.

▶ *An ad valorem tax is not concerned with the weight or size of an item, but only its value.*

ad valorem duty an import tax based on the value of the item rather than its weight, size, or quantity. ▶ *The ad valorem duty on this item is substantial.*

adjudication the determination of a dispute and the pronouncement of judgment, especially in a legal sense. ▶ *We received notice yesterday of the court's final adjudication regarding the alleged patent infringement.*

adjustable rate mortgage AND **ARM** a mortgage loan that permits the interest rate to be increased or decreased at specific intervals over the life of the loan. ▶ *Jane was able to get an adjustable rate mortgage when she bought her new condo.*

adjusted gross income AND **AGI** the income on which Federal income tax is computed. ▶ *Alimony payments reduce a person's adjusted gross income.*

adjusting entry a journal entry to update an income or expense account because of the accruing or deferring of an item in that account. ▶ *Sam made an adjusting entry to reflect the unanticipated payment.*

adjustment a change in an income or expense account produced by an adjusting entry. ▶ *After adjustment, the utility expense for April appears to be unusually high.*

administered price a price that is set by management and held constant for a period of time without considering the demand forces in the marketplace. ▶ *When a company maintains a posted price at which it will make sales, or when a company simply has its own prices at which buyers may purchase or not as they desire, the result is an administered price.*

administration 1. the process of managing an organization or component thereof. ▶ *Proper administration is essential to the survival of an organization.* 2. the management of a decedent's estate by an administrator or executor. ▶ *The administration of Uncle Willard's estate is being handled by an attorney from New York.*

administrative expense an expense chargeable to the managerial and policy-making segments of an enterprise. ▶ *Administrative expense would include such items as executive salaries, secretarial salaries, and general corporate expenses pertaining to directors' fees, franchise taxes, and donations to charity.*

Administrative Management Society AND **AMS** a professional association of administrators and managers. ▶ *The Administrative Management Society promotes the application of scientific methods in business administration for the purposes of increasing productivity, lowering costs, and improving quality.*

administrator 1. a person who manages any type of organization or segment thereof. ▶ *The top manager in a hospital is usually referred to as the administrator.*

2. a person authorized to settle a decedent's estate in the absence of a will. ▶ *The probate court has appointed an administrator for John Elton's estate.*

admonition a warning against something. ▶ *The manager issued a stern admonition against long lunch hours.*

ADR See *American Depository Receipt.*

advance order the process of ordering goods from a manufacturer during the manufacturer's slow operating season. ▶ *An advance order usually brings a lower price, better service, or a combination of the two since it allows the manufacturer to operate efficiently during the off-season.*

adverse impact a negative effect; negative consequences. ▶ *The use of poor materials will have an adverse impact on sales.*

adverse opinion an outside auditor's opinion that a firm's financial statements are not in conformance with generally accepted accounting principles or that they do not fairly represent operating results. (Also in general use for any negative opinion.) ▶ *We received an adverse opinion in our last outside audit, but we are taking action to see that such a situation does not occur again.*

advertisement a nonpersonal sales presentation directed to potential customers through print or broadcast media, direct mail, signs, displays, etc. ▶ *Terry saw an advertisement in the classified section for a systems analyst.*

advertising a form of paid, non-personal promotion of goods, services, or ideas to a group by an identifiable sponsor. ▶ *Advertising is a widely used means of promoting consumer products.*

advertising alley See *Madison Avenue.*

advertising allowance the sum that a manufacturer gives wholesalers or distributors to encourage them to advertise. ▶ *An advertising allowance is generally given at the end of the year and is a percentage of the total amount spent for advertising up to a specified limit.*

advertising manager the person who oversees the advertising effort of an enterprise. ▶ *The duties of an advertising manager vary from overseeing and conducting advertising campaigns to acting as a liaison between the company and its advertising agency.*

advertising medium a vehicle used to present advertising to the public; e.g., newspapers, television, radio, billboards, and handbills. ▶ *The advertising medium should be carefully selected to fit the target audience.*

advise fate a request made by a collecting bank desiring to know as soon as possible whether or not a particular draft will clear. (The equivalent of "please advise me on the probable fate of this draft as to clearance.") ▶ *Please advise fate on the enclosed draft in the amount of $5,000.*

affective behavior the behavior relative to feelings, emotions, attitudes, etc. ▶ *Sales ability can often be improved through training* *aimed at a salesperson's affective behavior.*

affidavit   a voluntary statement of facts, written and sworn to or affirmed before some officer authorized to administer oaths. ► *A notary public is legally authorized to certify an affidavit.*

affiliate banking   a commercial banking arrangement whereby one bank (the affiliate) is organized by the board of directors of another bank. ► *In affiliate banking, the organizing bank provides executive officers and financial assistance for the new bank.*

Affirmative Action Plan AND **AAP** a program undertaken by an organization to improve job opportunities for and increase the utilization of protected classes in its work force. (Such a program may be initiated: (1) voluntarily, (2) as a condition of doing business with the Federal government, (3) by Federal court order, or (4) through a consent decree with the *Equal Employment Opportunity Commission*.) ► *An Affirmative Action Plan is tangible proof of an employer's commitment to equal opportunity employment practices.*

AFL-CIO   See *American Federation of Labor-Congress of Industrial Organizations.*

AFT   See *American Federation of Teachers.*

after-sale service   the maintenance of a product by the manufacturer or an authorized representative after it has been purchased. ► *After-sale service is an important consideration in deciding where to buy an automobile.*

after-tax basis   a figure that reflects the effects of taxation on a sum of money. (Often used in comparing the rates of return on a taxable corporate bond with a municipal bond that is tax free.) ► *On an after-tax basis, the return on this corporate bond is not as high as the return on that municipal bond.*

after-tax real rate of return   the rate of return on an investment, adjusted for inflation, and after payment of all taxes. ► *The after-tax real rate of return is a measure of the true earnings on the money a person has invested.*

aftermarket   **1.** the stock exchanges and over-the-counter markets where securities are bought and sold after their original issue. ► *After the bonds were issued, they were actively traded in the aftermarket.* **2.** after the original sale. (Refers to items that can be added to existing merchandise or equipment.) ► *Automobile air conditioners are usually more costly as aftermarket expenditures than they are as original equipment.*

AFTRA   See *American Federation of Television and Radio Artists.*

against the box   the *short sale* of a security by someone who also owns the same security. ► *Billy Ray decided to go against the box because he felt the price of the stock would keep dropping.*

agate   a size of printing type five and one half points in depth. (There are 72 points to an inch.) ► *Please make certain that this page is set in agate.*

agate line   a unit of measurement

used in print advertising. ▶ *An agate line is one column wide by one-fourteenth of an inch.*

age discrimination the denial of employment opportunities or the infringement of the terms and conditions of employment because of a person's age, especially if the person is age 40 or over. ▶ *Age discrimination is a serious problem in American industry today.*

agency agreement an agreement between two parties whereby one party is authorized to represent the second party in transactions with a third party. ▶ *The agency agreement is prevalent in negotiating contracts in professional sports.*

agency shop a workplace where all employees within a collective bargaining unit who do not join the union still are required to pay a fee equal to the cost of dues to the union for the collective bargaining services provided by the union. ▶ *Under an agency shop arrangement nonunion employees are, in effect, paying the union for bargaining on their behalf.*

agenda a list of items to be considered at a meeting or conference. ▶ *The agenda should be prepared and distributed prior to the meeting.*

agent 1. a person who is authorized to represent or act for another person, referred to as the *principal,* in dealing with a third party. ▶ *A good agent is highly skilled at negotiations.* 2. an individual who sells and services insurance policies. ▶ *I want to call my agent about increasing my homeowners insurance.*

AGI See *adjusted gross income.*

agricultural marketing cooperative a democratic association of individual agricultural producers that assists its members in the collective marketing of their products. ▶ *An agricultural marketing cooperative helps its members obtain the best possible prices for their products.*

AIB See *American Institute of Banking.*

aided recall method a method of evaluating how well an audience (reader, viewer, or listener) remembers an advertisement when a clue is given to assist the respondent in remembering that advertisement. ▶ *The aided recall method is only one of several approaches used to evaluate advertisements.*

air date the date of the first television or radio broadcast of a commercial. ▶ *The air date for our new television spot will be January 31.*

airtime 1. the amount of time allotted a television or radio commercial advertisement. ▶ *We have only thirty seconds of airtime, so we have to make every word count.* 2. the specific time at which a television or radio commercial is broadcast. ▶ *The airtime for our new commercial is 6:23 P.M.*

alcoholism a disease characterized by excessive, uncontrolled, or compulsive consumption of alcoholic beverages that interferes with a person's work, family, or social relationships. ▶ *Alcoholism affects people at all levels of society.*

algorithm a series of procedural

steps for solving a specific problem. ▶ *A computer spelling checker uses a clever algorithm to develop a list of possible replacements for a misspelled word.*

alien corporation a corporation that was organized in one country and is doing business in another country. ▶ *Any foreign corporation doing business in the United States is an alien corporation.*

all or none order a limited price stock market order that is to be executed completely or not at all. ▶ *If an all or none order is not executed, it is not cancelled, but continues in effect until it can be completed.*

allied lines See the following entry.

allied products AND **allied lines** products or groups of products that are closely associated with each other in the same field. ▶ *Lipstick, face powder, and cold cream are allied products in the cosmetics category.*

allied trades the industrial trades, crafts, or occupations that are closely related to each other because of their utilization of similar equipment, raw materials, or workers with similar skills and experience. ▶ *Carpentry and drywall hanging are allied trades in the home construction field.*

allonge a sheet of paper attached to a negotiable instrument to provide additional space for endorsements. ▶ *An allonge is seldom used in contemporary business transactions.*

allowance an increment of time included in the standard time for

completing an operation in order to compensate for production time lost as a result of worker fatigue and interruptions, such as unavoidable delays or attending to personal needs. ▶ *An allowance is expressed as a percentage of the normal time for the operation.*

allowed time the *leveled time* for an operation plus an allowance for personal needs, fatigue, and delay. ▶ *The allowed time is based on the time a competent worker would need to complete an operation.*

alphameric See the following entry.

alphanumeric AND **alphameric** a group of data in which the coded characters contain both letters and digits. ▶ *A list of names and addresses is alphanumeric.*

altered check a check on which the date, payee, or amount has been changed. (A commercial bank pays an altered check at its own risk and may be liable for any damages suffered by the drawer as a result of the check being paid.) ▶ *My bank will not accept an altered check.*

alternative order AND **either/or order** an order that offers alternative courses of action for a stockbroker to follow. ▶ *When one part of the order is executed the alternative order is treated as cancelled.*

AMA See *American Management Association; American Marketing Association.*

ambiance the atmosphere or environment surrounding a person, place, or organization. ▶ *The ambiance in this restaurant is excellent.*

American Bankers Association
AND **ABA** a banking organization
founded in 1875 whose purposes
are to keep its members informed
of the changing need for banking
services, to assist in developing
and maintaining educated and competent personnel for banks, to
spread economic knowledge, and
to raise the standards of bank management and service. ▶ *The American Bankers Association sponsors
several graduate schools of banking at universities across the
United States.*

American Bar Association AND
ABA an association of lawyers,
judges, law students, and teachers
founded in 1878 and pledged to up-
hold education and ethics in the
field of law. ▶ *The American Bar
Association determines the ac-
creditation for law schools.*

American Depository Receipt AND
**ADR; American Depositary Re-
ceipt** a receipt issued by banks
in the United States as a substitute
for direct ownership of stock in
foreign companies. ▶ *An American
Depository Receipt may be bought
or sold in the over-the-counter
market.*

American Express AND **Amex** a
major United States credit card
company offering diversified services in countries around the
world. ▶ *An American Express
credit card bill is payable in full
at the time it is received.*

**American Federation of Labor-
Congress of Industrial Organizations** AND **AFL-CIO** two
major U.S. unions that merged in
1955, forming the largest union in
the United States. (Prior to that
time the AFL had been comprised
of craft unions and the CIO had
been comprised of industrial
unions.) ▶ *The AFL-CIO remains a
powerful force in the American
labor movement.*

American Federation of Teachers
AND **AFT** an organization of education workers that promotes professionalism, pay standards, equal
opportunity, and job security as
well as addresses classroom issues,
such as class size. (Founded in
1916.) ▶ *The AFT seeks to increase
professionalism in American education.*

**American Federation of Televi-
sion and Radio Artists** AND
AFTRA the labor union for people working in live and videotaped
television programming, commer-
cials, and radio broadcasting. ▶
*Since Jane joined the American
Federation of Television and
Radio Artists, she has been getting
a number of auditions.*

American Institute of Banking
AND **AIB** the educational section
of the American Bankers Association organized in 1900 to provide
educational opportunities in banking for bank employees. (Activities
are carried on through local chap-
ters and study groups throughout
the United States.) ▶ *Membership
in the American Institute of Banking is open to employees and officers of ABA member institutions.*

**American Institute of Industrial
Engineers** a professional society for industrial engineers founded in 1948. (Members of the American Institute of Industrial
Engineers are concerned with the
design, improvement, and installa-

tion of integrated systems of human resources, materials, and equipment.) ▶ *Walter received an award from the American Institute of Industrial Engineers for his plan.*

American Management Association AND **AMA** an association of professional managers and university teachers of management. (Founded in 1923.) ▶ *The American Management Association seeks to provide the training, research, publications, and information services that are necessary for managers.*

American Marketing Association AND **AMA** an association of marketing managers, teachers, and others interested in the field of marketing. ▶ *The American Marketing Association fosters research, sponsors seminars, conferences, and student clubs.*

American National Standards Institute an association of industrial firms, trade associations, technical societies, consumer organizations, and government agencies. ▶ *The American National Standards Institute serves as a clearinghouse for nationally coordinated voluntary safety, engineering, and industrial standards for various parts and products.*

American plan AND **AP** an arrangement whereby a hotel charges a guest a price that includes room, meals, and other services. ▶ *We booked our stay in Tokyo on the American plan because it was the best rate we could get.*

American Society for Training and Development a profession-

al organization for people involved in the training and development of business, industry, and government personnel. ▶ *The American Society for Training and Development is the world's largest training organization with over 26,000 members.*

American Standard Computer Information Interchange AND **ASCII** a coding system used on most microcomputers, computer terminals, and printers. (Acronym.) ▶ *The manuscript for the report was processed and stored in ASCII.*

American Stock Exchange AND **AMEX** the second largest stock exchange in the United States. ▶ *The American Stock Exchange was once called the New York Curb Exchange.*

Americans with Disabilities Act of 1990 a Federal antidiscrimination act that protects qualified individuals who have a physical or mental impairment that substantially limits one or more major life activities. ▶ *Complying with the Americans with Disabilities Act of 1990 will have a significant impact on state and local governments as well as industry.*

Amex See *American Express.*

AMEX See *American Stock Exchange.*

amortization **1.** the periodic writing off of long-lived intangible assets such as goodwill, copyrights, and patents. ▶ *Amortization is a method of allocating costs to appropriate accounting periods.* **2.** the periodic reduction of a debt. ▶ *Amortization is accomplished*

13

through periodic payments to the debt holder.

AMS See *Administrative Management Society.*

analog computer a computer that performs arithmetical functions upon numbers where the numbers are represented by some physical quantity rather than combinations of discrete data. ▶ *An analog computer is used in scientific applications rather than in business applications.*

analysis the systematic study, classification, evaluation, or separation of a subject or a field of operation into its principal parts or components. ▶ *We need to perform a cost analysis on the proposed manufacturing changes to see if we can afford them.*

analyst a person who, by reason of training, skill, and experience, engages in the study, classification, evaluation, or separation of something into its principal parts or components. ▶ *This project should be assigned to a cost analyst.*

analytic process 1. the procedures, techniques, or approaches used to perform an analysis of something. ▶ *Through an analytic process, a company decides if it should invest in new equipment.* 2. a manufacturing process in which raw material is separated into several components. ▶ *The analytic process is used in the petroleum industry.*

anchor tenant the major tenant in a shopping center or mall. ▶ *The anchor tenant has drawing power and attracts people to the shopping center or mall.*

andragogy that area of the field of learning theory concerned with how adults learn, as opposed to how children learn. ▶ *According to a basic principle of andragogy, adult learners require active involvement in the learning process in order to learn effectively.*

annual audit the yearly examination of a company's accounting books and records by an independent auditor. ▶ *The annual audit coincides with a company's fiscal year.*

annual basis a statistical technique whereby data for a period of time less than one year is extended to cover the entire year. ▶ *We will need to see these numbers on an annual basis to see if the changes we made are cost effective.*

annual percentage rate AND **APR** the cost of credit expressed as a simple yearly percentage. ▶ *Due to the way in which interest rates are calculated, the annual percentage rate is usually much higher than the stated rate of interest.*

annual report a formal statement of the financial condition and operating results of an enterprise that is prepared and submitted to stockholders and other interested parties on a yearly basis. ▶ *The annual report typically contains a formal statement from the company's chief executive officer.*

annuitant the recipient of the proceeds of an annuity. ▶ *An annuitant is often a spouse or heir.*

annuity the payment of a fixed sum of money at uniform intervals of time. Normally, the payments are made from a fund created over a period of time by deposits of money. ▶ *Insurance companies offer annuities as a means of saving for retirement.*

antitrust laws legislation designed to eliminate or prevent monopoly and restraint of trade. ▶ *Two of the oldest Federal antitrust laws are the Sherman Act of 1890 and the Clayton Act of 1914.*

AP See *American plan.*

applause mail the letters of appreciation from the listening or viewing audience received by radio or television stations or sponsors. ▶ *Our new television commercial has generated a great amount of applause mail.*

appraisal 1. the act of estimating the value, usefulness, or performance of something. ▶ *Through appraisal, Don determined that the diamond was not worth as much as we originally thought.* 2. the value of something as determined through an estimate. ▶ *The appraisal on that property is $2 million.*

appraisal surplus AND **appreciation surplus** an increase in the owner's equity account arising from an increase in the appraised value of an asset. ▶ *Appraisal surplus should be recognized only under very unusual circumstances.*

appreciation an increase in the market value of an asset over its cost. (Normally, the increase in value is due to changes in economic or other conditions.) ▶ *An increase in the value of an asset as a result of improvements or additions to the asset is not considered*

to be appreciation.

appreciation surplus See *appraisal surplus.*

apprentice 1. a person who works for another with the obligation of learning a trade or a skill. ▶ *Before he became a stonemason, Wagner was an apprentice to a bricklayer for four years.* 2. a novice or a learner. ▶ *An apprentice worker initially makes a lot of mistakes on the job.*

apprenticeship training an approach to training used in craft occupations such as plumber, carpenter, and printer wherein on-the-job training is combined with classroom instruction over a stipulated period of time. ▶ *The apprenticeship training period for a pattern maker is five years.*

appropriated surplus a part of the owner's equity account that has been restricted for some general or specific purpose and is therefore not available for distribution to stockholders. ▶ *Appropriated surplus is created by an action of the board of directors.*

APR See *annual percentage rate.*

aptitude test a psychological test used to measure an individual's latent or potential ability to perform certain functions, provided proper training is afforded the individual. ▶ *An aptitude test can be helpful in making career decisions.*

arbitrage the simultaneous purchase and sale of securities to take advantage of a discrepancy in prices between two or more markets. ▶ *Arbitrage tends to equalize prices in different markets.*

arbitration an arrangement

whereby unresolved disputes are submitted to an impartial third party whose decision in the case is binding on both parties to the dispute. ▶ *Long used in labor relations to settle disputes between union and management, arbitration is now being used increasingly as an alternative to lawsuits.*

arbitration award   the decision reached by an arbitrator in a dispute between two parties. ▶ *As outlined in the arbitration award, Smith is to be reinstated immediately and given six months back pay.*

arbitrator   a person who has been appointed to act as judge or referee in a dispute between two parties. ▶ *An arbitrator has a great deal of freedom in arriving at decisions.*

archives   **1.** the site of all records, journals, documents, letters, etc., being stored for legal or historical purposes. ▶ *The first check ever written by this corporation is stored in the company archives.* **2.** the backup computer files maintained on magnetic tape or disks. ▶ *If the original data is lost, we can always get from archives a tape that has the information on it.*

area sampling   a form of statistical random sampling in which different areas are scientifically selected to represent the different elements that make up the whole being studied. ▶ *Area sampling is sometimes used to assure that sufficient geographical segments of a population have been polled.*

arithmetic mean AND **(simple) average**   the result obtained from dividing the sum of two or more quantities by the number of items. ▶ *Please figure out the arithmetic mean of this list of numbers.*

ARM   See *adjustable rate mortgage.*

arm's length   not favoring anyone; open and above board. (Said of a transaction in which both buyer and seller are independent persons acting freely, with each seeking to further their own economic interests.) ▶ *An arm's length transaction involves no favoritism or irregularity.*

ARP   See *account reconciliation plan.*

array   an arrangement of values according to magnitude, normally from the smallest to the largest. ▶ *Numerical data presented in an array are easier to understand than data presented in random order.*

arrears   the state of an overdue debt. ▶ *Mrs. Johnson's account is two months in arrears.*

articles of incorporation   See *certificate of incorporation.*

as is   [available for sale] in its present condition without warranty or guarantee. ▶ *When goods are sold as is, the seller is not responsible for any existing damages or defects.*

ASAP   as soon as possible, denoting that something is to be done immediately. (Acronym.) ▶ *Tell Willard that we must have this order shipped ASAP!*

ASCII   See *American Standard Computer Information Interchange.*

asking price   the price at which the owner offers to sell a commodity or a piece of property. ▶ *The price at which a piece of property sells is frequently much lower than the asking price.*

assembly   two or more subassemblies joined together to form a complete article. ▶ *The bumper assembly on an automobile contains several different parts and subassemblies.*

assembly line   See *production line.*

assessed value   the value of property as determined for taxation or other purposes. ▶ *The assessed value of real estate is usually much lower than its actual value.*

assessment center   the site of a series of processes used in identifying and selecting candidates for promotion that requires the candidates to participate in a series of activities similar to those they may be expected to perform on the actual job. ▶ *The assessment center concept was first used by AT&T.*

asset   anything that can be assigned a monetary value, such as cash, securities, real estate, machinery, furniture, etc., and can be held by an institution or an individual. ▶ *We will have to sell an asset to raise cash to make the loan payment.*

asset allocation   the investing of money in various types of investments to assure the greatest overall return as well as the safety of the assets. ▶ *Asset allocation is a prudent approach to investing.*

assignee   someone to whom an assignment has been made. ▶ *The contract has been transferred to the new assignee.*

assignment   the transfer of rights or benefits by and from one entity to another, usually as specified in a contract. ▶ *To secure a loan, Joan made an assignment of her life insurance policy to the lender.*

assignor   someone who makes an assignment to another. ▶ *When the owner of a life insurance policy uses the policy to secure a loan, the owner is the assignor and the lender is the assignee.*

Association for Systems Management   an international professional organization dedicated to the advancement of knowledge in the field of business systems analysis. ▶ *Founded in 1947, the Association for Systems Management consists largely of individuals from data processing or related fields.*

Association of Consulting Management Engineers   a professional association of management consulting firms that conducts conferences and seminars for its members, promotes public relations, and makes surveys on various aspects of management consulting. ▶ *The Association of Consulting Management Engineers also prescribes standards of conduct for its members.*

assumed liability   an obligation of one party for which responsibility for payment is taken over by a second party. ▶ *When one company acquires another, the outstanding notes of the acquired company become the assumed liability of the acquiring company.*

at sight   a designation on the face of a negotiable instrument indicating that payment is due on presentation. ▶ *Any draft marked at sight must be paid in full when it is presented for collection.*

at the close order   a stock market order to a broker, to buy or sell a security or commodity, that is to be executed at the close of the trading day or as close to it as possible. ▶ *Time constraints may preclude the execution of an at the close order.*

at the market order   a stock market order to a broker to buy or sell a security or commodity immediately for the best price possible. ▶ *An at the market order is to be executed at the current price, whatever the price may be.*

at the opening (only) order   a stock market order to a broker to buy or sell a security or commodity at the price that applies when the market opens. ▶ *An at the opening only order that is not executed as ordered is cancelled.*

ATM   See *automated teller machine.*

AT&T   American Telephone and Telegraph Company, a very large information processing and telecommunications company that provides communication products and services worldwide. ▶ *AT&T has long been one of the most stable corporations in the United States.*

attached account   a commercial banking deposit account against which a court order has been issued, permitting disbursement of the balance only with the consent of the court. ▶ *An attached account can no longer be used freely by the depositor.*

attachment   1. the legal process of seizing a debtor's property for nonpayment of a debt. ▶ *Garnishment is the attachment of a worker's wages.* 2. any document added to another document. ▶ *An attachment to an insurance policy explains additional coverages or exclusions not enumerated in the policy itself.*

attitude scale   a means of assessing employees' feelings toward their jobs and the employing firm and its policies. ▶ *An attitude scale frequently produces very informative findings for management.*

attractive nuisance   property that entices or attracts children and is inherently dangerous to them because they cannot appreciate the risks involved. ▶ *A swimming pool is an attractive nuisance and must be fenced to protect against its unauthorized use by children.*

attribute   1. a quality or a group of qualities reduced to quantitative form for statistical analysis. ▶ *An attribute is essentially a characteristic.* 2. a personal quality inherent in the makeup of an individual. ▶ *Honesty is a good attribute to possess.*

auction company   a firm that conducts a sale for a second party in which merchandise offered is sold to the highest bidder. ▶ *An auction company is normally required to have a license.*

audit   1. the examination of contracts, orders, or other types of original documents for the purpose of substantiating or verifying individual transactions. ▶ *An audit is one of the ways of discovering errors in documents or transactions.* **2.** the systematic investigation of procedures and operations, or the appraisal thereof, for the purpose of determining conformity with prescribed criteria. ▶ *A procedures audit should be conducted on a regular basis to determine if managers are implementing policies correctly.* **3.** the periodic or continuous inspection of an enterprise's accounting records, statements, accounts, and procedures for purposes of verifying the accuracy and completeness of the records and the processes for maintaining them. ▶ *Embezzlement is often first detected through an audit.*

audit period   the period of time covered by an audit, normally one year. ▶ *The audit period generally remains constant over time.*

audit trail   the means whereby data can be traced from one processing step to the next or from final product back to the source document. ▶ *Establishing an audit trail is particularly important now that so much data is processed by computer.*

auditor   a person who audits account books or records kept by others. (An *auditor* may be a regular employee of an organization, an *internal auditor,* or a member of an independent firm that specializes in auditing the books and records of organizations, an *external auditor.*) ▶ *An auditor should have a college degree in accounting.*

authority   **1.** the power or right to act independently or to command others. ▶ *Managers have the authority to discipline employees in their units.* **2.** a knowledgeable person. ▶ *Sally is an authority on computers.*

authorized shares   the number of shares of capital stock that may be issued by a corporation under its articles of incorporation. ▶ *The number of shares issued can never be greater than the number of authorized shares.*

author's alt(eration)s   See the following entry.

author's corrections AND **author's errors; author's alt(eration)s**   the additions, corrections, or deletions that are made by an author on printed proofs. ▶ *Author's alts are inevitable because even the most careful writer makes mistakes.*

author's errors   See the previous entry.

automated teller machine AND **ATM; automatic teller**   a device that automatically handles simple banking transactions such as deposits and withdrawals without the need for a human teller. ▶ *Since the ATM would not accept Tom's bankcard, he could not withdraw any money.*

automatic overdraft   a banking procedure wherein checks that normally would overdraw an account are automatically paid instead. ▶ *Sally needs automatic overdraft because she is constantly writing checks that do not clear.*

automatic teller   See *automated teller machine.*

automation 1. the act or process of introducing automatic machinery or robotics into the workplace, thereby reducing or replacing human workers. ▶ *Automation will replace many workers in the automobile industry in the next three years.* 2. an area of design and engineering concerned with automatic machinery and its use in the workplace. ▶ *In the next century, almost all manufacturing will be accomplished through automation.*

autonomy the condition of being self-governing or independent. ▶ *Contemporary management theorists believe that giving workers autonomy makes them more productive.*

auxiliary 1. giving assistance or support. ▶ *Tom can be used in an auxiliary capacity if you need help.* 2. a person or thing that assists. ▶ *Don will be your auxiliary on this project.* 3. subsidiary or supplemental. ▶ *The auxiliary engine will supply additional power when it is needed.*

available assets the assets that are unencumbered and are not serving as collateral for any debt. ▶ *This company is deeply in debt and has no available assets.*

available audience the number of potential consumers who are apt to be interested in a given advertising message. ▶ *It is not always easy to determine the available audience for a new commercial.*

average 1. an index representing the valuation of groups of securities, especially the Dow Jones or Standard and Poor's evaluation of stock and bond prices. ▶ *The Dow Jones transportation average was down yesterday.* 2. See *arithmetic mean.*

average down to buy shares of stock in a declining market in fixed dollar amounts, such as $1,000. (As the price drops, more shares will be bought and the average price paid per share will be lower.) ▶ *Joan has been averaging down in the expectation that the market will rise in the future, and she will be able to sell her shares at a profit.*

average outgoing quality level the maximum average or acceptable quality of products passed by a quality assurance system employing sampling methods. ▶ *Average outgoing quality level is usually expressed in terms of the percentage of defective items to total items.*

average quality level the ratio of defective parts or products to the total parts or products produced during a given period. ▶ *The average quality level has been improving since we instituted quality circles.*

average work force a measure of the average number of workers employed by a firm calculated as follows: the number of workers at the beginning of a period plus the number of workers at the end of the period divided by two. ▶ *Since we had 25 employees at the beginning of the month and 31 at the end, the average work force for the month was 28.*

averaging up the practice of selling short shares of stock in a rising market in fixed dollar amounts, such as $1,000. (As the price increases fewer shares will be sold short. *Averaging up* is done so that prices can fall only part of the way back toward the original starting price, and will produce a net profit if the shares are bought to cover those sold short before the original prices are reached again.) ▶ *Averaging up is a practice that should be used only by professional investors.*

avoidable delay the time during a work period that the worker is idle or doing things that are not necessary to the completion of the job. ▶ *Productivity can be increased by reducing avoidable delay.*

B

baby bond a bond with a par value of less than $1,000. ▶ *A baby bond typically has a par value of $25 to $500.*

baby boomer an individual born between 1946 and 1962. ▶ *A baby boomer tends to expect instant gratification from consumer products.*

back haul the hauling of goods away from the destination at the beginning of a trip or the hauling of goods beyond the destination at the end of a trip in order to meet connections, etc. ▶ *Fred will have to back haul on this trip, but it shouldn't result in too much lost time.*

back office the departments not actively involved with customers, especially in banking and brokerage houses. ▶ *The back office is involved in accounting, record keeping, etc.*

back order that portion of a customer's order that is undelivered for any reason, but normally because the product or merchandise is not in stock at the time of the order. ▶ *Many items are sold out or on back order now because of the holiday season.*

back pay unpaid salaries and wages from a prior pay period. ▶ *The company owes Robert three weeks back pay from last month, but it still can't afford to pay him.*

back-to-work movement an attempt by a group of workers to break a labor strike by persuading a majority of striking workers to express their willingness to return to work. ▶ *Management was hoping for a back-to-work movement, but none materialized.*

backdate to date a document or a negotiable instrument with a date earlier than the current date or the date the instrument was drawn. ▶ *If we backdate this letter, it will* *look as if we answered that complaint in a timely fashion.*

backdoor financing **1.** the congressional sanction of Federal spending without formal appropriation. ▶ *Backdoor financing is not typically used to fund major government projects.* **2.** legislation permitting the issuance of bonds to the public or borrowing from the U.S. Treasury as the need arises. ▶ *Backdoor financing is used to inject cash into the money market.*

backlog the volume of work that has accumulated, but has not yet been processed. ▶ *The backlog is the difference between work volume input and output.*

backup withholding a procedure used to assure that Federal income tax is paid on earnings when a recipient cannot be identified by Social Security number. ▶ *Backup withholding amounts to 20 percent of the amount earned in interest, dividends, fees, etc.*

backward integration the expansion of a firm toward its source of goods or raw materials. ▶ *A steel manufacturer used backward integration when it acquired an iron ore mine and the means of transporting the ore from the mine to the steel mill.*

backwardation a situation in which commodity prices tend to be higher for quick delivery than for delivery at a later date. ▶ *Backwardation occurs when current demand is stronger than anticipated future demand.*

bad debt AND **uncollectible account** **1.** an account receivable that is determined to be uncollectible. ▶ *We may as well consider the Smith account a bad debt because they have not made a payment in six months.* **2.** the ledger account to which uncollectible accounts receivable are periodically charged. ▶ *The Brown Company account should be charged to the bad debt account in the general ledger as soon as possible.*

bailee a person who temporarily receives personal property owned by another person. ▶ *When you loan a book to a friend, the friend technically becomes a bailee.*

bailment a contract providing for the surrender of personal property by the owner (the bailor) to another (the bailee) to be returned to the owner at a later date. ▶ *Under the terms of a bailment, the bailee is responsible for returning the property in good condition to the bailor.*

bailor the owner of personal property who, for a period of time, surrenders the property to another for return at a later time. ▶ *When you loan a book to a friend, you technically become a bailor.*

bait and switch advertising a method of false advertising that is done to bring a customer into a store by advertising a product the seller does not desire to sell and then attempting to sell the customer a higher priced item. ▶ *The store was accused of bait and switch advertising when it advertised a T.V. for $50 but then told customers the T.V.s were sold out.*

balance of payments a record of all the economic transactions between one nation and the rest of the world in a given period, normally one year. (The transactions included are: (1) trade and services between countries, (2) long- and short-term capital flows, (3) gold and silver movements, and (4) unilateral transfers or gifts by individuals or governments.) ▶ *If a country's receipts exceed its payments to other countries, the balance of payments is favorable; if payments exceed receipts, the balance of payments is unfavorable.*

balance of trade the difference between the value of goods exported and the value of goods imported by a country. ▶ *If a country exports more than it imports, its balance of trade is favorable; if it imports more than it exports, its balance of trade is unfavorable.*

balance sheet an itemized statement of financial condition listing total assets, total liabilities, and the net worth of a business enterprise at a given point in time. ▶ *We would like to see a copy of your balance sheet for last year.*

balloon **1.** a graphic technique that simulates speech from a drawn character. ▶ *A balloon is often used in print media that contains comic strip-like characters.* **2.** any payment on a loan that is substantially larger than the amount of a regular payment. ▶ *The last payment on your new refrigerator will be the largest because it is a balloon.*

balloon note a loan in which the last payment is substantially larger than the amount of a regular payment and pays the loan in full. ▶

Monthly payments—except for the final one—are lower with a balloon note.

ballpark figure a rough estimation of the amount or value of something. ▶ *My ballpark figure for this month's sales increase is 10 percent. We'll know the actual figure next week.*

bank acceptance a draft drawn on a bank and accepted by the bank. ▶ *A bank acceptance is used in international trade to finance imports and exports.*

bank call See under *call report.*

bank charter a document issued by a national or state regulatory agency that gives a bank the right to do business. ▶ *A bank charter enumerates the functions of the bank and prescribes the conditions under which it may operate.*

bank check a check drawn by a bank on itself or on its account with another bank. ▶ *Please have the loan department issue a bank check for the proceeds of this loan.*

bank deposit money placed on account at a bank for safekeeping or for earning interest. ▶ *An individual bank deposit may be very small or it may be a substantial sum.*

bank draft a check drawn by one bank against funds deposited to its account in another bank. ▶ *The First National Bank is going to draw a bank draft against its account with the Second United Fidelity Bank.*

bank examiner a representative of a Federal or a state supervisory agency who audits banks with respect to their financial condition, investment and loan policies, and management. ▶ *My brother Tom is a bank examiner in Utah.*

bank note   a promissory note bearing no interest, issued for general circulation as money and payable to the bearer on demand ▶ *The Federal Reserve Bank is the only bank in the United States that can issue a bank note.*

bank rate   the discount rate of the Federal Reserve System; i.e., the rate of interest at which the Federal Reserve makes loans to member banks. ▶ *The bank rate is currently the lowest it has been in many years.*

bank run   a situation in which bank depositors, fearing that a bank may fail, hurriedly withdraw their funds from the bank. ▶ *In its seventy-two years of existence, the Legendary National Bank has never experienced a bank run.*

bank statement   a statement of a customer's demand deposit account that a bank furnishes periodically, usually monthly. (This document shows all checks paid and all deposits made during the period covered by the statement.) ▶ *If there is ever an error in your bank statement, please call our customer service department and they will assist you.*

bankruptcy   a procedure provided by the Federal Bankruptcy Act to make it possible under certain conditions for an insolvent person or company to be relieved of its financial obligations. (The procedure involves the Federal court, through a designated officer, taking control of all of the bankrupt entity's property, converting it into cash, and equitably paying all expenses and debts to the limit of the cash available.) ▶ *During the 1980s, many Americans, because of economic hardship, had to file bankruptcy.*

bar chart   a graphic representation of statistical data arranged in vertical or horizontal lines forming rectangles. ▶ *This income data can probably be presented more effectively in a bar chart.*

bar graph   a pictorial representation of statistical information in either horizontal or vertical columns. ▶ *A bar graph would be helpful in explaining these numbers to the sales staff.*

bargain   1. an agreement. ▶ *I made a bargain with Tom that I would give him half my earnings if he would lend me the money to buy the stock.* 2. to negotiate; to deal; to reach an agreement. ▶ *We bargained for three hours and never could reach an accord.* 3. a purchase that is a very good value for the amount spent. ▶ *I picked up an excellent computer stock, and a year later, it turned out to be a real bargain.*

bargain basement   1. an area in a department store, originally located in the basement, in which goods are marked down for sale at lower than normal prices. ▶ *Jane bought her wedding dress in the bargain basement at the department store.* 2. low-priced [goods, services, or securities]. (Can refer to good value or poor value.) ▶ *If you invest in bargain basement stocks, you are taking a risk.*

bargain hunter   1. a purchaser who is very sensitive to price. ▶ *A* *bargain hunter will buy from the cheapest source possible.* **2.** an investor who purchases undervalued stock in the expectation of a price increase. ▶ *A skilled bargain hunter can make a great deal of money in the stock market.*

bargaining **1.** a way of reaching an agreement by means of compromise, negotiation, and give-and-take. ▶ *It took a lot of bargaining to get Thompson Corporation to agree to the delivery date.* **2.** the process of negotiations between union and management. ▶ *Bargaining will probably be a lengthy process this year because of the hard-line positions being taken by the union as well as the company.*

bargaining agent a union certified by an authorized agency or recognized by an employer to act as the exclusive representative for a designated bargaining unit. ▶ *The UAW has been certified as the bargaining agent for the tire makers.*

bargaining right the right of a duly recognized collective bargaining unit to represent its members in negotiations with an employer. ▶ *As the authorized agent for the tire makers, the UAW has the bargaining right for any term or condition affecting any of its members.*

bargaining unit **1.** a group of employees who have joined together to bargain collectively with their employer. ▶ *A bargaining unit must be certified by the National Labor Relations Board.* **2.** a particular group of jobs covered by a collective bargaining agreement. ▶ *In some plants it is very common to have more than one bargaining unit.*

barge a flat-bottomed boat capable of carrying a large cargo, normally towed or pushed by a tugboat. ▶ *The heavy equipment was transported down the river by barge.*

barrier to entry a factor that inhibits or precludes the entry of a new firm into a particular industry. ▶ *The barrier to entry in many industries is the high investment needed for plant and equipment.*

BARS See *Behaviorally Anchored Rating Scales.*

barter the exchange of goods and services for other goods and services without the use of a medium of exchange such as money. (Barter is often used by small businesses that are short on cash.) ▶ *We used barter to obtain a new car from the dealer in exchange for free advertising in our newspaper.*

base pay AND **base rate** the amount per hour, or other unit of time, established to compensate a worker for performing a specified job. ▶ *The base pay for this job is somewhat low, but the opportunity for sizable incentive pay more than makes up for it.*

base period a period of time used as a reference point for evaluating changes in business and economic data. ▶ *On a percentage scale, the base period is represented as 100 percent.*

base price the price used as a starting point for goods or services. ▶ *Freight, credit services, and other charges may be added to the base price, or trade discounts and other deductions may be subtracted.*

base rate   See *base pay.*

Basic Motion Timestudy AND **BMT** a system of determining basic time standards for specific tasks. ► *In the Basic Motion Timestudy system, each motion begins and ends at rest.*

basing point   a point to and from which transportation rates are computed. ► *The rate on that shipment will be calculated using Fort Worth as the basing point.*

basis grade   the basic grades of commodities deliverable on contracts at par, without premium or discount. ► *There may be more than one basis grade for a commodity. For example, wheat has seven.*

basis point   the smallest measure used in quoting yields on mortgages, notes, and bonds. ► *One basis point is equal to 0.01 percent of the yield.*

batch   a quantity of materials or goods chosen as a unit for processing purposes. ► *When the first batch of parts is finished, the machine settings will have to be adjusted.*

batch costing   a cost accounting procedure wherein costs incurred in producing or processing a particular quantity of goods are assigned or allocated to that quantity of goods. ► *Some industries, such as petroleum refining, must use a batch costing system because their products are not produced as individual units.*

batch processing   1. a method of production in which a limited quantity of an item is processed during a given time. ► *Batch processing*

may require that equipment be reset after each batch is processed. **2.** a type of computer processing where each processing job is fed into the computer as a stack of punched cards. (Now rarely found in modern data processing systems.) ► *With the advent of the modern computer terminal, batch processing has become obsolete.* **3.** a type of computer processing where the computer operates unattended to complete long programs or operations, such as printing payroll checks. ► *The batch processing capabilities of this system require a minimum of personnel.*

baud   a unit of electronic data transmission speed equal to the number of code elements per second. (From the name *Baudot.* See the following entry.) ► *A good modem will operate at a minimum of 1200 baud.*

Baudot code   a five-level (bit) code widely used for encoding symbols in teletypewriter operations. ► *Emil Baudot, for whom the Baudot code is named, produced the first major teleprinter code in the nineteenth century.*

Bay Street   the Toronto Stock Exchange, specifically, and Toronto financial institutions, generally. ► *Prices of high technology stocks were up on Bay Street today.*

BCD   See *binary coded decimal.*

beachhead demands   the initial demands of a union during labor negotiations. ► *Beachhead demands are used to test management's resistance to the union's demands.*

beans   soybeans. (Slang.) ► *The*

beans went sky high when the market opened today.

bear a person who believes that one or more of the financial markets will decline. (Compare with *bull*.) ▶ *My broker generally tends to be a bear.*

bear market a period of prolonged decline in a stock, bond, or commodity market. (Compare with *bull market*.) ▶ *We're experiencing a bear market in gold again this year as in the past two years.*

bear raid the heavy short selling of a stock by one or more big traders in the hope of driving down the price of the stock in a short period of time. (See *short sale*.) ▶ *A bear raid is illegal under the rules of the Securities and Exchange Commission.*

bearer bond a bond whose owner's name does not appear on the issuing firm's books, and is payable to the holder. ▶ *A bearer bond does not require an endorsement.*

bearer instrument a negotiable item, such as a bond or a check, that does not carry the name of the payee on the face of the instrument. ▶ *Anyone can cash a bearer instrument without having to endorse it.*

Bedaux point system a wage incentive system that compensates a worker on the basis of time saved rather than on the basis of output. ▶ *If the standard time for performing a task is twelve hours and a worker performs it in eight hours, the incentive bonus under the Bedaux point system would be calculated on four hours.*

bedroom community a suburban residential community offering few employment opportunities but located close to a large metropolitan area, which is a significant employment center. ▶ *The typical bedroom community has little or no industry of its own.*

behavior modification an attempt to alter a person's behavior by providing rewards to reinforce desirable behaviors or punishments to eliminate undesirable behaviors. ▶ *It is generally believed that behavior modification operates more effectively when it focuses on positive reinforcement rather than punishment.*

Behaviorally Anchored Rating Scales AND **BARS** a method of personnel performance appraisal that uses a precise identification of various kinds of job behavior as performance factors. ▶ *Behaviorally Anchored Rating Scales were developed to overcome weaknesses in other performance appraisal methods by focusing on specific job behaviors and expectations.*

behind the power curve the condition of lagging behind the leading edge of innovation, development, marketing a product, entry into a market, etc. ▶ *We are definitely behind the power curve on the development of the atomic weather vane.*

bell-shaped curve See *normal curve.*

bellwether a security that is considered an indicator of the overall movement of a market. ▶ *AT&T has long been considered one of the best bellwethers on the New York Stock Exchange.*

below par at a price below the face or nominal value of a security. ▶ *Our preferred bonds are currently selling at $10 below par.*

below the line out of the ordinary balance sheet, revenue, or expense items as opposed to customary items. (The opposite of *above the line*.) ▶ *The capital gain on the sale of the old plant is shown below the line.*

benchmark problem a program or problem used as a means of evaluating the performance and speed of different computers or computer systems. ▶ *Performance on the benchmark problem was much better for the APEX-Co computer than it was for the Dytel computer.*

bequest a gift of personal property through a will. ▶ *Tom received a $10,000 bequest through his Uncle Cleveland's will.*

Better Business Bureau an organization sponsored by local business interests whose chief function is to foster and maintain ethical business practices. ▶ *The Better Business Bureau handles complaints from consumers about business practices in the local area.*

betterment an expenditure, whether of time or money, that (1) helps to extend the useful life of an asset, (2) increases an asset's rate of output, (3) lowers an asset's operating costs, or (4) adds to the overall benefits of the asset. ▶ *A betterment is an improvement, not a repair.*

BFOQ See *bona fide occupational qualification.*

Bible Belt the southern portion of the United States that includes the former states of the Confederacy. (The so-called *Bible Belt* derives its name from the traditional importance of Protestantism in the southern U.S.) ▶ *Virginia and Alabama are two states in the Bible Belt.*

bid and ask(ed) in the stock market, the price offered by a willing buyer and the price at which a seller is willing to sell. (The difference between the two prices is the dealer's markup.) ▶ *Over-the-counter stock exchanges list the bid and asked price for all shares traded.*

bid (price) the price offered by a willing buyer. (Compare with *asking price*. See also *bid and ask(ed)*.) ▶ *The bid for the Picasso sketch was $45,000.*

biennial occurring every two years. ▶ *Most state legislatures have biennial sessions.*

bifurcate to divide into two parts. ▶ *In criminal trials, a decision has been made to bifurcate the process into: (1) a determination of guilt or innocence and (2) a determination, if necessary, of the proper penalty.*

Big Blue the International Business Machines Corporation, (IBM). (The name *Big Blue* comes from the color used in IBM's logo.) ▶ *Big Blue was down 4 points today.*

Big Board the *New York Stock Exchange* listings of stock prices. ▶ *Industrials closed up five points today on the Big Board.*

Big Business large business enterprises in the United States considered collectively. ▶ *Big Business is* *a significant employer in the American economy.*

Big Eight the eight largest public accounting firms in the United States. ▶ *The Big Eight do the accounting, auditing, and tax work for most major U.S. corporations.*

Big Steel the United States Steel Company. ▶ *Big Steel is no longer the powerful company it once was.*

Big Three the three largest automobile manufacturing firms in the United States. ▶ *General Motors, Ford Motor Company, and Chrysler Corporation comprise the Big Three.*

big-ticket item a high-priced and usually large-sized retail item. ▶ *A refrigerator is an example of a big-ticket item.*

bill **1.** an invoice for goods or services. ▶ *The bill for the printing must be paid today.* **2.** to prepare and submit an invoice for goods or services to a customer. ▶ *Bob, would you please bill Otto Services Company today for the goods we shipped last week?*

bill broker a person who arranges for the purchase or sale of negotiable paper. ▶ *Does anyone know a bill broker who can help us sell the negotiable instruments we are holding?*

bill of credit a written instrument requesting the party to whom it is addressed to extend credit to the bearer on the security or credit of the signer. ▶ *A bill of credit is only as strong as the party signing it.*

bill of exchange a written order addressed by one party (the drawer) to another party (the drawee)

directing the drawee to pay a specified sum of money to the order of a third party (the payee). ▶ *A bill of exchange may be payable on demand or at some future date.*

bill of goods something worthless or of little value. (Usually in the idiom, *to sell someone a bill of goods.*) ▶ *Acme Corporation sold us a bill of goods when we purchased the distribution rights to the atomic weather vane.*

bill of lading a document signed by a carrier to deliver goods described in the agreement to some person (the consignee) designated by the shipper (the consignor). ▶ *A bill of lading is evidence of a contract between the shipper and the carrier.*

bill of materials a list of materials, parts, subassemblies, or assemblies that are needed to manufacture a product. ▶ *As indicated on the bill of materials, six dozen steel hex nuts are needed for this product model.*

bill of sale a legal document attesting to the sale or transfer of goods or property from a seller to a buyer. ▶ *A bill of sale passes the title of personal property from the seller to the buyer.*

bill of specific performance a document filed by a court to compel a party to a contract to perform exactly as promised. ▶ *If Frank doesn't finish the building soon, we intend to ask the court for a bill of specific performance.*

billboard an advertising medium taking the form of a large sign or poster. ▶ *A billboard is a common sight along highways and roads.*

billing cycle   the time interval at which statements of account and requests for payment are prepared and sent to customers. ▶ *Most corporations use a monthly billing cycle.*

bimodal distribution   a statistical frequency distribution with two modes. ▶ *Bimodal distribution may result, for instance, from combining different distributions from two different geographical regions.*

binary code   a number system using "2" as its base and employing only the digits "0" and "1." ▶ *The number "2" would be written as "10" in binary code.*

binary coded decimal AND **BCD**   a number that has been coded using a binary coding system whereby each individual decimal digit is represented by the corresponding group of binary digits. ▶ *The number "15" in binary coded decimal is written as "0001 0101."*

binder   a memorandum that assures temporary insurance coverage until the formal policy can be issued. ▶ *In some instances, an insurance agent can issue a binder without obtaining specific approval from the insurance company issuing the policy.*

binominal distribution   a frequency distribution of discrete data where two possibilities, such as yes/no or positive/negative, exist. ▶ *The binomial distribution is one of the most widely observed probability distributions in statistics.*

birth rate   the number of live births per 1,000 persons. ▶ *The birth rate is higher in some coun-*tries *than it is in other countries.*

bit   **1.** an abbreviation of binary digit. ▶ *A bit represents the smallest unit of information.* **2.** a single character in a binary number. ▶ *In a binary system, "2" is a bit.* **3.** a unit of information capacity of a storage device. ▶ *Bit density measures the number of bits contained on a magnetic tape or disk.*

bivarate analysis   the analysis of two variables. ▶ *Through bivariate analysis, the company determined that the probability that a person would buy their product was based on sex and age.*

black ink   profit. (When bookkeeping was done manually, *black ink* was used to indicate credits and *red ink* for debits. The opposite of *red ink*.) ▶ *We hope to see black ink on the bottom line next quarter.*

black market   a market for the illegal sale of merchandise in which illicit items, rationed items, or items that are in short supply, are bought and sold at high prices. ▶ *A drug that cannot be sold legally to consumers can normally be purchased on the black market.*

Black Tuesday   the day of the great stock market crash on October 29, 1929. ▶ *People who remember Black Tuesday still fear the stock market.*

blacklist   an identification of persons, organizations, etc., to be avoided for specific reasons such as inability to pay debts, pro-union sympathies, or other similar factors. ▶ *Seldom is a blacklist written down.*

blank   **1.** a part, formed but unfinished in the manufacturing process, that will eventually be completed in a manner to satisfy a particular need. ▶ *A key blank has to be ground to certain specifications to make a key that fits a particular lock.* **2.** a printed document or form with spaces to be filled in. ▶ *Please fill out the application blank and leave it with the personnel secretary.* **3.** a space or an area to be filled in on a printed document or form. ▶ *This blank doesn't have enough room for a complete address.*

blank endorsement an endorsement that specifies no particular endorsee and may consist of a mere signature. ▶ *A blank endorsement makes an instrument payable to the bearer.*

blanket bond a bond that indemnifies an employer for loss caused by infidelity or non-performance of duty by any employee. ▶ *A blanket bond protects an employer against defalcation and misfeasance.*

blanket rate **1.** a shipping rate that applies to and/or from a number of shipping points. ▶ *The cost of shipping automobiles to Fort Worth may be covered by a blanket rate for the North Texas Region.* **2.** a rate for shipping several different articles moving in one shipment. ▶ *All goods shipped in a unitized container, regardless of what they may be, are transported under our blanket rate for stovepipes.* **3.** an insurance premium rate applied when there is more than one property covered or more than one type of coverage is provided. ▶ *Fire and casualty losses are insured under a blanket rate.*

blanking a metal forming process that uses a die to stamp out a form from a flat stock. (See *blank*.) ▶ *Blanking in a manufacturing plant is typically very noisy because of the kind of equipment used.*

blind testing **1.** the psychological assessment of a person without ever meeting the person being evaluated. ▶ *Since Richard is in the West Indies and will not be available in person for some time, we will have to do his psychological profile through blind testing.* **2.** the testing or evaluation of an unidentified product or service. ▶ *A program of blind testing demonstrated that consumers prefer the product that we manufacture.*

bloc a coalition of factions, parties, sides, or interests for a particular purpose. ▶ *The distributors are united as a bloc in their opposition to our reduction of the commission rate.*

block control a means of production control wherein identical amounts of work are released to the factory for processing at regular intervals of time. ▶ *The manufacturing improvement committee has recommended that we consider block control for the new batch processing plant.*

block diagram a graphic representation of a system, instrument, computer, or program in which selected portions are indicated by annotated boxes and interconnecting lines. ▶ *A block diagram enables a person to see the linkages between the various parts of a system.*

blocked account a bank account

balance or other credit, the use of which has been restricted or prohibited by action of the government of the country in which the account or credit is located. ▶ *Funds in a blocked account cannot be transferred to another country.*

blocked credit the state of one's credit in a *blocked account.* ▶ *The belligerent country could not use its blocked credit.*

blocked currency currency and bank deposits whose use has been restricted by the government of the country where the currency or deposits are located. ▶ *Blocked currency cannot legally be shipped to another country.*

blowup **1.** a process whereby printed material is enlarged for display. ▶ *We need to blowup this photograph.* **2.** an enlargement of a photograph or other printed material. ▶ *We need a blowup of this photograph to put by the front door.*

blue-chip stock a stock that sells at a relatively high price because of a long history of earnings, sales, dividends, growth, good management, and organizational stability. ▶ *Any stock that is referred to as a blue-chip stock is an equity of the highest quality and a relatively safe investment.*

blue-collar worker a factory worker, a craftsperson, an operative employee, a nonfarm laborer, etc., whose job involves manual work. (Compare with *white-collar worker.*) ▶ *A blue-collar worker often earns considerably more than a white-collar worker.*

blue laws state or local laws or ordinances that prohibit or restrict doing business on Sunday. ▶ *Now, businesses complain that blue laws are unfair to certain businesses.*

blue list a daily listing of municipal bonds offered for sale. ▶ *The latest blue list shows an increase in price for the Yucca City sewer bonds.*

blue-sky laws statutes enacted by various states which, in an attempt to prevent fraud, regulate the sale and issuance of securities. ▶ *Blue-sky laws protect the public from fraudulent stock deals.*

blueprint **1.** a graphic representation of technical drawings, architectural plans, or other specifications, printed in white lines on blue paper. (The original version is usually a pencil rendering on white paper. Many modern *blueprints* are blue or purple lines on white paper.) ▶ *A specialized machine is required to produce and copy a blueprint.* **2.** any comprehensive plan or scheme. ▶ *The president outlined a blueprint for the company's growth during the next ten years.*

BMT See *Basic Motion Time-study.*

board lot the customary unit of shares that makes up a normal transaction on a stock exchange. ▶ *On the New York Stock Exchange a board lot is 100 shares of stock.*

board of directors the governing body of a corporation. ▶ *The board of directors is elected by the stockholders and represents their interests in the corporation.*

boardroom 1. a room where a corporation's board of directors meets. (Refers to *a board* of directors.) ▶ *Since the boardroom is being renovated, the directors will have to hold their meeting in the cafeteria.* 2. a room provided by stockbrokers for their customers. (Refers to the *chalkboards* on which current prices were written before the age of automated displays.) ▶ *The boardroom is equipped with the latest devices that provide information on stock prices and volumes of shares traded.*

bogey an output standard that a worker sets for himself or herself or an informal time standard that is used until a formal standard can be set. ▶ *The bogey on this particular grinding job is five and one-half minutes.*

boiler room an office or room devoted to high pressure sales of stocks, bonds, commodities, etc., usually of questionable value, by telephone. ▶ *A boiler room operation is likely to involve stocks that are worthless.*

boilerplate 1. standardized language, especially on contracts, offered with the expectation that the contract will be signed without a careful reading of the information. ▶ *Boilerplate is more likely to be written in favor of the party writing the contract than in favor of the party signing it.* 2. all standardized or preprinted forms or agreements. ▶ *Most legal forms are nothing more than boilerplate.*

boldface type a form of (printing) type that retains the characteristics of the style but has heavier lines or shading. ▶ *Boldface type is fre-quently used to emphasize certain key words or points.*

bona fide "in good faith." (Latin.) ▶ *As used in business, bona fide indicates that something is real, actual, genuine, honest, or objective.*

bona fide occupational qualification AND **BFOQ** an exception to the antidiscrimination rules in Title VII of the Civil Rights Act of 1964, as Amended, where the exception is an actual requirement for performing the job in question. ▶ *Sex is a bona fide occupational qualification when a company is hiring a restroom attendant for the women's lounge.*

bond a document that evidences debt. (A *bond* may be issued by an industrial concern, the Federal government, a state, a county, a municipal government, or any other entity.) ▶ *A bond is traded in the same manner as a share of stock.*

bond indenture the details of a legal contract set forth in an agreement between those issuing bonds and those buying bonds. ▶ *Please read the bond indenture to make certain that you understand the terms and conditions of this issue.*

bond power a power of attorney used in connection with the sale and transfer of registered bonds. ▶ *My brother has bond power for all of my tax-free and municipal bond holdings.*

bond premium the net amount, in excess of its face value, yielded by the sale of a bond. ▶ *The bond premium on the sale of the Yucca City sewer bonds amounted to $250 per bond.*

bond rate   the rate of interest that a bond pays its holder. ▶ *Assuming a par value of $1,000, a bond whose indenture commits it to a bond rate of 5 percent would pay the holder $50 per year.*

bond yield   the income that will be realized by a bond purchaser. (Three factors influence the *bond yield:* (1) purchase price, (2) nominal or coupon rate of interest, and (3) length of time to maturity.) ▶ *My broker is advising me to purchase Waterford Corp. bonds now because the bond yield is 7.25 percent.*

bonded warehouse   **1.** a warehouse required by the Federal government to have a license and bond to insure against loss of internal revenue taxes or customs duties on items stored there. ▶ *Goods being imported usually have to be stored in a bonded warehouse until the customs duties are paid.* **2.** a public warehouse licensed and bonded for the storage of agricultural commodities. ▶ *With the arrival of that last shipment, we now have 372 bales of cotton stored in a bonded warehouse.*

bonus   extra compensation paid to a worker. (A *bonus* may be one of two types: (1) a production bonus, which is a regularly scheduled reward granted for exceeding standard performance, or (2) a non-production bonus, which is not regularly scheduled but is basically a gratuity; for example, a Christmas bonus.) ▶ *All employees will receive a bonus amounting to 10 percent of their monthly salary.*

bonus stock   stock given as a pre-mium with the purchase of bonds or stock. ▶ *Anyone who purchases 100 shares of the new stock issue will receive five additional shares as bonus stock.*

book of original entry   See *journal.*

book value   the net amount at which an asset is carried on a firm's books; that is, the gross value or cost less accumulated depreciation. ▶ *The book value on that particular vehicle is only $2,500.*

book value per share (of stock) AND **book value of a share (of stock)**   the net assets of a corporation divided by the number of shares of stock outstanding. ▶ *The book value of a share of Tylex stock is $4.25, whereas it is currently trading at $6.50.*

bookkeeping   the process of analyzing, classifying, and recording the financial transactions of an enterprise. ▶ *Accurate bookkeeping is very important in organizations of any size.*

boom   a period of high economic prosperity. ▶ *In the years following World War II, the American economy experienced an unprecedented boom.*

boondoggle   a project of dubious value whose only apparent usefulness is to provide employment, especially in government. ▶ *The government's research and development project on the modification of the atomic weather vane is a real boondoggle.*

boot up   to start up a computer. ▶ *Older PCs take longer to boot up than do more modern computers.*

borrowed hours   personnel hours obtained from one work center for use in another work center. ▶ *Borrowed hours are deducted from the available hours of the work center from which they are borrowed.*

bottom line   net profit; net loss; net result. ▶ *The bottom line on that project is that it will not be profitable.*

Boulwareism   a policy of developing, from management's standpoint, firm and fair offers to a labor union and sticking to these offers regardless of the intensity or length of negotiations. (This collective bargaining strategy was developed by a former vice president, Lemuel Boulware, of the General Electric Company.) ▶ *Boulwareism is a strategy of making management's first offer its last offer.*

bounce a check   to write a check on a depository account with prior knowledge that the account lacks sufficient funds for the check to clear. ▶ *We will not be able to pay the office rent this month unless we bounce a check.*

box top offer   an offer for a premium item, which is accepted by mailing a part of a product packaging to the producer of the product. ▶ *A box top offer usually can be found on a package of cereal.*

boxcar   a railroad car that is totally enclosed and can be padlocked and sealed. ▶ *Goods that must be protected from the weather can only be shipped by rail in a boxcar.*

boycott   an attempt to restrict the patronage of a business enterprise by influencing people not to do business with it. ▶ *A boycott is*

sometimes used by labor unions against employers.

brain drain   the loss of a country's well-educated individuals, professional people, technicians, or skilled craftspeople to other countries. ▶ *The brain drain typically occurs because employment opportunities, living conditions, tax rates, and pay are more favorable in another country.*

brainstorming   an approach to problem solving utilizing groups of people, free association of ideas, unrestricted group interaction, and complete restraint of criticism. ▶ *Brainstorming can be an effective way to solve a problem by generating as many potential solutions as possible within a short period of time.*

brainwashing   a systematic indoctrination designed to change the convictions or beliefs of others. ▶ *If Carl doesn't go along with our new advertising campaign soon, we may have to resort to brainwashing to get him to agree.*

branch bank   **1.** a bank that has a central office and one or more offices at locations removed from the central office. ▶ *It is not unusual for a branch bank to have ten or more locations.* **2.** any office of a bank removed from its central office. ▶ *Since many of our customers can no longer get downtown to conduct their banking business, we should establish a new branch bank in the northern part of town.*

branch banking   an arrangement whereby a single bank maintains more than one office. ▶ *Branch* *banking has long been common-place in California.*

brand the name or mark used to identify goods or services so as to distinguish them from other competing goods and services. ▶ *A catchy or unusual name sometimes helps people to remember a particular brand.*

brand image the impression of a particular brand of goods or services that has been created in the minds of actual and potential customers. ▶ *IBM has a very strong brand image in the field of computers.*

brand loyalty the degree to which customers repeatedly choose one brand over competing brands. ▶ *One of the objectives of advertising is to intensify consumer brand loyalty.*

brand mark distinctive letters, words, or phrases that identify a product or a manufacturer. (Similar to *logo*.) ▶ *M&M's is a brand mark in candy.*

brand name the protected, proprietary designation of a good or service. ▶ *Levi's is a well known brand name in blue jeans.*

BRC See *business reply card.*

breach of contract the failure of one of the parties to a contractual agreement to perform as specified in the agreement. ▶ *Failure to deliver goods by the date specified is a breach of contract.*

break-even analysis a method or procedure of analyzing the interrelationships of cost, volume, and profit to determine the point at which the stream of income produced equals total costs. ▶ *According to the break-even analysis, we will not completely recover our costs until we have produced 10,549 units.*

break-even chart AND **profit-volume graph; profitgraph; p/v graph** a graphic representation of the total cost of manufactured goods and of the income from sales thereof at various levels. ▶ *The purpose of the break-even chart is to show the number of units that must be sold before all expenses are covered.*

break-even point the point at which income from the sale of goods or services equals their total cost. ▶ *The break-even point for the new microchips is 12,532 units.*

break-off point the point at which separate items or grades of a product emerge from a common raw material as a result of a common processing procedure or operation. ▶ *Catalytic conversion is a significant break-off point in the processing of crude oil.*

break-up value the value of the assets of a company should the company be dissolved. ▶ *It is not unusual to find a corporation with a break-up value greater than its current book value.*

bridge loan a short-term loan to cover the gap between the sale of one asset and the purchase of another. ▶ *The bridge loan arrangement is commonly used in the residential housing market to assist a home buyer who must purchase another home prior to the sale of a currently owned home.*

broadside a multi-folded, often multi-colored sheet that, when unfolded, conveys an advertising message. ▶ *The design of the new broadside for the electric fireplace tongs is really outstanding.*

brochure a booklet, often illustrated, that has been given special production and editorial attention to create interest in a product or service, or the idea it offers. ▶ *The advertising agency has been working on a new brochure for the fog-less window panes.*

broken lot goods or merchandise offered for sale in smaller lots than usually constitute the unit of sale. ▶ *If you wait until the end of the season, you may be able to purchase a broken lot of 50 units rather than the customary lot of 100 units.*

broker a middleman who brings together buyers and sellers of goods or securities or other commodities and endeavors to execute the necessary transactions. ▶ *For bringing buyers and sellers together, a broker is paid a commission.*

brokerage 1. the fee paid to a broker. ▶ *Our brokerage income is up significantly this year.* 2. the business of a broker. ▶ *Real estate brokerage is a highly profitable business, but it is very risky.*

brokerage house an investment securities firm. ▶ *My friend Thomas sells bonds for a Wall Street brokerage house.*

broker's loan a bank loan made to a stockbroker and secured by stock. ▶ *If we can obtain a broker's loan from the bank, we will have sufficient working capital for sixty days.*

brotherhood an international or national union. (The term alludes to the fact that originally some unions began as fraternal or benefit associations.) ▶ *The International Brotherhood of Electrical Workers represents workers in a number of different industries.*

bucket shop an illegal stock market operation that takes a customer's order to buy or sell securities but never executes the order. (The broker in this illegal transaction would hope to profit by pocketing any loss a customer would have suffered. If the customer would have made a profit, the broker would pay that profit out of his pocket.) ▶ *A broker running a bucket shop assumes that the customer will be wrong most of the time.*

buddy rating a technique for rating personnel performance that was developed by the U.S. Navy during World War II. (This technique requires that every member of a group rate the other members of the group on certain aspects of their work performance.) ▶ *Buddy rating could create social problems in some work environments.*

budget a statement of anticipated results expressed in numerical terms. (A *budget* may be stated in dollars, in numbers of items, in numbers of machine hours, in numbers of people, or any other quantitative terms.) ▶ *A budget may show cash flow (the cash budget), it may show projected expenditures (the expense budget), or it may refer to anticipated capital outlays (capital expenditures budget).*

budget period the period of time covered by a budget. ▶ *For most organizations, the normal budget period is one year.*

budgetary control the process of comparing actual results with budget projections. (This can lead to changes in budgetary projections or other actions that reduce expenditures.) ▶ *Some organizations have a special department that monitors budgets and exercises budgetary control.*

budgetary variance the difference between the amount budgeted and the amount actually spent or used ▶ *Our president was pleased because this month's budgetary variance was the smallest we have ever had.*

budgeting the process whereby quantitative planning is committed to paper in an orderly, systematic, and methodical fashion. ▶ *All departments are hereby requested to complete their budgeting for next year by November 15.*

buffer a special section of computer memory used for the temporary storage of information. ▶ *Many computer programs set up temporary buffers as part of the program* ▶ *Since a computer is much faster than a printer, the computer's output is first sent to a buffer before it is sent to the printer.*

buffer stock See *safety stock.*

bug 1. an error in a computer program. ▶ *We have spent three days looking for the bug in the new accounts program.* 2. an electronic eavesdropping device. ▶ *If we plant a bug in the boardroom, we can find out what the directors*

think of the new advertising campaign.

bull a stock market investor who believes that the market will rise. (Compare with *bear.*) ▶ *My stockbroker tends to be a bull most of the time.*

bull market a rising stock market. (Compare with *bear market.*) ▶ *The average investor is looking forward to a bull market after election day.*

bulldog edition that edition of a morning newspaper that is printed the previous evening for shipment to out-of-town readers. ▶ *Late breaking news will not be covered in the bulldog edition.*

bumping an arrangement during a layoff whereby an employee with seniority can demand the job of another employee with less seniority. ▶ *Bumping rights are clearly spelled out in the labor agreement.*

bureau a department, office, or agency, especially of the Federal government. ▶ *The Federal Bureau of Investigation is headquartered in Washington, D.C., but has many offices around the country.*

bureaucracy a form of organization characterized by rigid adherence to formalized policies, procedures, and rules. ▶ *Through its rigidity, a bureaucracy strives to maintain consistency, uniformity, and fairness.*

bureaucrat 1. an official or manager in a *bureaucracy.* ▶ *Every manager in the Federal government is a bureaucrat.* 2. an official or manager in a nonbureaucratic organization who manages by fixed routine and rules, exercising little or no initiative or judgment. ▶ *Even the most progressive organization has a bureaucrat or two somewhere in the chain of command.*

buried offer an offer of something free, hidden in advertising copy. ▶ *The advertising copy must be read very carefully in order to discover the buried offer.*

burnout a chronic state of fatigue, frustration, disillusionment, disappointment, or boredom resulting from work or relationships that do not provide the expected rewards. (Some of the symptoms of *burnout* include fatigue, anger, cynicism, irritability, and frequent headaches.) ▶ *Many people at our plant are suffering from burnout.*

burster a device used to separate individual pages or forms in a set of continuous paper. ▶ *A burster eliminates a great deal of manual effort.*

business activity the volume or level of production and distribution of goods and services as indicated by the number of business transactions of various types, rates of employment, and other quantitative measures. ▶ *By all estimates, business activity should begin to increase after Inauguration Day.*

business agent a full-time employee of a local union whose duties include negotiating labor agreements with the employer, overseeing the way in which the collective bargaining agreement is carried out, handling union member grievances against the employer, and conducting union membership drives. ▶ *The business agent is responsible for the day-to-day operations of a local union.*

business cycle the ups and downs in business activities as they occur periodically. ▶ *Generally, a business cycle follows a somewhat regular pattern.*

business entity a single for-profit firm. ▶ *A business entity may be large or small as well as national or international, but its purpose is to make money.*

business entity concept a concept which holds that a business is treated, for accounting purposes, separately from the person or persons who own the business. ▶ *The business entity concept separates a business organization from the people who own it.*

business environment the economic, political, social, cultural, and institutional conditions within which a business enterprise exists and conducts its operations. ▶ *Forces and events in the business environment have a dramatic impact on the day-to-day operations of an organization.*

business game a training device utilizing a simulated business situation. (The players make various operating decisions and receive quantitative feedback on their decisions from the game.) ▶ *A business game is commonly played on or in conjunction with a computer.*

business indicators the various quantitative elements that reveal the general health of the business and the national economy. ▶ *Housing starts and unemployment rates are examples of business indicators.*

business law the statutes, rules,

codes, and regulations that are enforceable by court action, and within which business must operate. ► *Business law has become increasingly complex over the last decade.*

business reply card AND **BRC** a preaddressed post card accompanying direct mail advertising that may be returned to order a product, request more information, or request a call from a salesperson. ► *We find that the responses to our direct mail solicitations are much higher when we include a business reply card.*

bust a period of economic downturn. ► *The stock market has gone from boom to bust in a few short months.*

buy on closing order a stock market order to a broker to purchase a security or commodity at the price prevailing when the market closes. ► *A buy on closing order is usually made in anticipation of a rise in the price of stock.*

buy on opening order a stock market order to a broker to purchase a security or commodity at the price prevailing when the market opens. ► *A buy on opening order may allow an investor to buy at the best price possible during the day.*

buy order an order to a broker to purchase a specified amount of a security at the market price, or at a stipulated price. ► *A buy order is good until executed or cancelled.*

buyer's market a market in which conditions are more favorable to the buyer than to the seller. (Normally, a *buyer's market* results from an oversupply of goods, which consequently drives down the price.) ► *In a buyer's market, the buyer can afford to be more selective in the purchase of goods.*

buying the process of acquiring goods and services for consumption or use. ► *Manufacturers use advertising in an attempt to influence the buying habits of individual consumers.*

buying agent a specialized middleman who seeks out sources of supply for his or her principals. ► *Joan is a buying agent and is compensated in the form of a commission from her principals.*

buying club a group of retailers who combine their purchasing needs in order to buy in larger quantities and secure more advantageous prices. ► *Belonging to a buying club is essential to survival for some retailers.*

buying power the ability to buy in large quantities. ► *A large retailer has more buying power than a small retailer.*

by-product a secondary product resulting from the manufacture of a major product. ► *Wax is a by-product resulting from the manufacture of gasoline.*

bylaws the rules adopted by an organization by which it conducts its affairs. (Corporations and organizations of all types have *bylaws*.) ► *Any change in a corporation's bylaws must be approved by the board of directors as well as the stockholders.*

byte a storage unit of primary data that represents and stores one character of data. ► *A byte is composed of eight bits.*

C

cable transfer the transfer of funds to or from a foreign country through instructions sent by cable. ▶ *We need to cable transfer $250,000 to our account in Geneva before noon today.*

CAD See *computer aided design.*

CAD/CAM computer aided design/computer aided manufacturing. (This refers to the application and use of computers to design parts, components, and products and to facilitate and control manufacturing processes. See also *computer aided design; computer aided manufacturing.*) ▶ *CAD/CAM has expedited product design and manufacturing.*

CAF See *cost and freight.*

calendar advertising a form of advertising that utilizes a calendar as the medium. (The advertiser's name, address, products, etc., are displayed on the calendar and serve as a continual reminder to the customer.) ▶ *Many insurance agents use calendar advertising.*

calendar year a continuous twelve-month period beginning on January 1 and ending on December 31. ▶ *Some companies use a calendar year for accounting purposes while other companies use a fiscal year.*

call **1.** to demand payment of an installment of the price of bonds or stocks that have been subscribed for. ▶ *We are going to call the second installment on the Branford stocks.* **2.** to demand payment of a loan secured by collateral because of failure on the part of the borrower to comply with the terms of the loan. ▶ *The bank is going to call our loan because we failed to make the interest payments as scheduled.* **3.** the visit paid by a salesperson to a customer or a prospective customer. ▶ *According to Lawrence, the call on Swenson*

Electronics went very well. **4.** a transferable option to buy a specified number of shares of stock at a stipulated price during a given period of time. ▶ *A call is purchased by investors who hope to make a profit from an increase in the price of shares above the call price.*

call-back pay additional compensation, usually paid at a premium rate, given to a worker for reporting back to work for additional hours after the worker has completed a regular shift. ▶ *Call-back pay is usually necessitated by emergency situations.*

call forwarding a special service offered by telephone companies whereby incoming calls are automatically transferred to another number. ▶ *Call forwarding is available in most areas of the U.S. at an additional cost.*

call letters a series of identifying letters assigned to a radio or television station by the Federal Communications Commission. (With a few exceptions, the call letters of stations east of the Mississippi river begin with the letter "W" and those west of the river begin with the letter "K." The exceptions are stations in existence before the Dill-White Radio Control Act of 1927.) ▶ *Today call letters are always composed of four letters.*

call loan a loan made on a day-to-day basis, callable on twenty-four hours' notice by the lender. ▶ *A call loan is confined to security and commodity brokers and is made for the purpose of facilitating the purchase of securities and commodities.*

call money money loaned to brokers by banks that is subject to payment at the discretion of the lender. ▶ *Call money is the result of a call loan.*

call (option) a right to buy 100 shares of a particular stock at a predetermined price before a preset deadline. ▶ *An investor who buys a call option does so in the expectation that the price of the stock will increase dramatically in the future.*

call pay **1.** AND **reporting pay** a payment made to a worker for reporting to work when there is no work available and the worker was not given advance notice not to report to work. ▶ *Call pay, in effect, compensates a worker for the effort expended in showing up for work.* **2.** an additional payment given to a worker as an incentive for being asked to report to work outside the normal working hours. ▶ *Acme Foods found it had to offer call pay if it wanted employees to work on Saturdays.*

call premium the amount over the face or par value of a security, especially a bond, that the issuing entity must pay the holder when the security is redeemed prior to the maturity date. ▶ *The call premium is, in effect, a penalty a firm pays for redeeming a bond early.*

call price the price at which a callable bond may be redeemed before maturity. ▶ *The call price on that series of bonds is $950.*

call report **1.** a form completed by an outside salesperson that lists the various customers contacted within a specified period, usually one week. ▶ *According to Jane's call report, she developed some very strong leads for new business last week.* **2.** AND **bank call** a bank's statement of financial condition submitted in response to a request by the bank's supervisory agency. ▶ *The Comptroller of the Currency has directed the First National Bank to submit a call report as of December 15.*

call waiting a special service offered by telephone companies whereby a tone sounds when a person is using the telephone and another person calls. ▶ *Call waiting allows a single telephone line to function as two or more lines.*

callable 1. [a bond issue] redeemable in whole or in part by the issuing corporation before actual maturity. ▶ *The Yucca City sewer bonds are a callable issue.* **2.** [a preferred stock issue] redeemable by the issuing corporation. ▶ *Callable preferred stock may be entitled to a premium if the issue is called.*

CAM See *computer aided manufacturing.*

cancellation notice a written advisement that a contract, arrangement, agreement, etc., is being cancelled. ▶ *Contracts often contain a provision whereby the contract can be terminated under certain conditions through a cancellation notice to the other party.*

cancelled check a check that has been paid and charged to a bank depositor's account and then stamped with the drawee bank's name and date. ▶ *A cancelled check serves as proof that a bill has been*

paid and when it was paid.

canned program a prewritten computer program. ▶ *A canned program is often available for purchase from a software dealer.*

canvassing the visiting of customers in a given market to gather information about the sales situation, competitive activity, opportunities, etc. ▶ *Canvassing is an important step in developing a sound marketing strategy.*

cap a limitation or ceiling, especially one placed on an interest rate. ▶ *An interest rate cap places a limitation on the amount of interest that may be charged on an adjustable rate mortgage.* ▶ *The interest on our ARM can never exceed 8 percent, its interest rate cap.*

capability the ability to perform. ▶ *A corporation has the legal capability to execute contracts.*

capability statement a listing of an organization's areas of expertise or ability to perform certain services, especially in consulting. ▶ *The attached capability statement outlines our major service areas for clients.*

capacity 1. the legal ability to do something. ▶ *An individual under 18 years of age may not have the capacity to enter into a legally binding contract.* **2.** the ability, particularly of a manufacturing organization, to produce products at a certain volume or within a specified time frame. ▶ *The plant is operating at full capacity and cannot accept any other orders at this time.*

capital the net assets of an enterprise, partnership, corporation, or other business entity including not only the original investment but all additional investments as well as earnings retained for use in the business. ▶ *Adequate capital is required to start a new business.*

capital account   an account that shows the amount of assets invested in a business by its owners. ▶ *Due to significant increases in retained earnings, the capital account has increased by 225 percent in the last two years.*

capital assets   the land, buildings, equipment, mineral deposits, leaseholds, timber preserves, goodwill, trademarks, franchises, and investments intended for continued use or possession. ▶ *Capital assets typically have a long life.*

capital budget   a budget that shows all proposed additions to capital assets during the budgeting period. ▶ *Expenditures for any new equipment to be acquired in the next twelve months must be included in the capital budget.*

capital consumption allowance the amount of depreciation included in the gross national product. ▶ *The capital consumption allowance is deducted from the gross national product (GNP) and represents an estimation of the amount of depreciation and obsolescence of capital goods resulting from use during the period.*

capital control   the monitoring system that a firm uses to regulate the use of its capital. ▶ *Requiring that an anticipated capital expense be included in the capital expenditure budget is an example*

of capital control.

capital expenditure AND **capital spending**   **1.** the procurement of long-term equipment, land, or buildings that are used to produce income for a business enterprise. ▶ *The purchase of a new computer system is a major capital expenditure.* **2.** any expenditure benefiting a future accounting period rather than the current period. ▶ *They delayed the delivery of the truck until next year, making it a capital expenditure.*

capital gain   a profit from the sale or exchange of a capital asset. ▶ *A capital gain is said to be long term if the asset sold or exchanged has been held for six months or longer.*

capital gains tax   a Federal tax on profits realized from the sale of capital assets. ▶ *The capital gains tax rate is higher for short-term gains than it is for long-term gains.*

capital goods   goods, such as machines, equipment, industrial plants, highways, etc., used in the production of other goods. ▶ *The aggregate of capital goods determines, in large measure, a nation's productive capacity.*

capital improvement   the betterment of a building or equipment that extends the life of the building or equipment. ▶ *Capital improvement differs from repair in that the purpose of repair is to restore an asset to operating condition whereas improvement seeks to extend the life of the asset.* ▶ *The expansion of our warehouse is a capital improvement.*

capital intensive   an industrial

condition wherein large investments are required in capital assets. ▶ *The automobile industry is very capital intensive.*

capital investment 1. money invested to acquire something of permanent use or value. ▶ *Purchasing the new manufacturing plant will require a large capital investment.* 2. money paid out to purchase stock or acquire an interest in a business venture. ▶ *George's capital investment in Tobago Industries gives him 12 percent of the outstanding shares of stock.*

capital loss a loss from the sale of a capital asset. ▶ *The capital loss on the sale of the Nevada silver mine was in excess of $2 million dollars.*

capital procurement obtaining funds necessary to enable a firm to grow, operate profitably, buy capital equipment, or satisfy some other need. ▶ *Capital procurement is often difficult during recessionary periods.*

capital spending See *capital expenditure.*

capital stock the shares of stock, common and preferred, which represent ownership of a firm. ▶ *The capital stock of the new company was divided into 80 percent common and 20 percent preferred.*

capital surplus that part of the paid-in surplus of a corporation not assigned to capital stock. ▶ *Contributions by stockholders in excess of par or stated value of the issued shares is considered to be capital surplus.*

capital turnover the ratio of sales to the total of all bonds outstanding

and net worth. ▶ *Capital turnover is a measure of how well a corporation uses its capital.*

capitalism AND **free enterprise** an economic system characterized by private ownership of the means of production and the free play of the market conducting business affairs. ▶ *Under capitalism, decisions about the use of resources are often based on supply and demand considerations.*

capitalization the sum of all securities issued by a corporation, including stocks, both common and preferred; bonds; and the total surplus account. ▶ *Capitalization represents the investment in a corporation.*

capitalization ratio the percentage of long-term debt, preferred stock, common stock, and surplus to a firm's total investment. ▶ *The capitalization ratio is a measure of a firm's leverage.*

carload rate a transportation rate that applies to a railroad shipment that occupies an entire railroad car rather than a portion thereof. ▶ *A carload rate is the most favorable rate available for railroad shipments.*

car loadings the number of railroad freight cars loaded during a given period. ▶ *Car loadings are used as an indicator of the level of business activity.*

carbon copy a duplicate of something. ▶ *The plant in Fargo is a carbon copy of the one in Marionsville.*

career anchors motives that account for the way people select and prepare for a career. (The specific *career anchors* identified by Edgar Schein are managerial competence, technical or functional competence, security, creativity, and autonomy and independence.) ▶ *It was determined that Joel possessed all the career anchors necessary for success.*

career ladder a vertical sequence of jobs that allows an employee to advance in an organization. ▶ *A career ladder in an advertising agency includes the positions of account executive, supervisor, and vice president.*

cargo the freight or merchandise shipped on a transportation vehicle. ▶ *Passengers are not considered cargo.*

carrier a receiver of goods who agrees under contract to transport them from one point to another for a fee. ▶ *A railroad, a truckline, an airline, or a bus line is a carrier.*

carrier rate the rate charged by a transporter for carrying goods. (The *carrier rate* is normally computed on the basis of units of weight, but may also be based on size or bulkiness of the item shipped.) ▶ *We compared the carrier rates of a dozen different lines and found them all to be excessive.*

carrier's lien the legal right of a transporter to retain freight or merchandise shipped as collateral for payment of transportation charges. ▶ *A carrier's lien provides a cargo carrier some assurance that freight charges will be paid.*

carrot and stick approach an approach to motivation offering a positive reward (the carrot) if a de-sired result is accomplished or a desired action is taken, or, conversely punishment (the stick). (From the visual image of a carrot tied by a string to the end of a stick that is held in front of a horse. The horse moves forward in hopes of getting to eat the carrot. If this does not work, the stick is used to strike the horse.) ▶ *The carrot and stick approach is not as effective a motivational approach as it once was.*

carrying charge an amount added to the purchase price of goods or services to cover interest and other charges for installment credit. ▶ *The carrying charge on a credit purchase can often be substantial.*

carrying value the net value of an asset as shown on a firm's books. ▶ *The acquisition cost of an asset less accumulated depreciation equals the carrying value of the asset.*

carryover merchandise the merchandise that is left over from one selling season to the next season. ▶ *In retailing, too much carryover merchandise can create cash flow problems.*

cartel an association of business organizations, located in one or more countries, formed for the purpose of regulating prices, quantities of goods sold, or marketing territories. ▶ *A cartel is illegal in the United States.*

case law that body of law established by court decisions in prior cases. ▶ *It is through case law that the meanings and applications of statutes are determined.*

case method a method of teaching

business and law students in which the student develops solutions to actual or hypothetical business or law problems. ▶ *Andrew's law course was built around the case method, and required rigorous reading.*

cash coin, currency, checks, money orders, bank drafts, and commercial bank deposits. ▶ *Normally, any medium of exchange that a bank will accept at face value upon deposit is considered to be cash.*

cash account an account with a brokerage house that requires that the purchaser of securities pay the full amount due for purchases within a short period of time, usually five business days. ▶ *A cash account practically dictates that securities be paid for as they are purchased.*

cash balance the amount of actual cash on hand at any given time. ▶ *Our cash balance is getting very low.*

cash basis a method of accounting in which income is recognized when it is received and expenses are recognized when they are paid. (Contrast with *accrual basis*.) ▶ *Many small businesses operate on a cash basis.*

cash before delivery AND **CBD** a stipulation that goods must be paid for before delivery will be made. ▶ *Most mail order sales require cash before delivery.*

cash book a book or ledger in which a record of cash receipts and disbursements is kept. ▶ *The balance in the cash book should be the same as the balance in the general ledger cash account.*

cash budget a budget that shows the projected sources and uses of cash during the budgeting period. ▶ *The board of directors spent all morning blaming the cash budget for the company's woes.*

cash cow a business that produces high profits and generates a continuing and substantial cash flow. ▶ *A cash cow is frequently not a glamorous business, but it is one that is stable.*

cash customer a purchaser who pays cash for goods or services. ▶ *A cash customer is sometimes given a purchase discount by the seller.*

cash disbursements book a book or ledger in which cash expenditures are recorded. ▶ *The cash disbursements book shows every cash expenditure made by a firm.*

cash discount a discount from the purchase price of goods allowed for prompt payment. ▶ *A cash discount encourages purchasers to pay with cash or by check instead of credit cards.*

cash dividend a corporate dividend paid in cash as opposed to a dividend paid in stock, bonds, or property. ▶ *Many investors prefer a cash dividend rather than a stock dividend.*

cash flow the reported net income of a firm, plus depreciation, depletion, amortization, and extraordinary charges to reserves not paid in cash. ▶ *Cash flow is a measurement of the funds that pass through an enterprise during a given period of time.*

cash flow statement a statement

that shows the cash receipts and the uses to which cash is put during a given period. ▶ *A cash flow statement helps a business enterprise understand where its cash comes from and how it is used.*

cash in lieu   cash in place of something. (Cash offered in the place of something else that had previously been offered, or cash offered as an alternative to something of a non-cash nature.) ▶ *This year's stock dividend will be one share for every ten shares held, or $10 cash in lieu.*

cash market   a market in which transactions are promptly completed with transfer of ownership and payment is executed immediately or very quickly. (See also *spot market*.) ▶ *In a cash market in commodities a transaction is completed on the spot for cash.*

cash on delivery AND **COD**   a type of sale wherein the seller requires full payment for the merchandise upon delivery. ▶ *Cash on delivery is a method of selling to either poor credit risks, customers who do not have open credit accounts, or accounts where future payment cannot be guaranteed.*

cash on hand   the amount of money actually in a cash register, cash box, safe, or otherwise held on a firm's premises. ▶ *After a holiday sale, a retailer may have a large amount of cash on hand.*

cash price   the price charged when payment is made immediately or within a specified interval of time. (See also *spot price*.) ▶ *The cash price of a good may be lower than the credit price for the same good.*

cash receipts book   a book or ledger in which cash receipts are recorded. ▶ *The entries in a cash receipts book are in chronological order.*

cash reserve   cash kept by a business or an individual that is in excess of the cash required for immediate needs. ▶ *This week's cash reserve is $2,000.*

cash sale   a sale of goods for which payment is made in cash. ▶ *The biggest advantage of a cash sale is that the seller receives payment immediately.*

cash settlement   a transaction in which payment is to be executed immediately or in very short order. ▶ *High quality securities bought on the London Stock Exchange are subject to cash settlement.*

cash statement   a periodic report showing opening and closing balances of cash on hand and in the bank, receipts and disbursements during the period, and the particulars of any deposits, withdrawals, or other changes in the cash account. ▶ *A cash statement is usually prepared monthly.*

cash surrender value   the amount the insurer will pay the insured upon cancellation of a life insurance policy before the death of the insured. ▶ *The cash surrender value increases with the age of the policy.*

cashier   **1.** the person in a business who accepts payments, provides change if needed, and records each such transaction. ▶ *Please take your purchase to the cashier and she will process it for you.* **2.** a bank officer who is responsible for the custody of a bank's assets and whose signature is required on all official documents of the bank. ▶ *A bank cashier is usually in charge of all the backroom activities of the bank.*

cashier's check a bank's own check drawn upon itself and signed by the cashier or another authorized bank official. ▶ *Some transactions require payment to be made by cashier's check rather than by personal check.*

casting the act of making a product by pouring a molten substance into a mold and allowing it to cool or solidify. ▶ *Either metal or plastic may be used for casting.*

casual worker a temporary worker. ▶ *A casual worker usually receives no benefits and acquires no seniority.*

casualty insurance generally, all insurance except life, marine, and sometimes, fire. (*Casualty insurance* exists for automobiles, public liability, accident and health, and worker's compensation.) ▶ *The cost of casualty insurance increased greatly owing to a number of natural disasters.*

catalog selling a form of retailing in which customers order from a seller's catalog rather than make purchases at a store. ▶ *Because of the convenience to customers, catalog selling is a very popular method of retailing in the United States today.*

cats and dogs the issues of stocks of companies having short histories of sales, earnings, and dividend payouts. (Slang). ▶ *In a bull mar-* *ket, even the prices of the cats and dogs go up.*

caveat emptor "let the buyer beware." (Latin. The expression suggests that one buys goods or services at one's own risk.) ▶ *Whenever I consider buying a used car, I always think* caveat emptor.

caveat venditor "let the seller beware." (Latin. The term suggests that the purchaser has recourse to the seller in the event that goods purchased are not as represented.) ▶ *There are many new laws that involve the selling of real estate that justify the phrase* caveat venditor.

CBD See *cash before delivery.*

CBOT See *Chicago Board of Trade.*

CDT See *Central Daylight Time.*

cease and desist order an order issued by a court or an administrative agency requiring an individual or organization to stop a particular activity. ▶ *The Federal Trade Commission may issue a cease and desist order to prohibit a manufacturer from making false or misleading claims about a competitor's product.*

ceiling an upper limitation, such as a ceiling price or a wage ceiling. ▶ *An adjustable rate mortgage may have a ceiling above which the interest rate cannot rise.*

cellular phone a portable telephone that can be carried from place to place. ▶ *A cellular phone is a boon to the salesperson who is always on the go.*

center spread two facing pages

located in the center of a publication. (This is considered a very desirable position by advertisers.) ▶ *The center spread of* Time *magazine would be an excellent place for our new advertisement.*

central bank the official bank of a country that is responsible for issuing currency, administering monetary policy, holding the deposits and reserves of the nation's banks, and engaging in transactions that facilitate business and protect the public's interest. ▶ *The Federal Reserve Bank is the central bank of the United States.*

central business district the downtown section of a city that houses retail establishments, offices, banks, government agencies, hotels, entertainment facilities, etc. ▶ *The central business district in many U.S. cities is not as predominant as it once was.*

central buying a purchasing practice wherein a large retailer purchases goods and services for all of its outlets from a main office. ▶ *Central buying permits a greater degree of inventory and price control than would exist if each location did its own buying.*

Central Daylight Time AND **CDT** the adjusted time in the central part of the United States from early April to late October. ▶ *Bank transactions completed after 2:00 P.M. Central Daylight Time will be posted on the next business day.*

central processing unit AND **CPU** that portion of a computer system containing the arithmetic unit, the internal memory unit, and the control unit. ▶ *The central processing*

unit is the heart of a computer system.

Central Standard Time AND **CST** the standard time in the central United States from late October to early April. ▶ *Central Standard Time is six hours behind Greenwich Mean Time.*

central tendency the tendency for data in a frequency distribution to group themselves around some middle value in the distribution. ▶ *The mean and the medium are two measures of central tendency.*

centralization 1. the locating of organizational functions at the home office of an organization. ▶ *Centralization increases the size of a corporation's headquarters staff.* 2. the retention of decision-making authority and responsibility in the upper echelons of an organization. ▶ *Our company is so centralized that middle managers have little authority to make decisions.*

CEO See *chief executive officer.*

certificate a document attesting to the truth of something, or to status, qualifications, privileges, etc. ▶ *A stock certificate attests to a stockholder's ownership of a certain number of shares and the right to participate in the corporation's profits.*

certificate of deposit a formal receipt for funds left with a bank as a special deposit. (If they bear interest, they are payable at a definite future date or after a specified notice of withdrawal. If they do not bear interest, they may be payable on demand or at a specified future date.) ▶ *A certificate of deposit is* *carried by a bank on its general ledger in a certificate of deposit account rather than on individual ledgers under the name of the party to whom the certificate was issued.*

certificate of incorporation AND **articles of incorporation** the charter or franchise granted by a state to the original petitioners of a corporation, authorizing the corporation to transact business as a legal entity. ▶ *We should frame our certificate of incorporation and hang it in the lobby.*

certificate of origin a document required by countries that have treaty agreements with the United States for shipments arriving in their countries. (The purpose is to certify that the goods covered actually originated in the United States.) ▶ *A certificate of origin is often used to replace a consular invoice although some countries require both.*

certification the authorization of a union by a Federal or state agency to act as the collective bargaining agent for a specified bargaining unit. ▶ *A union cannot act as a collective bargaining agent without certification.*

certified check a personal check bearing the bank's certification that there is money in the account to cover the check. (The money to cover the account is essentially frozen in the account until the check is cashed.) ▶ *With a certified check, the bank is guaranteeing that the depositor's account contains sufficient funds to pay the check when it is presented for payment.*

Certified Public Accountant AND **CPA** a professional designation conferred upon an individual who has met a state's legal requirements for the public practice of accountancy. ▶ *Possession of the title Certified Public Accountant attests to the holder's competence in installing accounting systems, preparing accounting reports, and analyzing accounting data.*

ceteris paribus "assuming that everything else remains unchanged." (Latin.) ▶ *If the price of a product continues to fall,* ceteris paribus, *people will buy more of that product.*

CFO See *chief financial officer.*

CFTC See *Commodities Futures Trading Association.*

chad the piece of material removed from a card or a paper tape when a hole or a notch is made. ▶ *Please be careful when emptying the receptacle because the chad is difficult to get out of the carpet.*

chain banking the ownership or control of two or more banks by one or more individuals. ▶ *A chain banking system is built around a key bank that is usually larger than any other bank in the chain.*

chain of command the sequence of superior-subordinate relationships through which formal authority is exercised in an organization. ▶ *When complaining about working conditions, it is company policy that employees adhere strictly to the chain of command.*

chain picketing the picketing of several retail outlets of one specific company. ▶ *The union has decided to use chain picketing on all of the*

Acme Grocery Store outlets in the city.

chain store   one of two or more retail stores in the same line of business owned and operated by the same firm. ▶ *Each chain store typically has the same merchandise as every other store in the chain.*

chairman of the board   the member of a corporation's board of directors who presides over its meetings. (In actual practice, the board chairman is usually the most powerful member of the policy-making group in a corporation.) ▶ *The chairman of the board is often the chief executive officer of a firm.*

Chamber of Commerce   a local association of business firms and professionals that promotes the area's business and industry. ▶ *The Chamber of Commerce is holding its monthly meeting next Wednesday.*

champion   an organizational innovator who promotes, supports, and encourages new ideas, products, systems, etc. ▶ *A champion is in favor of change, whether in products or approaches.*

change agent   one who instigates or implements change in an organization. (This person may be from within the organization or an outsider.) ▶ *A change agent often challenges an organization's traditional ways of doing things* ▶ *The outside change agent may bring new ideas to an organization.*

channel of distribution   the route taken by a product as it moves from producer to ultimate con-

sumer. ▶ *In some industries the channel of distribution is short.* ▶ *Most often, the channel of distribution followed by the title to a good is the same as the one followed by the good itself.*

Chapter VII   a section of the Federal Bankruptcy Act of 1978 that allows a petitioner to seek liquidation. ▶ *Under Chapter VII, the court appoints a trustee who is empowered to make broad decisions and operate the business in such a way as to prevent loss.*

Chapter XI   a section of the Federal Bankruptcy Act of 1978 that allows a petitioner to seek a reorganization of a business. ▶ *Under Chapter XI, the owners and managers of the business may remain in control of the organization.*

Chapter XIII   a section of the Federal Bankruptcy Act of 1978 under which an individual or a small business is allowed to pay off a portion of its debt, receives extra time to pay off its debt, or both. ▶ *Once the court has approved a debt repayment plan under Chapter XIII, all unsecured creditors must accept the plan.*

charge account   an arrangement that allows a customer to buy merchandise now and pay for it later. ▶ *My Uncle Andrew has a charge account at Acme Dry Goods.*

charge-off   **1.** to write-off or treat as a loss. ▶ *Please instruct the Accounting Department to charge-off Mr. Brown's loan.* **2.** the amount written-off or treated as a loss. ▶ *The charge-off on Mr. Brown's loan is $750.*

charter   **1.** an instrument issued

by a sovereign legislature or other public authority granting a public or private corporation or institution the right to operate as such, and defining the restrictions under which it may do so. ▶ *According to our corporate charter, we can engage in almost any business of our choosing.* **2.** to hire a vehicle for exclusive use. ▶ *To get to Las Vegas in time for the convention, we will have to charter an airplane.* **3.** a statement of expectations or a mandate from management given to an individual in an organization whereby the individual accomplishes the job to be done. ▶ *John's charter from the president is to straighten out the mess in the Accounting Department.*

chattel an item of personal property. ▶ *Anything tangible that is owned, with the exception of real estate, is a chattel.*

chattel mortgage a transfer of title to personal property as security for the payment of a debt. ▶ *Tom's car could not be traded in since the bank held a chattel mortgage on it as security for his vacation loan.*

cheap money a situation in which, due to a money supply that exceeds the needs of the economy, money loses its purchasing power and interest rates are low. ▶ *The appropriate time for a major plant renovation may be during a period of cheap money because interest rates are low.*

check **1.** a draft drawn on a bank by a depositor instructing the bank to pay a certain sum of money to the person or persons named on

the check or to the bearer of the check. ▶ *A check is payable upon demand.* **2.** to verify or to investigate the correctness or accuracy of something. ▶ *Elaine, would you have the Purchasing Department check on the accuracy of this invoice?*

check-off an arrangement whereby an employer agrees to deduct union dues from the employee's paycheck and submit this money to the union. ▶ *The check-off procedure simplifies dues collection for the union.*

check signer a machine that signs checks automatically. ▶ *With the new check signer we just purchased we will be able to process the month-end bills faster.*

check stub a perforated attachment to a check that contains information about the check. (The *check stub* remains as a record of the writing of the check after the check itself has been removed. The *check stub* indicates the amount of the check, the payee, the date, and other pertinent information.) ▶ *I have to look at my check stub to determine the amount of the last check I wrote.*

checking account a bank account that checks may be drawn against. ▶ *Robert has just opened a checking account at the First National Bank.*

checking copy a copy of a publication sent by a publisher to the advertising agency or to the advertiser so that an advertisement as it appears in the publication may be checked for accuracy. ▶ *A checking copy is often the last chance an* *advertiser will have to catch any errors in an advertisement.*

chi-square test a statistical procedure to determine whether or not two or more variables are (1) independent or (2) homogeneous. (The *chi-square test* formula for determining independence is the same as the formula for determining homogeneity.) ▶ *By applying the chi-square formula, it was determined that personal income and purchasing power were homogeneous variables.*

Chicago Board of Trade AND **CBOT** a commodity exchange organized in 1848. ▶ *The Chicago Board of Trade is the foremost grain market in the United States.*

chief executive the top officer of a corporation. ▶ *The job of chief executive is normally held by either the chairman of the board or the president of a corporation.*

chief executive officer AND **CEO** the corporate officer who has ultimate management responsibility for the organization and its operation. ▶ *The chief executive officer reports directly to the board of directors.*

chief financial officer AND **CFO** the corporate officer who has full and final financial authority to make appropriations and expenditures for an organization. ▶ *The chief financial officer usually reports to the chief executive officer.*

chief operating officer AND **COO** the corporate officer who has the overall responsibility for the day-to-day activities and operations of an organization. ▶ *In some cases, the chief operating officer may*

also have the title of president.

child labor laws legislation concerned with the employment of children in the labor market designed to protect them from hazardous work, to assure them a minimum amount of schooling, and to establish age limits and conditions of work. ▶ *According to the child labor laws, hazardous work cannot be performed by anyone under 18 years old.*

chopped ticket that portion of a price ticket that is removed from sold merchandise and sent to the vendor daily as a procedural step in a vendor's computerized stock control system. ▶ *To have an accurate record of inventory, it is important that each chopped ticket be processed, batched, and forwarded to the vendor on a daily basis.*

Christmas bonus a nonproduction payment given to a worker at Christmas time. ▶ *The typical Christmas bonus in this organization is two weeks' pay.*

chronic unemployment unemployment that lasts longer than six months. ▶ *Chronic unemployment is becoming a serious problem during the current recession.*

churning the execution of a large number of transactions in a customer's account solely for the purpose of generating brokerage commissions. ▶ *Churning a customer's accounts is illegal.*

CIF See *cost, insurance, and freight.*

circular a small printed advertisement that contains a sales message and is delivered by hand or by mail. ▶ *The owner of the new store down* *the street left a circular under the windshield wiper of my car yesterday.*

circulating capital See *floating capital.*

circulation guarantee the number of copies of a periodical the publisher guarantees will be sold or circulated. (It is an indication of the potential audience a prospective advertiser may reach by advertising in the publication.) ▶ *The rates charged for advertising are based on the size of the circulation guarantee.*

civil action a judicial proceeding in which an individual, and not the state, acts as the accuser. (A *civil action* may involve a contractual dispute, a question of property rights, or a personal wrong for which monetary damages are sought.) ▶ *When he slipped on the ice and broke his leg in his neighbor's driveway, John brought a civil action against the neighbor.*

civil rights the rights of a citizen that are protected by the U.S. Constitution. (An individual's basic *civil rights* are the rights to own property, to use the court system to seek redress of alleged wrongs, to marry, to contract, and to obtain any other benefits set out by law.) ▶ *I think my civil rights were violated when the contractor refused to sell me the house.*

civil wrong an act or the failure to act that violates a legal duty. ▶ *The victim of an alleged civil wrong can seek redress through a civil action in the courts.*

claim 1. a demand for something. ▶ *We need to claim the items that* are being held in storage. 2. a request to an insurer to indemnify the insured for a loss suffered. ▶ *To file an insurance claim you must use the proper form.*

claim for refund a request by a taxpayer to the *Internal Revenue Service* to refund all or part of overpaid taxes. ▶ *A claim for refund must be initiated within three years of the date of the tax return.*

class interval the statistical difference between the upper limit value and the lower limit value of a series of grouped data. ▶ *The class interval for any series of grouped data is normally uniform.*

class price the price charged one group of buyers. ▶ *A different class price may be charged a different class of buyers.*

class rate 1. a method of classifying rates for advertising on radio or television. ▶ *The class rate for the most desirable times is the highest rate charged.* 2. a transportation rate applicable to a classification of commodities. ▶ *The class rate for ore differs from the class rate for crude oil.*

classical school that school of economic thought originating with Adam Smith and including the writings of Say, Ricardo, Malthus, and J.S. Mill. ▶ *The classical school advocated a policy of non-intervention on the part of government.*

classified advertising AND **want ads** a form of print advertising using only text that generally appears in a special section of a newspaper or magazine. ▶ *Classified advertising is widely used to* *advertise job openings, houses for sale or rent, and automobiles for sale.*

classified stock   common stock that is divided into two or more classes. ▶ *Classified stock may consist of Class A, stock that may be used to raise capital, and Class B stock, which may be used to assign voting rights.*

clause   a designated part of a written document, such as a contract, will, insurance policy, statute, etc., that contains a separate and major point. ▶ *According to Clause 15, damage from flood is limited to $15,000.*

Clayton Act of 1914   an act that makes it unlawful, where the effect will be substantially to lessen competition or tend to create monopoly, to: (1) discriminate in price between purchasers of like grade, quality, or quantity of the good sold, (2) sell or lease goods on the condition that the purchaser or lessee refrain from using or dealing in goods provided by a competitor of the seller or lessor, (3) interlock directorates in directly competing corporations of more than $1 million capital, banks and common carriers excluded, and (4) acquire the stock of another corporation. ▶ *The Clayton Act of 1914 excluded labor unions from prosecution under the antitrust laws.*

clean bill   a *bill of exchange* without any documents attached to it. ▶ *They refused our bill of exchange because of the attachments and demanded a clean bill.*

clean draft   a sight or time draft without any documents attached to it. ▶ *A clean draft has no modifying documents accompanying it.*

clearance sale   a promotion designed to sell, at reduced prices, slow-moving or demonstration-model goods and thereby reduce inventory. ▶ *A clearance sale usually occurs at the end of a selling season and offers merchandise at greatly reduced prices.*

clearinghouse   an association of banks within a particular city formed to expedite the settlement of checks, drafts, notes, and other items among the members of the association. ▶ *The primary objective of a clearinghouse is to enable banks to settle their balances with each other as quickly and conveniently as possible.*

client   a person, firm, enterprise, agency, or organization that uses the professional services of another; a customer. ▶ *The advertising agency had to lay off several employees when it lost its largest client.*

Clifford trust   a trust established for at least ten years and a day, which gives income to a second party but allows the first party to retain ownership of the assets. ▶ *Parents can use a Clifford trust to transfer income to their children.*

clique   a small group of persons who share common interests. ▶ *A clique may help or hinder the work efforts of an organization.*

closeout   a special sale to dispose of the remainder of a line of merchandise that the seller intends to discontinue. ▶ *Our closeout was a big success.*

closed account   **1.** a bank or

charge account that has been closed. ▶ *Checks cannot be written on a closed account.* **2.** a ledger or journal account that has had the balance transferred to another account. ▶ *The sales account becomes a closed account once the balance has been posted to the profit and loss account.*

closed loop system   a system in which control of the system is exercised in terms of the operation rather than in terms of outside or predetermined arrangements. ▶ *A streetlight system that goes off and on by means of a timer is an example of a closed loop system.*

closed shop   an arrangement whereby an enterprise hires only union members. ▶ *The closed shop is illegal under provisions of the Taft-Hartley Act of 1947.*

closed union   a union that does not accept new members or that imposes restrictions that make it difficult for new members to be admitted. ▶ *A closed union restricts its membership in order to protect job opportunities for its members.*

closing costs   the various fees and expenses payable by a buyer and seller at the time of the consummation of a real estate transaction. ▶ *The closing costs on this transaction will be fairly small.*

closing date   the date on which the seller of real estate delivers the deed to the buyer and the buyer remits payment to the seller. ▶ *The closing date is the date on which a real estate transaction is consummated.*

closing entry   a journal entry made to a revenue or expense ac-

count for the purpose of transferring the amount remaining there to a profit and loss account (or whatever the firm may call its income summary account). ▶ *A closing entry is made at the end of a fiscal period.*

closing price   the price of the last sale of a security on a given day. ▶ *The closing price today for Acme Limited was $30.50.*

closing time   the date by which all advertising material must be received in order to appear in a certain issue of a print publication. (Also, the time by which all advertising material must be received in order for it to be programmed for broadcast or telecast.) ▶ *If the new advertisement is not finished tonight, we will probably not be able to make the closing time tomorrow.*

cloud on title   a claim or encumbrance on property that, if valid, would render the owner's title to the property defective. ▶ *In real estate transactions a title search is conducted to determine if there is a cloud on title or if the title is free and clear.*

club plan selling   a marketing arrangement whereby a consumer is awarded merchandise prizes or granted discount buying privileges for obtaining new members for a group of customers (the club) serviced by the selling organization. ▶ *Club plan selling has great appeal in certain socioeconomic groups.*

cluster sampling   a method of sampling in which groups of items in a universe rather than individual items are sampled. ▶ *A sample of* *households rather than each individual residing in a given area is an example of cluster sampling.*

CMO See *collateralized mortgage obligation.*

co-maker an individual who signs the note of another as an additional maker in order to strengthen the credit of the principal maker. ▶ *In the event that the first party is unable to repay the note, the co-maker is liable for repayment.*

coaching an on-the-job training approach whereby a superior teaches job knowledge and skills to a subordinate by assigning work to the subordinate and then providing suggestions and guidance as to how the work should be done. ▶ *Coaching allows a senior worker to pass along job knowledge gained over a period of time to a newer worker.*

COD See *cash on delivery; collect on delivery.*

code of ethics a statement of principles and expectations governing the behavior of individuals in a particular profession. (*Codes of ethics* are designed to protect the members of a profession from unfair competition.) ▶ *The American Institute of Certified Public Accountants has a strict code of ethics for its members.*

codicil a document making an addition to, or a change in, a will. ▶ *A codicil modifies a will but does not revoke it.*

coding the process of writing a set of instructions for a computer in a computer programming language. ▶ *Harvey is doing a much better job of coding since he took that*

course in COBOL.

coffee break a pause or recess in the work day allowing workers to rest and refresh themselves. (From the fact that many workers drink coffee during their rest period.) ▶ *The coffee break has long been an American workplace tradition.*

coined word a word made up from scratch; an invented word formed by combining letters or syllables. ▶ *Many brand names are coined words.*

coinsurance an insurance arrangement in which the insurer pays for only a certain percentage of the insured's loss. ▶ *Under the coinsurance provision in our health insurance policy, the insurer pays 80 percent of a claim and the employee pays 20 percent.*

COLA See *cost-of-living adjustment.*

collapsible corporation a corporation formed for the sole purpose of purchasing property and will be transformed or dissolved before a substantial amount of income is derived from the property. (This can disguise the true purpose to which the property will be put, often keeping the price for the property lower.) ▶ *A collapsible corporation is usually dissolved within three years.*

collateral stocks, bonds, money, property, or other assets that a borrower pledges as security for a loan. ▶ *An automobile may serve as collateral for a loan.*

collateral bond a debt that is secured by a pledge of other securities such as stocks. ▶ *A collateral bond may be secured by bonds of a* *subsidiary corporation pledged as collateral.*

collateral loan   a short-term loan for which the borrower has pledged to the lender an asset that may be sold to repay the loan if the borrower forfeits. ▶ *An automobile loan is a collateral loan in that the lender retains title to the automobile until the loan is repaid.*

collateral trust bond   a debt secured by specified property or securities, the title to which is deposited with a trustee. ▶ *The collateral trust bond is not widely used today as a financing method.*

collateralized mortgage obligation AND **CMO**   a security backed by mortgages that have been separated into short-, medium-, and long-term mortgage pools. ▶ *A collateralized mortgage obligation is guaranteed by the Government National Mortgage Association.*

colleague   an associate or coworker, particularly in administrative, professional, or managerial work. ▶ *A colleague is frequently in a good position to judge the quality of the work produced by a coworker.*

collect on delivery AND **COD**   a specification attached to a shipment of goods requiring payment in cash by the buyer at the time the goods are turned over to the buyer. ▶ *Collect on delivery is a sales method that assures the seller that payment will be received when the goods are turned over to the purchaser.*

collection period   the average length of time it takes a business enterprise to collect its accounts receivable. (An approximation of a firm's *collection period* can be determined by dividing accounts receivable—as shown on the balance sheet—by average daily sales [net sales divided by 365 days].) ▶ *A long collection period can be a financial hardship on a company.*

collective bargaining   the process of negotiating, administering, and interpreting agreements between employers and unions. ▶ *Collective bargaining produces a labor agreement that specifies wages, hours of work, and other conditions of employment.*

college recruiting   the recruitment method whereby representatives of business and government visit colleges and universities in order to convince graduating students to work for their organizations. ▶ *Engineering graduates are often hired as a result of college recruiting.*

collusion   a secret agreement between two or more parties for an illegal purpose such as price fixing. ▶ *A secret agreement to commit fraud is collusion.*

column inch   a unit of measurement of printed copy that is one column wide and one inch deep. ▶ *A column inch contains 14 agate lines.*

combination   a unification of two or more separate business enterprises. ▶ *A combination that may result in a monopoly is illegal under the Sherman Act of 1890.*

combination rate   **1.** a shipping rate arrived at by adding together two or more rates. ▶ *A combination rate is used when a shipment travels via two or more trans-*

portation modes such as roadway and air. **2.** a special advertising rate offered by the owner of two or more publications to entice advertisers to use two or more of these publications. ▶ *The combination rate for the two magazines was only 20 percent higher than the advertising rate for one of the magazines.*

comic strip technique the use of cartoons in advertising to assist in the delivery of a sales message. ▶ *The comic strip technique often uses a humorous approach to advertising.*

command economy an economy in which production and prices are regulated by a central governmental authority. ▶ *A communist country tends to have a command economy.*

commercial an advertising message presented on radio or television. ▶ *A radio commercial is a great deal less expensive than a television commercial.*

commercial bank an organization chartered, by either the Comptroller of the Currency or the state in which the organization is located, to engage in the business of banking, i.e., accept deposits subject to withdrawal by checks and make short-term loans to business enterprises. ▶ *A commercial bank may offer consumer loans and safe deposit boxes.*

commercial credit short-term credit used to finance the production, manufacture, and distribution of goods, or to operate a business enterprise. ▶ *Commercial credit keeps a business enterprise oper-*

ating on a day-to-day basis.

commercial crisis a period of economic distress characterized by financial stringency, increased bankruptcies, a declining rate of new investments, and a general breakdown or impairment of the smooth functioning of commercial institutions. ▶ *A commercial crisis is a severe recession.*

commercial law that branch of law relating to business enterprise and commercial transactions. ▶ *Commercial law is becoming increasingly complex due to the passage of more and more laws affecting the way business is transacted.*

commercial loan a short-term loan made to a business enterprise for use in financing the production, manufacture, or distribution of goods, or in the financing of related services. ▶ *A commercial loan may be used to finance inventory needs.*

commercial paper short-term negotiable notes, drafts, bills of exchange, and acceptances arising from transactions involving the production, manufacture, or distribution of goods. ▶ *Commercial paper typically has a maturity ranging from 2 to 270 days.*

commingling a situation that exists when a trustee or fiduciary mixes his or her own funds with those of a client or customer. ▶ *Commingling of funds is generally prohibited by law.*

commission **1.** the fee paid to a broker for the purchase, sale, or trade of securities, real estate, commodities, or other property. ▶ *The* *broker's commission is usually a stipulated percentage of the total amount of the transaction.* **2.** the fee paid to a salesperson for selling a firm's goods and services. ► *A salesperson may be compensated by commission only or by salary plus commission.*

commission agent a person who buys or sells goods or who arranges for the purchase or sale of goods for another person or entity, receiving a stipulated percentage of the transaction as payment for services rendered. ► *A real estate broker is a type of commission agent.*

commission merchant a limited function wholesaler who takes possession of, but not title to, the products or commodities handled as part of a business transaction. ► *A commission merchant arranges for shipment, temporary storage, and delivery of goods, and receives a commission for these services.*

commission plan a method of compensating salespersons whereby each salesperson receives a percentage of sales revenue generated. (The higher the total sales, the greater the income received by the salesperson.) ► *A commission plan is widely used by automobile dealers who sell new and used cars.*

committee a group of people who meet to act on a specific item or class of business. (The fundamental characteristic of a committee is group action. Some committees may undertake managerial functions, some committees may make decisions on problems while other committees may only make recommendations.) ► *A committee may be established on a formal basis and meet at regularly scheduled times or it may be informally constituted and meet at irregular intervals.*

Commodities Futures Trading Association AND **CFTC** an organization established in 1973 to regulate trading on United States futures exchanges, the activities of commodity exchange workers, and other matters. ► *The Commodities Futures Trading Association is concerned, among other things, with protection of customer funds.*

commodity **1.** any good, ware, or merchandise that is for sale. ► *In the largest sense, anything a person purchases is a commodity.* **2.** any one of many raw materials or agricultural products such as corn, wheat, cocoa, or frozen pork bellies that are traded speculatively in a commodities market. ► *Although gold is not an agricultural product, it is a commodity and is traded in a commodity exchange.*

commodity exchange a market where listed commodities are bought and sold. ► *The Chicago Board of Trade is the largest commodity exchange in the United States.*

commodity paper drafts, promissory notes, or other documents representing a loan secured by bills of lading or warehouse receipts on commodities. ► *A trade acceptance accompanied and secured by shipping documents is an example of commodity paper.*

commodity price forecast a prediction of future prices of certain raw materials or agricultural products classified as *commodities.* ▶ *The commodity price forecast for frozen pork bellies anticipates that prices will continue falling for the next six months.*

commodity rate a transportation rate that applies to specific materials that move in large volumes and therefore receive lower rates. ▶ *Coal, iron ore, cotton, and wheat are goods that receive a commodity rate.*

commodity warehouse a storage place for raw materials or agricultural products classified as *commodities.* ▶ *We have ten tons of rice stored in a commodity warehouse.*

common carrier a carrier engaged in transporting goods for compensation. (*Common carriers* must accept all goods offered to them for shipment.) ▶ *A common carrier is recognized as a public utility and is governed by Federal and state regulations called "tariffs."*

common law AND **unwritten law** law that is established through usage and precedent, but which is not reduced to codes. ▶ *Common law originated in England and was later applied in the United States.*

Common Market See *(European) Common Market.*

common situs picketing the picketing of an entire construction site by a union that has a dispute with one, but not all, of the contractors. ▶ *Common situs picketing is generally illegal.*

common stock a share in the ownership of a corporation. (Ownership of a share of *common stock* entitles the holder to vote for directors of the corporation and to share in the profits of the corporation. In the event of liquidation, the common stock shareholder shares in the final distribution of assets [after all prior claims have been settled] in proportion to the amount of stock held.) ▶ *Common stock is traded on the New York Stock Exchange, the American Stock Exchange, and various over-the-counter exchanges in the United States.*

communism an economic system based on government or community ownership of all wealth. ▶ *As an economic system, communism tends to reduce worker incentive and seems to be less efficient and productive than capitalism.*

community property the property acquired by a husband or wife after marriage, each sharing equally in the income produced by or derived from the property. (*Community property* laws are not recognized in every state of the United States.) ▶ *Even though my husband paid for the car with his inheritance, it is community property.*

commuter an individual who travels between two places, especially one who resides in one location and works in another. ▶ *A commuter may spend two or more hours per day traveling to and from work.*

commuter tax a tax imposed on individuals who work in one location but live in another. ▶ *New York City imposes a tax on those who* *work in the city but reside in other counties or states.*

company a business concern. ► *A company may be a sole proprietorship, a partnership, or a corporation.*

company car an automobile owned by the company but available for use by an employee or a group of employees. ► *Fred's employer furnishes him a company car.*

comparable worth (principle) a principle that maintains that the rate of compensation for a job should be determined by its relative value to the organization rather than by market value, and without consideration of the sex, race, age, etc., of the individual holding the job. ► *Women particularly support the principle of comparable worth because they feel they have long been underpaid.*

comparative advantage the special ability of a country to provide one product or one service more cheaply than other products or services. ► *The principle of comparative advantage suggests that the manufacture of a product will gravitate to the country that can produce the product at the lowest cost.*

comparison shopping a process whereby a consumer compares goods and services, prices, availability, credit terms, and other factors in order to decide what to purchase and where to purchase it. ► *Comparison shopping can be time consuming, but it usually results in a more informed purchase.*

compensable factor one of the characteristics of a job that determines the wage rate for that job, such as skill, effort, responsibility, and working conditions. ► *More than two years of experience is not a compensable factor for this entry-level factory job.*

compensating balance funds, over and above the depositor's normal balance, left on deposit with a commercial bank in order to compensate the bank for the performance of services for which it charges the depositor no fee. ► *In some cases the depositor must maintain a stipulated compensating balance in order to obtain a loan.*

compensation payment given or received for services, debt, loss, etc. ► *A compensation plan is an organization's arrangement for paying its employees.*

compensatory damages benefits awarded by a court to a claimant that restore, in whole or part, that which the claimant has lost. ► *The court settlement included a fine as well as $250,000 in compensatory damages to offset the medical costs incurred.*

comp(ensatory) time time off allowed an employee in lieu of additional compensation for overtime worked. ► *Compensatory time may be advantageous for a company because it does not have to expend funds for overtime.*

competent party a person legally capable of entering a contract. (This has nothing to do with abilities in general.) ► *A person who is under legal age is not a competent party.*

competition rivalry between two or more business enterprises to secure the patronage of prospective buyers. ► *Competition often results in lower prices for the consumer.*

competitive bid an offer, containing prices, terms, and conditions, submitted by a prospective contractor to a purchaser, which is in competition with bids submitted by other prospective contractors. ► *The Interstate Bank would like for us to be one of three companies to submit a competitive bid on installing an employee compensation system.*

competitive strategy an advertising strategy designed for use against rival brands or products. ► *Part of our competitive strategy is to emphasize the benefits of our product that are lacking in our competitor's product.*

competitor a rival company that manufactures or sells a product or service that is sold in the same market. ► *Kingsley Manufacturing is our major competitor.*

compiler program a computer program that translates a high-level programming language such as FORTRAN into machine language. ► *A compiler program makes it easier for a programmer to write computer programs.*

complementary product a product in a firm's line of goods that supplements another product or products. ► *Nails are a complementary product to screws and other types of wall fasteners.*

composition an alternative to bankruptcy in which creditors agree to accept partial payment of their claims as full settlement of their total claims. ► *Composition is used most often by small, unincorporated firms.*

compound interest interest computed on the principal as well as on any interest earned or accrued during a previous period or periods. ► *Compound interest may be computed on a daily, quarterly, semiannual, or annual basis.*

comprehensive health insurance insurance coverage that combines basic medical and major medical coverage and provides complete coverage of hospital and physician charges, subject to appropriate deductibles and coinsurance, if any. ► *Comprehensive health insurance coverage is an important benefit provided by many employers.*

comprehensive liability insurance a liability insurance policy that provides a business with coverage against bodily injury and property damage and medical expenses resulting from injury or damage. ► *Our comprehensive liability insurance will protect us if someone should suffer an accident on our property.*

comprehensive policy an insurance policy that protects the insured against any loss suffered from any cause not specifically excluded from the policy. ► *A comprehensive policy on an automobile protects the owner against loss from fire, theft, hail, or other damage.*

compromise the trading-off of one item of value for another item of value. ► *Most labor agreements are* *the result of compromise by both union and management.*

comptroller See *controller.*

Comptroller of the Currency a Federal official, appointed by the President of the United States, who is responsible for chartering national banks and exercises primary supervisory authority over them. ▶ *The Comptroller of the Currency is an officer in the U.S. Treasury Department.*

compulsory arbitration a labor relations arrangement whereby work stoppages are prohibited and the parties to a collective bargaining agreement are required to submit unresolved issues to final and binding arbitration. ▶ *The primary advantage of compulsory arbitration is that it prevents strikes.*

compulsory retirement the forced resignation of one's employment at an age specified by union contract, Federal requirement (as in the case of commercial airline pilots), or company policy. ▶ *In most instances, private sector employers can no longer have compulsory retirement policies that require employees to retire before age 70.*

computer a device capable of accepting data, processing the data in accordance with prescribed procedures, and providing the results of the processing. ▶ *Generally, a computer consists of input and output devices, storage, arithmetic and logic units, and a control unit.*

computer aided design AND **CAD** the use of computers to assist in the design of parts, products, systems, etc., through the use of modeling, analysis, simulation, and other approaches. (See also *CAD/CAM.*) ▶ *Computer aided design has significantly enhanced the product design process.*

computer aided manufacturing AND **CAM** the use of computers and numerical control equipment to aid in manufacturing processes. (See also *CAD/CAM.*) ▶ *Computer aided manufacturing is part of the general trend toward automation in the factory.*

computer conferencing the interchange of messages on a particular topic through the use of a computer network. ▶ *Computer conferencing can save time and money and will become even more popular in the years to come.*

computer program the set of instructions by which a computer processes data. ▶ *A computer program must be written in a language that the computer understands.*

computer trading the use of a computer to initiate automatic buy and sell orders of securities. ▶ *Computer trading has had a significant impact on the way securities are traded.*

concentration ratio the percentage of total business in a given industry that is handled by a specified number of the largest firms in that industry. ▶ *The concentration ratio is of concern to the Federal Trade Commission, a body concerned with competition and free trade.*

concession 1. the act of yielding or conceding something. ▶ *The* *union gained a concession from management when it agreed to a dues checkoff.* **2.** something conceded by a government entity. ▶ *The state granted Albert a concession to operate a bait and tackle shop on the lake.* **3.** a space or a privilege within a certain area for operation of a business. ▶ *Pete has a concession stand in the lobby of the Parker Building.*

conciliation AND **mediation** the process by which an outside party helps to break a deadlock in negotiations between labor and management. (The outside party, having no authority to force a settlement, works with labor and management to find a mutually agreeable basis for settlement.) ▶ *Conciliation requires great skill on the part of the conciliator as well as a willingness on the part of both management and labor to compromise.*

condemnation a legal proceeding that is authorized by legislative bodies for the purpose of taking private property for public use after the payment of a sum of money. ▶ *Rights of way for highways are often obtained through condemnation of personal or commercial property.*

conditional sales contract an agreement made by a buyer and seller that is subject to certain conditions that must be fulfilled before the agreement is valid. ▶ *A conditional sales contract to purchase a used automobile may depend upon the car's ability to pass a motor vehicle inspection.*

conference a meeting for the purpose of consultation or discussion. ▶ *The conference on sexual ha-*

rassment will be held at 10:00 A.M. tomorrow.

conference call a telephone call in which two are more lines are connected so that three or more people can converse with each other. ▶ *A conference call often expedites discussion of a problem because it eliminates the need for making multiple telephone calls.*

confidence game a scheme by which a swindler gains someone's money through fraud or deception. (The swindler first gains the confidence of the victim and then takes advantage of the confidence that was gained earlier.) ▶ *My Uncle Hubert was the victim of a confidence game played by a phony aluminum siding salesman.*

confidence limits in a statistical sample, the range of either side of the true value of a population within which a measure of that value (such as the arithmetic mean) will fall with an established probability (such as 90 times out of a 100). ▶ *Confidence limits, in the simplest of terms, suggest how seriously the analysis of a sample should be taken.*

con(fidence) man a man who practices a *confidence game.* ▶ *Uncle Thaddeus was cheated by a con man.*

confirmation **1.** a written description of a securities transaction given by a broker to a customer or another broker. ▶ *We just received confirmation of the sale of the Trenton Company shares.* **2.** a formal approval, especially one given in writing. ▶ *Enclosed is our confirmation of your order dated*

June 16. **3.** the transfer of title to land to a person who has possession of the land. ▶ *Confirmation may result in enlarging a particular estate.* **4.** an agreement that something is correct, such as the balance of an outstanding account. ▶ *Please indicate on the enclosed confirmation notice whether or not the balance on your books agrees with ours.* **5.** the approval of a presidential appointment by Congress. ▶ *We have just learned of the confirmation by Congress of the new Comptroller of the Currency.*

confiscation the expropriation of private property by a government without appropriate compensation. ▶ *Confiscation is a type of punitive action.*

conflict of interest a relationship whereby an individual may benefit from a transaction of one's employer where one is identified with or has influenced in any way or manner its initiation, specification, terms, conditions, completion, or acceptance. (A *conflict of interest* may be asserted even if no material benefit has been gained by an individual, but the mere possibility of some future benefit at an indefinite time exists.) ▶ *Avoiding even the appearance of having a conflict of interest is wise in any business or political activity.*

conformed copy a copy of an original document with the essential legal features typed in or indicated in writing. ▶ *We will need a conformed copy of the deed by tomorrow morning.*

conglomerate a corporation that diversifies its operations by entering many different industries. ▶ *Research suggests that a conglomerate may not be any more successful than a company that has only one line of business.*

consent decree an admission by a defendant in a lawsuit of certain charges and the acceptance of certain remedies proposed by the plaintiff, subject to the approval of the court. ▶ *The case was settled by consent decree wherein the defendant agreed not to engage in the future sale of pineapples.*

consent election an election held at the joint request of management and union to determine which of two or more competing unions represent a particular bargaining unit. ▶ *The UAW won the consent election and is now the authorized bargaining representative for the machinists.*

conservatism concept the notion that assets should be valued on a firm's books at cost or market value, whichever is lower. ▶ *The conservatism concept may tend to understate asset value in the long run.*

consideration the benefit that a contracting party derives when entering into a contract. ▶ *Consideration must be present for a contract to be valid.*

consignee the receiver of a shipment of goods. (See also *consignment.*) ▶ *The consignee refused to pay for the damaged merchandise.*

consignment an arrangement whereby the shipper of goods (the *consignor*) retains title to the goods shipped to the receiver (the *consignee*) until the latter has sold such goods. (The *consignor* is paid by the *consignee*.) ▶ *With a consignment arrangement, the dealer must return unsold goods to the owner.*

consignor the sender of a shipment of goods. (See also *consignment*.) ▶ *The consignor sent the shipment to the wrong address.*

consistency concept continued uniformity, during an accounting period or from one period to another, in methods of accounting, evaluating inventories or other assets, and accruing items of income or expense as reflected in the financial statements of an enterprise. ▶ *The consistency concept creates a uniformity that makes it easier to understand financial statements from period to period.*

consolidated balance sheet a combined statement of financial position for a parent company and its subsidiaries. ▶ *A consolidated balance sheet may combine the financial positions of a great many legally separate entities.*

consolidation the combination of two or more corporations to form an entirely new corporation as opposed to a merger, which is the absorption of one company by another. ▶ *The U.S. Steel Company is the result of a consolidation of many smaller companies into one very large entity.*

consortium a group of organizations or individuals brought together to engage in a project that will benefit all members of the group. ▶ *The purpose of forming a consortium may be to pool resources to accomplish something that no one*

consortium member could do alone.

conspicuous consumption the purchase and use of consumer goods in a manner designed to impress others or to display one's position or status, rather than for the satisfaction of a normal consumer demand. (The term was coined by the American economist Thorstein Veblen.) ▶ *Sue lives in a modest neighborhood where conspicuous consumption is a rarity.*

constant dollars a unit of measurement expressed in dollars of a base year. ▶ *Constant dollars are used as a measurement of real purchasing power.*

construction copy a variety of advertising copy that shows the step-by-step process of making a product. ▶ *Construction copy shows the benefits of the advertised product over a competitive product at certain points in its production.*

consular invoice an invoice covering a shipment of goods certified by the consul of the country for which the goods are destined. ▶ *Customs officials of the receiving country use the consular invoice to verify the value, quantity, and nature of the goods imported.*

consultant a specialist in a particular field who provides professional advice for a fee. (A *consultant* may be an individual practitioner or a person employed by a firm specializing in such work.) ▶ *The computer consultant recommended that we purchase a larger mainframe computer.*

consumer one who purchases or

uses goods and services. (See also *industrial consumer; ultimate consumer.*) ▶ *In order to market goods effectively, one must understand what the consumer wants and needs.*

consumer behavior   the reasons why consumers purchase goods and services and how consumers act in the marketplace. ▶ *An understanding of consumer behavior is important to the successful marketing of products.*

consumer credit   the power or ability used by an individual or a family to obtain goods, services, or money for the satisfaction of their wants or needs in exchange for a promise to pay at a later date. ▶ *The interest rate charged for consumer credit is usually much higher than that charged to commercial loan customers.*

Consumer Credit Protection Act of 1968 AND **Truth in Lending Act**   a Federal act ensuring that consumers be informed about the details of credit transactions such as annual percentage rates, potential total cost, and any special loan terms. ▶ *Under the Truth in Lending Act, borrowers must be told about the interest rate and interest charges.*

consumer debt   money owed by individual consumers or households as opposed to money owed by business enterprises or governments. ▶ *Consumer debt is much higher today than it was twenty years ago.*

consumer finance company   a financial institution that makes loans to consumers and small businesses.

▶ *We obtained our auto loan through a consumer finance company.*

consumer goods   goods bought by individuals or families for their own use or consumption. ▶ *Toothpaste, cooking oil, detergent, fresh fish, and bacon are all consumer goods.*

consumer loan   a loan made to an individual for the purpose of purchasing *consumer goods.* (The rate of interest on a *consumer loan* is usually much higher than the rate of interest on a *commercial loan.*) ▶ *Tom got a consumer loan to purchase his new car.*

consumer motivation   the motives that move a consumer to purchase certain goods or patronize certain stores. ▶ *A producer must have an understanding of consumer motivation in order to manufacture the types of products consumers really desire.*

Consumer Price Index AND **CPI; Cost-of-Living Index**   a measure, compiled by the U.S. Bureau of Labor Statistics, of the changes in the prices of goods and services consumed by urban families and individuals. ▶ *According to the Consumer Price Index, prices rose 5 percent last month.*

Consumer Product Safety Commission   a Federal agency created to protect the public from unreasonable risk of injury from consumer products. ▶ *The Consumer Product Safety Commission today ruled that the atomic weather vane is an unsafe product.*

consumer protection laws   the statutes enacted to protect consumers from goods and services that are improperly manufactured, delivered, described, etc. ▶ *Consumer protection laws have made many manufacturers more cautious in their design of products.*

consumer research the research conducted to obtain information about consumers, their motives, and their purchasing habits. ▶ *Consumer research helps a company target its markets more easily.*

consumerism the actions and concerns of various groups that are working to protect the interests of consumers. ▶ *Consumerism is of more concern today than it was a few years ago.*

consumer's risk the calculated probability that, under a given statistical quality control sampling plan, a batch of unacceptable quality will be accepted by the plan. (This means, essentially, that sometimes a few defective products reach the consumer.) ▶ *In many cases the consumer's risk cannot be entirely eliminated because it would be too expensive for the manufacturer to do so.*

consumption the purchase and utilization of goods and services. ▶ *A healthy economy needs a high level of consumption.*

consumption function the relationship between the level of income and the level of consumption. ▶ *According to the consumption function, consumption is greatly influenced by income.*

containerization a method of transporting goods whereby they are packed in a sealed container at the point of origin and are not removed from the container until the

final destination is reached. ▶ *Containerization permits goods to be shipped by different modes of transportation without having to unpack and repack the container in which the goods are shipped.*

contingency a possible future event or condition that may arise from causes unknown, or from causes undeterminable at the present time. ▶ *Long-range planning must always take contingencies into account even though they cannot be clearly discerned.*

contingency fee a fee paid, in whole or in part, based on a future result or financial outcome. ▶ *In my worker's compensation case, my attorney is charging a contingency fee of 20 percent of the final settlement.*

contingent liability a liability that is not presently an obligation but which may become one in the future if certain events transpire. ▶ *A cosigner of a note has a contingent liability because the cosigner will be liable for repayment of the note if the maker defaults.*

continuing education the non-credit courses offered by community colleges, colleges, and universities on a variety of topics designed to appeal to the needs of adult learners. ▶ *Robert is taking a continuing education course in wine-making.*

continuous process an industrial process that operates on an around-the-clock basis. ▶ *Petroleum refining is a continuous process operation.*

continuous sample a sample that is taken on a sustained basis over a period of time. ▶ *A continuous sample procedure is used extensively in processing industries to assure quality.*

contra account an account that partially or wholly offsets another account. ▶ *The reserve for depreciation is a contra account to plant and equipment.*

contract a legally enforceable agreement between two or more competent parties in which one or more of the parties agrees for a consideration, to do or not to do some particular thing. ▶ *A contract is invalid if one of the parties to the contract is incompetent to execute a legal contract.*

contract carrier a transportation company that serves shippers on an individual contract basis. ▶ *A contract carrier usually has defined standards as to the type of shipments that will be accepted.*

contraction a widespread decline in economic activity. ▶ *We are experiencing a contraction now, which will probably develop into a recession if the Federal government doesn't take action soon.*

contrarian an investor who buys and sells securities contrary to current trends. ▶ *A contrarian believes that popular opinion is likely to be wrong.*

contribution margin the excess of sales price over the unit variable cost, which contributes to the recovery of fixed expenses and, eventually, to the realization of profit. ▶ *Last month's contribution margin was even greater than that of the month before. This will be a profitable quarter.*

contributory negligence a legal principle recognizing that an injured party may have contributed to the injury sustained. (This can lead to a reduced settlement or a dismissal of a lawsuit.) ▶ *Someone who enters a building on which is posted a "Do Not Enter" sign and is injured, may be guilty of contributory negligence.*

control account an account in the general ledger that takes the place of individual ledger accounts removed to a subsidiary ledger. ▶ *A control account shows summary totals for all of the transactions shown in detail in the subsidiary ledger.*

control chart a diagram used to discriminate between random and nonrandom causes of variation in products or processes. ▶ *A control chart is used as a means of analyzing performance and controlling quality.*

controllable cost **1.** a cost that varies with volume, efficiency, or choice of alternatives and is generally subject to determination by management. ▶ *Postage expense is an example of a controllable cost.* **2.** any cost that a part of an organization has the authority to incur. ▶ *Subscription expenses for magazines and trade journals are a controllable cost for the research and development department.*

controlled economy an economic system characterized by government control of business and government affairs. ▶ *Socialism results in a controlled economy.*

controller AND **comptroller** a company officer who is responsible for the overall accounting system used by an organization. (Normally, a *controller* is responsible for general accounting, cost accounting, budgetary control, statistical analysis, development of economic forecasts, and preparation of local, state, and Federal taxes.) ▶ *The controller is usually the highest ranking accounting official in an organization.* ▶ *The comptroller refused to sign the contract.*

controlling interest the ownership of more than 50 percent of the stock of a corporation. ▶ *In a large corporation, it is rare that any one individual owns a controlling interest.*

convenience goods AND **convenience merchandise** the items purchased by consumers with a minimum of shopping and price or brand comparison because the gain from shopping or making comparisons is normally very small. ▶ *Tobacco, candy, chewing gum, and milk are examples of convenience goods.*

convenience merchandise See the previous entry.

convenience store a small retail outlet that sells a limited variety of groceries, staples, convenience goods, and impulse merchandise. ▶ *A convenience store charges higher prices than a supermarket.*

conversational mode a method of computer operation in which the user is in direct communication with the computer. ▶ *Conversational mode is an on-line interaction between a computer and a user.*

conversion **1.** a feature of bonds

or *preferred stock* that allows the holder to change (convert) the holdings to *common stock.* ▶ *The conversion rate is three shares of preferred stock to one share of common stock.* **2.** the transformation of raw materials into goods suitable for sale. ▶ *Crude oil undergoes a conversion process and emerges as gasoline, motor oil, and other products.* **3.** any act that deprives an owner of property without just cause. ▶ *Stealing is an act of conversion.*

conversion cost the total direct labor and overhead cost incurred in the process of converting a raw material into a salable product. ▶ *The conversion cost associated with the processing of crude oil is substantial.*

conversion price the price at which a stock or bond, as stipulated in a previous agreement, may be exchanged at the option of the holder for another security. ▶ *The conversion price for that issue of preferred stock is $22 per share.*

convertible pertaining to a bond, debenture, or preferred stock that can be exchanged for common stock, warrants, or some other security, as provided by the conditions set forth by the issuing corporation. ▶ *These convertible bonds are attractive investment vehicles.*

conveyance the transfer of property from one party to another by means of mortgage, deed, bill of sale, etc. ▶ *In a transfer of real property, the conveyance must take place by deed.*

COO See *chief operating officer.*

cooling-off laws a type of law designed to require a *cooling-off period* in a dispute. ▶ *There are very few cooling-off laws on the books.*

cooling-off period **1.** a period of time fixed by Federal law or state law or contract, during which employees cannot strike and employers cannot resort to lockout as a means of forcing a settlement in a labor dispute. ▶ *The Taft-Hartley Act of 1947 calls for an 80-day cooling-off period in instances where a work stoppage may create a national emergency.* **2.** the interval between the filing of a preliminary prospectus with the *Securities and Exchange Commission* and the actual date at which securities are offered for sale to the public. ▶ *A cooling-off period gives the Securities and Exchange Commission time to review a proposed security offering.* **3.** a period of time in which a purchaser may cancel a sale. ▶ *Many states allow a purchaser a cooling-off period of three days during which the purchaser may cancel a sale made door-to-door or by telephone.*

cooperative a voluntary business enterprise or association formed by a group of people to serve their own needs. (Each member of the *cooperative* has an equal vote in the operations of the organization.) ▶ *Profits are shared among the members of a cooperative on an equal basis.*

copy the written part of an advertisement. ▶ *The copy portion of an ad must be written very carefully in order to appeal to the target market.*

copy protected disk a computer disk that cannot be fully copied by the programs typically used to copy disks. ▶ *The purpose of a copy protected disk is to preclude unauthorized duplication of software.*

copyright a form of legal protection accorded by the government to a writer against duplication, infringement, or other use of what the writer has written. ▶ *An application for a copyright can be obtained from the Register of Copyrights in Washington, D.C.*

core dump AND **memory dump; storage dump** a listing of the contents of a computer storage device or selected portions of it. ▶ *A core dump is sometimes necessary to locate an error in a program.*

core memory the main memory of a computer. (The term is derived from the doughnut-shaped magnetic rings used by early computers.) ▶ *There was not enough core memory to run the program.*

corner a market to buy goods, commodities, or securities in large enough quantities to give the purchaser control over the prices. ▶ *Attempting to corner a market is illegal.*

corporate bylaws the rules established by the stockholders of a corporation for conducting the business of the enterprise. (See also *bylaws.*) ▶ *The procedure for electing officers is spelled out in the corporate bylaws.*

corporate campaign an advertising campaign designed to improve the public image of a corporation rather than sell any specific products or services. ▶ *A corporate campaign may be particularly important for an organization that is* *not well known to the public.*

corporate structure the organizational arrangement of a corporation in terms of divisions, department, groups, units, etc. ▶ *The corporate structure of a large organization is usually very complex.*

corporation a legal entity separate and distinct from its members and regarded by courts as an artificial person. (A *corporation* may own property, incur debts, and sue or be sued in its own name. The chief characteristics of a *corporation* are the limited liability of stockholders, the easy transferability of ownership interests, and the continuity of existence.) ▶ *A corporation may be chartered by a state or by the Federal government.*

corpus the body of an investment or note. ▶ *The corpus is the principal or capital as opposed to the interest or income derived from the principal.*

corrective maintenance repairs on equipment. (See *maintenance.* The opposite of *preventative maintenance.*) ▶ *The entire production line had to shut down for corrective maintenance on the machine tools.*

correlation a measure of the degree of association between two or more variables. ▶ *There are two variables in a simple correlation: an independent variable and a dependent variable.*

correspondent bank a commercial bank that is the depository for another commercial bank. ▶ *Most banks find it convenient to maintain an account with a correspon-*

dent bank in another city.

cost the amount paid or required as payment for a given product or service. ▶ *The total cost of the machine, including delivery and set-up, is $12,345.*

cost accounting **1.** the branch of accounting concerned with classifying, recording, allocating, summarizing, and reporting current and future costs. ▶ *Cost accounting is a complex field of study.* **2.** the department within an organization concerned with classifying, recording, allocating, summarizing, and reporting current and future costs. ▶ *We have not received this month's departmental expense report from Cost Accounting.*

cost and freight AND **CAF** a designation indicating that the quoted price of a good includes any and all charges for handling and freight up to delivery to a port, at which time the purchaser assumes costs of unloading, insurance, transportation, etc. ▶ *The price of a turret lathe, cost and freight, is $7,289.*

cost avoidance dollar savings achieved as a result of not incurring additional costs. (The term is used to denote savings resulting from the ability to handle an increased work load volume without adding additional employees.) ▶ *The practice of cost avoidance soon resulted in many people quitting because their work loads were too high.*

cost basis the original acquisition price of an asset. ▶ *The cost basis determines the basis for all subsequent accounting for an asset.*

cost-benefit analysis a comparison of all the costs and risks of a project to the values or benefits to be derived from the project. ► *A project should be undertaken only if a cost-benefit analysis shows that benefits outweigh costs significantly.*

cost center a subdivision of an organization that is established or identified for the purpose of assigning or allocating costs. ► *An entire department or any appropriate subunit thereof may be a cost center.*

cost conscious an awareness of the need to keep expenses as low as possible, consistent with the best performance of a specified task or activity. ► *Some managers are more cost conscious than other managers.*

cost containment the process of maintaining organizational expenses within a specified amount, typically expressed in a budget. ► *Cost containment is especially important during periods of declining sales.*

cost displacement dollar savings achieved as a result of cutting expenditures. ► *Cost displacement results from trimming the unnecessary expenses from an operation.*

cost effective a condition that exists when the benefits accruing from goods or projects exceed their cost. ► *Advertising is cost effective if it attracts new customers and retains existing ones.*

cost, insurance, and freight AND **CIF** a designation that the quoted price of goods includes any and all charges for handling, insurance, and freight up to delivery to a port, at which time the purchaser must assume the costs of additional handling, insurance, and freight. ► *The price of a turret lathe, cost, insurance, and freight, is $8,372.*

cost ledger a book used in collecting and summarizing the costs of goods produced or of services rendered. ► *These freight charges should be posted to the cost ledger.*

cost of capital the cost of raising funds in the money market at any given time. ► *The cost of capital has been increasing steadily over the last twelve months.*

cost of doing business the costs typically associated with conducting normal business affairs. ► *A minimal level of advertising is often looked upon as a cost of doing business.*

cost of goods sold the total costs incurred in producing marketable products. ► *In a manufacturing company, the cost of goods sold includes the costs of the raw material, the labor, and all the manufacturing charges incurred in a given period.*

cost-of-living the overall costs necessary to maintain a certain standard of living. ► *As reported by the Consumer Price Index, the cost-of-living rose sharply last month.*

cost-of-living adjustment AND **COLA** a wage or salary adjustment made in compensation rates in order to equate the wage or salary with changes made in the cost of living as measured by the *Consumer Price Index.* ► *A cost-*

of-living adjustment is usually made as a percentage applied across-the-board to salaries.

Cost-of-Living Index See *Consumer Price Index.*

cost-plus contract a contract that specifies that the selling price of an item is the total cost incurred by the producer in making that item, plus either a stated percentage of profit or a fixed fee. ▶ *A disadvantage of the cost-plus contract is that it does not encourage the manufacturer to attempt to reduce manufacturing costs.*

cost-plus pricing a method of setting the selling prices of goods or services by adding a fixed amount or a certain percentage of the cost to the goods or services. ▶ *A common cost-plus pricing arrangement is to double the cost of the item to determine what it should sell for at retail.*

cost-price squeeze a condition in which the producer or seller of goods encounters increased costs of production or purchase, and these increased costs cannot be passed on to the consumer in the form of higher prices. ▶ *A manufacturer caught in a cost-price squeeze should seek ways to reduce manufacturing costs.*

cost progress chart a graphic devise illustrating chronologically the relative time and cost increments incurred by a product at various stages of its manufacture. ▶ *A cost progress chart is often helpful because it allows one to visualize the costs incurred by a product as it progresses through the manufacturing cycle.*

cost-push inflation a rise in the general level of prices caused by increases in the cost of production. ▶ *Cost-push inflation begins with increases in the prices of raw materials, which in turn increase the prices of manufactured goods, which causes increases in retail prices.*

cost records the ledgers, statements, schedules, reports, invoices, vouchers, and similar documents evidencing the cost of a product, process, operation, job, project, service, function, or production center. ▶ *We need to review all of the cost records carefully to make certain that all expenses have been accounted for.*

cost recovery the recapture of cost through expense recognition. ▶ *Accurate cost recovery depends upon careful recording of expenses.*

cost saving the saving achieved as a result of not incurring additional costs or as a result of cutting expenditures. ▶ *By eliminating two steps in the production process, we can achieve a significant cost saving.*

cost standard a statement of what the cost should be for manufacturing a product, rendering a service, etc., under the most efficient methods of operation that can be attained and sustained. ▶ *A cost standard is a goal to be achieved.*

cost variance the difference, either negative or positive, between a budgeted cost and the actual cost incurred during a given period. ▶ *With the drop in raw material* *prices below the budgeted cost, our cost variance was positive.*

costing the process of determining the actual cost of something. ▶ *Before we prepare a bid on the manufacture of those electromagnetic turbines, we should do some costing on their electronic components.*

cottage industry an industry in which production takes place in the home of the producer. ▶ *A cottage industry is often an industry in its infancy.*

Council of Economic Advisors a panel of three prominent economists appointed by the President of the United States to advise him on economic affairs. ▶ *The Council of Economic Advisors was created by the Employment Act of 1946.*

counterfeit forged; produced without approval, particularly with the intent to pass the imitation off as genuine. ▶ *The market is being flooded with counterfeit Acme watches from South America.*

counteroffer the rejection of an offer to sell or to buy accompanied with a new offer for the sale or purchase of the same good or service. ▶ *George rejected the original price and made a counteroffer of $17 per share.*

countervailing power the forces that arise in an economy to offset some of the bargaining power enjoyed in the marketplace by large buyers and sellers of goods. (The term was originated by John Kenneth Galbraith.) ▶ *An example of countervailing power is the emergence of large labor unions that offset the power of large corpora-*tions by influencing the amounts corporations must pay for labor.*

coupon a small certificate that entitles the bearer to a certain privilege, money, or discount. (See also the following entry.) ▶ *Manufacturers often use a "cents off" coupon to get consumers to try a product.*

coupon bond a bond with attached certificates that are redeemable at specified intervals for an interest payment when presented to designated financial institutions. ▶ *The coupon bond is becoming a thing of the past.*

coupon rate See *nominal yield.*

covenant a promise in writing that is frequently used as a substitute for a contract. ▶ *A covenant may be entered into concerning the use of land and attached to a property deed as a restriction.*

coverage insurance protection against specific losses as stated in the policy. ▶ *The coverage stipulates the dollar amount of the insurance one has against a particular risk.*

covered option an option for which the seller actually owns the securities. ▶ *A covered option may be the safest route to go.*

covering the purchase of a security by a trader who has earlier gone short; that is, sold a security at an agreed upon price for future delivery. ▶ *Covering is an effort to take profits or accept losses in order to prevent further loss.*

CPA See *Certified Public Accountant.*

CPI See *Consumer Price Index.*

CPU See *central processing unit.*

craft 1. an art, trade, or occupation requiring special skill. ▶ *Fred took several years to master his craft.* 2. a boat or ship. ▶ *Johnson has the largest craft in the harbor.* 3. an airplane. ▶ *The F-16 is one of the fastest crafts in the air today.*

craft union a labor union that includes all workers in a single occupation regardless of the industry in which they work. ▶ *The Carpenters and Joiners Union is an example of a craft union.*

crash 1. a sharp decline in economic activity and stock prices. ▶ *The stock market crash of 1929 resulted in the Great Depression.* 2. a hardware failure or a program error, which causes a computer to become inoperable. ▶ *We will not be able to process payroll checks today because we had a computer crash last night and have not been able to get the system back in operation yet.*

credit 1. an arrangement whereby a seller allows a buyer to purchase goods or services, taking delivery immediately but paying for them sometime in the future. ▶ *Bill is buying a refrigerator from the furniture store on credit.* 2. to lower a balance in an asset or expense account and to increase a balance in a liability, owner's equity, or revenue account. ▶ *We must credit the profit and loss account with this $2,000 entry for miscellaneous sales.* 3. available but unused borrowing ability. ▶ *We still have another $25,000 line of credit with the First State Bank that we could use to help finance this project.* 4. an adjustment in a customer's favor. ▶ *We are terribly sorry that you are not pleased with the handwoven carpet and will issue you a credit immediately.* 5. recognition; acknowledgment. ▶ *Harold should be given full credit for developing the new product.*

credit balance an account receivable balance in the customer's favor; i.e., the firm owes money to the customer. ▶ *According to our records, Mr. Smith, you have a credit balance of $2.17, which we will refund to you.*

credit bureau an organization that assembles and maintains credit and other information on consumers and furnishes that information to authorized users for a fee. ▶ *A bank usually obtains a report from the credit bureau before granting a personal loan.*

credit card an identification card, usually made of plastic, which allows a purchaser to buy goods or services on credit. ▶ *Issuance of a credit card to an individual is contingent upon the person's credit rating.*

credit insurance coverage that insures a firm against unusually high losses resulting from the extension of credit to customers. (*Credit insurance* usually carries a deductible provision whereby the insured firm absorbs a stated amount of loss and everything above that amount is covered by the insurer.) ▶ *Our credit insurance covers losses over $1,000.*

credit life insurance insurance that guarantees that the amount owed on a contract or a personal loan will be paid in full in the event of the borrower's death. ▶ *Credit life insurance is paid for by the borrower.*

credit line 1. an agreement by a bank to make a loan, not to exceed a specified amount, when needed by a customer. ▶ *The Vandoss Company has a $25,000 credit line at the Williamsport Bank.* 2. the total amount that a purchaser is allowed to buy on credit with a particular institution. ▶ *Sam's credit line with the department store is $5,000.* 3. a statement appearing in a journal article, book, or other written document, usually in the form of a note or acknowledgement, that mentions the source of material cited and indicates that permission to quote from the source has been given. ▶ *The credit line should reflect that the material cited is from our newsletter.*

credit price the price charged for a product if the product is to be bought on credit rather than for cash. (See also *cash price.*) ▶ *The credit price of gasoline is different from the cash price.*

credit rating an evaluation, usually by a professional rating service, of a purchaser's ability or potential to pay for goods and services bought on credit. ▶ *An individual's credit rating determines whether the person can borrow from a financial institution.*

credit risk a borrower considered as representing a possible loss to a lender. (A good *credit risk* offers less possibility of loss than a bad one.) ▶ *The bank denied the loan to Miller because they considered him to be a poor credit risk.*

credit sale a sale involving the extension of credit for payment. ▶ *A credit sale may be more profitable than a cash sale because the selling institution can charge interest for the use of the credit.*

credit terms the conditions under which a credit sale is made. (*Credit terms* usually specify the interest rate charged, the length of time the account is to be carried, and how the account is to be repaid.) ▶ *The credit terms of the sale specify an 18 percent interest rate compounded annually.*

credit union a cooperative organization that receives deposits from members and makes loans to them at low interest rates. ▶ *Since deregulation of the banking industry, a credit union may perform almost all of the activities previously reserved for banks.*

creditor one to whom a debt is owed. ▶ *Allan's major creditor is Fuller's Department Store.*

criminal action legal proceedings against a person or persons who have broken statutes that forbid certain conduct detrimental to the best interests of the state and general public. ▶ *When a corporation violates certain Federal or state laws, it may be subject to criminal action.*

critical incidents appraisal a method of employee performance appraisal whereby the person conducting the appraisal records in a notebook all the significant incidents in the behavior of the person being rated. ▶ *With the critical incidents method, the rater keeps, in essence, a diary on the ratee, not-*

ing accomplishments, improvements, or failures.

crop insurance insurance coverage that protects a farmer against the failure of or the damage to an agricultural crop. ▶ *Crop insurance is most frequently used to insure against loss from hail damage.*

cropping trimming an illustration, graph, photograph, etc., to eliminate unnecessary parts in order to fit the item into a given space. ▶ *We will have to do some major cropping in order to fit this picture of the Golden Gate Bridge into our advertisement.*

cross footing the totaling of rows and columns in a spreadsheet and the comparing of the totals to see that they are in agreement. ▶ *Cross footing is a means of assuring accuracy in a spreadsheet.*

cross-merchandising a technique of merchandising in which in-store displays feature complementary products in an attempt to get a consumer to buy an additional product. ▶ *A display of toothbrushes next to a shelf of toothpaste is an example of cross-merchandising.*

cross-picketing picketing by two or more unions that claim to represent the same workers. ▶ *The cross-picketing problem will be resolved as soon as the certification election is held.*

cross-selling an attempt by a salesperson to convince a consumer to purchase other goods or services in addition to the ones the consumer is currently purchasing. ▶ *Effective cross-selling can dramatically increase a store's sales volume.*

crown jewels valuable assets or properties that make a firm vulnerable to takeover by another firm. (Slang.) ▶ *The crown jewels make a company valuable.*

crude quantity theory See *quantity theory of money.*

cryogenics the study and use of devices utilizing properties of materials near absolute zero temperature. ▶ *Tom became very interested in cryogenics while pursuing a Ph.D. in physics.*

CST See *Central Standard Time.*

cube rate a transportation rate that determines the shipping charge for small shipments. (It is based on the total number of pieces in the shipment and the total cubic volume; the greater the density and the fewer the pieces, the lower the charges.) ▶ *Please see if we can get a cube rate on these parcels going to Detroit.*

cum dividend with dividend. ▶ *Stocks are said to be cum dividend when the price quoted includes the payment to the buyer of any declared dividend.*

cum rights with rights. ▶ *Stock sold cum rights is sold with rights to subscribe to a current new issue of stock offered by the corporation.*

cumulative preferred a type of preferred stock whose dividends accumulate and are paid in subsequent years should they be skipped for any reason in any year. ▶ *My cumulative preferred stock failed again to pay its dividend, but I know I'll get the money someday.*

cumulative voting an arrangement whereby a corporation allows stockholders voting rights that are disproportionate to the number of shares held. (Shareholders may cast each of their votes for a single member, one for each individual member, or any combination between these extremes.) ▶ *The proposal for cumulative voting, introduced at the stockholder's meeting, received strong opposition from the board of directors.*

current assets the cash or other assets that are likely to be converted into cash or useful goods and services within a short period of time, usually one year. ▶ *Inventory is frequently a large component of current assets.*

current income the earnings and revenue that is realized and accounted for in the present operating period. ▶ *Current income for this period is 10 percent higher than it was last period.*

current liabilities amounts that are owed and payable within a short period of time, usually one year or less. (Examples of *current liabilities* are debts owed to trade creditors for materials and supplies, debts owed to banks on promissory notes, and accrued salaries, taxes, and interest.) ▶ *Our current income is barely exceeding our current liabilities.*

current ratio a measure of a firm's liquidity obtained by dividing the total current assets by the total current liabilities. (While the *current ratio* will vary from firm to firm and from industry to industry, a ratio of 2:1 is a generally accepted rule of thumb for an adequate

ratio.) ▶ *When the stockholders learned of the firm's current ratio, some of them threatened lawsuits.*

current return See the following entry.

current yield AND **current return** the ratio of current income from an investment to the purchase price or the current price of that investment. ▶ *The current yield on a share of Apex stock is 5.27 percent.*

curriculum vitae a biographical *résumé* of a person's career, including education credentials and professional experience and accomplishments. ▶ *A curriculum vitae is typically called for when applying for an academic position.*

cursor a symbol on a computer terminal screen that shows where the next character will be typed. ▶ *A cursor typically appears as a dash or a rectangle.*

custom made made to order for a particular customer. ▶ *Billy Ray's new stereo cabinet was custom made to hold his new receiver and speakers.*

customer one who purchases goods or services. ▶ *A customer may be an industrial consumer or an ultimate consumer.*

customer service 1. all those activities performed in an organization with the objective of assuring a customer's maximum satisfaction with the products or services offered and with the experience of doing business with the organization. ▶ *Customer service is a powerful competitive weapon in today's marketing arsenal.* 2. a department or function of an organization that responds to customer inquiries or complaints. ▶ *Our customer service department handles all inquiries about defective merchandise.*

customer service representative an individual in an organization who handles customer inquiries and complaints. ▶ *A customer service representative has to use a great deal of tact in responding to irate customers.*

customs duty a tax levied on goods imported into a country. ▶ *An automobile imported into the United States from Japan is subject to a substantial customs duty.*

cut-throat competition competition between two or more firms characterized by drastic price reductions that are intended to cause competitors to experience losses and force them out of business. ▶ *The firm that survives cut-throat competition will attempt to recoup its losses by charging higher prices in the future.*

cutback a reduction in the total number of people employed by an organization. ▶ *The cutback in personnel staffing will be a flat 15 percent across the board, effective September 1.*

cutout a point of sale display, usually made of heavy paper board, designed so that a part of the display is removed—cut out—in order to produce a desired effect. ▶ *A cutout may be designed so as to display in a prominent fashion a replica of the product being promoted.*

cybernetics the comparative study of control and communication processes of information handling machines and nervous systems of animals and man in order to understand and improve communication processes. ▶ *The twenty-first century will undoubtedly see some exciting developments in cybernetics.*

cycle billing a method of preparing and mailing account statements in which each customer is sent a statement on a certain date during the month rather than at the end of the month. ▶ *The primary purpose of cycle billing is to distribute the billing work load more or less evenly over the month, thereby eliminating the problem of a large month-end work load.*

cyclical fluctuation the periodic, alternating recurrence of periods of economic prosperity and recession. ▶ *Cyclical fluctuation refers to the rhythmic expansion and contraction of business activity.*

cyclical industry an industry in which variation in activity occurs in a cyclical pattern. ▶ *Construction is a cyclical industry—higher activity in the summer and lower activity in the winter.*

cyclical unemployment unemployment caused by cyclic downturns in business activity. ▶ *Cyclical unemployment occurs in the winter in the construction industry.*

D

dashboard reporting concept
the notion that reports submitted
to managers should contain only
key bits of information just as the
dashboard in an automobile displays only key indicators of the operation of the car. ▶ *Utilizing the
dashboard reporting concept
would greatly simplify many
managerial reports.*

data   the facts, numbers, letters,
and symbols that refer to or describe an object, idea, condition,
situation, or other factors. (This
form is the Latin plural. The Latin
singular is **datum**. Expressions
such as *these data* represent the
correct use of this Latin loan word
in English, although *this data* is
widely used.) ▶ *Frequently a manager has to sort through vast
amounts of data to find the facts
needed to make an assessment of a
situation.*

data base   an organized collection

of information stored on a computer for access or retrieval as needed.
▶ *A data base provides information that can be used in a number
of different ways.*

data processing   **1.** in general, all
operations performed on data in
order to produce information or to
achieve a specified result such as
the alphabetical ordering of a set of
records. ▶ *Data processing can be
accomplished manually.* **2.** specifically, the performance of (1) above
through the use of computers. ▶
*Data processing can be accom-
plished at tremendous rates of
speed through the use of computers.* **3.** that department within the
organization that performs the operations in (1) above through the
use of computers. ▶ *Helen, would
you take these documents to data
processing and see if we can get a
final report this afternoon?*

data reduction   the process of

selecting, editing, combining, and summarizing data in order to produce meaningful information. ▶ *Without sufficient data reduction, a manager would be swamped with superfluous information.*

data retrieval   See *information retrieval.*

data transmission   the automatic transfer of data from one computer to another, or the transfer of data to and from a central computer and remote data collection points. ▶ *Data transmission often utilizes telephone lines.*

Data Universal Numbering System   a listing of firms published by Dun & Bradstreet that provides such information as number of employees, finances, management, personnel, and corporate affiliations. ▶ *The Data Universal Numbering System is used to find the facts you need to evaluate a company.*

date of maturity   See *maturity date.*

datum   a specific fact or figure. (This is the Latin singular of *data.*) ▶ *Fred quoted datum after datum, trying to make his point.*

day laborer   a person who works and is paid by the day, and who has no long-term contract or working arrangement with an employer. ▶ *A day laborer is, in effect, an intermittent part-time worker.*

day loan   a loan made to stockbrokers for one day only. ▶ *A day loan is granted for the purpose of purchasing securities.*

day order   a stock market order to buy or sell that must be executed during a specified trading day. ▶ *If*

a day order is not executed during the designated trading day, it expires.

day rate   the rate of compensation for performing *day work* as differentiated from *incentive pay.* ▶ *A worker who is not producing work subject to incentive pay is compensated at a predetermined day rate.*

day shift   See *first shift.*

day trader   one who purchases and sells the same security in a margin account on the same day. ▶ *A day trader usually does not have to pay commissions on the sale and purchase of shares of stock.*

day work   a wage payment method whereby an employee is paid a fixed hourly or daily rate regardless of how much the employee produces. ▶ *One advantage of day work is that the employee always knows how big each paycheck will be.*

daybook   a chronological record of business transactions or events. ▶ *We will have to check the daybook to see when that order was processed.*

daylight saving time   the period of time between early April and late October when clocks in most of the United States are set an hour ahead, providing an extra hour of daylight in the evening. (Hawaii, and a few other locations, do not utilize daylight saving time.) ▶ *When does daylight saving time start this year?*

days of grace AND **grace period**   the reasonable length of time allowed, without incurring a penalty or a loss, for postponing payment of an obligation or for the present-ment of certain financial docu-ments. ▶ *This insurance policy gives me five days of grace to make my premium payment.*

DBA doing business as. (Doing business under a name assumed for business purposes.) ▶ *Most states require that a DBA be registered with the state.*

de facto "in actual fact." (Latin.) ▶ *John operates a garage sale from his home every weekend and is, de facto, a retailer.*

de jure "by law." (Latin.) ▶ *A cor-porate charter establishes de jure the corporation's right to conduct business.*

de novo "from the beginning." (Latin.) ▶ *When a corporation di-versifies, it sometimes acquires existing businesses rather than starting a business de novo.*

dead-end job a job with few or no promotion opportunities. (A *dead-end job* leads nowhere in the orga-nization.) ▶ *My first job out of high school was a dead-end job and that's why I decided to go to college.*

dead stock merchandise that can-not be readily sold, if at all. ▶ *The dead stock in inventory will have to be disposed of to make room for the new goods that are arriving tomorrow.*

dead time that portion of a day during which an employee is idle due to machine breakdown, insuffi-ciency of materials, or other fac-tors beyond the employee's con-trol. ▶ *Our production costs are increasing because we are experi-encing too much dead time.*

deadbeat someone who gives no fee or provides no service for the value received. (Slang.) ▶ *Since Jones did not pay us the finder's fee we were entitled to, we must consider him a deadbeat.*

deadhead **1.** an employee who is next in line for promotion but who is not qualified to assume the responsibilities of the higher posi-tion. (Slang.) ▶ *We would like to promote Smith, but he is a real deadhead.* **2.** to move a truck, bus, airplane, etc., from one place to an-other without a *payload*. ▶ *To deadhead a truck is costly because revenue-paying cargo is not being hauled.*

deadheading pay compensation paid to workers to cover the time spent in transportation to and from a workstation that is removed from the workers' normal workstation. ▶ *In some industries deadheading pay is less than a worker's stan-dard hourly rate.*

deadweight the weight of freight-carrying vehicles when they are empty. ▶ *When a vehicle is fully loaded, the deadweight is subtract-ed from the total weight to deter-mine the weight of the cargo.*

deadwood a nonproductive per-son or persons in an organization. ▶ *We need a reduction in force to eliminate the deadwood in this or-ganization.*

dealer **1.** one who purchases goods for resale to consumers. ▶ *My cousin Steve is a furniture dealer in Omaha.* **2.** a securities trader who buys and sells for his or her own account rather than as an agent for someone else's account. ▶

A bond dealer has more opportunity to earn large sums of money than does a bond trader.

dealer aid   promotional aid supplied to a retailer by a dealer or a manufacturer. ▶ *The displays at the checkout counter of a supermarket are examples of dealer aid.*

dealer brand   a brand name that belongs to a wholesaler rather than a manufacturer or a retailer. ▶ *A dealer brand creates more creditability than an unbranded product.*

dealer display   a promotional display or arrangement provided to a retailer by a wholesaler or a manufacturer. ▶ *A dealer display may be used at the checkout counter to encourage impulse buying.*

dealer servicing salesperson   a representative of a firm, usually a wholesale establishment, who has the responsibility of calling on retailers, checking their inventories, and maintaining their stocks of goods at the proper levels. ▶ *A dealer servicing salesperson establishes a relationship with the customer by providing service and advice.*

debasement   the act of reducing the quality, purity, or content, or otherwise altering the intrinsic value of the coinage of a government. ▶ *Substituting nonprecious metals for the gold or silver in a country's coinage is an act of debasement.*

debenture bond   a bond secured by the general credit of the issuer. (In the case of default the holder has no specific claim on any particular assets of the company, but instead must share in the distribution of assets on a *pro rata* basis.) ▶ *A debenture bond issued by an organization whose credit is questionable may sell at a greatly reduced price.*

debit   1. the left-hand side of the records of an account. ▶ *The debit side of an account is always located on the left-hand side.* 2. an amount entered on the left-hand side of an account. ▶ *The amount of the debit is $15.* 3. to enter an amount on the left-hand side of an account. ▶ *We should debit this account for the full amount of the refund.* 4. the collection of insurance premiums on a route basis. ▶ *My brother used to make a fairly good living running an insurance debit.*

debt   an amount, either secured or unsecured, owed to another. ▶ *A debt should always be settled in a timely manner.*

debt retirement   the repayment of debt, especially mortgages and bonds. (The most common method of *debt retirement* is to set aside funds each year to repay the debt.) ▶ *To improve its solvency the company started a plan of debt retirement.*

debt service   the payment of interest and such installments of principal as are currently due on a debt. ▶ *The inability to provide adequate debt service gets individuals as well as corporations into financial difficulty.*

debt to equity ratio   total liabilities divided by shareholders' equity. ▶ *The debt to equity ratio is a measure of the extent to which a corporation is leveraged.*

debugging the process of locating and correcting errors in a computer program or in the operation of the computer itself. ▶ *Debugging requires a great deal of skill and patience.*

decentralization 1. the locating of organizational functions at places geographically removed from the home office of the organization. ▶ *When our decentralization program is complete we will have operating units in twenty-five states and two foreign countries.* 2. the delegation of decision-making authority and responsibility. ▶ *Decentralization results in decisions being made at the lowest possible organizational levels.*

deceptive advertising advertising that makes false assertions or creates a false impression about the capabilities of a product or service. ▶ *Product testimonials from nonexistent people are one form of deceptive advertising.*

deceptive packaging packaging that creates an impression that the goods contained in the package are more than they actually are, either in terms of quantity or quality. ▶ *Deceptive packaging is an unethical means of attempting to increase sales.*

decile any of the values that divide a frequency distribution into ten parts. ▶ *The first decile contains 10 percent of the items comprising the frequency distribution.*

decision making the process of selecting a course of action from among two or more alternatives. ▶ *Decision making, while not time consuming, is perhaps the riskiest*

part of a manager's job.

decision table a tabular representation of a procedure or system in which alternative courses of action or numerical results are specified for various combinations of conditions. ▶ *A decision table identifies all possible outcomes.*

decision theory a technique for assigning numerical significance to the values of alternative courses of action. ▶ *Decision theory is essential to the development and evaluation of organizational strategies.*

decision tree a graphic method whereby courses of action, risks, information needs, and possible outcomes in a problem situation can be identified and presented visually for a decision maker. ▶ *A decision tree helps one see the interrelationships between the factors that influence a decision.*

declining balance method a method of depreciating capital goods in an accelerated manner. ▶ *Rules for using the declining balance method are specified in the Internal Revenue Code.*

deed a written agreement used to convey the legal title of real property from one person to another. ▶ *The deed to that particular piece of property is in my safe deposit box at the bank.*

deed of trust an instrument by which title to real property is conveyed to a trustee to hold as security for the holders of notes or bonds. ▶ *A deed of trust should be prepared by a qualified attorney.*

deep discount bond a bond that sells at a discount of 25 percent or more of its face value. ▶ *A $1,000 bond selling at $650 is referred to as a deep discount bond.*

deep discounting the selling of a good or service at a price significantly lower than the standard or normal price of the good or service. ▶ *Deep discounting is sometimes used to dispose of slow-moving merchandise.*

defalcation misappropriation of money or embezzlement by a person in a position of trust. ▶ *An indemnity bond protects an organization against defalcation.*

default the failure to perform contractual obligations or to pay a debt. ▶ *Since Robert has not made a loan payment in three months, he is in default on his loan.*

defective having a fault or imperfection. ▶ *The purpose of quality assurance is to catch defective parts or products before they leave the plant.*

defendant one who, in law, is called upon to respond to a formal complaint and provide satisfaction for an alleged wrong. ▶ *The defendant in a lawsuit may have to spend a great deal of money just to prove that there was no wrongdoing involved in an alleged action.*

deferred annuity an annuity policy from which payments are due after a specified period has elapsed. ▶ *My deferred annuity will pay me $2,000 per month after twenty years.*

deferred billing the delayed invoicing of a customer at the request of the seller. ▶ *Under our deferred billing arrangement, any* *purchases made this month will not be invoiced until February.*

deferred charge an expenditure that is not recognized as a cost of doing business in the period in which it is incurred, but is carried forward to be written-off in subsequent periods. ▶ *An annual insurance premium is an example of a deferred charge.*

deferred income income received or recorded before it is earned. ▶ *Rent received in advance of the period to which it applies is an example of deferred income.*

deferred liability **1.** a debt the payment of which is delayed beyond a legal or customary date. ▶ *Through negotiations with the lender, the loan has been reclassified from a current liability to a deferred liability.* **2.** any long-term liability. ▶ *Any long-term liability is a deferred liability because it does not have to be settled in the current period.*

deferred tax a tax liability on income accrued in the current period. (The tax will not be paid until the next period when the income is actually received.) ▶ *A deferred tax is incurred in one period but is not payable until a future period.*

deficit **1.** a debit balance in the surplus or retained earnings account. ▶ *A net operating loss in a given year may produce a deficit in the retained earnings account on the balance sheet.* **2.** the excess of liabilities and capital stock over assets. ▶ *The sudden increase in liabilities has resulted in a deficit.*

deficit financing AND **deficit**

89

spending the practice of spending more money than is received in revenue by a government. ▶ *Deficit financing is sometimes necessary to keep a government operational.*

deficit spending See the previous entry.

deflation a general reduction in the level of prices. ▶ *Deflation is brought about artificially by decreasing the money supply or by decreasing the volume of money spent.*

degree of freedom any of the independent variables that make up any statistic. ▶ *Two degrees of freedom would mean that two of the conditions that make up a statistic could vary independently of one another.*

delay a period during the performance of a task in which conditions do not permit or do not require the immediate performance of the next step in the task. ▶ *Eliminating a delay in the performance of a task reduces the cost of performance.*

delay allowance 1. an increment of time, usually expressed as a percentage, added to the normal time for performing a task in order to compensate for delays beyond the control of the worker. ▶ *The delay allowance for this task is 15 percent.* 2. a separate time or money credit used to compensate a worker on incentive wages for a delay not covered by the piece rate or standard for the job. ▶ *Because of the fire in the knitting area, everyone will be paid a delay allowance.*

delegate 1. a person authorized to act as the representative of another person or persons. ▶ *Because Smith could not attend the meeting, she sent Johnson as her delegate.* 2. to assign work to someone, usually a subordinate. ▶ *Tom delegates as much as possible to his subordinates.*

delegation the process of assigning work to another, usually a subordinate. ▶ *Every manager should learn the art of delegation.*

delegation of authority the act of assigning work to a subordinate and granting the subordinate the necessary power to take action to accomplish the work. ▶ *Delegation of authority must always include the power to take action.*

delivered price a price that includes the cost of transporting a product from the point of shipment to a point designated by the customer. ▶ *The delivered price actually represents the total cost of the product.*

delivery the transfer of goods from one person to another. ▶ *Thompson plans to take delivery of the turret lathe at the end of next week.*

delphi technique a method used to forecast future developments in technology. ▶ *The delphi technique utilizes a panel of experts who pool their best judgments.*

deluxe goods the higher priced, exclusive styles or models of goods, which are typically purchased by the wealthiest of customers. ▶ *In automobiles, Jaguars and Masertis are considered to be deluxe goods.*

demand 1. the desire to own or

acquire goods or services. ▶ *An individual consumer has a demand for a product.* **2.** the sum total of all desires for particular goods or services. ▶ *There is a great deal of consumer demand for the electronic hydromulcher.* **3.** an action by a creditor causing the maturity of a note. ▶ *Acme Financial Services is exercising its right of demand regarding your past due note.* **4.** a union request about a term or condition of employment. ▶ *The latest union demand is for a four-day workweek.*

demand curve a graphic representation of variations in the quantity of a product that will be purchased at different prices. (This assumes that consumers will buy more of a product at a low price than they will at a high price.) ▶ *The demand curve demonstrates the importance of realistic pricing.*

demand deposit account funds on deposit at a commercial bank that can be withdrawn by check and are payable upon the request of the depositor. ▶ *A demand deposit account sometimes pays interest.*

demand loan a loan that has no fixed maturity date, but which is payable upon request of the lender. ▶ *A demand loan is frequently an unsecured signature loan.*

demarketing the process of discouraging consumers from buying or using a product. ▶ *Cigarettes have been the object of demarketing by the U.S. government for a number of years.*

demographics aspects or characteristics of the human population. ▶

Rate of population growth, population density, population distribution, and the average per capita income are examples of demographics.

demotion the transfer of an employee to a position of lower pay, status, or responsibility. ▶ *Because of the morale problems it creates, demotion should be used sparingly.*

demurrage a charge incurred by the consignee of a shipment, generally by rail or water, for detaining the shipment vehicle longer than a stipulated length of time. ▶ *Demurrage should be avoided because it is very expensive.*

department a distinct area or sphere of activity within an enterprise over which someone has authority for the performance of tasks. ▶ *Depending upon its size, a department may have an assistant manager as well as a manager.*

department store a retail organization carrying several lines of merchandise and organized into separate departments for purposes of sales promotion, accounting, control, etc. ▶ *Macy's is one of the best known department stores in New York City.*

departmentation the process of grouping activities into organizational components such as divisions, departments, branches, sections, or units. ▶ *The most common ways of achieving departmentation are by products, services, processes, functions, customers, locations, and time.*

departmentized specialty store a large retail store selling men's and/or women's ready-to-wear clothing and a full line of accessories that has been separated into departments for purposes of sales promotion, service, accounting, control, etc. ▶ *A departmentized specialty store differs from a regular department store in that it does not sell furniture or home appliances and does not normally handle piece goods.*

dependent variable a variable that is determined by another variable. ▶ *In a time series depicting corn output per year and annual rainfall, corn output is the dependent variable.*

depletion a periodic reduction in the value of an asset that cannot be replaced. ▶ *Depletion differs from depreciation in that the asset being depleted cannot be replace (for example, oil or coal), whereas a normal asset being depreciated can be replaced.*

deposit 1. to place property in the hands of another party for safekeeping. ▶ *We would like to deposit the truckload of bumper springs with you until we can arrange for their sale.* 2. money given as partial payment, down payment, earnest money, or security for a purchase. ▶ *A deposit of $250 will hold that refrigerator for you until financing can be arranged.* 3. cash, checks, drafts, and other negotiable instruments placed in a financial institution for credit to a particular account. ▶ *We have a considerable amount of money on deposit at the First National Bank.*

deposit account an account with a financial institution from which

money cannot be withdrawn by check. ▶ *A savings account with a savings and loan association is a deposit account.*

deposit in transit cash, checks, drafts, and other negotiable instruments en route to a financial institution but not yet credited to the appropriate account. ▶ *A deposit in transit will not show up on a bank statement if the deposit was made the same day as the statement date.*

depository (institution) 1. a bank in which funds or securities are deposited under terms of a legal agreement. ▶ *A savings bank is a depository for consumers.* 2. a bank in which Federal, state, or local government funds are deposited, or in which other banks are permitted by law to maintain legal reserves. ▶ *The Federal Reserve Bank is a depository institution.*

Depository Institutions Deregulation and Monetary Control Act of 1980 a comprehensive Federal statute that provided for the deregulation of the U.S. banking system. ▶ *The Depository Institutions Deregulation and Monetary Control Act of 1980 has had a tremendous impact on all U.S. bank, savings and loan associations, and credit unions.*

depreciation the method whereby the costs of fixed assets are converted into expenses. ▶ *The Internal Revenue Code recognizes several methods of depreciation.*

depressed area a specific geographical area where economic conditions are unfavorable. ▶ *In a* *depressed area incomes are low and unemployment is high.*

depression an economic condition that is characterized by high unemployment, falling prices, and a decrease in business activity. ▶ *The length and severity of a depression cannot normally be foreseen in advance.*

deregulation the removal of governmental controls on markets, industries, and businesses. ▶ *Banking and transportation are two industries that have undergone significant deregulation.*

derived demand the demand for a product or service that is created by the demand for another product. ▶ *The demand for lumber is a derived demand stemming from the demand for new houses.*

descriptive label a label that lists the significant and measurable characteristics of goods. ▶ *Items such as size, variety, sugar content, seasoning, etc., on a can of vegetables are the kinds of characteristics typically shown on a descriptive label.*

desk jobber a person or firm who performs a wholesaling function without taking title or possession of the goods. ▶ *A desk jobber may rely on drop shipment to move merchandise from a manufacturer to a retailer.*

desktop publishing a computer application that allows individuals and firms to produce reports, advertising, newsletters, etc., at a quality level approaching typeset copy. ▶ *Desktop publishing has resulted in a proliferation of innovative and inexpensive newsletters*

devoted to specialized topics.

deterioration a kind of depreciation caused by physical or chemical action occurring over time, or by the physical process of wearing out. ▶ *Rust is a form of deterioration that affects products made of iron and steel.*

deterministic model a representation of reality in which all the variables are controlled and chance plays a small role. ▶ *Development of a deterministic model is dependent upon being able to identify and control all variables.*

deutsch mark the unit of German currency. ▶ *The exchange rate of the deutsch mark and the U.S. dollar is 1.62 deutsch marks per dollar today.*

devaluation the lowering of the value of a currency by decreasing its worth in relation to gold or other currencies. (See also *revaluation*.) ▶ *Devaluation may be necessary in times of galloping inflation.*

devil's advocate a person or group who presents an opposing view or argument. ▶ *Wilson has been playing the devil's advocate on our plan to expand the Pittsburgh plant.*

Dictionary of Occupational Titles a publication of the U.S. Department of Labor that lists and describes some 22,000 jobs. ▶ *Almost any job title currently in use can be found in the Dictionary of Occupational Titles.*

dictum 1. in general, a succinctly worded, authoritative statement. ▶ *We have just received a dictum about the use of overtime from* *corporate headquarters.* **2.** an opinion handed down by a judge. (Legal.) ▶ *Judge Howard will deliver his dictum at 2:00 P.M. today.*

die a device used to cut out, stamp, or otherwise form metal, paper, plastic, or other substances. ▶ *A die can be used to cut metal into different shapes.*

differential cost See *marginal cost.*

differently abled an individual who has a physical, a mental, an emotional, or other handicap that substantially limits one or more major life activities. ▶ *"Differently abled" is used as a replacement for "handicapped."*

dilution (of earnings) the weakening of a share of stock's proportion of earnings or asset value caused by an increase in the number of shares outstanding, without a corresponding increase in total earnings or asset value. ▶ *Issuing more stock now will only result in dilution.*

dime store See *variety store.*

Dimensional Motion Times AND **DMT** a system of predetermined elemental time standards. ▶ *Dimensional Motion Times can only be used by a person who has been thoroughly trained in the use of this system.*

diminishing returns See *(law of) diminishing returns.*

dink "dual income, no kids." (Slang acronym. A term for an employed married couple who have no children.) ▶ *After Tom and Mary are married, they will be another dink.*

direct advertising printed advertisements, such as catalogs, booklets, letters, circulars, etc., distributed to prospective customers by mail or by hand. ▶ *Today's consumers are literally bombarded by a barrage of direct advertising designed to get them to purchase a variety of products.*

direct cost the labor and materials that can be identified and charged to a specific product or products. ▶ *The direct cost of the radar detector is eighty percent of the total cost of manufacturing the product.*

direct costing system a method of cost accounting in which manufacturing costs are segregated into two categories: those that are fixed and those that vary directly with volume. (Only the prime manufacturing costs plus variable factory costs are used to value inventory and cost of sales. The remaining factory expenses are charged to profit and loss.) ▶ *Our accountant recommends that we install a direct costing system.*

direct distribution AND **direct marketing** the sale of a product direct from the manufacturer to the consumer. ▶ *Direct distribution eliminates the wholesaler and other middlemen from the channel of distribution.*

direct labor the work that alters in some fashion the product being manufactured, the cost of which can be identified with or assigned to a particular part, product, or group of products. ▶ *The efforts of a machinist are part of direct labor.*

direct labor budget an estimate for some future period of the cost of labor applied directly to the manufacture of a product. ▶ *The direct labor budget for next year should be finished by the end of the week.*

direct labor cost the salaries and wages of workers engaged in production or processing operations. ▶ *Direct labor cost can be identified with specific products or groups of products.*

direct labor standard a specified output or a time allowance established for performing direct labor. ▶ *The direct labor standard will have to be reset now that the new machine is operational.*

direct mail advertising advertising distributed by mail. ▶ *Direct mail advertising is a popular method of advertising to ultimate consumers.*

direct marketing See *direct distribution.*

direct material cost the cost of all materials that will become part of a finished product. ▶ *Direct material cost is often less than direct labor cost.*

direct overhead that portion of overhead cost allocated to all manufacturing operations. ▶ *Each product line should bear its proportionate share of direct overhead.*

direct production the creation of consumable goods by the application of labor to land or natural wealth. ▶ *Farming is an example of direct production.*

directing the process of guiding, supervising, and overseeing subordinates. ▶ *Directing is one of the most difficult activities a manager has to perform.*

director a person elected by the stockholders to serve on the governing board of a corporation. ▶ *We are pleased to announce that Sam Patterson has been elected a director of the Apex Corporation.*

disbursement the act of paying out money. ▶ *Please make the disbursement for the flowers out of the petty cash fund.*

discharge 1. to carry out or fulfill one's obligation. ▶ *We expect you to discharge your duty as specified in the contract.* 2. the involuntary termination of a worker. ▶ *Larry's discharge was due to his poor attendance.*

disciplinary penalty the punishment of an employee for violation of a company's rules or policies. ▶ *Termination of employment is the most severe disciplinary penalty that can be given to an employee.*

disclaimer a repudiation or denial of a claim. ▶ *A disclaimer is often included in a sales contract to limit the seller's responsibilities.*

discount 1. an allowance given for the settlement of a debt before it is due. ▶ *Our normal trade discount is 10 percent if the invoice is paid within five working days.* 2. the excess of par or face value of a security over the amount paid or received for it. ▶ *The discount on the bond was $100.* 3. the commission deducted by a broker for selling an issue of securities. ▶ *The broker's discount on that issue is 10 percent.* 4. a reduction of a principal amount. ▶ *Although the in-*

voice price on that automobile is $12,500, we will be able to grant a discount of $1,500.

discount merchandising low margin retailing, generally self-service, wherein goods are sold at less than list, normal, or standard prices. ► *Discount merchandising is extremely popular with low income consumers.*

discount rate the interest rate the Federal Reserve charges member banks for loans using government securities or eligible paper as collateral. ► *The Federal Reserve revises the discount rate periodically to either encourage or discourage borrowing by member banks.*

discount store a store selling to the public at prices that are lower than normal prices. ► *People who are cost conscious tend to shop at a discount store.*

discounted cash flow a method of evaluating the earning power of proposed capital expenditures. (This is done by discounting the anticipated annual earnings resulting from the expenditures at a rate that makes the accumulated present values of these earnings equal to the sum originally expended on the project.) ► *The discounted cash flow method takes into consideration the fact that money received earlier has a greater value than money received at a later time.*

discretionary income the spendable income a consumer has remaining after the purchase of food, clothing, and shelter, and the payment of taxes. ► *Expensive goods do not sell well when consumers*

have little or no discretionary income.

discretionary order a situation in which a customer gives a stockbroker the power to buy or sell any security that the broker considers to be in the best interests of the customer. ► *When a person gives a discretionary order to a stockbroker, it is an indication that the person has a great deal of trust in the broker's judgment.*

discrimination the failure to treat individuals fairly and equally in employment because of factors of race, color, sex, creed, national origin, religion, physical handicap, or other similar irrelevant criteria. ► *Discrimination is still a problem in American industry.*

diseconomy of scale the tendency for certain costs to grow disproportionately as a company becomes larger or its volume of business grows. ► *Diseconomy of scale exists when a larger plant is less cost efficient than a smaller plant.*

dishonor 1. the refusal by the drawee to accept or to pay a check, draft, or bill of exchange when it is presented. (Usually in the phrase **notice of dishonor.**) ► *We have received a notice of dishonor from Neumann alleging that presentment of the draft was not made in a timely fashion.* **2.** to refuse to pay a note when it is presented for payment. ► *We anticipate that Wright will dishonor the note because the date is missing.*

disinflation a condition during an economic downturn when economic activity lessens enough to discourage inflation but not sufficiently to increase unemployment. ▶ *In disinflation price increases slow down or stop, but prices do not drop.*

disintermediation a situation wherein money moves from conventional financial institutions into investment vehicles because rates are higher in those investments than they are in financial institutions. ▶ *Disintermediation may cause problems for banks because of the outflow of funds.*

disk a computer memory device. ▶ *A microcomputer uses a floppy disk.*

disk operating system AND **DOS** the collection of programs that allows a personal computer to run its programs, to store and retrieve data, and to communicate with its peripheral units. (Acronym.) ▶ *IBM, Digital Research, and Microsoft are three companies that make operating systems known as DOS.*

dismal science the field of economics. (The term was coined by Thomas Carlyle in 1798.) ▶ *Contemporary economics is no longer referred to as the dismal science, even though it does have its depressing aspects.*

dismissal the permanent termination of an individual's employment with an organization initiated by the organization. ▶ *Dismissal may be accompanied with severance pay if the discharged employee has sufficient tenure.*

dispatching the process of assigning work to employees or machines. ▶ *Keeping machines and*

employees fully utilized depends upon effective dispatching.

display advertising a presentation made to the consumer in the form of an attractive exhibit, usually at the point of purchase. ▶ *Display advertising combines a printed message with immediately available products to encourage consumers to make instant purchases.*

disposable income income that is available for use in an unrestricted manner. ▶ *As disposable income increases, people tend to purchase luxury goods.*

disposal sale a method of removing merchandise from stock at a lower than normal price. ▶ *A disposal sale helps to clear slow moving items from a firm's inventory.*

distinctive competency something that a particular organization does better than other competing organizations. ▶ *A distinctive competency creates a competitive advantage for a firm.*

distress selling the selling of goods under conditions that are not in the best interest of the seller. ▶ *Distress selling may occur when a seller has to sell merchandise very quickly in order to raise cash to meet an urgent financial need.*

distribution 1. marketing. ▶ *Distribution, in the broadest sense, is concerned with every step in the process of moving goods from the manufacturer to the final users of those goods.* 2. the physical movement of goods from producer to consumer. ▶ *Warehousing is a key step in the distribution system.* 3. any payment of cash, property, or shares of stock to stockholders or owners of a business. ► *This year's dividend distribution will be made in shares of stock rather than in cash.*

distribution center a point from which merchandise is dispersed to retail outlets. ► *A distribution center is usually a very large warehouse.*

distribution channel AND **marketing channel** the route taken by a good as it moves from the producer to the consumer. ► *Direct distribution by a manufacturer shortens the distribution channel.*

distributor 1. specifically, a wholesale middleman who supplies retailers with merchandise. ► *A good distributor is of value to the manufacturer as well as the retailer.* 2. generally, the retailers who sell a manufacturer's products. ► *Each distributor must have a copy of the new product booklet to show purchasers.*

diversification the participation of a single business enterprise in the manufacture or distribution of a widely divergent assortment of goods or services. ► *Diversification broadens an organization's product lines.*

diversion in transit privilege the option of a consignor or a consignee of goods to change the destination of a shipment at some point between its point of origin and its destination. ► *If we secure a diversion in transit privilege, we will be able to ship the machines to either Little Rock or Shreveport, depending on which plant needs them the most.*

divestiture 1. the selling off or otherwise disposing of a portion of a firm or one of its major assets. ► *Divestiture is a method for disposing of unprofitable divisions.* 2. a court order instructing an organization to dispose of something. (Legal.) ► *The court has decreed a divestiture of the Amplex division by December 15.*

dividend a periodic distribution of profits or other property among the stockholders of a corporation. ► *Due to the company's poor performance this year, there will be no dividend.*

dividend in arrears AND **accumulated dividend** the undeclared dividends on preferred stock. ► *A dividend in arrears situation may depress the price of a share of stock.*

dividend payout ratio a ratio obtained by dividing the total amount of cash dividends paid on both common and preferred stock by the total cash earnings of a corporation for a given fiscal or calendar year. ► *Webber Tools and Equipment has the lowest dividend payout ratio of any firm in its industry.*

division a major functional area or activity within an organization. ► *Within a large corporation, one will customarily find a marketing division, a finance division, a production division, and a research and development division.*

division of labor the separation of work into specialized tasks. ► *Division of labor may result in lower production costs.*

DMT See *Dimensional Motion*

Times.

do not reduce order a stock market order to buy or sell securities under certain conditions, with the stipulation that the security price is not to be reduced by the ordinary cash dividend on the ex-dividend date. ▶ *Percy just gave his broker a do not reduce order for 100 shares of Apple Computer.*

dock to deduct money from a worker's salary or wage as a *disciplinary penalty* for certain infractions of an employer's rules. ▶ *Tom was docked for three hours' pay for reporting to work late.*

dock receipt a document issued by a steamship agent verifying the receipt of goods to be exported. ▶ *We know the goods have arrived in New Orleans because we have received a dock receipt.*

document 1. any specific paper or written instrument. ▶ *A deed is a type of legal document.* 2. to substantiate as to source or veracity. ▶ *There is a rumor that the Flint, Michigan plant will be closed, but we have not been able to document it.*

dollar cost averaging a methodical way of buying securities at regular intervals in fixed dollar amounts. (By using this method the investor will buy fewer shares at higher prices and more shares at lower prices, thus over time, the investor will pay a lower average price per share.) ▶ *My broker has advised me to begin a dollar cost averaging program as soon as possible.*

dollar sales per square foot a measure of retail productiveness obtained by dividing a store or department's net sales by the number of square feet of selling space occupied by the store or department. ▶ *Dollar sales per square foot will vary from store to store.*

domestic bill 1. a draft or bill of exchange payable in the same state in which it is drawn. ▶ *Since this is a domestic bill payable in Colorado, we will not have to send it out of state for collection.* 2. in foreign trade, a draft or bill of exchange payable within the country in which it is drawn. ▶ *Anne's draft is a domestic bill payable in Switzerland.*

domestic corporation 1. a corporation established under the laws of a given state or country that operates within that state or country. ▶ *A Delaware corporation is considered a domestic corporation when it does business in Delaware.* 2. a corporation established under the laws of the United States as opposed to one established under the laws of another country. ▶ *Burlington Northern Railroad is a domestic corporation.*

domestic production 1. the goods produced within a country as opposed to goods that are imported. ▶ *When domestic production is sufficient, we do not have to import tomatoes from Mexico.* 2. household production. (The output by a household and its members for their consumption, usually from raw materials that have been raised or collected by the household.) ▶ *Our domestic production of carrots will be sufficient to last us all winter.*

domicile the permanent home or principal establishment of an individual. ▶ *An individual may have several residences but only one domicile.*

donated surplus an increase in the shareholder's equity account arising from gifts made to the corporation by stockholders or others. ▶ *Donated surplus is not commonly found in large publicly traded corporations.*

door-to-door selling a method of personal selling whereby a salesperson calls on each house in a residential neighborhood. ▶ *Some items lend themselves to door-to-door selling, and some do not.*

dormant account 1. a credit account that is set up but is inactive either through lack of use or the customer's request. ▶ *A dormant account should be reviewed periodically to determine if it could be made an active account.* 2. a bank account that has been inactive for a long period of time. ▶ *A dormant account may, after a specified number of years, be subject to escheat by the state.*

DOS See *disk operating system.*

dot matrix a two-dimensional array of dots in printing that form characters or graphics. ▶ *Dot matrix letters are fairly easy to read.*

double entry system an accounting system that requires that two entries, a debit and a credit, be made for each transaction recorded. (Debit entries record increases in assets and expenses or decreases in liabilities or owner's equity. Credit entries record increases in liabilities or owner's equity, and decreases in assets and expenses.) ▶ *Under the double entry system, debit entries must always equal credit entries.*

double-name paper See *two-name paper.*

double taxation a situation that exists when the Federal government taxes corporations on their profits that are at least partially distributed to stockholders who then must pay taxes on the dividends earned by their shares. ▶ *Double taxation means, in essence, that a corporation's earnings are taxed twice.*

double time compensation paid at twice the normal rate. ▶ *Double time may be paid for overtime, holiday, or Sunday work.*

Dow Jones Averages a stock market index compiled by the Dow Jones Irwin Company. (The three averages are the industrials, the transportations, and the utilities.) ▶ *The Dow Jones Average is composed of a selected number of relatively high grade stocks listed on the New York Stock Exchange.*

Dow theory a method of forecasting the action of the stock market by using the *Dow Jones Averages.* (This involves confirmations of new highs among the three averages—industrials, transportations, and utilities.) ▶ *The Dow theory was originated in 1897 by Charles Dow.*

down payment that part of the purchase price of goods that the buyer gives the seller at the time of purchase. (The remainder of the price is then paid at a future date, usually through some form of credit arrangement or when delivery is taken of the goods.) ▶ *The typical down payment on a new car is 10 percent of the purchase price.*

down tick a stock market transaction in a particular security that is lower than the transaction immediately preceding it. ▶ *A down tick does not necessarily mean that the price of the stock is about to fall significantly.*

downscale to reduce the size of an organization, division, department, project, etc. ▶ *We should downscale the Riverside division to make it efficient*

downsizing the act of reducing the size of an organization, division, department, project, etc. ▶ *Many large American corporations went through a period of downsizing during the 1990s.*

downtime a period of time during which a work operation is halted due to a lack of materials, a machine breakdown, etc. ▶ *The downtime on the new machine is significantly less than the downtime on the old machine.*

draft a written order signed by one party (the *drawer*) requesting a second party (the *drawee*) to make payment of a specified sum of money to a third party (the *payee*). ▶ *A draft may be payable upon presentation or it may be payable after a stipulated period of time.*

drawee a party, such as an individual, a proprietorship, a partnership, or a corporation, upon whom a draft is drawn and from whom payment of the draft is expected. ▶ *The drawee is usually the purchaser of goods.*

drawer AND **maker** a party, such as an individual, a proprietorship, a partnership, or a corporation, who draws a draft, check, or bill of exchange upon another party for the payment of funds. ▶ *The drawer expects full and immediate payment.*

drawing account **1.** a temporary owner's equity account used in proprietorships and partnerships to show amounts withdrawn from the business by the owners. ▶ *According to the drawing account, Smith has taken $25,000 out of the business during the first six months of the year.* **2.** a method of compensating salespeople paid on a commission basis. (A salesperson is allowed to receive salary up to a certain amount each pay period even though the salesperson's present commission pay does not cover the amount of salary drawn.) ▶ *A drawing account allows a salesperson to have an even level of income.*

drayage a charge made for transportation of goods from one location to another. ▶ *We received a drayage bill from Acme Moving Company this morning.*

drive-in a sales or service facility designed to accommodate customers who conduct business at the facility from their automobiles. ▶ *Practically every bank in the United States has a drive-in facility.*

drop shipment a shipment from a manufacturer or a wholesaler made directly to a customer of a distributor without passing through the hands of the distributor. ▶ *A drop shipment can speed up the* *delivery process considerably.*

drop shipper a functional wholesaler who takes title to, but not possession of, the goods handled. ▶ *A drop shipper takes orders from buyers and sends these orders to manufacturers or other suppliers who ship the goods directly to the buyer.*

dry cargo packaged or nonfluid goods transported on a tanker, which normally carries fluid goods. ▶ *Dry cargo is stored in special areas of the tanker's hold.*

dry goods textiles, clothing, and other related goods and materials. ▶ *Lace, threads, buttons, and beads are considered to be dry goods.*

dry goods store a retail store that generally handles only clothing and piece goods. ▶ *The dry goods store is gradually disappearing from the American retailing scene in favor of full service stores that offer a complete line of goods.*

dry hole 1. specifically, an oil or gas well that does not result in the discovery of oil or gas. ▶ *Acme Petroleum drilled another dry hole in Parker County last month.* 2. generally, any venture that does not produce results. ▶ *Our efforts on the atomic powered weather vane will probably be another dry hole.*

dual banking system a situation in which a bank can be chartered by either the Federal government or by a state government. ▶ *The United States has a dual banking system.*

dual pay system a compensation plan under which employees may select the more advantageous of two methods of computing earnings. ▶ *In the railroad industry, a dual pay system allows employees to choose to be paid on the basis of miles traveled or hours worked.*

dues checkoff a system in which a company withholds union dues from an employee's paycheck and submits the dues directly to the union. ▶ *Dues checkoff is an item subject to collective bargaining.*

dummy stockholder a person in whose name shares of stock are registered although the shares actually belong to someone else. (Frequently, large stockholders hold shares in the names of their brokers in order to conceal the actual ownership of the stock.) ▶ *Ray is using his broker as a dummy stockholder for his shares of Patella Computers.*

dump the printout of the contents, or a portion of the contents, of a computer file. ▶ *A dump may be required to find an error in a computer program.*

dumping the sale of excess production in a foreign market at a price that is lower than the price in the domestic market. ▶ *It is illegal for a U.S. company to engage in dumping.*

Dun and Bradstreet, Inc. an international firm whose primary business is collecting and reporting credit information. ▶ *Dun and Bradstreet, Inc. gives a credit rating to corporations.*

dun letter a notice or letter sent to a person who is delinquent in paying a debt reminding the person that the debt is past due. ▶ *A dun* *letter may threaten legal action if payment is not forthcoming.*

duopoly a market situation in which there are only two sellers of a particular item or service. ▶ *A duopoly exists in theoretical economics, but is not readily found in reality.*

duopsony a market situation in which there are only two buyers of a particular item or service. ▶ *A duopsony is a theoretical economic condition.*

durable goods AND **hard goods** goods of a long-lived nature that are capable of being used again and again. ▶ *Washing machines and refrigerators are examples of durable goods used by ultimate consumers.*

duress force or illegal compulsion. ▶ *Contracts signed or agreements entered into under duress are not binding.*

Dutch auction an auction in which the price of an item begins at its highest level and is continuously reduced until a prospective buyer is induced to purchase. ▶ *U.S. Treasury bills are sold at Dutch auction.*

dynamic analysis a study of a situation, an operation, or some other process under realistic operating conditions. ▶ *Dynamic analysis is performed while the process being studied is actually happening.*

dynamic programming a mathematical approach to solving multistage problems in which decisions at one stage become the conditions for succeeding stages. ▶ *Dynamic programming would be virtually impossible to use on complex problems without a computer.*

dynamiter a high pressure salesman who sells fraudulent securities by telephone. (Slang.) ▶ *A dynamiter typically operates out of a boiler room.*

E

E-mail See *electronic mail.*

early markdown a reduction in the price of merchandise made early in the season or while demand for the merchandise is fairly active. ▶ *Summer clothing may experience an early markdown at the end of the Easter season.*

early retirement the act of leaving a job by way of retirement before the normal retirement age. ▶ *Bob elected early retirement when he left the company at age 52.*

early retirement benefits the payments and other privileges to which a person is entitled when retiring before the customary retirement age. ▶ *Corporations sometimes increase early retirement benefits to encourage workers to retire.*

earned hours the time in standard hours credited to a worker or a work group as a result of their completion of a given task or series of tasks. ▶ *Earned hours are greater than actual hours worked this month.*

earned income income realized as a result of the normal operation of a business. ▶ *Earned income for February shows an increase of 10 percent over January.*

earned surplus extra funds accumulated from the profits of a corporation. (See also *surplus.*) ▶ *The earned surplus remained in the company's treasury.*

earnest money the monetary funds given by one party to a contract and accepted by the other party in order to bind the contractual agreement. ▶ *Earnest money is forfeited by the payer if he fails to live up to his part of the contract.*

earning power **1.** the capacity of an asset to return a profit. ▶ *The earning power of finished goods inventory is greater than that of* *cash.* **2.** the capacity of a person to earn a wage or salary. ▶ *An accountant's earning power is greater than a janitor's earning power.*

earnings **1.** gross revenue, profit, or income. ▶ *General Motors reports that earnings for the year are up.* **2.** net income. ▶ *While gross revenues are higher this year, earnings are lower.*

earnings per share the net income of a corporation divided by the average number of shares of stock outstanding during the period in which the income was earned. ▶ *Earnings per share show an increase of two cents this quarter.*

earnings report See *income statement.*

earnings statement See *income statement.*

easement **1.** the right of a person, corporation, or governmental agency to use land owned by another. ▶ *An easement is used by a utility company to lay pipes across a housing development.* **2.** a specific portion of land, as described above. ▶ *The electric company laid new cable in the easement.*

Eastern Daylight Time AND **EDT** the adjusted time in the easternmost time zone of the United States from early April to late October. ▶ *Eastern Daylight Time is four hours behind Greenwich Time.*

Eastern Standard Time AND **EST** the time in the easternmost zone of the United States from late October to early April. ▶ *Eastern Standard Time is five hours behind Greenwich Time.*

Eastern Time the time in the easternmost zone of the United States. ▶ *New York is on Eastern Time.*

easy money readily available money; ample funds in the money supply so that interest rates are lower and loans are easier to get; easily earned money. ▶ *Easy money tends to encourage economic growth.*

echo check a method of verifying the accuracy of data transmitted over telephone lines or by microwaves. ▶ *An echo check involves retransmitting received data to the sending unit for comparison with the original data.*

ECM See *European Economic Community.*

econometrics that part of the field of economics concerned with the study of economic measurements for the purpose of developing and testing models or theories. ▶ *Econometrics involves the use of computers and high-level statistical approaches.*

economic Darwinism the principle, derived from Charles Darwin, that in business only the fittest of enterprises will survive in the long run. ▶ *According to economic Darwinism, many organizations in existence today will not survive the next five years.*

Economic Development Administration an agency within the Department of Commerce that protects jobs and encourages economic growth in low income areas. ▶ *The run-down neighborhoods received a great deal of aid from the Economic Development*

Administration.

economic forecast an estimation of general levels of business activity for a specified period of time in the future. ▶ *The government's economic forecast for the third quarter indicates a slowing of the growth rate experienced in the second quarter.*

economic freedom the lack of, or a minimum of, governmental regulations, restrictions, or interference in the economic system. ▶ *Economic freedom is one of the basic tenets of the capitalistic system.*

economic goods products or services that are useful and thus have a market value. ▶ *Economic goods that are scarce command higher prices in the marketplace than those that are in abundance.*

economic growth an increase from period to period in a country's production of goods and services. ▶ *In the United States, economic growth is measured by increases in the Gross Domestic Product.*

economic indicator a statistical index that has been found to represent changes in business conditions in a fairly accurate manner. ▶ *A commonly used economic indicator is the number of claims for unemployment insurance.*

economic interest the ownership of all or part of a business enterprise or other profit-making venture, or ownership of an obligation of a business enterprise or venture. ▶ *A share of stock presents an economic interest in a corporation.*

economic life the period of time over which an asset can be expected to generate a profit or be used

effectively. ▶ *The economic life of computers has steadily decreased because of the rapidity of technological advances in hardware and software.*

economic lot size the number of units of a material or product that can be purchased or produced within the lowest unit cost range. ▶ *Economic lot size increases as production volume rises.*

economic man concept the notion that human beings are motivated solely by economic considerations and act solely in their own interest. (Refers both to men and women.) ▶ *The economic man concept is no longer accepted as valid in the United States.*

economic motivation the willingness to exert effort toward the accomplishment of some objective because of monetary gain. ▶ *A sales commission is a frequently used form of economic motivation.*

economic order quantity the number of units to be ordered in a single purchase so that costs are minimized or benefits are maximized. ▶ *The economic order quantity is determined by such factors as cost of placing and receiving an order and cost of carrying the inventory.*

Economic Recovery Tax Act of 1981 a Federal act that reduced taxes and encouraged savings and investments. ▶ *Many of the provisions of the Economic Recovery Tax Act of 1981 were later altered by the passage of the Tax Reform Act of 1986.*

economic sanction a restriction

on international trade and finance imposed by one or more countries upon another country or countries for political reasons. ▶ *An economic sanction is typically used to punish a country for performing acts or pursuing policies of which the sanctioning country disapproves.*

economic strike a labor strike by workers for the purpose of gaining economic concessions from an employer. ▶ *The United Car Makers are engaged in an economic strike against a major automotive manufacturer.*

economic warfare economic activities designed to harass or handicap another country. (*Economic warfare* includes placing embargoes on goods exported to a country, influencing other countries not to trade with that country, and blockading transportation to or from that country.) ▶ *Economic warfare devastated the small country.*

economics the study of the means used by society to produce, distribute, and consume goods and services. ▶ *Tom plans to major in economics when he goes to college.*

economy **1.** the careful or thrifty use of materials, capital, or labor. ▶ *Economy in the use of resources is very important to a small business.* **2.** the business activity in a given area, state, or nation. ▶ *The economy in Texas has been depressed for several years.*

economy of scale the reduction in average unit cost of manufacturing a product as the size of the plant or the level of production is in-

creased. ▶ *Enlarging a factory should result in a greater economy of scale.*

ECU See *European Currency Unit.*

Edge Act Corporation an organization chartered by the Federal Reserve Board to engage in international banking operations, approve applications for banks to establish subsidiaries under provisions of the *Edge Act of 1919,* and examine such subsidiaries. ▶ *The Edge Act Corporation is named for Senator Walter Edge who sponsored the original Federal legislation.*

Edge Act of 1919 a Federal statute that gives national banks the right to conduct foreign banking activities through Federal or state chartered subsidiaries. ▶ *The Edge Act of 1919 was strengthened by the International Banking Act of 1978.*

EDP See *electronic data processing.*

EDT See *Eastern Daylight Time.*

EEC See *European Economic Community.*

EEOC See *Equal Employment Opportunity Commission.*

effective date **1.** the date on which an agreement takes place. ▶ *The effective date of the sale, according to the contract, is February 15.* **2.** the date on which an insurance policy goes into effect. ▶ *The effective date of the insurance is contingent upon issuance of the policy by the company.* **3.** the date on which an offering of securities registered with the *Securities and Exchange Commission* may be sold. ▶ *The effective date on the new stock issue is November 15.*

effective demand the actual purchases of goods and services being made, as distinguished from purchases that could be made. ▶ *Increases in sales are due to changes in effective demand.*

effective rate the yield on a debt instrument as calculated from the purchase price rather than the face amount. ▶ *The effective rate is higher when the purchase price of an instrument is less than the face amount.*

efficiency 1. competency in performance. ▶ *Task specialization usually produces greater worker efficiency.* 2. the ratio of work produced to amount of energy supplied. ▶ *Automation increases manufacturing efficiency.*

efficiency rating See *performance appraisal.*

efficiency ratio See *utilization index.*

efficiency report 1. a periodic report that shows the ratio of work produced to amount of energy supplied. ▶ *This month's efficiency report suggests that we are not fully utilizing the human resource hours we have available.* 2. an individual's performance appraisal report. ▶ *Your efficiency report for this quarter shows that you have increased the number of units you assemble each day.*

effort 1. the will to work. ▶ *Sales commissions are used as incentives to increase the effort of a salesperson.* 2. the total mental and physical exertion required to perform a task. ▶ *A great deal of effort will be required to complete this job by Friday.*

EFTA See *European Free Trade Association.*

eighty-twenty rule See *Pareto's Law.*

either/or order See *alternative order.*

elastic demand the relative responsiveness of demand to changes in supply. ▶ *Some products, such as snow shovels, exhibit an elastic demand.*

electronic data processing AND **EDP** 1. data processing performed by electronic devices as opposed to mechanical or electromechanical devices. ▶ *An abacus processes data, but it is not an electronic data processing device.* 2. data processing performed by a computer and its peripheral equipment. ▶ *The laptop computer has made it possible to perform electronic data processing in remote locations.*

electronic funds transfer the movement of funds initiated by means other than check. ▶ *Withdrawals from automated teller machines are considered a form of electronic funds transfer.*

electronic mail AND **E-mail** a system that allows individuals to communicate with each other by computer terminals. ▶ *Electronic mail is usually sent over telephone lines.*

eleemosynary corporation a corporation organized for charitable purposes. ▶ *The United Way is an eleemosynary corporation.*

element a subdivision of a work task, normally consisting of one or more fundamental body motions, that has distinct beginning and ending points. ▶ *To improve efficiency, industrial engineers analyze each element that is required to perform work.*

eligible paper   the notes, bills, or other securities acceptable by Federal Reserve Banks for rediscount or as collateral for loans from member banks. ▶ *A commercial bank may secure a loan from a Federal Reserve Bank by using eligible paper as collateral.*

embargo   **1.** the regulation or prohibition of imports and exports. ▶ *An embargo is often used during wartime to limit the goods moving into and out of a particular country.* **2.** a governmental order restricting, prohibiting, or otherwise impairing the movement of freight. ▶ *Because of potential health hazards the state of Louisiana has placed an embargo on tomatoes grown in Arkansas.*

embezzlement   the appropriation for personal use of money or property belonging to another. (It is a criminal act.) ▶ *The accountant was charged with embezzlement after a shortage of $50,000 was discovered.*

embossing   a printing process in which the printed words are higher than the rest of the printing surface. ▶ *Embossing is sometimes done without ink.*

eminent domain   the right of certain legally constituted government bodies to take title to and possession of real property for the public good after justly compensating the owner. ▶ *The city exercised its right of eminent domain to ac-*

quire the land for the new municipal auditorium.

emolument   compensation for services rendered. ▶ *Salary or fees received is an emolument.*

empire building   an attempt to increase one's self-importance in an organization by increasing unnecessarily the number of one's subordinates either by developing additional organizational units or taking over existing units. ▶ *Empire building is a common practice in large organizations.*

employee   **1.** one who works for another and receives wages or salary for the time and effort expended. ▶ *My cousin is an employee of Lamborgini Cinema.* **2.** someone other than a supervisor or manager in an organization. ▶ *An employee typically reports to a first-line supervisor.*

employee leasing   a procedure whereby one company obtains its workers by contracting for the services of a second company's employees. ▶ *Employee leasing differs from temporary help services in that it focuses on placing employees on a permanent basis.*

Employee Retirement Income Security Act of 1974 AND **ERISA**   a Federal statute that regulates the operation of most private pension, retirement, and benefit plans. ▶ *The Employee Retirement Income Security Act of 1974 eased pension rules for employee eligibility.*

employee stock option   an arrangement whereby employees have the opportunity to purchase stock in the company for which they work. ▶ *An employee stock op-*

tion usually gives an employee the right to purchase stock at a discount from the market price of the stock.

employee stock ownership plan AND **ESOP** a program that allows employees to purchase stock in the company for which they work. ▶ *With an employee stock ownership plan, employees may actively participate in the management of the company.*

employer an individual or organization that hires workers and pays wages or salaries. ▶ *An employer has the authority, within legal guidelines, to decide how much to pay employees.*

Employment Act of 1946 an act of Congress that makes the Federal government officially responsible for promoting a stable economy and achieving full employment. ▶ *The Employment Act of 1946 was passed during the Truman administration.*

employment agency a public or private organization that provides various services to individuals seeking employment. ▶ *A person who is really serious about finding a job should contact an employment agency.*

employment history the chronological record of an individual's past work experience. ▶ *Employment history is a major consideration in evaluating applicants for a job.*

employment security See *job security.*

employment test an examination, usually written, given to a prospective employee to assist in determining whether or not to hire that individual. ▶ *An employment test may require that the employment candidate perform sample work.*

enclosure 1. land that has been fenced off. ▶ *Barbed wire is often used to create an enclosure on a ranch.* 2. an item that is included with a letter, for example, a résumé or a snapshot. ▶ *The enclosure provides a detailed record of my employment history.*

encumbrance 1. any lien or liability attached to real property. ▶ *An encumbrance on a piece of property may increase the difficulty in selling it.* 2. an obligation or commitment. ▶ *Signing a promissory note creates an encumbrance for the borrower.*

end-user the final consumer or user of a product or service. ▶ *Successful products are designed with the end-user in mind.*

endorse 1. the act of placing one's signature on a check, note, or other instrument as evidence of ownership or approval of the contents of the instrument. ▶ *To cash a payroll check at a bank, you must first endorse it.* 2. the approval of a particular candidate for political office. ▶ *The local newspaper plans to endorse the Democratic candidate for mayor.*

endorsement the act of endorsing. ▶ *An endorsement is an evidence of ownership or a form of approval.*

endowment (fund) money or other valuable property that has been donated to an institution, an individual, or some entity as a source of income. ▶ *Harvard University has a very large endowment fund.*

endowment policy a type of insurance contract (policy) that matures or reaches its face value at a stipulated time and is paid to the insured at that time. ▶ *Should the insured die before an endorsement policy matures, the named beneficiary is paid the face amount of the contract.*

engraving a process, performed by hand or machine, by which the surface of a metal plate is cut producing printing or an illustration on it. ▶ *Engraving by hand is a meticulous process requiring a skilled craftsperson.*

entrepreneur a person who initiates a business by securing the necessary capital and assuming the risks, with the expectation of it becoming a profitable enterprise. ▶ *Sam Walton, the late founder of Wal-Mart, was an outstanding entrepreneur.*

entry-level job a job requiring little or no experience. ▶ *An entry-level job is an individual's first step in pursuing a career with an organization.*

Environmental Protection Agency AND **EPA** an agency of the Federal government established in 1970 to protect the environment by controlling pollution and regulating disposal of waste. ▶ *Neighbors of the toxic waste dump contacted the Environmental Protection Agency to have the site closed and cleaned up.*

EOE See *equal opportunity employer.*

EPA See *Environmental Protection Agency.*

Equal Employment Opportunity Commission AND **EEOC** A government agency that handles discrimination complaints in employment situations. ▶ *Fred filed a complaint with the EEOC.*

equal opportunity employer AND **EOE** an employer who has made a commitment to practice nondiscrimination in every aspect of employment. ▶ *The phrase, equal opportunity employer, is used in employment ads to show commitment to nondiscrimination.*

equal pay for equal work the principle that pay rates should apply to jobs and not to individuals. ▶ *If all firms adhered to the principle of equal pay for equal work, pay discrimination would not be a problem.*

Equal Rights Amendment AND **ERA** a proposed constitutional amendment that would eliminate sex as a basis for any decisions made by any state of the United States. ▶ *The ERA has been the topic of very heated debates.*

equifinality the principle that it is possible to achieve similar results by pursuing different means. ▶ *Equifinality is a tactic that has been long practiced by politicians.*

equilibrium (condition) a state of balance in which the actions of different forces counteract each other. ▶ *When supply and demand are equal, a state of equilibrium exists.*

equipment the machinery, tools, apparatus, and appliances used in industry and business. ▶ *The new* *equipment will be expensive, but it will increase productivity.*

equipment bond AND **equipment trust certificate** a supplemental mortgage on machinery, railroad rolling stock, airplanes, etc., incurred by a company to finance the purchase of the equipment or to raise cash for another purpose. ▶ *The purchase of the company airplane was financed with an equipment bond.*

equipment investment analysis the process of determining, usually quantitatively, whether particular capital equipment expenditures should be made. ▶ *According to our equipment investment analysis, the purchase of a new computer system would be a wise use of corporate funds.*

equipment trust certificate See *equipment bond.*

equities shares of the value of a corporation; stocks, as opposed to bonds or other debt instruments. ▶ *Equities took a dive in the market today, but bonds held firm.*

equity the net value of a property as determined by subtracting the total claims or charges against the property. ▶ *On a balance sheet, the owner's equity is determined by subtracting total liabilities from total assets.*

equity financing the sale of stock by a corporation to raise capital. ▶ *Equity financing is often preferable to borrowing money from institutional lenders.*

equity funding a method of raising funds for a business by selling stock or ownership. ▶ *Equity funding is a common method of fi-*

nancing a new business.

equity market the stock market; a stock market. ▶ *The equity markets were closed last Friday.*

ERA See *Equal Rights Amendment.*

ergonomics AND **human engineering** the study of humans and machines with a view to determining how machines can be better designed and more effectively used by their human operators. ▶ *Ergonomics can make people more comfortable and more efficient.*

ERISA See *Employee Retirement Income Security Act of 1974.*

escalator clause a stipulation in a contract that provides for increases in certain numerical items of that contract. ▶ *An escalator clause is commonly used in contracts between labor unions and management to provide for salary adjustments based on increases in the cost of living.*

escape clause a provision allowing a party to a contract to withdraw from the contract or to modify promised performance. ▶ *Exercising an escape clause may render a contract null and void.*

escheat the legal process whereby money, land, or other assets are turned over to the state in the absence of legal heirs or claimants. ▶ *Money left in dormant bank accounts is periodically acquired by the state of Texas by escheat.*

escrow an agreement whereby one party places the agreement instrument in the hands of a third party until certain specified things have been done. ▶ *Funds are frequently* *held in escrow pending the final execution of a contract.*

ESOP See *employee stock ownership plan.*

esprit de corps a sense of unity, interests, and shared responsibilities among individuals associated together. ▶ *Organizations with high esprit de corps are typically organizations with outstanding performance.*

EST See *Eastern Standard Time.*

estate the property, real or personal, owned by a person, either living or deceased. ▶ *A person's estate is distributed according to the provisions of the deceased person's will, if any.*

estate accounting the financial record keeping concerned with the preparation and maintenance of accounts for property in the hands of executors, administrators, or trustees acting under the jurisdiction of a probate court. ▶ *The probate judge requested all of the estate accounting files for last year.*

estate tax a tax imposed by the Federal government and several of the states on the estates of deceased persons. ▶ *The amount of the estate tax in some states depends on the size of the estate.*

estimated tax **1.** the predicted tax liability for the coming year. ▶ *In computing estimated tax, one must consider any possible tax credit that might reduce the total tax liability.* **2.** income taxes paid on a quarterly basis by a taxpayer whose income is not subject to withholding taxes. ▶ *The amount of estimated tax paid during the*

year must closely approximate the ultimate tax liability to avoid possible penalty.

estoppel a legal doctrine that prevents a person from asserting a fact or claim inconsistent with the position the person has previously taken. ▶ *Estoppel is a type of legal restraint.*

etching a process using chemicals to make cuts in the surface of a metal plate thereby producing printing or an illustration on it. ▶ *Etching is a process very similar to engraving.*

ethics principles of proper action or standards of conduct, either written or unwritten, set forth to guide individuals in their behavior. ▶ *Business schools are now paying more attention to ethics than they have in the recent past.*

Eurobond a bond that pays interest and principal in *Eurodollars.* ▶ *A Eurobond may be purchased by a non-European investor.*

Eurodollars American dollars on deposit in European banks. ▶ *Eurodollars are most frequently created by the purchase of European goods by Americans.*

(European) Common Market See *European Economic Community.*

European Currency Unit AND **ECU** the denominator of the European Monetary System's *exchange rate* mechanism. ▶ *Each national currency of the European Monetary System is related to the European Currency Unit on a parity basis.*

European Economic Community AND **EEC; (European) Common Market; ECM** an economic alliance formed in 1957 by Belgium, France, Italy, The Netherlands, Luxemburg, and the former West Germany to increase trade and cooperation among its members. ▶ *Since 1957 additional countries have been added to the original countries of the European Economic Community.*

European Free Trade Association AND **EFTA**   a defunct organization established by the United Kingdom, Sweden, Norway, Denmark, Switzerland, Austria, and Portugal as an answer to the *Common Market.* ▶ *When the European Free Trade Association failed, some of its members sought membership in the Common Market.*

European Monetary System   the monetary system established by the *European Common Market* to limit fluctuations in *exchange rates* of the currencies of its members. ▶ *The European Monetary System helps provide currency stability among the Common Market countries.*

evaluation   the act of placing a value on any item. ▶ *Job evaluation is the process whereby an organization determines the worth or value of each of its jobs to the success of the organization.*

Evalucomp   a propriety approach to job evaluation and job pricing developed and offered by the Wyatt Company, a management consulting organization. ▶ *Evalucomp makes extensive use of labor market surveys in determining job worth and pay structures.*

even lot   See *round lot.*

ex-all   the sale of a security without dividends, rights, warrants, or any other privileges. ▶ *All shares of International Computer are currently selling ex-all.*

ex-dividend   without dividend. ▶ *Stocks are said to be ex-dividend when the price quoted excludes the payment of any declared dividend to the buyer and the dividend reverts to the seller.*

ex-dividend date   the date after which the purchaser of a security would not be entitled to the dividend declared on that security. ▶ *The ex-dividend date is normally four days prior to the record date.*

ex-rights   without rights. ▶ *Shares of stock sold ex-rights are sold without the right to subscribe to a current new issue of stock offered by the corporation.*

excess profits tax   additional Federal tax levied on the undistributed excess earnings of a business. ▶ *The excess profits tax prevents companies from avoiding the payment of taxable dividends.*

exchange   **1.** to give one product or service in return for another. ▶ *Department stores usually permit an exchange of merchandise if the purchaser has a receipt.* **2.** a place where traders meet to buy and sell commodities or securities. ▶ *Millions of shares of stock are traded each day on the New York Stock Exchange.*

exchange rate AND **rate of exchange**   the price of one currency in terms of another currency. ▶ *The exchange rate between the U.S. dollar and the Mexican peso fluctuates on a daily basis.*

excise tax a tax levied on a certain act, occupation, privilege, sale, or use of goods and services. ► *Gasoline, tobacco, and alcoholic beverages are examples of products subject to an excise tax.*

exclusive agent **1.** one who has the sole right to sell a product or service within a designated area. ► *Rogers Insurance Agency is the exclusive agent for Farmers Insurance Company in Titusville.* **2.** one who has the sole right to represent a second party in dealings with a third party. ► *A major league baseball player often negotiates salary with his team through an exclusive agent.*

exclusive dealing an arrangement whereby a manufacturer or a wholesaler designates a particular wholesaler or retailer as the sole distributor of a certain product or class of products within a specified area. ► *Exclusive dealing is not as prevalent today as it once was.*

executive a high ranking official in an organization who has major decision-making authority and responsibility. ► *An executive may have any one of many organizational titles; e.g., president, senior vice president, or managing partner.*

executive committee a group appointed by the board of directors of a corporation, from among their own members, to act for the board, to the extent legally possible, between meetings of the board. ► *An executive committee meets more frequently than does a board of directors.*

executive recruiter an individual who specializes in locating managerial and professional personnel for organizations for a fee. ► *An executive recruiter may be paid as much as one-third of the first year's salary and benefits of the position to be filled.*

executor a person named in a will to manage the estate of a decedent in accordance with terms set forth in the will. (Can be used for both males and females. See also *executrix*.) ► *A surviving spouse often functions as an executor for the deceased spouse.*

executrix a woman named in a will to manage the estate of a decedent in accordance with terms set forth in the will. (This is the Latin-based feminine form of *executor*.) ► *Helen is the executrix of Franklin's estate.*

exercise price See *strike price*.

exhibit **1.** a supporting document such as a chart, graph, accounting statement, illustration, etc., accompanying a report. ► *Exhibit XII shows the trend in profits for the last five years.* **2.** a display at a trade show, conference, etc. ► *Be sure to visit our exhibit of new products while you are at the conference.*

exit interview an interview with an employee who is leaving an organization. ► *The purpose of the exit interview is to collect information that may be useful to the firm in revising policies or procedures.*

expatriate employee a citizen of one country working in another country. ► *A U.S. citizen working in Thailand is an expatriate* *employee.*

expedite to hurry along a process; to hasten a delivery; to make a process go faster. ▶ *I have asked the warehouse to expedite the shipment.*

expediter 1. a person who searches out and corrects those conditions or situations that cause discrepancies between planned production and actual production. ▶ *An expediter must be familiar with the company's manufacturing processes and procedures.* 2. a person who rushes production orders that must be completed in less than normal lead time to assure their timely completion. ▶ *Give this rush order to an expediter.*

expendable fund an asset that may be applied to any specific or general purpose by administrative action. ▶ *Petty cash is an expendable fund.*

expenditure the actual outlay of funds to purchase goods or services. ▶ *Due to problems with cash flow, we are unable to make the expenditures for new office furniture now.*

expense 1. an expired cost. ▶ *Periodic depreciation expense represents a cost relative to a certain piece of equipment.* 2. an expenditure recognized as an operating cost of a current or past accounting period. ▶ *The postage expense for last month exceeded budget.* 3. any expenditure that benefits the present rather than the future. ▶ *It is important that we incur the expense during this tax year.* 4. the designation of a current or past expenditure as an

operating cost or a loss. ▶ *Bad debts are written off periodically as an expense.*

expense account 1. an account where particular expenses are recorded. ▶ *The costs of printing are shown in the office supplies expense account.* 2. AND **expense report** a statement of an individual's financial outlays for business purposes for a given period of time. ▶ *Here is my expense account for May.* 3. an allowance given to executives, salespersons, or other company personnel for business related costs that may have to be incurred by the individual. ▶ *The size of the expense account provided may be a deciding factor in accepting a job offer.*

expense budget a statement of projected expenses covering an expected level or volume of activity. ▶ *The manufacturing expense budget for 10,000 units is $5,000.*

expense center an organizational component where expenses are accumulated and recorded. ▶ *An expense center incurs costs, but often produces no income.*

expense report See under *expense account.*

experience merit rating the adjustment of an insurance premium rate to reflect past risk experience of the insured. ▶ *Experience merit rating is widely used to adjust premium rates for worker's compensation insurance.*

expired utility that portion of the anticipated usefulness of goods that is no longer available because of deterioration or some other factor. ▶ *Expired utility reduces the* *value of goods.*

export **1.** to ship goods to another country for sale or exchange. ► *We will export this product to Germany next month.* **2.** goods actually shipped to another country for sale or exchange. ► *Export sales are much higher this month.*

export credit a commercial letter of credit issued for the purpose of financing the shipment of goods to another country. ► *We will have to arrange for export credit if we are to ship these goods to Brazil.*

Export-Import Bank an independent federally chartered bank that makes loans to companies as well as foreign governments to finance the flow of imports and exports. ► *The Export-Import Bank finances projects that cannot be funded through private capital.*

exposure **1.** the number of times a particular advertisement is seen by the public or a targeted audience. ► *Bankers Monthly provides good exposure for the services we sell.* **2.** paid or free advertising of goods or services. ► *Media interviews are an excellent way to gain product exposure.* **3.** the amount of financial risk to which one is subject. ► *Our exposure on this project is in excess of $2 million.*

express mail a service offered by the U.S. Postal Service that guarantees next day delivery for shipments between major U.S. cities. ► *If we send this proposal by express mail, they will receive it in New York tomorrow.*

express trust a trust created by specific provision in a written instrument. ► *Under the terms of Jonathan's will, an express trust was created to provide for his son's education.*

express warranty a manufacturer's written guarantee that a product meets certain standards and will perform according to those standards. ► *An express warranty gives the purchaser the right to return an item for full refund if it fails to perform as specified.*

expropriation the compulsory purchase of land or other property by a governmental body in return for fair compensation. ► *The city will acquire the necessary land for the park through expropriation.*

extended coverage an addition to a standard fire insurance policy that adds the additional coverages of damage due to riots, civil commotion, smoke, aircraft and vehicles, windstorms, hail, and explosions. ► *Extended coverage can be added to a policy for a modest monthly expenditure.*

extended term insurance option an option in an insurance policy that uses the cash surrender value of an ordinary life policy to purchase a paid-in-full term life policy. ► *Using the extended term insurance option in her policy, Jane bought a larger term policy that covers her for the next five years.*

exterior display a billboard, roadside sign, or car card displayed on trains, buses, and automobiles used to advertise products or services. ► *Exterior displays are widely used to advertise consumer products such as beer, cigarettes, and liquor.*

external audit an examination

made by an outside auditor of the books and accounting methods of an enterprise to determine if they conform to generally accepted accounting practices and if they reflect accurately the condition of the enterprise. ▶ *Large corporations undergo an external audit annually.*

external auditor an *auditor* who is not employed by the company being audited. (Compare with *internal auditor.*) ▶ *The external auditors accepted our financial statement.*

external premises the factors, conditions, situations, and considerations outside a firm that affect the formulation and implementation of its plans. ▶ *Government regulations, competition, and labor supply are examples of important external premises.*

extra (dividend) a dividend paid by a corporation—either in cash or securities, to its shareholders—over and above its regular dividend. ▶ *General Appliances Corporation has not paid an extra dividend in the last ten years.*

extractive industry a firm that takes materials directly from the earth or its waters and thereby depletes the stock of natural resources. ▶ *Coal mining is an extractive industry.*

extractive process the manner or means by which raw materials are taken from the earth or its waters. ▶ *The drilling of wells is the extractive process by which oil, water, and gas are obtained.*

extrapolation a statistical extension, projection, or estimate of a value or number lying outside the range of known values or numbers. ▶ *Trend lines may be extended into the future through the process of extrapolation.*

F

401(k) plan   an employer-sponsored retirement savings program permitted by Section 401(k) of the *Internal Revenue Code* that allows employees to invest pre-tax dollars that may or may not be matched by their employer. ▶ *The 401(k) plan allows an employee to save for retirement and reduce current Federal taxes.*

FAA   See   *Federal   Aviation Agency.*

fabricating   the act of manufacturing a finished product from parts furnished by another manufacturer. ▶ *Once we receive the parts from Coleman Manufacturing we can begin fabricating the right wing assembly.*

face value   the actual value shown on a note, bond, bill, or certificate. ▶ *The face value of the bond is $25.*

facsimile   an exact copy that preserves all the markings of the original. (See also the following entry.) ▶ *We must have a facsimile of your check before we can credit your account.*

facsimile (transmission) AND **FAX; telefacsimile   1.** the use of electronic means to send printed materials. ▶ *Please FAX a copy of this invoice to Roger Howard immediately.* **2.** a copy of printed material sent by electronic means. ▶ *We just received a FAX of the Jones deed from James Vernon.*

fact-finding board   a committee appointed to conduct a complete investigation into the facts, issues, and problems of a situation, especially a labor dispute. ▶ *A fact-finding board in a labor dispute may be appointed by the Federal government or by a state government.*

fact tag   a tag attached to a product that conveys factual information about that product to the consumer. ▶ *A fact tag often outlines* *the benefits of using the product.*

factor a person or firm that buys accounts receivable at a discount. ▶ *If we sell our accounts receivable to a factor we can raise the cash we need to pay off the loan that is due.*

factor comparison method a job evaluation technique in which jobs are valued in terms of a few common compensable factors. ▶ *The factor comparison method is seldom used today.*

factoring the purchasing of accounts receivable at a discount from a seller. ▶ *The company called in a specialist in factoring in an attempt to raise cash quickly.*

factory a building or group of buildings in which a firm manufactures its products or goods. ▶ *The new factory has a much more efficient layout than the old factory.*

factory costs the costs directly associated with the operation of a manufacturing facility. ▶ *Factory costs encompass direct materials, direct labor, and building costs.*

factory overhead that portion of a firm's manufacturing costs that cannot be identified or associated with specific products or groups of products and must therefore be allocated or prorated among all products on some arbitrary basis. ▶ *Under orders from management, factory overhead was cut back considerably.*

(factory) second a finished product containing some minor defect or flaw, which is sold at a lower price than a like product that is free of defects or flaws. (See also *irregular.*) ▶ *Factory seconds are frequently sold through outlet stores.* ▶ *In many instances, seconds are as good as the unflawed product.*

fad an accepted or popular style of relatively short duration. ▶ *A fad usually appears suddenly, gains rapid acceptance, and disappears or falls from favor quickly.*

fad item an item that is the subject of a fad. ▶ *The hula hoop was a very famous fad item.*

fair day's work the amount of work that can be produced by a qualified worker with average skill who follows a prescribed method, works under specified conditions, and expends average effort. ▶ *What is considered a fair day's work varies from job to job.*

fair list a list of employers considered to be fair, or favorable, to organized labor. ▶ *Many unions compile and publish a fair list.*

fair market value the price of an item, good, or service as determined by a willing buyer and a willing seller. ▶ *The fair market value of the property was determined through negotiations between the two parties involved in the transaction.*

fair trade agreement an arrangement between a manufacturer and a retailer wherein the retailer agrees to sell the manufacturer's product at or above a stipulated retail price. ▶ *The fair trade agreement, under provisions of the Consumer Goods Pricing Act of 1975, cannot be used in interstate commerce.*

false advertising a form of advertising by an identifiable sponsor in which the description of the goods, services, or ideas is misleading or deceitful. ▶ *An advertisement that leads consumers to believe that a store has an abundance of a particular item, when in fact it doesn't, is false advertising.*

Fannie Mae See *Federal National Mortgage Association.*

FAS See *free alongside ship.*

FASB See *Financial Accounting Standards Board.*

fascism a system of government generally characterized by dictatorship, a single political party, and the denial of civil liberties. ▶ *Fascism exists in many developing countries.*

fashion an accepted or popular style. ▶ *According to the latest fashion, Western boots may be worn with business suits.*

fashion cycle the waxing and waning of public acceptance of a style of clothing or accessories. (The duration of a *fashion cycle* is measured from the point of public adoption of a fashion to the disappearance of that fashion.) ▶ *Fortunately, the fashion cycle of leisure suits was short.*

fashion good a consumer good that is subject to relatively rapid changes in style. ▶ *A woman's dress is an example of a fashion good.*

fast food industry a segment of the restaurant industry comprised of establishments that offer limited and standardized menus, and serve food that requires a limited amount of preparation. ▶ *McDonald's and Burger King are two of the giants in the fast food industry.*

fast track the means by which designated individuals move rapidly up the corporate hierarchy. ▶ *Stanley was selected for the fast track because of his outgoing personality and his academic achievements at the Harvard Law School.*

fatigue a person's physical or mental weariness, real or imaginary, that adversely affects the person's ability to perform work. ▶ *Fatigue can be alleviated through regularly scheduled rest periods.*

fatigue allowance AND **rest allowance** an increment of time that is added to the normal time for performing a task in order to allow for decreases or losses in production attributable to fatigue. (The increment is often expressed as a percentage of the normal time allowed to perform the task. It is usually determined through a work sampling study. See also *idle time.*) ▶ *The normal production time for this part is sixty minutes and the fatigue allowance is 10 percent.*

FAX See *facsimile (transmission).*

FDIC See *Federal Deposit Insurance Corporation.*

featherbedding a situation resulting from union rules or practices designed to provide easy jobs or to increase unnecessarily the number of workers required for performing a task. ▶ *Featherbedding results in excessive labor costs.*

Federal Aviation Agency AND **FAA** an agency of the Federal government that regulates airline operations and the safety with which those operations are carried out. ▶ *The Federal Aviation Agency requires commercial airline pilots to retire at age sixty.*

federal deficit the condition that exists when the Federal government spends more in a fiscal year than it receives in revenue. ▶ *The federal deficit, according to many economists, is responsible for high interest rates and inflation.*

Federal Deposit Insurance Corporation AND **FDIC** a corporation established by the U.S. government to insure a depositor's account up to $100,000 against loss due to the insolvency of the bank carrying the account. ▶ *All banks belonging to the Federal Reserve System must also belong to the Federal Deposit Insurance Corporation.*

Federal Home Loan Mortgage Corporation AND **Freddie Mac** a publicly chartered corporation established to develop a secondary market for conventional residential mortgages. It purchases mortgages from financial institutions and resells them as securities backed by the pooled mortgages. ▶ *The stock of the Federal Home Loan Mortgage Corporation is owned by savings institutions in the United States.*

Federal Housing Administration AND **FHA** a Federal government agency formed to carry out the provisions of the National Housing Act. (The FHA insures loans to homeowners for the purchase of residences, construction of new homes, and renovation or remodeling of residences and other types of buildings.) ▶ *The Federal Housing Administration was founded in 1934.*

Federal Insurance Contributions Act AND **FICA** the 1935 Federal legislation that requires money to be withheld from income to go toward Social Security. ▶ *Under the provisions of the Federal Insurance Contributions Act, periodic deductions are made from every employee's paycheck.*

Federal Mediation and Conciliation Service AND **FMCS** an independent Federal agency that has the authority to offer its services in cases of labor-management disputes. (The agency was established by the Taft-Hartley Act of 1947.) ▶ *A union or a company may request assistance from the Federal Mediation and Conciliation Service.*

Federal National Mortgage Association AND **FNMA; Fannie Mae** an independent Federal agency whose principal activity is purchasing mortgages from banks and other lenders, thereby creating a revolving fund of money available for mortgage lending. ▶ *Because of Fannie Mae, a lot of money is available to prospective home owners.*

Federal Open Market Committee AND **FOMC** the committee in the *Federal Reserve System* that sets short-term monetary policy for the *Federal Reserve System.* ▶ *The actions of the Federal Open Market Committee are closely watched by economists.*

Federal Power Commission an agency of the United State government that is responsible for the regulation of the interstate energy industry. ▶ *In 1977 the Federal Power Commission became the Department of Energy.*

Federal Reserve Bank one of 12 banks created by and operating under the Federal Reserve System as a source of credit and a depository of reserves for state and national member banks. ▶ *There is a Federal Reserve Bank in each of twelve different U.S. cities.*

Federal Reserve Board the governing body of the Federal Reserve System. (The seven members of the Board are appointed by the President of the United States and serve fourteen-year terms.) ▶ *The Federal Reserve Board sets current margin requirements, bank reserve requirements, determines the discount rate, and executes open market operations.*

Federal Reserve System the central banking system of the United States given the power to (1) regulate the money supply in the United States, (2) hold the legal reserves of member banks, (3) furnish currency with complete elasticity for the economic demands of the nation, (4) affect transfers of funds between banks, (5) promote and facilitate the clearance and collection of checks, (6) supervise and examine member banks, (7) collect and interpret economic information, and (8) act as fiscal agent, custodian of government funds, and depository for the U.S. Treasury and all other Federal government agencies. (It was established by the Federal Reserve Act of 1913.) ▶ *The Federal Reserve System is the closest thing to a Federal bank in the United States.*

Federal Savings and Loan Insurance Corporation AND **FSLIC** an agency of the Federal government established in 1934 that insures depositors in savings and loan associations against loss of deposited funds. ▶ *The Federal Savings and Loan Insurance Corporation protects most deposit accounts up to a stipulated maximum amount.*

Federal Trade Commission AND **FTC** a regulatory agency established in 1915 to investigate and prevent unfair business practices that might lead to restraint of trade in interstate commerce. ▶ *The Federal Trade Commission will have to approve the proposed merger of the two computer giants.*

fee simple the full and unconditional ownership of land. ▶ *One who holds property in fee simple has complete control over the property and can do anything with it.*

feeder line a small transportation company that serves small communities or outlying districts and connects them with main transportation facilities. ▶ *Market analysis shows that there is a need for a feeder line to service the Belto-Killeen area.*

FHA See *Federal Housing Administration.*

fiat money coins or currency whose face value is fixed by government decree at a level that bears no relation to intrinsic value. ▶ *Fiat money is money because a government declares it to be so.*

FICA See *Federal Insurance Contributions Act.*

fidelity bond insurance coverage protecting an employer against loss due to dishonest acts of employees. ▶ *The premium on our fidelity bond is going to increase next year because of the claims we had on the two embezzlements.*

fiduciary a person or corporation who holds property in trust for the benefit of another person; a trustee. ▶ *The bank acted as fiduciary for Ellen's deceased mother's funds.*

fiduciary money money that is not fully backed by silver or gold, but which is convertible into silver and gold. ▶ *Fiduciary money is backed by trust in the monetary system.*

field the section of a computer record that is designated for the storage of specified information. ▶ *A fixed field has a defined length, whereas a variable field can be assigned different lengths.*

field warehousing a means of using inventories to secure business loans. (Under this approach, a warehouser leases part of the borrower's warehouse and assigns a custodian to oversee the goods in the warehouse. The warehouser is in exclusive possession of the goods, releasing them to the borrower only upon the lender's order.) ▶ *Field warehousing uses goods as a collateral for a loan.*

FIFO See *first in-first out.*

fifth season the slow period, in retailing, between July and September. ▶ *The five seasons in retailing are fall, winter, spring, summer, and the fifth season.*

fill or kill (order) AND **FOK** a stock market order that is to be filled in its entirety immediately upon presentation to the trader or not at all. ▶ *Buy 300 shares of Blue Ribbon Buffet, fill or kill.*

final assembly the assembling of all components into a finished product. ▶ *After final assembly the product is ready to be shipped to the dealer for sale to the consumer.*

finance 1. to supply with funds through floating loans, acquiring trade credit, selling stocks or bonds, or transferring or appropriating funds from internal sources. ▶ *We will have to issue bonds to finance the acquisition of the coal mine.* 2. the theory and practice of dealing in money and investments. ▶ *Joe Bob Harris has an undergraduate degree in accounting and a master's degree in finance.*

finance bill a bill of exchange drawn by a bank in one country on a bank in another country against securities held by the latter bank. ▶ *Please draw a finance bill for $1,000,000 on the Frankford Banc immediately.*

financial accounting the accounting for revenues, expenses, assets, and liabilities that is commonly carried out in an organization. ▶ *Financial accounting provides periodic reports on the operations of a business.*

Financial Accounting Standards Board AND **FASB** an independent board that is responsible for establishing, maintaining, and interpreting generally accepted accounting principles. ▶ *The Financial Accounting Standards Board has is-*

sued new rule for accounting for retirees' future medical expenses.

financial costs the expenses incurred when borrowing capital. ▶ *Interest, service charges, and loan origination fees are examples of financial costs.*

financial institution a business firm that furnishes financial assistance to companies that are in need of such help. (A *financial institution* usually specializes in the provision of long-term capital [more than one year] or short-term capital [less than one-year]. Examples of long-term financial institutions are investment banking companies, brokerage firms, savings banks, investment companies, trust companies, insurance companies, and savings and loan institutions. Examples of short-term institutions are commercial banks, commercial paper houses, and factoring companies.) ▶ *A financial institution plays a critical role in supporting American business.*

financial market the overall market for the exchange of capital and credit in the economy. ▶ *The New York Stock Exchange is an example of a financial market.*

financial policy a general guideline established by the management of an enterprise specifying how funds are to be acquired and used. ▶ *It is the company's financial policy not to engage in ventures that seem highly speculative.*

financial ratio the relationship of one amount to another derived from comparing balance sheet items, or comparing balance sheet items with items on the profit and loss statement. (See also *operating ratio*.) ▶ *Net sales to inventory is a commonly used financial ratio.*

financial risk the investment risk associated with default in performance of an obligation as opposed to other types of risk, such as *credit risk.* ▶ *When given a choice, the investment opportunity with the lowest financial risk is the one this company will choose.*

financial statements a group of financial reports issued by a business entity, usually on an annual basis, that shows its financial position at a point in time (*balance sheet*) and its income and expenses during the year (*income statement*). (Sometimes *financial statements* also contain the balance sheet and the income statement from the previous year.) ▶ *To provide current information, interim financial statements may be issued between annual reports.*

finder's fee a fee paid to an individual or company for bringing two or more parties together in a business deal. ▶ *A typical finder's fee amounts to 10 percent of the total amount of the consummated deal.*

finished goods finished products manufactured by a concern and held in inventory ready for sale. ▶ *If we don't slow down the manufacturing process, we may have difficulty finding a place to store the finished goods.*

finished goods inventory stocks of manufactured products ready for sale as distinct from stocks of semifinished products or stocks of raw materials. ▶ *The finished goods inventory is increasing* *faster than the other inventories at the Carthage Golf Ball Plant.*

fink 1. a worker who engages in strikebreaking. ▶ *Only a fink would cross a union picket line.* 2. a union member who reports to an employer on the activities of other union members. ▶ *Smith is a fink; he told management everything Jones said at last week's union meeting.*

fire sale a sale of goods at reduced prices due to fire, water, or other damage or to any emergency. ▶ *A struggling company may have a fire sale, even when goods are not damaged, in order to raise cash quickly.*

firm a business enterprise. (The same as *company* in most uses.) ▶ *A firm may be a sole proprietorship, a partnership, or a corporation.*

firm offer a written offer to buy or sell that is irrevocable for a stipulated period of time. ▶ *Richard made a firm offer to purchase two sailboats for $45,000.*

first class mail a class of service offered by the U.S. Postal Service that receives quick handling and delivery, free forwarding, and is not subject to opening for postal inspection. ▶ *Have Vernon send this letter to Pittsburgh by first class mail so that it will arrive there by Monday.*

first in-first out AND **FIFO** a method of inventory identification and valuation that calculates the value of inventory on hand by using the costs of items most recently purchased. (Also used generically for any situation where the first

thing in is also the first thing out.) ▶ *In times of rapid inflation, first in-first out, when applied to inventory valuation, inflates profits.*

first lien See *first mortgage.*

first-line supervisor a member of the first rank of management. ▶ *A first-line supervisor is a very important link in the chain of command.*

first mortgage AND **first lien** a mortgage that has priority as a lien over all other mortgages against a specific property. ▶ *In the event of foreclosure, the first mortgage will be satisfied before any other mortgages.*

first preferred stock a preferred stock having the first claim to dividends. ▶ *First preferred stock is entitled to receive dividends ahead of a second or later issue of preferred or common stock.*

first shift AND **day shift** an eight-hour work period that begins at approximately eight o'clock in the morning. ▶ *If I can't work the first shift, I will look for another job!*

fiscal pertaining to financial matters. ▶ *The company president seemed to have no sense of fiscal responsibility and was fired.*

fiscal agent a person or entity who has the responsibility and authority to manage the money and financial affairs of another person or institution. ▶ *A bank or a trust company may function as a fiscal agent for a corporation.*

fiscal year 1. an accounting period of 12 consecutive months, 52 consecutive weeks, or 13 consecutive four-week periods. ▶ *A company's fiscal year usually en-*

compasses 365 days. **2.** a 12-month accounting period ending with the last day of any month other than December. ▶ *Many municipalities end their fiscal year on September 30.*

fishy-back service a method of transportation whereby highway-going trailers are transported fully loaded over water, usually on barges. (Based on *piggyback service.*) ▶ *With fishy-back service, a barge is met at the dock and the trailer is then pulled by truck overland to its destination.*

five and ten cent store See *variety store.*

fixed asset AND **fixed capital** tangible property, which will not be consumed or converted into cash in the normal course of events, used in carrying on the operation of an organization. ▶ *A fixed asset, such as a computer, has a useful life in excess of one year.*

fixed budget a statement of the assumed cost of an activity that does not vary. ▶ *A fixed budget assumes a defined level of sales or production.*

fixed capital See *fixed asset.*

fixed charge an expense that is constant throughout time or volume of production and tends to remain constant through at least the accounting period. (From an accounting point of view. See also *fixed cost.*) ▶ *Rent is an example of a fixed charge.*

fixed cost an operating expense that does not vary with business volume or level of production. (See also *fixed charge.*) ▶ *An insurance premium is a fixed cost.*

fixed deduction a cost, charge, expense, or any other item that is deleted in a constant or permanent manner. ▶ *The cost of health insurance is a fixed deduction for an employee because the same amount is withheld from each paycheck.*

fixed income income that has been set in amount by law, contract, or circumstances. ▶ *A fixed income is a real problem during times of high inflation.*

fixed obligation a charge, expense, or other cost that remains constant throughout its life. ▶ *Bond interest is a fixed obligation for the corporation that issued the bonds.*

fixed rate mortgage a mortgage on which the rate of interest does not vary for the term of the mortgage. ▶ *When buying a home, many purchasers prefer the certainty of a fixed rate mortgage.*

fixed stock an inventory of goods that has already been produced and is ready for sale, and whose volume cannot be increased without large expenditures of time or money, and can only be decreased by sale. ▶ *A Christmas tree lot has a fixed stock of trees to sell.*

fixed sum game a competitive situation in which the stakes are not subject to variation. ▶ *In a fixed sum game, the algebraic sums of winnings and losses equal zero.*

fixture **1.** any personal property that has been attached to real property but may not be removed. ▶ *A pencil sharpener attached by screws to a wall of a house is a fixture.* **2.** a device mounted on a machine table to hold a piece of work firmly in place during a machine operation. ▶ *A good fixture is essential to precision machine work.*

flat without the addition of interest. ▶ *A bond is said to be sold flat when the sale price does not include accrued interest.*

flatcar a railroad car without sides or a roof. ▶ *A flatcar is used for transporting such large items as power generators and aircraft wings.*

flat rate **1.** a uniform rate of pay or remuneration where no allowance is made for volume, frequency, or other factors. ▶ *This job pays a flat rate of $6.00 per hour, regardless of how much an employee produces.* **2.** a per unit price that remains constant regardless of volume, frequency, or other considerations. ▶ *The flat rate is $10 whether you buy one or a thousand.*

flat tax a tax that is applied at the same rate to all levels of income. ▶ *A flat tax would be advantageous to those earning large amounts of money.*

flex time an arrangement wherein employees determine, with certain limitations, their own daily work schedules. ▶ *With flex time one employee may choose to report to work at 7:00 A.M. and another employee may choose to report at 8:00 A.M.*

flexibility the ability to change plans without undue cost or without excessive friction, and to keep moving toward a goal. ▶ *Flexibility is very important in achieving long-term plans.*

flexible budget a statement of expected costs and expenses at varying levels of output, instead of one set of budget figures, a range of figures is provided so that different levels of cost can be associated with different rates of output or volumes of sales. ▶ *A flexible budget helps managers understand how costs vary with production volumes.*

float the amount of money outstanding in checks that have been written but not collected. ▶ *Float arises from the delay between the time a check is written and the time it is actually collected against deposited funds.*

floater policy an insurance policy that covers goods against loss wherever they may go or wherever they may be located. ▶ *A floater policy covers goods that move on a scheduled as well as an unscheduled basis.*

floating capital AND **circulating capital** funds available for general expenses. ▶ *Without more floating capital, we risk not being able to meet the payroll in the months with the most workdays.*

floating exchange rate an exchange rate between the currencies of two countries that is allowed to move up or down in response to supply and demand conditions in the foreign exchange market. ▶ *The Mexican peso and the U.S. dollar have a floating exchange rate.*

floating supply that quantity of securities or commodities that can be obtained in the open market at any given point in time. ▶ *Since the* *floating supply of Bramble Corp. stock is so small, we should probably give serious consideration to making a tender offer.*

floor See *(trading) floor.*

floor broker a member of a stock exchange who actually executes orders to buy and sell stocks and bonds on the floor of a stock exchange. ▶ *A floor broker is right in the middle of the action on a stock exchange.*

floor planning a type of financing that supplies the funds necessary for a dealer in a certain product to acquire samples of the product to display for sale. (When the product is sold, the loan is liquidated.) ▶ *Automobile and boat dealers use floor planning extensively.*

floor trader a member of a stock exchange who acts for himself or herself in the hope of turning a quick profit. ▶ *A floor trader pays no commissions on sales or purchases and is therefore able to profit from small movements in the price of a stock.*

floppy disk a computer storage device made of plastic coated with a magnetic surface. ▶ *The floppy disk is widely used with microcomputers because of its convenience and low cost.*

flow control the process of controlling the movement of production items from one workstation to another in a continuous or assembly line-type of manufacturing operation. ▶ *Our flow control plans call for moving 59 automobiles per hour through the paint section to the trim section.*

flow diagram a graphic represen-

tation of the flow of work, either people or materials, and the location of workstations, desks, equipment, etc., superimposed on a physical floor plan of that part of the factory or office under study. ▶ *A flow diagram can reveal inefficiencies in the movement of items.*

flow process chart a graphic representation of a procedure or work process depicting the sequence of operations, transportations, inspections, delays, and storages. (A *flow process chart* may show the activities of a worker in accomplishing the steps in a procedure or it may show the events that occur to the material being processed.) ▶ *The flow process chart is a basic tool of work simplification.*

flowchart a graphic representation of the movement of people, materials, or information. ▶ *Stan, would you ask Jane to prepare a flowchart that will give us some idea of the work going on in the stamping department?*

flower bond a type of U.S. government bond that is acceptable at par in payment of estate taxes if the deceased was the legal holder of the bond at the time of death. ▶ *A flower bond is acceptable at par regardless of what the purchaser may have paid for it.*

flyer a handbill distributed as a supplement to other advertising or used as an informal announcement of special interest. ▶ *The print shop just called and left word that the flyer on the ten-speed bikes is ready.*

FMCS See *Federal Mediation and Conciliation Service.*

FNMA See *Federal National Mortgage Association.*

~~**FOB** See *free on board.*~~

focus group a group of consumers, selected according to particular demographic characteristics, who are asked to respond to questions about a product or service. ► *A manufacturer who is contemplating the introduction of a new product will sometimes use a focus group to determine how the product may be received by its target market.*

FOK See *fill or kill.*

follow-up 1. of any letter, note, visit, or phone call carrying through on previous communication. ► *I will make a follow-up call to all the people I contacted at the convention.* ► *We must make certain that we send Bob Miller a follow-up letter regarding our meeting last Thursday.* 2. any act of carrying through on previous communication. ► *Each of those telephone inquiries we received about the Bermuda vacation package should receive a follow-up by Tuesday.*

FOMC See *Federal Open Market Committee.*

foot candle a unit of illumination equal to the light produced by a standard candle at a distance of one foot. ► *A foot candle measurement is used to determine whether or not lighting in an office is adequate.*

forced choice rating a method of employee performance evaluation in which the rater checks one statement out of a series of several that is most descriptive, and one that is least descriptive of each particular trait or behavior being evaluated. ► *A forced choice rating system is considered to be objective because there is no way that individual subjective notions can be expressed.*

forced distribution rating a method of performance appraisal that requires the rater to distribute performance ratings in a pattern conforming to a normal frequency distribution. (Thus, 10 percent of the employee rated must be allocated to the top performance category, 20 percent to the next highest category, 40 percent to the middle category, 20 percent to the next lowest category, and 10 percent to the bottom category.) ► *Forced distribution rating attempts to eliminate the problem of too many high performance evaluations.*

forced sale a sale, usually for a lower price, that the seller must execute immediately without the opportunity to locate a buyer who might pay the full market price for the item being sold. ► *A forced sale is sometimes used to avoid foreclosure on a piece of property.*

forecasting the estimation of future events or values from known past events or values. ► *Statistical forecasting uses a mathematical approach to determining future values.*

foreclosure the process by which a mortgagor acquires title to property in order to satisfy the outstanding debt on that property. ► *Ted was forced to sell his house at a price well below market in order to avoid foreclosure.*

foreign bill of exchange a draft

drawn by a resident of one state or country on a resident of another state or country. ▶ *A foreign bill of exchange cannot be processed through the bank clearinghouse. It must be sent for collection.*

foreign corporation a corporation established under the laws of a given state or country that is doing business in another state or country. ▶ *General Motors is a foreign corporation in Mexico.*

foreign exchange 1. the money of one nation in another nation. ▶ *When an American tourist buys dollars in Mexico, the tourist is purchasing foreign exchange.* 2. the system by which balances resulting from transactions between nations are settled. ▶ *The foreign exchange system uses drafts and bills of exchange extensively.*

foreign exchange rate the price relationship between the currencies of two countries; that is, the rate at which the currency of one country can be exchanged for the currency of another country. ▶ *The foreign exchange rate between the U.S. dollar and the Mexican peso is 1 to 3,114 today.*

foreign investment the investment by individuals or the government of one country in the property, industries, or securities of another country. ▶ *Foreign investment is a means of supplying needed capital for domestic industries.*

foreign trade 1. the trade between persons or corporations who are residents of different countries. ▶ *Foreign trade is the natural result of global marketing.* 2. the

trade between the governments of different countries. ▶ *The United States and Canada are engaging in extensive foreign trade with South Korea.*

foreman 1. a member of the first level of management of an organization. ▶ *A worker who becomes a foreman is no longer an employee.* 2. one who supervises operative level employees in manufacturing activities. ▶ *Grant Hayes is the new foreman in the grinding department.*

forgery false writing intended to defraud or to deceive. ▶ *The bank refused to pay the check because it appeared to be a forgery.*

forging 1. the act of falsifying in writing with the intent to defraud or deceive. ▶ *Noah was arrested for forging the signatures on fourteen company checks.* 2. a metalworking process whereby metals are heated and then shaped into various items while they are soft. ▶ *Forging is a dirty, noisy, and dangerous process.*

form letter a standardized, already prepared letter that can be mailed to a number of people, with only the date and the recipient's name and address having to be typed in. ▶ *With a word processor and a laser printer, a form letter can appear to be a personalized letter.*

form utility the ability of a good to satisfy a human want or need as the result of the alteration of the good's shape, structure, or composition. ▶ *When raw materials or parts are fashioned into finished products, form utility is created.*

formal authority the power or right to act or to command others that an organization confers upon an individual because of the position that the individual holds. ▶ *Although he had the formal authority to do so, Dick decided not to terminate George.*

formal conference a conference in which an official record of the discussions and proceedings is kept. ▶ *One advantage of a formal conference is that a record of the proceedings is available to refer to later, if there is any question about an item of discussion.*

formal organization **1.** a type of organization characterized by a rigid designation of officers and managers, the establishment of departments along clearly delineated lines of authority and responsibility, and specific delegation and assignment of duties. ▶ *The U.S. Army is a highly formal organization.* **2.** the structure and relationships within an organization as described by the organization chart or organization manual. ▶ *The formal organization is a paradigm of how an enterprise should function.*

former buyer a previous customer who has not made any additional purchases within a specified period of time. ▶ *A former buyer is frequently overlooked as a source of sales opportunities.*

formula investing a method of purchasing securities in accordance with some fixed pattern. ▶ *Investing a fixed dollar amount each payday is an example of formula investing.*

Fortune 500 the annual listing by *Fortune* magazine of the 500 largest manufacturing corporations in the United States. ▶ *To make the Fortune 500 is a significant achievement for a corporation.*

forward integration the expansion of a firm to serve the consumer. ▶ *A manufacturer who acquires distribution and marketing facilities in order to sell directly to consumers is engaging in forward integration.*

forward pricing method a method of pricing used by open-end investment companies whereby the share price is determined by the net asset value of the outstanding shares. ▶ *The forward pricing method provides a daily update on the value of each share.*

forwarding agent AND **freight forwarder** **1.** an individual or a firm that picks up rail shipments and delivers them to locations not served by railroad. ▶ *We will have to use a forwarding agent to get that order moved from the Omaha station to Rustwater.* **2.** an individual or firm that assembles small freight shipments and consolidates them into carload lots for shipment. ▶ *The forwarding agent in Rustwater works with a number of small manufacturers in that area and assists them in shipping their products.*

four-color process a printing process that produces color illustrations. ▶ *In the four-color process, the colors used are red, yellow, blue, and black.*

fractional share less than one share of stock. ▶ *In the event of a* *stock dividend, a shareholder may be entitled to cash for the fractional share resulting from the dividend declaration.*

franchise **1.** a privilege granted by a governmental authority. ▸ *The state of Texas grants a franchise to a corporation for a stipulated annual fee.* **2.** the privilege conferred on a dealer by a manufacturer or service provider to sell products or services within a certain territory. ▸ *My Uncle Herman has a McDonald's franchise in Oklahoma City.* **3.** a certificate of incorporation. ▸ *We plan to have our franchise framed and displayed in the lobby.*

franchise agreement the contract between a manufacturer or a service provider (the franchisor) giving a dealer (the franchisee) the right to sell the products or service of the franchisor within a certain territory. ▸ *Before signing a franchise agreement, it is advisable to have it reviewed by an attorney.*

franchise tax a tax imposed on a corporation for the right to do business under its corporate name. ▸ *Many corporations incorporate in Delaware because of its favorable franchise tax.*

fraud the intentional deception by one party that results in injury or loss to a second party. ▸ *Nondisclosure of a material fact is a type of fraud.*

Freddie Mac See *Federal Home Loan Mortgage Corporation.*

free alongside ship AND **FAS** a designation indicating that the seller of goods will not charge for shipping the goods to the dock beside a ship. (The buyer pays the shipping and other charges associated with transporting the goods and assumes all risk of damage in transit not caused by the seller, or not covered by the liability insurance of the carrier.) ▸ *The designation free alongside ship means that the purchaser must pay all shipping charges once the goods reach the dock.*

free and open market a market in which buyers and sellers are free to trade without restrictions that regulate prices charged or quantities traded. ▸ *A free and open market is a highly competitive market.*

free currency currency or other payment media of a country that can be used without restriction by residents of that country or by those in other countries in international transactions. ▸ *The U.S. dollar is a free currency.*

free enterprise See *capitalism.*

free good a good supplied by nature in such abundance that all demand for it is satisfied without work. ▸ *The air we breathe is a free good.*

free list the list of all commodities on which no import duties are levied. ▸ *Bob was irate when he discovered that tequila and rum were not on the free list.*

free market a market in which there is little or no interference or control by government or any other entity. ▸ *In a free market the price of a good is determined solely by supply and demand factors.*

free on board AND **FOB** a designation indicating that the seller of goods will not charge for the shipping of goods up to the point of loading them onto the transporting vehicle. (The seller of goods places the goods on board a railroad car, truck, or other vehicle and the buyer pays the shipping and other charges associated with transporting the goods and assumes all risk of damage in transit not caused by the seller and not covered by the liability insurance of the carrier.) ▶ *The designation free on board means essentially that the purchaser pays all transportation charges.*

free trade international trade that is unhampered by tariffs, restrictions, and protectionism. ▶ *Free trade is very important in an increasingly global economy.*

freestanding store a retail establishment, not attached to any other buildings and not part of a mall, that stands alone and attracts customers to it by reason of its location, name recognition, or products. ▶ *Most major retailers will not build a freestanding store today because they prefer to be located in a shopping center or a mall.*

freight absorption the payment of freight charges by the seller of a good. ▶ *Freight absorption shifts the freight cost from the purchaser to the seller.*

freight bill a bill prepared by or for the carrier of goods for transportation charges associated with the shipment of goods. ▶ *We have just received a freight bill from Acme Transportation for that shipment of chairs to Atlanta.*

freight forwarder See *forwarding agent.*

freight-in an account used to break down shipping charges of items received. ▶ *Freight-in applies to inventory as well as capital equipment.*

frequency distribution the classification of statistical data so as to show the number of items having the same value, for example, 15 a's, 10 b's, and 5 c's. ▶ *A frequency distribution helps a person to more clearly understand a set of data.*

frequency polygon a graphic representation of a frequency distribution formed by joining the midpoints of the tops of the bars of a histogram. ▶ *This income data would probably make more sense if it was presented as a frequency polygon.*

frictional unemployment **1.** the unemployment caused by a temporary imbalance between the supply of specialized labor and the demand for specialized labor. ▶ *Any decrease in the demand for airplanes may cause frictional unemployment among aircraft workers.* **2.** temporary unemployment caused by workers changing jobs. ▶ *Our economic system will always be subject to frictional unemployment.*

fringe benefits employer-paid programs and services benefiting employees. (Included in *fringe benefits* are pensions, insurance, profit sharing, sick leave, vacations, holidays, and other supplemental benefits.) ▶ *Fringe benefits represent a major cost to employers.*

front money cash paid in advance in order to start a project. ▶ *Sam has agreed to undertake the land* *development project, but he will need some front money to rent the necessary equipment.*

frozen account a bank account that has been suspended in payment until a court order or legal process makes the account available for withdrawal. ▶ *The bank told Dick the check would not clear because it was drawn on a frozen account.*

frozen asset **1.** any asset that cannot be used by the owner or disposed of because of legal action. ▶ *A building that has been condemned as a public hazard is a frozen asset because the building cannot be occupied or sold until the restriction of its use is lifted.* **2.** an asset that is believed to have value but which cannot be converted readily into cash. ▶ *Given the poor state of the market right now, my art collection is essentially a frozen asset.*

FSLIC See *Federal Savings and Loan Insurance Corporation.*

FTC See *Federal Trade Commission.*

full-bodied money money that has an intrinsic value equal to its face value. ▶ *If a twenty-dollar gold piece actually contains twenty dollars worth of gold, it is full-bodied money.*

full costing See *absorption costing.*

full crew rule a union practice requiring the employment of a certain number of union workers for a given job. ▶ *The full crew rule may substantially increase personnel costs.*

full employment the condition existing when all of those who are able and willing to work can find remunerative work. ▶ *Full employment is a condition that is almost impossible to achieve.*

full faith and credit a phrase signifying that the full taxing and borrowing power plus revenue, other than taxes of a government entity, is pledged in repayment of a bond issue as well as in payment of interest. ▶ *U.S. government securities are backed by the full faith and credit of the Federal government.*

full-line forcing the practice of requiring a retailer or a wholesaler to handle the full line of items supplied by a manufacturer or wholesaler as a condition of obtaining any items. ▶ *With full-line forcing, a retailer carries the complete range of a manufacturer's products or the merchant carries none of them.*

full service broker a broker who offers a broad range of services, in addition to buying and selling securities, to clients. ▶ *A full service broker offers investment advice to clients.*

functional authority the power or right to command, given to a department or an individual, which is exercised over processes, practices, policies, or personnel in departments other than its own. ▶ *The human resource department in an organization has functional authority over matters of all departments.*

functional middleman a wholesale agent, such as a selling agent, manufacturer's agent, commission broker, broker, or auctioneer, who negotiates purchases or sales but who does not take title to the goods being handled. ► *The functional middleman is remunerated in the form of a commission.*

functional obsolescence the decline in usefulness of an item due to technical innovations or changing tastes. ► *Typewriters are experiencing functional obsolescence now that word processors have become commonplace.*

functional organization an enterprise that is structured according to the basic functions it performs, such as manufacturing, marketing, finance, and accounting. ► *The functional organization structure is probably the most widely used form of organization.*

funded debt a debt that is evidenced by long-term notes or outstanding bonds. ► *Funded debt is long-term debt.*

funds cash or other forms of money. ► *The company decided not to take that project on because of a lack of funds.*

funds flow statement a statement of all monies received and expended during an accounting period. ► *The funds flow statement will help identify how our money is being spent.*

fungible goods goods that are standardized or interchangeable. ► *In a shipment of fungible goods, each unit is like every other unit.*

futures contract an agreement to buy or sell a commodity at some future point in time. ► *A futures contract may be sold to a third party.*

futures market a commodity exchange where futures contracts are bought and sold. ► *Trading was very active on the futures market today, especially in oats and barley.*

futures trading the buying and selling of future values of commodities. ► *Franklin is interested in a career in futures trading.*

G

GAAP See *Generally Accepted Accounting Practices.*

gain sharing an incentive wage payment plan whereby the bonus earned for work beyond the standard is shared, according to some predetermined proportion, between management and workers. ▶ *Any premium or bonus incentive plan may be referred to as a type of gain sharing.*

galloping inflation a rate of inflation that is considered to be excessive, especially when the rate is increasing from period to period. ▶ *The United States experienced a period of galloping inflation in the 1970s.*

game theory the area of decision theory applicable to situations in which two or more persons are in competition with each other. ▶ *According to game theory, both players are rational and will make their decisions in a logical manner.*

Gantt chart a bar chart frequently used in production scheduling to compare actual performance with planned performance. (The *Gantt chart* was developed by Henry L. Gantt, one of the early management pioneers.) ▶ *The Gantt charts for last quarter revealed where our weaknesses are.*

GAO See *General Accounting Office.*

garage sale a sale held by one or more individual or organizations to dispose of personal property no longer needed or wanted. (Often held in or near the driveway or garage of one of the sponsors of the sale.) ▶ *There was a big garage sale in my neighborhood last Saturday, and I bought two rocking chairs for $3.00 each.*

garnishment the withholding of all or part of an employee's wage or salary by an employer for the payment of a debt owed to an outside agency or person. ▶ *The amount of compensation that may be withheld through garnishment is limited by Federal law.*

gatekeeper   an employee, usually a secretary or administrative assistant, who shields an executive or manager from unscheduled and unwanted visitors. ▶ *If you want to see the executive vice president, you must first get past Jane, her gatekeeper.*

GATT   See *General Agreements on Tariffs and Trade.*

Gaussian distribution   See *normal curve.*

GDP   See *Gross Domestic Product.*

general accounting   **1.** the practice of all phases of accounting as opposed to solely specialized functions. ▶ *Some CPAs have a general accounting practice while others specialize in tax or audit.* **2.** a department within an organization where all phases of accounting are practiced. ▶ *General accounting prepares income statements, balance sheets, and other reports for the company.*

General Accounting Office AND **GAO**   an office of the Federal government that provides legal, accounting, and auditing services for the United States Congress. ▶ *The General Accounting Office was established by the Budget and Accounting Act of 1921.*

General Agreements on Tariffs and Trade AND **GATT**   a somewhat informal, multilateral agreement, signed in Geneva in 1947, designed to encourage and increase international trade by reducing or eliminating duties and quotas. ▶

The nations that are members of the General Agreements on Tariffs and Trade group account for approximately 80 percent of the world's trade.

general merchandise store   a retail outlet carrying two or more unrelated lines of goods. ▶ *A department store, a dry goods store, and a variety store are examples of a general merchandise store.*

general mortgage bond   a bond that is secured by a mortgage on company property. ▶ *A series of general mortgage bonds is secured by our various factories and office buildings just outside the city.*

general obligation bond   a municipal bond backed by the taxing authority and credit of a municipality. ▶ *A city must repay a general obligation bond from its general revenue fund*

(general) partnership   the association of two or more persons to pursue a business for profit as joint participants. ▶ *In a partnership, participants are personally liable for all business debts.*

general store   a small, nondepartmentalized retail outlet, usually found in areas of scattered or isolated population, which carries two or more unrelated lines of goods. ▶ *A general store typically carries a wide variety of merchandise to satisfy a range of consumer needs.*

generalist   an individual who performs tasks in many areas of one field, or in several fields, rather than in one area of one field or one field itself. ▶ *A human resource generalist must understand compensation, selection, recruitment,* *performance appraisal, labor negotiations, and all other aspects of personnel management.*

Generally Accepted Accounting Practices AND **GAAP** the practices, procedures, rules, conventions, and guidelines that define accepted practice in the field of accounting. ▶ *This report has been filed with the Department of Revenue according to Generally Accepted Accounting Practices.*

generic pertaining to, relating to, or describing an entire class. ▶ *Accounting, production, and marketing are three generic functions of a business enterprise.*

generic brand the non-trademark name of a product sold at a lower price than the trademarked product. ▶ *This generic brand of vitamins is much less expensive than that well-known brand and is probably just as good.*

generic market an entire product or service category. ▶ *The generic market for tobacco products is declining in the United States.*

Giffin good a product or service that experiences an increase in demand as the price rises. ▶ *A Giffin good does not adhere to the normal demand and price interaction.*

GIGO "garbage in, garbage out" (Slang acronym. It refers to the principle that reliable input is a necessity for reliable output.) ▶ *Of course, the final figure is all wrong! You fed in the wrong figures. A classic case of GIGO!*

gilt-edged stock a security of the highest grade of investment safety. ▶ *A gilt-edged stock is as good as gold.*

Ginnie Mae See *Government National Mortgage Association.*

giveaways premiums or samples that are given to prospective buyers. ▶ *Giveaways are a marketing device for getting potential customers to use a product with the anticipation that after trying it they will buy it.*

glamor stock a heavily traded stock whose price tends to increase consistently. ▶ *You are most likely to find a glamor stock in a high-tech industry today.*

glass ceiling the invisible barrier of tradition, resistance to change, covert discrimination, and other factors that prevent minorities and women from rising above a certain level in a corporation or a government organization. ▶ *The glass ceiling is becoming more and more of a problem as the composition of the work force changes.*

glut the overproduction of a good or service resulting in a situation where the available supply will not be bought at the current price. ▶ *A glut in a particular product works to the advantage of consumers since they are able to get it at a lower price.*

GNMA See *Government National Mortgage Association.*

GNP See *Gross National Product.*

go-go stock a speculative stock whose price increases very rapidly in a short period of time. ▶ *A go-go stock often falls in price as quickly as it increased in price.*

go-no-go gauge a device used in manufacturing to determine if a part is within allowable limits without attempting to measure its specific dimensions. (A means of choosing whether something is okay, a "go," or unacceptable, a "no go.") ▶ *Where it can be used, a go-no-go gauge is an inexpensive and simple quality assurance tool.*

go private to go from publicly held ownership to privately held ownership through the repurchase of shares, purchase of shares by an outside investor, or removal of the stock from an exchange. ▶ *Some companies may find it advantageous to go private because their actions are then not subject to as much scrutiny by outsiders.*

go public for a privately held company to sell its stock to the general public. ▶ *A company may decide to go public to raise additional capital.*

goal an end point toward which effort is directed. ▶ *Our short-term goal is to increase sales by 10 percent.*

goal setting the process of establishing end points toward which organizational effort will be directed. ▶ *In some companies, employees are expected to participate in goal setting.*

gobbledygook language that is roundabout, uses too many words, is confusing, or is filled with jargon. ▶ *Legal documents frequently border on gobbledygook.*

going concern an enterprise that is functioning or succeeding; a company that is prospering. ▶ *Even a financially weak company on the edge of bankruptcy is considered a going concern.*

going rate **1.** the general selling price of a product, class of prod-ucts, or a service. ▶ *The going rate for tubular steel is higher in California than it is in West Virginia.* **2.** the wage rate or salary most commonly paid to workers in a given occupation and a given labor market. ▶ *The going rate for plumbers in Tampa has increased rapidly over the past two years.*

gold certificate a currency formerly issued to the public by the U.S. Treasury and redeemable in gold. ▶ *A gold certificate today can only be held by a Federal Reserve Bank.*

gold circle rate an actual pay rate that exceeds the maximum rate of pay established for a particular class of jobs. ▶ *When the new salary classification plan was implemented, there was only one instance of a gold circle rate.*

gold fixing the daily determination of the price of gold by experts in London, Paris, and Zurich. ▶ *The daily gold fixing has an influence on the price at which stocks trade on the New York Stock Exchange.*

goldbricking the shirking of one's assigned responsibilities. ▶ *A person who is goldbricking is wasting time.*

golden handcuffs a situation in which, because of incentives or other generous financial considerations with a current employer, an employee cannot realistically afford to change jobs. ▶ *Golden handcuffs effectively tie a person to a company.*

golden handshake early retirement inducements given to an employee to encourage that employee to retire. ▶ *A golden handshake* *may provide a significant financial benefit for retiring early.*

golden parachute   a lucrative package of severance pay, stock options, bonuses, and other items given to an executive to provide financial security in the event that the company is taken over by another company and the executive is terminated. ▶ *A golden parachute arrangement allows high ranking managers to maintain a given standard of living if they are suddenly fired by an acquiring company.*

good delivery   a designation that all necessary conditions to affect the transfer of a security have been satisfied. ▶ *Required endorsements are one of the essentials for good delivery.*

good faith   **1.** honesty. ▶ *Business transactions depend upon good faith.* **2.** the observance of reasonable standards of conduct in carrying out the activities of a trade. ▶ *Since we do not understand the technicalities involved, we must rely on the good faith of the plumber when he says we need a new hot water heater.*

good-till-cancelled order AND **open order**   a stock exchange order that may be placed for a specified period or may remain in effect until it is executed or cancelled. ▶ *A good-till-cancelled order remains effective until it is executed by the broker or cancelled by the investor.*

goodness of fit   the degree to which statistical data plotted as a frequency distribution correspond to a normal frequency distribution

curve. ▶ *In statistics, the chi-square test is used to determine goodness of fit.*

goods-in-process   See *work-in-process.*

goodwill   a value in excess of the total tangible assets of a company. ▶ *Goodwill is normally the result of superior earning power over an extended period of time.*

goon   a person hired by management to intimidate workers. (Slang.) ▶ *Historically, goons were sometimes maintained by management to thwart employees' efforts at unionization; however, such a practice is illegal today.*

Gordon technique   a variation of brainstorming, developed by William J. J. Gordon. ▶ *With the Gordon technique, only the leader of a problem-solving group knows the specific problem and it is not revealed to the group.*

government bonds   unsecured bonds issued by Federal, state, local, or foreign governments. ▶ *Government bonds are secured by the general credit of the governmental agency issuing them.*

Government National Mortgage Association AND **GNMA; Ginnie Mae**   a Federal corporation that assists the financing of federally guaranteed home mortgages. ▶ *The Government National Mortgage Association guarantees payments on bonds secured by mortgages assembled by lenders.*

government obligations   securities issued by various Federal agencies. ▶ *Government obligations include Treasury bills, bonds, notes, and savings bonds.*

governmental accounting the principles, practices, customs, procedures, and theories associated with accounting for municipal, state, and national government units. ▶ *Governmental accounting differs considerably from accounting in the private sector.*

grace period See *days of grace.*

grade labeling the practice of indicating the quality of a product on the label of the package. ▶ *Grade labeling can be observed on such products as meat, poultry, and fish.*

grading the process of testing and separating commodities or products into various classes according to predetermined physical standards. ▶ *Grading of fresh fruits and vegetables is usually done according to size and ripeness.*

grain pit the trading floor of an agricultural commodity exchange. ▶ *Traders in the grain pit buy and sell wheat, soybean, and oat futures.*

grand strategy the means by which a business enterprise expects to attain its overall goals. ▶ *A grand strategy must be set before supporting functional area strategies can be developed.*

grandfather clause a provision in a new law, regulation, or rule that exempts present practitioners from qualifying under the new restrictions. ▶ *The grandfather clause allows those currently plying a trade to continue to ply that trade even though they might not qualify under the new provisions.*

grapevine the informal, unofficial communication system in an organization. ▶ *While much of the information passed through the grapevine is of doubtful validity, some of it can be very accurate.*

graph a drawing that reflects the relationship between the different points of its message. ▶ *The accompanying graph will show the relationship between absenteeism and recent decreases in output.*

gratuity a payment over and above a formal cost or charge usually given as a token of appreciation for service received. ▶ *It is customary in the United States to give a gratuity to a waiter or a bellhop.*

graveyard shift See *third shift.*

gray market the sale and purchase of scarce goods through unethical, but technically legal, practices such as the payment of premium prices or the combined sale of wanted and unwanted goods. ▶ *An excessively high demand for new products may shift their distribution from normal channels to the gray market.*

Great Depression that period from late 1929 to the early 1940s when the United States experienced a tremendous slowdown in economic activity and a dramatic increase in unemployment. ▶ *The Great Depression ended with the onset of World War II.*

Greater Fool Theory the notion, especially in investing, that no matter how high a price one person paid for something, there is always someone else who will pay even more. ▶ *While the Greater Fool Theory may have an element of truth to it, it should not be used as* *a rationale for buying an item that is overpriced.*

Green Card a permit issued by the U.S. Immigration and Naturalization Service that allows aliens to work in the United States. ▶ *If an employer hires an alien worker who does not have a Green Card, the employer may be subject to a fine.*

green hand an inexperienced worker. ▶ *Because of the high demand for workers, the only person we have been able to hire lately is a green hand.*

Green River ordinance an ordinance enacted by municipalities to regulate or forbid house-to-house selling, canvassing, or soliciting. (The first such law controlling door-to-door salespersons was enacted in Green River, Wyoming.) ▶ *After many complaints from residents, the city council passed a Green River ordinance.*

greenbacks the paper currency of the United States. (Slang or colloquial.) ▶ *Greenbacks derived their name from the color of the ink used on American currency.*

Greenwich Mean Time the standard time of the meridian that passes through Greenwich, England, and serves as the basis for global time. ▶ *The eclipse begins at 4:15 P.M. Greenwich Mean Time.*

Gresham's Law an economic principle that postulates that bad money drives out good money. ▶ *According to Gresham's Law, when metals of differing values have equal power as legal tender, the cheaper metal will become the circulating medium and the other*

metal will be hoarded or exported.

grievance dissatisfaction or the feeling of injustice in connection with a worker's employment situation that the worker brings to the attention of management, especially in writing. ▶ *A grievance may arise out of a perceived violation of the terms and conditions of the labor agreement between the union and management.*

grievance procedure the formal means by which an employee lodges a complaint against his or her employer and has that complaint resolved. ▶ *Every union contract contains a formalized, specific grievance procedure.*

grinding the use of friction in metalworking to achieve a fine surface edge or finish. ▶ *The grinding area of a machine shop is noisy and dirty.*

gripe box a receptacle where employees may deposit their written complaints about company policies, procedures, operations, or other matters, and also leave suggestions for improvement. ▶ *A gripe box permits employees to vent their feelings about things they do not like in the company.*

Gross Domestic Product AND **GDP** a measure of economic welfare determined by the total value of a country's output of goods and services produced within the borders of the country within a given period of time, usually one year. ▶ *Unlike the Gross National Product, the Gross Domestic Product does not reflect earnings from income earned abroad.*

gross income **1.** the entire revenues of a business before any expenditures are made. ▶ *Gross income is up 10 percent this month.* **2.** the total income of a taxpayer, received from all sources before deductions or exemptions. ▶ *My gross income this year was $25,000.* **3.** the total earnings of a worker before deductions for taxes, health insurance, pension plan, etc. ▶ *Take-home pay is sometimes significantly less than gross income due to the number of deductions taken out.*

gross margin See *gross profit.*

Gross National Product AND **GNP** the money value of the total output of goods and services within a country during a given period of time (normally one year), before deduction of depreciation charges and other allowances. ▶ *The Gross National Product is one of the measures of a country's economic health.*

gross profit AND **gross margin** net sales less cost of goods sold, but before consideration of selling and general expenses. ▶ *Gross profit has increased significantly over the last several accounting periods.*

gross sales the total amount of sales before the deduction of returned sales. ▶ *Gross sales show an increase this quarter, but so do returned sales.*

group banking the ownership or control of one or more banks by a separate entity. ▶ *The concept of group banking is exemplified by the bank holding company.*

group bonus a wage premium paid to a group of workers operat-

ing as a unit for performance in excess of standard output. ▶ *A group bonus may lead to increased teamwork.*

group buying a practice whereby a number of smaller buyers combine their orders so that relatively large purchases can be made from suppliers at attractive prices. ▶ *Group buying allows small retailers to compete more effectively with large retailers.*

group by process to organize a working area so that similar tasks are performed close to one another. (See also *process layout.*) ▶ *This factory would be far more efficient if you would group by process rather than by product.*

group by product to group together all the equipment necessary to produce a specific product. (See also *product layout.*) ▶ *It is far less costly to group by product when only two or three products are manufactured.*

group dynamics **1.** the study or analysis of relationships and interactions among the individuals comprising a group. ▶ *Group dynamics has led to the development of new approaches to managing work groups.* **2.** the social interaction between the members of a group. ▶ *Group dynamics often leads to improved organizational communication.*

group incentive an inducement, normally monetary, offered to a group of workers for collectively surpassing a given standard of output or efficiency. ▶ *The Human Resource Department is considering a group incentive for the Produc-*

tion Department as a means of increasing output.

group insurance insurance taken out or arranged by an employer that covers all employees under one master policy, at a lower premium than the aggregate of premiums that would be charged for individual policies. ▶ *Life and health are examples of the types of coverage typically provided through group insurance.*

growth stock the stock of a corporation with excellent prospects for future growth at a rate greater than that anticipated for the average corporation. ▶ *My broker recommends ABC Corporation as a growth stock.*

guarantee a stipulation by a manufacturer that a product will perform as promised. ▶ *Under the terms of the guarantee, if the product fails to perform as specified it may be exchanged for a new unit.*

guaranteed annual wage an arrangement whereby a firm guarantees a full year's work or pay each year to all employees meeting certain minimum length of service requirements. ▶ *A person must be employed by Zentel Company four years in order to receive a guaranteed annual wage.*

guaranteed bond a bond whose interest or principal, or both, has been secured by a firm other than the one that issued the bond. ▶ *A guaranteed bond is usually a safe investment.*

guaranteed employment the assurance given by a business enterprise to its employees of a certain number of hours or weeks of work over a given period of time. ▶ *Guaranteed employment provides a measure of job security.*

guaranteed rate the rate of pay that is assured workers under an incentive pay system. ▶ *The guaranteed rate is always expressed in terms of dollars per hour.*

guaranteed stock a type of stock, usually a preferred issue, whose dividends are guaranteed by a firm other than the one that issued the stock. ▶ *Guaranteed stock is secure relative to the payment of dividends.*

guardian a person appointed by a court to administer the affairs or the property of a person who is not legally competent. ▶ *Judge Thomas appointed a guardian for my Uncle Otis last week.*

guild an association formed for the mutual aid and protection of persons engaged in a common pursuit or having common interests. ▶ *The Screen Actors Guild is a union of performing artists.*

gut-feel AND **gut-feeling** intuition. ▶ *My gut-feel is that it will rain today.*

H

hacker one who is proficient in the use of computers, especially in doing advanced or unusual things. ▶ *A hacker often discovers different uses for computers.*

halo effect a positive or negative opinion of a person based on excessive influence from performance in one area. ▶ *For a while, after his great success, the halo effect prevented us from seeing what a poor manager Tom really was.*

hand-to-mouth buying the practice of purchasing in very small quantities strictly as the need arises, thereby maintaining inventories at the lowest possible level. ▶ *When a firm is experiencing financial difficulties, it may resort to hand-to-mouth buying to conserve cash.*

hand tool an implement such as a hammer, saw, drill, or wrench, requiring the human hand for its operation. ▶ *A good hand tool will last for many years if it is used properly.*

hard copy documents, reports, letters, etc., printed or reproduced on paper. ▶ *We need to put a hard copy of this report in the Johnson Company file folder.*

hard-core deposits commercial banking time deposits that have remained on deposit for an extended period of time. ▶ *It is becoming increasingly difficult to attract hard-core deposits.*

hard-core unemployed that group of people who, as a whole, have been unable to find employment over an extended period of time. ▶ *The hard-core unemployed are usually disadvantaged people who lack the necessary skills, education, or training to be employed.*

hard currency money with a stable value, domestically and in international exchange. (Compare with *soft currency.*) ▶ *The U.S. dollar is considered to be a hard currency.*

hard drive   the internal storage portion of a computer system. ▶ *The operating system of a personal computer is stored on the computer's hard drive.*

hard goods   See *durable goods.*

hard money   coins as contrasted to currency. ▶ *Hard money is more difficult to carry than currency.*

hard sell   aggressive or high pressure sales tactics. (Compare with *soft sell.*) ▶ *Automobile salespeople sometimes resort to a hard sell.*

hardhat   **1.** a protective helmet worn by workers on a job site for safety reasons. ▶ *The purpose of a hardhat is to protect a worker from falling objects.* **2.** a construction or similar type of worker. ▶ *A hardhat does not wear a suit and tie to work.*

hardware   the physical equipment or devices comprising a computer and peripheral machines as opposed to computer programs. (Compare with *software.*) ▶ *Hardware is expensive, but prices have been decreasing lately.*

hardware store   a retail outlet that sells tools, nails, nuts, bolts, and similar goods as well as durable consumer goods. ▶ *We should go to the hardware store to see if they have a power mower.*

harvesting strategy   a business strategy whereby reinvestment in the business is held to a minimum and profits are maximized in the short run. ▶ *A harvesting strategy may be used to produce cash to be used in other businesses held by the same company.*

has-gets ratio   the distribution of shares of stock in a merger according to the ratio of ownership between the acquired company and the newly formed company. ▶ *The has-gets ratio may exert a significant influence on the attractiveness of a merger.*

Hawaiian-Aleutian Standard Time   the standard time in the Hawaiian and Aleutian Islands. ▶ *Hawaiian-Aleutian Standard Time is ten hours behind Greenwich Mean Time and two hours behind Pacific Standard Time.*

hazard pay   compensation over and above the base rate for a job, paid for performing work that is dangerous. ▶ *Tom draws hazard pay for his work as an oil field firefighter.*

head-on position   the panel of an outdoor advertising medium that faces oncoming traffic. ▶ *Advertisers prefer the head-on position in a billboard because it reaches the greatest number of people.*

head-shrinker   a psychiatrist or psychologist. ▶ *Bernie is seeing a head-shrinker to get help in quitting smoking.*

headhunter   an individual or firm that specializes in filling managerial, professional, or technical vacancies for client firms by luring people away from their present positions in other organizations. ▶ *We will probably have to use a headhunter to fill this specialized position.*

health maintenance organization AND **HMO**   a group health insurance arrangement whereby members agree to use the physicians, clinics, and hospitals that have been enlisted in the organization. (The members enjoy a lower cost in this type of managed health care. An *HMO* also attempts to keep future costs lower by practicing preventive medicine.) ▶ *A health maintenance organization emphasizes preventive medicine by encouraging its members to tend to their health problems before they become serious.*

hedging the act of purchasing or selling entered into for the purpose of balancing respectively, a sale or a purchase already made or contracted for, in order to offset price fluctuations. ▶ *Hedging is a common practice in industries that must purchase commodities for delivery at some time in the future.*

hemline theory the notion that stock prices move in the same direction as the hemlines on women's skirts and dresses. ▶ *While the hemline theory is untested scientifically, it is nonetheless an interesting and amusing idea.*

heuristic a strategy or rule of thumb, or any other device, which reduces the time required to arrive at a solution in a problem situation. ▶ *In essence, a heuristic is a problem-solving shortcut.*

hidden agenda the unidentified objectives, expectations, needs, and payoffs of an individual or a group when participating in some activity. ▶ *A hidden agenda may be revealed by the way a person acts or the language the person uses.*

hierarchy of needs a theory of human motivation postulated by Abraham H. Maslow in which human needs are arranged in a hierarchical pattern from lowest level needs to highest level needs. ▶ *The hierarchy of needs outlines five types of needs: physiological, safety, social, ego, and self-actualization.*

high end the more expensive portion of a product line or service category. ▶ *You can expect to pay much more for dinner in a high end restaurant than in a fast food restaurant.*

high finance any large scale, complex, or speculative financial dealings. ▶ *In the world of high finance, ten-million-dollar transactions are common.*

high flyer a speculative stock issue characterized by widely fluctuating prices. ▶ *A conservative investor is not normally attracted to a high flyer.*

high grade bond a bond of extremely high quality. ▶ *The interest rate on a high grade bond may be lower than the rate on other bonds, but it is more secure.*

high punch a punch in the first or second row above the zero row on a *Hollerith* card. ▶ *A high punch is typically used to designate something special about the information contained in the punch card.*

hiring hall a place frequented by certain types of union laborers seeking employment. ▶ *An employer needing dock workers would telephone or visit the dock workers' hiring hall to obtain the necessary workers.*

hiring rate **1.** the wage rate paid to a worker who is just starting out in a given job. ▶ *The hiring rate for this job is $5.25 per hour.* **2.** the number of additional workers hired during a given period of time, expressed as a percentage of total employment. ▶ *When business activity is expanding, the hiring rate rises.*

histogram a graphical representation of a frequency distribution that is constructed by drawing bars or rectangles at the class intervals in a manner that makes the areas of the bars proportional to the class frequency. ▶ *A histogram is used to plot discrete data, not continuous data.*

historical records approach a work measurement approach that correlates past volume and work hours to produce unit time standards or personnel requirements. ▶ *The historical records approach is the least expensive work measurement technique available.*

hit list a series of individuals, companies, or groups to be approached for a given purpose. ▶ *Salespeople often have a hit list of prospects that they call on first.*

hit the bricks to go to work to accomplish a particular purpose. ▶ *It looks like we will have to hit the bricks to make all of the sales calls we need to make this week.*

HMO See *health maintenance organization.*

hoarding a deliberate stockpiling of goods or currency beyond what is required for normal needs. ▶ *Fearing shortages of food, the people began hoarding flour.*

holder a person who is in possession of a negotiable instrument which has been issued, drawn, or endorsed to that person or to the bearer in blank. ▶ *Jane is the holder of a certified check for $10,000.*

holder in due course a person who has taken a negotiable instrument under the following conditions: (1) the person became a holder of the instrument before it was overdue, and without notice that the instrument had previously been dishonored; (2) the person took the instrument in good faith; and (3) at the time the person took the instrument, the person had no knowledge of any infirmity in the instrument or defect in the title of the person negotiating it. ▶ *A holder in due course acquires a negotiable instrument in good faith.*

holding company a business that owns or controls other businesses. ▶ *A holding company may own firms in many different industries.*

Hollerith card AND **punch card** **1.** a card punched with a pattern of holes, representing data, in accordance with an encoding system developed by Herman Hollerith. ▶ *The Hollerith card was first used at the U.S. Bureau of the Census where Herman Hollerith was employed.* **2.** a card before being encoded with the Hollerith code. ▶ *Everyone used Hollerith cards for note paper until they realized the cost.* **3.** any punched card. ▶ *Not every punched card is a true Hollerith card, but it might be referred to as one.*

homeostasis a state of equilibrium. ▶ *Homeostasis occurs when all systems are in balance.*

homogeneous commodity a product that the consumer identifies or perceives as being the same without regard to brand name. ▶ *Salt is a homogeneous commodity.*

honorarium a fee paid to a professional for rendering a service of some type. ▶ *Professor Jones received an honorarium for addressing the pathologists' convention.*

Hoover Commission a Federal commission created in 1947, and headed by former president Herbert C. Hoover, to consider the reorganization of the executive branch of the government. ▶ *The Hoover Commission has made a number of suggestions to improve the efficiency of the Federal government.*

horizontal combination AND **horizontal integration** the common ownership of two or more firms producing or marketing the same product or service. ▶ *The merger or acquisition of two or more firms to create a horizontal combination may be viewed with disfavor by the Federal Trade Commission if competition is reduced in the industry.*

horizontal integration See the previous entry.

horizontal market a market that exists for a product when that product is used by many kinds of firms in different industries. ▶ *The market for light bulbs is a horizontal market.*

host country a country other than the country of origin where a person works or a company operates. ▶ *Mexico is the host country for Lloyd's of London's new office.*

hot extrusion a process whereby metals and plastics are heated to a degree of softness and then are forced out of a mold by means of hydraulic pressure to the desired shape. ▶ *Many of the plastic products we use daily are made in part or whole by hot extrusion.*

hot item any product, service, idea, concept, etc., that is extremely popular. ▶ *Total Quality Management is a hot item in large companies today.*

hot money speculative capital that is moved rapidly from one country to another in anticipation of changes in exchange rates or to escape high taxation, economic difficulties, inflation, or losses due to war. ▶ *Hot money creates instability because it aggravates balance of payment problems.*

house brand See *private brand.*

house organ a publication printed by a company and distributed to its employees on a regular basis. ▶ *A house organ usually contains news about the company and its employees.*

house-to-house selling a method of distribution whereby sales are made directly to consumers in their homes by salespersons who personally visit every house in a neighborhood. ▶ *The Fuller Brush Co. is an example of an organization that uses house-to-house selling.*

human asset accounting the notion that, since a firm's most important assets are often its managers and employees, the worth of an organization's human assets should somehow be accounted for and reflected on the organization's balance sheet. ▶ *In practice, there are a number of things that make human asset accounting difficult to impossible.*

human engineering See *ergonomics.*

human relations the area of managerial effort and research concerned with social and psychological relations among people in the workplace. ▶ *Effective human relations are essential to a well-functioning organization.*

human relations school a school of management thought, developed by Elton Mayo and his followers, concerned with the study of human behavior in the workplace. ▶ *The human relations school developed out of studies begun in 1927.*

human resource management AND **personnel administration; personnel management** the area of management practice concerned with the effective use of human resources to achieve an organization's objectives. ▶ *Effective personnel management involves recruiting, selecting, compensating, and rewarding the people who work for an organization.*

human resources department AND **personnel department** the department that handles hiring, firing, benefits, and other personnel matters. (The first entry is the current term. The second entry is older but still in use.) ▶ *Please discuss your insurance questions with the human resources department.*

hush money a payoff, usually in cash, given to assure another person's silence about something. (Slang or colloquial.) ▶ *The trea-*surer tried to silence his secretary with hush money when she caught him embezzling funds.*

hypothecated account a savings account, trust account, etc., pledged as collateral for a loan. ▶ *A hypothecated account serves as security for a loan, but the borrower does not turn it over to the lender.*

hypothecation an agreement or contract that permits a creditor to cause personal property of the debtor to be sold in satisfaction of a debt. ▶ *Hypothecation allows a borrower to pledge personal assets as security for a loan.*

hypothesis a statement of belief that is used as a model for real phenomenon and is tested by comparing theoretical expectations with results obtained by sampling or experimentation. ▶ *A hypothesis is the starting point when conducting empirical research.*

I

ICC See *Interstate Commerce Commission.*

iconic model a representation of reality that looks like what it represents. ▶ *A scale model of an airplane is an iconic model.*

idle capacity an unused productive potential. ▶ *When a machine or a plant is in use only part of the time, it is said to have idle capacity.*

idle money money that is not invested or is not earning interest. ▶ *Funds kept in a noninterest bearing checking account in a bank represent idle money as far as the depositor is concerned.*

idle time **1.** that portion of a work period in which a worker, a piece of equipment, or both, do not perform work. ▶ *To increase productivity, we must reduce idle time.* **2.** the time interval in a motion study when a body member does not perform work. (See also *fa-*

tigue allowance.) ▶ *Our analysis of this task shows that the left hand has 50 percent more idle time than the right hand.*

ILGWU See *International Ladies' Garment Workers Union.*

illiquid **1.** the condition of not having sufficient cash flow to meet current obligations. ▶ *When a firm becomes illiquid, bankruptcy may be the only alternative available.* **2.** any asset not readily convertible into cash. ▶ *Real estate holdings are illiquid.*

ILO See *International Labor Organization.*

image advertising advertising that is directed at creating a specific public image of a company, product, service, or brand as distinguished from advertising that extols the specific features or attributes of a company, product, service, or brand. ▶ *Through image advertising Cadillac has created* *an aura of sophistication and luxury for its automobiles.*

IMF See *International Monetary Fund.*

IMM See *International Monetary Market*

impeachment the process for removing an elected official from office for misconduct or for commission of a crime. ▶ *The impeachment proceedings against the mayor are moving very slowly.*

implied contract an agreement that is inferred by circumstances or acts of the people involved. (An *implied contract* is not a written contract.) ▶ *The lawsuit claimed that because of the meeting that Fred held with Tom last May, Tom had an implied contract to begin the design project.*

implied policy an unwritten guide to action, which can be interpreted from the behavior and actions of a company, its employees, or its representatives. ▶ *For years IBM has had an implied policy concerning the wearing of white dress shirts.*

implied trust a trust where the intent of the parties to establish a trust is inferred from the transaction between them. ▶ *An implied trust exists when one party purchases land and has the conveyance made to another party.*

implied warranty a warranty that is not expressly defined in a contract or sale, but which is understood by the participating parties because of the nature of the agreement. ▶ *When Fred bought the car from Tom there was an implied warranty that Tom actually owned the car and had the legal*

right to sell it.

import credit a commercial letter of credit issued for the purpose of financing the shipment of goods into a country. ▶ *In order to purchase the shipment of chairs from Taiwan, we will have to get our bank to issue an import credit.*

import quota an imposed limit on the quantity of an item that may be brought into a country. ▶ *The Japanese have placed an import quota on American-made automobiles.*

impound to seize and hold in protective custody through legal processes, such as a court order. ▶ *The court has issued an order to impound the chairs from Taiwan until the import duty has been paid.*

imprest account See the following entry.

imprest fund AND **imprest account; petty cash** a small fund maintained in the form of currency and coins for the purpose of handling expenditures that must be made in cash. ▶ *The imprest fund must periodically be replenished.*

impulse buying the sudden, unpremeditated purchase of goods by a consumer. ▶ *Frequently, impulse buying is triggered by seeing the item on display.*

impulse goods AND **impulse merchandise** items that are purchased without planning or prior thought. ▶ *Impulse goods are typically displayed near checkout counters to induce consumers to purchase them.*

impulse merchandise See the previous entry.

imputed cost an estimated cost where no cash payment is involved. ▶ *The estimated cost of labor contributed to a business by a sole proprietor is an imputed cost.*

in-and-out buying and selling a stock within a short period of time, usually on the same day. ▶ *Otis went in-and-out on Wilson Hydromulch yesterday and made a nice profit.*

in-basket test a testing or training method in which a person is given a number of documents, memos, and letters, each pertaining to a problem or situation requiring an immediate decision. ▶ *The in-basket test provides an indication of a person's ability to recognize and establish priorities and make decisions under the pressure of time.*

in-house the performance of certain activities within an organization as opposed to having those activities performed by an outside contractor. ▶ *The Acme Company is very proud of its in-house printing capabilities.*

in play to be in an active condition or state. ▶ *The company's stock is now in play at the twenty-dollar price range.*

in the black the condition of having made a profit during some period. (Compare with *in the red*.) ▶ *Once we start selling the new units we will be in the black.*

in-the-money an option contract on a stock with a market price above the exercise price of a call option or below the exercise price of a put option. ▶ *Gustav will be in-the-money on those options he*

is holding.

in the red the condition of having made losses rather than profits during some period. (Compare with *in the black*.) ▶ *The Axton Corporation has been in the red for two years.*

in-transit privilege the right of a shipper to interrupt the movement of goods in order to perform some manufacturing or treating operation on the goods. ▶ *We will use our in-transit privilege to apply creosote to the telephone poles as they are being shipped from Alabama.*

inactive stock a stock issue traded in relatively low volume. ▶ *An inactive stock often has very low liquidity.*

Inc. See *incorporated*.

incentive wage a financial inducement other than base pay or overtime paid to an employee for exceeding an established goal. ▶ *An incentive wage is generally related to the quantity of output produced by a worker.*

incidental sampling See *chunk sampling*.

income bond AND **preference bond** a bond on which interest is paid only if it is earned during the year by the corporation issuing the bond. ▶ *An income bond is traded without accrued interest.*

income statement AND **earnings report; earnings statement; operating statement; profit and loss statement** a summary of the revenues and expenses of an enterprise, or a portion thereof, for a specified time period. ▶ *This month's income statement shows* *that earnings are continuing to grow at a faster rate than expenses.*

income tax   a tax levied by Federal, state, or local governments on the earnings of individuals or business enterprises. ► *The more money a person makes, the more income tax that person will have to pay.*

incorporated AND **Inc.**   a designation indicating that the owners of a concern have limited liability. (*Inc.* is used both as an abbreviation and an acronym.) ► *When the word* incorporated *follows the name of a business, it indicates that the firm is a corporation and not a proprietorship or a partnership.*

incorporation   the process by which a group of individuals unite to form a legal entity or corporation. ► *Each state has its own laws of incorporation, which govern the process and the requirements for forming a corporation.*

increment   an increasing unit of growth in size, value, etc., of an item. ► *The increment of increase in price is less than was anticipated.*

incremental revenue   See *marginal revenue.*

indemnity   **1.** an agreement whereby one party secures another party against loss from special events or actions. ► *The purpose of an indemnity is to restore one to one's original position after a financial loss.* **2.** the payment made to cover a loss under an insurance contract. ► *The indemnity Tom received will enable him to rebuild his tool shed.* **3.** an exemption from prosecution or liability incurred as

a result of one's actions. ► *Indemnity may be granted to public officials who perform unconstitutional acts.*

indenture   a written agreement between two or more parties involving reciprocal rights and duties. ► *The contract between bondholders and the issuing corporation is an indenture.*

independent contractor   a self-employed person who contracts to perform work for another. ► *An independent contractor is not subject to control by the employing party except as to work results.*

independent store   **1.** an individually owned and operated retail establishment. ► *Norman operates an independent store on the west side of town.* **2.** an individual store or a small chain of stores having no more than three branches. (As used in the A. C. Nielsen Company retail indexes.) ► *A retail chain with ten branches cannot be classified as an independent store.*

independent variable   a variable whose value is not dependent upon another variable. ► *In a time series depicting corn output per year and annual rainfall, rainfall is the independent variable.*

independents   retail outlets that are usually locally owned and operated, and are not part of a larger organization. ► *In the fast food industry, the independents constitute a very small portion of the total market.*

index number   a measure of the relative changes occurring in a series of values as compared with a base period. ► *The Consumer Price*

Index is an example of an index number.

indicated staff the number of personnel required in a work center at standard performance. ▶ *Actual staff is often much higher than indicated staff.*

indicated yield the coupon or dividend rate expressed as a percentage of the current market price of the security. ▶ *When bond prices drop, the indicated yield goes up.*

indirect cost an expenditure that is not specifically attributable to a product or department, but is attributable to the total manufacturing process. ▶ *Electricity is an example of an indirect cost.*

indirect labor budget an estimate, for some future period, of the cost of labor not directly applied to the manufacture of a product. ▶ *The indirect labor budget includes cost estimates for janitors, guards, accountants, etc.*

indirect labor cost the expenditures for labor not directly associated with the actual manufacture of goods. ▶ *Indirect labor cost is sometimes a significant portion of total cost.*

indirect labor standard a specified output or a time allowance established for performing indirect labor. ▶ *Each and every product that is manufactured has a direct labor standard and an indirect labor standard.*

indirect liability an obligation not yet incurred but for which responsibility may have to be assumed. ▶ *We may incur an indirect liability if we proceed with our plans to drill a well on Smith's property.*

indirect material cost the cost of material used in the manufacturing process that does not become part of the finished product. ▶ *The expenditure for cooling solution used in the machining of parts is an indirect material cost.*

indirect overhead cost an expenditure that is not specifically attributable to a product or department, but is attributable to the total manufacturing process as an overhead cost in the strictest sense. ▶ *Rent on the manufacturing plant is an indirect overhead cost.*

individual proprietorship See *sole proprietorship.*

Individual Retirement Account AND **IRA** an arrangement under Federal tax law whereby an individual employee who qualifies may set aside a portion of earnings for retirement purposes. (No taxes are due on the amounts set aside until the individual retires.) ▶ *An Individual Retirement Account will complement any money received from Social Security upon retirement.*

inducement an incentive, argument, reason, fact, etc., used to persuade a person or group to take a particular action. ▶ *A financial inducement offered to salespeople for exceeding quotas often leads to increases in sales.*

induction a method of reaching a conclusion about an entire population or universe by examining only a few values of that population or universe. ▶ *Through the process of induction, we are able to reach a conclusion concerning a person's* *personality by examining the colors of clothing the person wears.*

industrial consumer   a purchaser of goods and services for use in manufacturing concerns, retail outlets, wholesale houses, service businesses, financial organizations, and governmental institutions, and who buys for business purposes, on either a profit or nonprofit basis. ▶ *Advertising to the industrial consumer market is best done through trade publications.*

industrial democracy   **1.** the democratic governance of labor unions. ▶ *The Landrum-Griffin Act of 1959 was enacted largely for the purpose of restoring industrial democracy in the labor movement.* **2.** the limitation of management control of a firm resulting from collective bargaining, employee stock ownership, and profit sharing. ▶ *Industrial democracy implies a sharing of management's rights and powers with employees.*

industrial discipline   the framework of policies established and actions taken by an employer to encourage or compel employees to observe certain rules and regulations of the employer. ▶ *Wherever large groups of people work together, some form of industrial discipline is needed.*

industrial distributor   a wholesaler who sells primarily to business or institutional customers who purchase items for business use rather than resale. ▶ *A large firm buys in bulk from an industrial distributor.*

industrial engineer   a person who has the necessary education, training, experience, and personal attributes to perform the work involved in the field of industrial engineering. ▶ *An industrial engineer frequently conducts motion analysis and sets time standards.*

industrial engineering   the art and science of utilizing and coordinating human resources, equipment, materials, and information to attain a desired quantity and quality of output within a specified time and at optimum cost. (Included within this field is the gathering, analyzing, and acting upon facts pertaining to facilities, layouts, personnel, organization, operating procedures, methods, processes, schedules, time standards, costs, and systems for exercising control over the quantity and quality of goods and services produced.) ▶ *Computers have had a significant impact on the field of industrial engineering.*

industrial goods   goods or services purchased by a business enterprise to assist in or to enter into the production of other goods and services. ▶ *Industrial goods include a wide variety of products ranging from file cabinets to heavy equipment.*

industrial hygiene   **1.** that field of specialization dealing with the prevention of industrial diseases and the preservation of the worker's health and general well-being. ▶ *Industrial hygiene has become increasingly important over the years in helping to reduce absenteeism.* **2.** those factors in the total work environment that affect or contribute to the health and general well-being of workers. ▶ *Poor industrial hygiene often leads to excessive costs for health insurance.*

industrial psychology that branch of the field of psychology concerned with the study of human behavior in the workplace. ▶ *Industrial psychology deals with job analysis, testing, interviewing, and training as well as other personnel activities.*

industrial relations **1.** the negotiations and interactions between employers and union members or their representatives. ▶ *The industrial relations in the Detroit plant are at an all-time high.* **2.** all those areas of mutual concern to employees and employers. ▶ *In Japan, the cooperation between government, employers, and employees leads to outstanding industrial relations.*

industrial revolution **1.** that period of time during the eighteenth and nineteenth centuries when Western Europe changed from an agrarian-based society to an industrialized one. ▶ *By 1830, the industrial revolution had produced sweeping changes in England.* **2.** the change of any society from an agrarian-based one to an industrialized one. ▶ *The industrial revolution in the United States did not occur until the 1860s.*

industrial stock a share of stock in a corporation engaged in the manufacture or sale of goods and services as distinguished from a share of stock in a railroad, public utility, bank, or insurance company. ▶ *The concept of industrial stock has broadened, and the industrials in the Dow Jones Averages do not fit the definition in* *every case.*

industrial union a labor organization (union) that includes all types of workers in a given industry regardless of their specific occupations. ▶ *The United Auto Workers is an example of a very large industrial union.*

industrial waste the scraps, discards, emissions, effluents, and other unwanted items resulting from manufacturing or processing operations. ▶ *Disposing of industrial waste in an environmentally safe manner is of paramount importance today.*

industry **1.** a group of firms producing similar products. ▶ *The restaurant industry has grown at a phenomenal rate.* **2.** the overall production activities of a country. ▶ *Norway could see a vigorous growth in its industry over the next ten years.*

industry standard a generally accepted requirement used to guide producers in a given industrial segment and assure uniformity of products and services. ▶ *In the automobile industry, fourteen-inch wheels on passenger cars are an example of an industry standard.*

industry-wide bargaining an arrangement whereby a union or a group of unions negotiate a collective bargaining agreement with employers within a given industry. ▶ *The automobile industry frequently engages in industry-wide bargaining arrangements.*

inelastic demand a situation experienced when a decrease in price does not bring about a corresponding increase in sales. ▶ *Sugar is an* *example of a product with inelastic demand.*

inference 1. a logical conclusion based on the evidence available. ▶ *Deciding to market the new item resulted from an inference based upon the data presented in a research study.* 2. the conclusion that the characteristics of a universe are, or are not, represented by the evidence gathered by a sample. ▶ *Statistical studies require making an inference about a population from a sample of data.*

inferior goods products of which less is consumed as income increases. ▶ *Hot dogs are inferior goods because as income rises people can afford more exciting eating choices; hence they purchase fewer hot dogs.*

inflation an increase in the general price level of goods and services. ▶ *Inflation may occur when the amount of money in circulation is large compared with the amount of goods and services available for consumption.*

informal conference a conference in which no official transcript of the discussions and proceedings is kept. ▶ *A disadvantage of an informal conference is the absence of a record detailing what occurred.*

informal leader an individual whose power and authority over a group is conferred by the group itself rather than by the organization. ▶ *The informal leader of a work group is often a senior employee with many years of experience.*

informal organization the social relationships that arise from the co-operation of persons within the framework of a given activity. ▶ *The primary purpose of informal organization is to satisfy the needs of its participants.*

information management See *records management.*

information retrieval AND **data retrieval** 1. the recovering of desired information from a collection of documents or records. ▶ *A file cabinet is, in essence, an information retrieval system.* 2. the recovering of desired information by use of electronic means. ▶ *Information retrieval has become much faster and cheaper with the computer.*

information theory an analytical approach used to evaluate the effectiveness of information flow in a communications network. ▶ *A knowledge of information theory is important to people who design communications systems.*

informative labeling the practice of providing information about a product that does not include its specific characteristics. ▶ *Instructions on the label of a dress to dry clean only, or suggested dosages and possible side effects appearing on a medicine container are examples of informative labeling.*

infrastructure a nation's basic system of communications, transportation, utilities, waste disposal, etc., that constitute its physical makeup. ▶ *No nation can fully develop without a basic infrastructure.*

infringement the encroachment upon the right or privilege of another. ▶ *Infringement is most commonly used in conjunction with patents and copyrights.*

inherent delay the time during a production operation when a worker must be idle because of circumstances beyond the worker's control. ▶ *Inherent delay may occur when a worker is forced to wait for a machine to complete a mechanical operation.*

inherent skill the ability to perform a specific task without training. ▶ *Some people seem to have the inherent skill to sell things to others.*

inheritance tax a graduated tax assessed by any U.S. state on estates of deceased persons. ▶ *After paying the inheritance tax on Uncle Fred's estate, Wilbur had almost two million dollars left.*

initial public offering AND **IPO** the first sale of a new issue of corporate securities to the general public. ▶ *Fred bought shares in a fund that specializes in IPOs.*

injunction an order issued by a court directing that a person, a group of persons, or an enterprise refrain from a certain act or acts. ▶ *The Bardwell Company is asking for an injunction to keep the newspaper from printing further articles accusing Bardwell of dumping industrial waste into the river.*

innkeeper's lien the right of a hotel or motel operator to retain the baggage or property of a guest for an unpaid bill. ▶ *The hotel will not remove the innkeeper's lien on your luggage until the bill is paid in full.*

innovation the development of new products, ideas, procedures, systems, etc. ▶ *Ideas for innovation in a product often come directly from the users of that product.*

input-output analysis the examination of labor, energy, and materials going into a process in respect to the products and service provided by the process. ▶ *According to Carl's input-output analysis, the cost of items used in the process exceeds the value of the output.*

input-output bound a condition in which the speed of an overall operation is limited by the speed of the devices putting material into the operation or removing an item after it has been completed by the main processing unit. ▶ *A personal computer is input-output bound due to the low speed at which a person can type material into the system and the speed at which a printer can process the output.*

insider a person who, by reason of ownership, position, or similar factors, has information on a company and its operations not available to the general public. ▶ *It is illegal for an insider to use privileged information to make a profit from the selling or buying of the company's stock.*

insider trading buying or selling the stock of a company by a person who, by reason of ownership, position, or similar factors, has inside information on the company not available to the general public. ▶ *Discoveries of insider trading by employees of large brokerage houses have made people suspicious of the stock market in general.*

insolvency the state of being unable to meet debts or otherwise discharge liabilities when they become due. ▶ *An excess of liabilities over assets at any given time results in insolvency.*

inspection the act of examining a product, financial record, etc., with the objective of comparing it to some standard or of determining its condition, quality, or value. ▶ *The inspection of the building indicated that there was serious termite damage in the basement.*

inspector 1. one who inspects. ▶ *The building inspector discovered termites in the basement.* 2. a person who appraises the quality of manufactured products to determine if they meet the necessary specifications. ▶ *The inspector rejected three of the parts because the holes were too large.*

installment 1. a partial payment of a debt. ▶ *Typically, each installment calls for the same amount to be paid each month.* 2. any one of a series of steps or actions. ▶ *The first installment of this campaign will consist of full-page ads in the local newspaper.*

installment sale a sale made with the agreement that the purchaser will pay for the purchased goods in fractional amounts over a stipulated period of time. ▶ *An installment sale makes it possible for people to purchase items they could not otherwise afford.*

institutional advertising the advertising that is concerned primarily with establishing or maintaining a favorable public attitude toward the advertiser, rather than toward a specific product or service. ▶ *The basic purpose of institutional*

advertising is to make people aware of the company doing the advertising.

institutional lender a financial intermediary that makes loans or investments on behalf of its customers or depositors. ▶ *A commercial bank is an institutional lender.*

insurable interest a person's interest in or legal relationship to the property or person of another to the extent that damage to that property or person would cause the first person financial harm. ▶ *A husband's insurable interest in his wife permits the issuance of a life insurance policy.*

insurance policy a contractual means of indemnifying a person or legal entity for loss sustained through accident, fire, damage to property, bodily injury, loss of life, etc. ▶ *The contract protecting a person against loss is known as an insurance policy.*

insured one who is protected against loss through the purchase of insurance. ▶ *The insured is the person in whose name the insurance policy is issued.*

insured mail a package sent through the U.S. Postal Service that is protected by insurance from loss or damage. ▶ *Insured mail requires the payment of an insurance fee.*

insurer a company that assumes risks, and guarantees to indemnify policyholders for any losses covered under the terms and conditions of an insurance policy. ▶ *An insurer may offer several types of insurance protection.*

intangible asset a noncurrent, nonmaterial asset of a firm. ▶ *A patent is an intangible asset.*

integration the act of combining many things or parts into a workable whole. ▶ *Effective integration is essential when one company is merged into another company.*

intelligence test a psychological device for measuring a person's mental ability. ▶ *According to the Equal Employment Opportunity Commission, an intelligence test is not generally acceptable for screening job applicants.*

interest **1.** a payment given or received for the use of funds. ▶ *Credit cards have a high rate of interest.* **2.** a share, right, or title in property. ▶ *Clarence has an interest in two oil wells in Odessa.*

interest rate the percentage of a sum of money paid or received for its use. ▶ *The interest rate on savings accounts is at its lowest point in years.*

interface a common boundary or physical connection between two or more systems or between two or more parts of a single system. ▶ *A modem is an interface between a computer and the telephone lines used to carry data.*

interim certificate a diploma, warranty, policy, or other evidence of ownership that is issued until a permanent certificate can be prepared and issued. ▶ *This interim certificate is good for sixty days.*

interim report a report prepared at any time other than the end of a fiscal year. ▶ *The interim report for the first six months of the year* shows that earnings are exceeding expectations.

interlocking directorates a device formerly used for monopolistic purposes whereby members of a particular board of directors would also serve as members of other boards of directors, with members of those boards serving as members of the original organization's board. ▶ *Federal law precludes the use of interlocking directorates under provisions of the Clayton Act of 1914.*

internal audit an audit performed on a company by an individual who is an employee of the company. ▶ *The basic purpose of an internal audit is to assure compliance with accounting policies and procedures.*

internal auditor an *auditor* who is employed by the company being audited. (Compare with *external auditor*.) ▶ *The internal auditor was fired for missing some important matters.*

internal premises the planning assumptions that are controllable inside an enterprise. ▶ *Production rates, number of new employees, and rates of pay are examples of internal premises.*

Internal Revenue Code the tax regulations that are administered and enforced by the *Internal Revenue Service* of the United States government. ▶ *The Internal Revenue Code is periodically amended by acts of Congress.*

Internal Revenue Service AND **IRS** the part of the U.S. government charged with the administration of income tax laws and the collection of income taxes. ▶ *The Internal Revenue Service is part of the U.S. Department of the Treasury.*

International Bank an international organization that has two functions: (1) underwriting loans to developing countries, and (2) lending funds to countries in need. ▶ *The International Bank was started in 1944 with $9 billion in funds.*

International Brotherhood of Teamsters AND **Teamsters Union** a large international union comprised of truck drivers, vending machine repair persons, automobile salespersons, and persons in similar trades. ▶ *The International Brotherhood of Teamsters is one of the most powerful unions in the United States.*

international corporation a corporation conducting business in two or more countries. ▶ *With clients in Canada and Australia, we are now an international corporation.*

International Labor Organization AND **ILO** an agency established to promote employment, raise standards of living, create global standards of labor, improve working conditions, and provide technical assistance to developing countries. ▶ *Now a special agency of the United Nations, the International Labor Organization was originally established under the Treaty of Versailles in 1919.*

International Ladies' Garment Workers Union AND **ILGWU** a women's clothing workers union that is a member of the AFL-CIO. ▶ *Strikes led by the ILGWU in 1909 and 1910 resulted in improved working conditions, higher wages, and fewer hours of work per week.*

International Monetary Fund AND **IMF** an international institution that went into operation in 1947 to provide necessary contacts for consultation on international monetary problems, promote and regulate foreign trade, and supply members with funds to meet temporary negative balances of trade. ▶ *The International Monetary Fund is headquartered in Washington, D.C.*

International Monetary Market AND **IMM** a division of the Chicago Mercantile Exchange that trades in futures in U.S. Treasury bills, foreign currency, certificates of deposit, and *Eurodollar* deposits. ▶ *There has been brisk trading in foreign currency today in the International Monetary Market.*

interpolation the estimation of an unknown intermediate number between two known numbers. ▶ *If we know the mileage from Los Angeles to San Francisco, we can, through interpolation, determine the mileage from Los Angeles to San Jose.*

interstate commerce the business activity carried on between business entities in two or more states and therefore subject to regulation by the Federal government. ▶ *Interstate commerce also includes the transportation of people from one state to another state.*

Interstate Commerce Act of 1887 an act of Congress that regulates the transportation industry in order to make certain that it operates in the public interest. (This act established the *Interstate Commerce Commission*.) ▶ *The Interstate Commerce Act of 1887 was one of the first Federal attempts at regulating business activity in the country.*

Interstate Commerce Commission AND **ICC** a body of eleven members appointed by the President, whose duty it is to enforce the *Interstate Commerce Act of 1887*. (The jurisdiction of the *ICC* includes railroad, water, motor, and pipeline regulation.) ▶ *The Interstate Commerce Commission is involved in the affairs of many American firms because so much American business is done between entities in the various states.*

interview a conversation or verbal exchange, usually between two people, for a particular purpose. ▶ *Fritz was very excited about his upcoming job interview.*

intestate the condition of dying without having made a valid will. ▶ *My cousin Vincent died intestate.*

intrapreneurship entrepreneurial-like skills used within the framework of an existing organization, usually of large size. (Based on *entrepreneur*, using the prefix "intra," within, rather than "entre.") ▶ *By encouraging intrapreneurship, we hope to increase operating efficiency significantly.*

intrastate commerce the business activity carried on exclusively within a particular state and therefore subject to the regulations of that state and not the Federal government. ▶ *Intrastate commerce*

is not subject to the provisions of the Interstate Commerce Act of 1887.

intrinsic value the value or usefulness inherent in an object. ▶ *The intrinsic value of a gold coin depends upon the market price for gold.*

inventory **1.** a listing of all tangible property owned by an enterprise or a person. ▶ *The inventory of Frank's property shows two automobiles and three boats.* **2.** AND **stock on hand** a listing of goods that are to be consumed in the production of goods for sale (*raw materials*), goods currently in the process of being converted into goods for sale (*goods in process*), and goods held for sale in due course of business (*finished goods*). ▶ *Normally, the inventory lists the value of each item or class of items as well as the total value of all items.*

inventory control **1.** the techniques, procedures, methods, and systems used to maintain control over a firm's inventories. ▶ *The new computer system will enable us to maintain better inventory control.* **2.** the department or unit within a company that is assigned the responsibility for maintaining control over the company's various inventories. ▶ *Please send this document to inventory control immediately.*

inventory turnover AND **stock turnover** the number of times that the investment in stocks of goods and merchandise is replaced during a given period, usually one year. ▶ *Inventory turnover is determined by dividing sales by* *the average inventory during the period.*

investment **1.** an expenditure to acquire income-producing property. ▶ *We must make the investment now or we will not have the opportunity to earn the same rate of return later.* **2.** income-producing property. ▶ *My investment portfolio includes stocks, bonds, oil wells, and U.S. Treasury bills.* **3.** a security owned. ▶ *Tom has an investment in IBM stock.* **4.** owner's equity in a business enterprise. ▶ *My partners and I have an equal investment in this company.*

investment analysis the study of an investment to determine if the profit that it will return is great enough to warrant the risk incurred by its purchase. ▶ *According to this investment analysis, the potential profit from this project is very attractive.*

investment analyst a person who has the necessary education, training, and personal attributes to undertake *investment analysis.* ▶ *My uncle is an investment analyst for a Wall Street brokerage house.*

investment banker a financial intermediary who buys bond or stock issues in their entirety from the issuing corporation and then sells them to other security dealers or to the investing public. ▶ *The investment banker is the principal intermediary for bringing security issues to the investing public.*

investment center a division, department, section, unit, or other component part of a business enterprise over which a manager has

responsibility, not only for profit but also for the use of the assets employed in the divisions. ▶ *The manager of an investment center is responsible for an acceptable rate of return on all assets.*

investment company AND **investment trust** an organization that invests money for others. ▶ *A mutual fund is a type of investment company.*

investment counsel an individual whose principal business consists of advising investors on their holdings and on investment opportunities. ▶ *An investment counsel may be self-employed or may work for an investment company.*

investment tax credit **1.** a tax incentive given to encourage investment in equipment or buildings. ▶ *We should purchase the equipment now while we can still benefit from the investment tax credit.* **2.** a tax break for investing in certain types of tangible personal property and placing that property in use at any time during the tax year. ▶ *We have until December 31 to get that machine in use if we want to qualify for the investment tax credit.* **3.** a first year tax credit for the purchase of art. ▶ *When we purchase that Picasso for the corporate offices, we will get an investment tax credit.*

investment trust See *investment company.*

investor a person or firm that acquires income-producing property. ▶ *The individual investor has long been a part of the American economic scene.*

invisible hand a force that guides

society through enlightened self-interest. (Used by Adam Smith in *The Wealth of Nations*, published in 1776.) ▶ *The concept of the invisible hand sets forth the thesis that the welfare of society in general is assured when all the people in that society act in their own self-interest.*

invitation for bid a request by a business enterprise, governmental agency, or other institution inviting suppliers to submit price quotations on specified goods or services. ▶ *This invitation for bid from the Bass Company requires a response by next Monday.*

invoice 1. a statement itemizing goods bought or sold. ▶ *We have not yet received all of the items listed on this invoice.* 2. to issue a statement requesting payment for goods sold. ▶ *Please ask accounts payable to invoice Miller Corporation for three dozen power wrenches.*

invoice cost 1. the cost of goods or services incurred by a buyer as reflected on an invoice. ▶ *The invoice cost does not appear to be the same as the amount we agreed on last week.* 2. the billed cost less trade discount, but not cash discount. ▶ *Because of the trade discount we receive, our invoice cost is less than that of other purchasers.*

IOU "I owe you." (An informal acknowledgement of a cash debt.) ▶ *When a friend borrows money from another friend, he may give the lender an IOU.*

IPO See *initial public offering.*

IRA See *Individual Retirement Account.*

irregular any good that fails to meet specified standards of appearance, but not of service or use. (See also *(factory) second.*) ▶ *Today, a number of manufacturers are selling irregulars at reduced prices through their own retail stores in outlet malls.*

IRS See *Internal Revenue Service.*

island position a newspaper advertisement positioned so that it is entirely surrounded by non-advertising reading matter. ▶ *If we can get an island position for this ad, more people are likely to read it.*

isolationist one who opposes one's country's involvement in international affairs. ▶ *Because of the increasing interdependence of the countries of the world, it is difficult for a businessperson to be an isolationist today.*

issue the shares of stock or bonds sold by a corporation at a particular time. ▶ *The price on that new issue was much lower than we anticipated.*

issue price the original price to the public at which an individual share of stock or a bond from a new security offering sells. ▶ *The issue price on Apex Pinnacle's new preferred stock offering is very attractive.*

issued shares the number of shares of stock that a corporation has released for sale to the public. ▶ *The issued shares may be equal to or less than the number of shares authorized.*

issuer a legal entity, such as a corporation, municipality, or government, that has the power to issue and distribute a security. ▶ *The issuer of stock is responsible for periodic reports to shareholders.*

itinerant worker See *migrant worker.*

J

JIT See *just in time.*

job **1.** a grouping of work tasks. ▶ *A job may be assigned to one or more workers.* **2.** a group of positions having identical tasks or functions. ▶ *All of the people performing this job have the title "Space Engineer."*

job analysis AND **job study** the process of determining the nature of a specific job and reporting the results of the study. (*Job analysis* encompasses the determination of tasks comprising the job and worker skills, knowledge, abilities, and responsibilities necessary for successful job performance.) ▶ *A job analysis of the new position showed that we needed someone with at least a high school diploma and the ability to lift 50 pounds.*

job analyst an individual who, by reason of education, training, and other qualifications, performs the task of *job analysis.* ▶ *Another job analyst will have to be hired to complete this project on schedule.*

job bank a listing of job openings by category, usually maintained on a computer. ▶ *An employment agency uses a job bank to assist job applicants in locating suitable employment.*

job bidding the process of applying for jobs offered in one's own company. (See also *job posting.*) ▶ *Job bidding is more common in manufacturing industries than it is in nonmanufacturing industries.*

job breakdown the analysis of a job into its component tasks, duties, responsibilities, skill requirements, and other characteristics for the purpose of preparing a *job description* or a *job specification.* ▶ *According to the job breakdown, one of the specifications for this job should be a college degree in Spanish.*

job classification a grouping of jobs with similar content, responsibilities, requirements, etc., into classes or grades normally having similar rates of pay. ▶ *A job classification plan results from evaluating all of an organization's jobs.*

job cluster a group of jobs within an organization linked together by technology, administrative organization, and social custom. ▶ *All data entry clerk positions are in the same job cluster.*

job content the various tasks, duties, functions, responsibilities, and other factors comprising a job. ▶ *Job content must be examined and analyzed before an accurate job description can be written.*

job cost sheet a form used to accumulate material, labor, and other charges applicable to a certain costing point of a particular production run or lot. ▶ *According to the job cost sheet, labor cost is the largest cost component for this production run.*

job description a written statement of the tasks, duties, behaviors, accountabilities, responsibilities, and other factors found in a given job. (This can refer to an existing job or a job that an employer is trying to fill. See also *job specification; role prescription*.) ▶ *An accurate job description is essential to determining the proper rate of pay for a job.*

job design the process of determining what the specifications of a job should be. ▶ *Job design is often performed by industrial engineers.*

job enlargement the process of making an overly specialized job more meaningful and challenging to the worker through the addition of more tasks. (See also the following entry.) ▶ *Job enlargement adds variety to a job and can improve employee morale.*

job enrichment the process of making an overly specialized job more meaningful and challenging to the worker through the addition of greater responsibility or decision-making authority. (See also the previous entry.) ▶ *Job enrichment increases the depth of a job.*

job evaluation AND **job grading** a formalized systematic approach to determining the relative monetary value of a job within an organization. ▶ *The point method is the most widely used job evaluation system.* ▶ *Some local governmental agencies still use a job grading system to determine the monetary value of their jobs.*

job family a collection of two or more jobs that require similar worker characteristics or that contain parallel tasks. ▶ *Executive secretary and secretary are jobs within the same job family.*

job grading See *job evaluation.*

job hopper a worker who moves from employer to employer, spending little time with any one job. (Colloquial.) ▶ *Tom is a job hopper who has had five jobs in a twelve-month period.*

job lot a relatively small number of a specific type of item that is produced at one time. ▶ *Many small machine shops only do work in job lots.*

job opening a vacant position in an organization. ▶ *According to the personnel department, there is a job opening in accounting.*

job order production the manufacturing of items in small quantities, to customer or stock orders. ▶ *Job order production is the opposite of mass production.*

job posting posting notices of job vacancies on company bulletin boards or in company publications and allowing workers to apply for those jobs. (See also *job bidding*.) ▶ *Our company just started job posting, and now we know what other positions are available.*

job pricing the process of assigning wage or salary rates to job grades or classes. ▶ *Job pricing can only be accomplished after a salary survey has been done to ascertain pay for various jobs within the local labor market.*

job ranking a method of *job evaluation* that consists of ordering all of the jobs within an organization, from the most difficult to the least difficult. ▶ *Of all the job evaluation methods in use today, job ranking is by far the simplest.*

job rating the process of determining the relative rank of each job in an organization and of evaluating each job in terms of pay. ▶ *Job rating establishes the base pay for each of an organization's jobs.*

job rotation a form of training in which employees or managers are transferred, on a planned basis, from job to job within an organization in order to develop wider knowledge and skills. ▶ *Job rotation programs help new employees*

understand the variety of jobs within an enterprise.

job sampling a form of skill testing that requires a job applicant to perform some of the tasks that are actually part of the job for which the person is applying. ▶ *A typing test given to prospective secretaries is a form of job sampling.*

job security AND **employment security** the relative permanency and continuity of a person's employment. ▶ *College professors have a great deal of job security whereas clerical workers in the same university have little or none.* ▶ *In many types of companies, employment security is based on seniority.*

job sharing an arrangement whereby the duties and responsibilities of one job are divided and assigned to two people. (*Job sharing* can be used as an alternative to layoffs since it provides at least part-time employment for both individuals sharing a job.) ▶ *Since our company started job sharing, I work Monday, Tuesday, and half of Wednesday, and Leslie works the rest of the week.*

job shop a manufacturing firm that produces items, usually in small quantities, for specific customers. ▶ *In a job shop, parts are manufactured only to fill orders received from customers.*

job shopper an individual who works on a contract basis for an organization, especially in the defense industry. (Someone who works in a *job shop*.) ▶ *A job shopper is an independent contractor and is not entitled to participate* *in the employee benefits programs offered by the organization.*

job specification   a written statement of the skills, qualifications, and characteristics required by an individual to perform a given job. (This can refer to the specifications of a position that an employer is trying to fill. See also *job description*.) ▶ *A job description and a job specification are the two end products resulting from job analysis.*

job study   See *job analysis.*

jobber   **1.** a wholesaler who buys in *job lots* from manufacturers, importers, or other wholesalers and sells to retailers. ▶ *A jobber buys from different sources and sells to stores serving the ultimate consumer.* **2.** any wholesaler. ▶ *One of the large national jobbers ordered nearly 20,000 copies of the newly published book.*

jobless   **1.** to be unemployed. ▶ *My next-door neighbor was fired yesterday and is now jobless.* **2.** the unemployed as a whole. ▶ *At any point in time in the United States, the jobless number is in the millions.*

joint account   a bank account that authorizes either of two or more parties to write checks and make deposits. ▶ *John and Mary have a joint account at the First National Bank.*

joint agreement   a collective bargaining agreement signed by more than two parties. ▶ *A joint agreement may be signed by two employers and two unions, one employer and two unions, two employers and one union, or other*

similar combinations of parties.

joint contract   an agreement for a mutual purpose between two or more parties entered into with another party or parties. ▶ *Fred and Bob entered into a joint contract with the remodeling contractor.*

joint cost   the common cost of two or more operations or the common cost of two or more products resulting from a single operation or series of operations. ▶ *When two or more items result from a simultaneous process, there is a joint cost of manufacturing.*

joint products   two or more items or grades of an item made from a common raw material. ▶ *When gold and silver are extracted from the same ore, they are said to be joint products.*

joint rate   the shipping rate for a shipment that travels on two or more carriers. ▶ *Because it is necessary to ship that container by rail and truck, a joint rate will have to be determined to ascertain total shipping costs.*

joint rate setting   a process whereby wage rates are set by management and union representatives in conjunction with each other rather than by management alone. ▶ *Our company agreed to joint rate setting in an effort to placate the union.*

joint stock company   a firm whose capital stock is held in transferable shares by joint owners. ▶ *A joint stock company combines features of a partnership and a corporation.*

joint venture   an undertaking entered into by two or more parties who share the risks and the profits.

> *The parties undertaking a joint venture may be located in two different countries.*

journal AND **book of original entry** the accounting book in which transactions are first recorded and from which they are transferred to ledger accounts. ▶ *The journal is frequently referred to as the "book of original entry" since all accounting transactions are first recorded there.*

journeyman one who has completed an apprenticeship in an occupation but who has not yet, typically because of experience requirements, reached the level of master craftsman. ▶ *A journeyman is an accomplished worker in a trade.*

judgment sampling AND **purposive sampling** a type of non-probability sampling wherein a sample is selected based on knowledge, experience, and familiarity rather than randomness or the number of items to be sampled. ▶ *Outside auditors frequently use judgment sampling in performing audits of clients.*

junior bond AND **junior issue** a bond that, in the event of dissolution, is subordinate to one or more issues in regard to interest, principal, or redemption. ▶ *Because of their subordinate status, junior bonds may be less attractive to investors than other types of bonds.*

junior issue See the previous entry.

junk bond a bond with a speculative credit rating. ▶ *A junk bond is issued in leveraged buyouts by firms that do not have substantial sales and earnings histories.*

just in time AND **JIT** a production and inventory control system that enables parts and materials to be delivered from suppliers to manufacturers just as the parts and materials are needed. ▶ *A just in time system reduces the expense of carrying a large inventory.*

justify to adjust the position of words arranged for processing or printing so that both the left-hand and right-hand margins are in line. ▶ *When a common margin is desired in a document, the typical procedure is to justify the left-hand margin.*

K

Kefauver-Celler Act of 1950 an amendment to the *Clayton Act of 1914* forbidding the acquisition of the assets of one company by another in the same line of business. ▶ *The Kefauver-Celler Act of 1950 is an impediment to monopolistic mergers.*

Keogh Plan an arrangement made possible by the Self-Employed Individuals Retirement Act of 1962 that permits people who are self-employed to establish their own retirement plans. ▶ *As an independent contractor, Tom has set up a Keogh Plan to save for his retirement.*

key class a job class that is important to the determination of compensation rates for other classes within a compensation plan. ▶ *One of the factors that indicates a key class is the number of jobs it contains.*

key job a job used as a guide or benchmark for determining the value of other jobs. ▶ *In job evaluation, a key job actually represents a number of other jobs.*

key-man insurance life insurance on an important (key) executive, manager, or owner of a business enterprise, purchased by the company with the company designated as beneficiary. ▶ *Key-man insurance protects a company financially in the event of the death of a person vital to the company's success.*

keypunch 1. a special device that records information on cards or on tape by punching holes in the cards or tape to represent letters, numbers, or other characters. ▶ *Keypunch machines were essential in the early days of data processing.* 2. to operate a device for punching holes in cards or tape. ▶ *Once we get the data from accounting we will keypunch it so that we can* *run it through the data processing machine.*

keyboard   a device for entering, encoding, or printing numbers, letters, or other characters by means of depressing a key or depressing a key and a motor bar. ▶ *To use a personal computer effectively, one must have keyboard skills.*

Keynesian economics   the school of economic thought fathered by John Maynard Keynes. (One of the key ideas of *Keynesian economics* is that if savings are not offset by new capital investments, unemployment will result.) ▶ *According to Keynesian economics, the Federal government can prevent mass unemployment by stimulating spending or creating investments.*

keystone   a method of pricing in which the wholesale cost of an item is doubled to determine the retail price at which the item will be sold. ▶ *Keystone pricing is commonly used by the majority of small retailers in the United States because of its simplicity as a pricing scheme.*

Keyword-in-Context AND **KWIC**   a method of indexing documents, utilizing a computer to select, by means of statistics, the significant words in the document. ▶ *Keyword-in-Context was one of the earliest computer indexing approaches.*

kickback   a payment made to an individual, firm, or agency for the purpose of enlisting support in influencing an event in making a sale or purchase, or in obtaining some other kind of favor. ▶ *A kickback is an unethical business practice in the United States.*

kicked upstairs   the act of being promoted to a position of higher responsibility, usually at the executive level. ▶ *Johnson was kicked upstairs last week and is now executive vice president in charge of retail marketing.*

kinked demand   a demand curve that becomes discontinuous at the market price. (In an industry with few firms, but no price leader, if one firm raises prices, the other firms will not follow, but if one firm reduces prices, the others will follow suit.) ▶ *Kinked demand does not occur in every industry.*

kiting   the act of depositing and writing checks on accounts at two or more banks to take advantage of the delay in processing checks, creating the impression that there are sufficient funds in each account. ▶ *Kiting is a fraudulent practice.*

Kuder Preference Record   a psychological test used to measure a person's interest in different types of jobs. ▶ *According to the results of his Kuder Preference Record, Willard should major in mechanical engineering.*

kurtosis   a measure of the degree to which a frequency distribution is peaked or concentrated about a central value. ▶ *A high degree of kurtosis indicates that the values of a frequency distribution are clustered at one point.*

KWIC   See *Keyword-in-Context.*

L

labeling laws laws requiring safe packaging and warning labels on hazardous materials. ▶ *With the new labeling laws, we will have to redesign our packaging.*

labor **1.** the mental and physical effort expended by people to produce and distribute goods and services. ▶ *A good deal of labor went into the production of the new weather vane.* **2.** employees with little or no supervisory responsibility whose main task is the production of goods and services. ▶ *Plant A determined that a reduction in labor would cut costs.*

labor agitator a person who deliberately encourages unrest and agitates for unionization among workers. ▶ *Because of his hostile feelings toward unions, it was obvious he was not a labor agitator.*

labor agreement See *union contract.*

labor dispute a controversy between labor and management over terms and conditions of employment. ▶ *We are having a labor dispute over wages at this company.*

labor force all adults sixteen years of age and over in the United States who are gainfully employed. ▶ *Some would say the U.S. labor force is shrinking.*

labor force participation rate the percentage of the total labor force that is working or actively seeking work. ▶ *A 95 percent labor force participation rate is almost unknown.*

labor grade a category or level of a job as determined on the basis of skill, experience, education, and other job requirements. ▶ *A labor grade is usually applied to a category or level of a direct production job as opposed to an office or indirect labor job.*

labor intensive the activities in which labor costs are the highest component of the total cost of the activity. ▶ *Programming a computer is a labor intensive job.*

labor leader an individual who devotes full time and energies to the activities or affairs of a union as a paid official. ▶ *His status in the union verifies his position of a labor leader.*

Labor-Management Reporting and Disclosure Act of 1959 AND **Landrum-Griffin Act of 1959** a Federal labor relations act aimed at eliminating racketeering, corruption, and collusion between employers and union leaders. (This act requires the reporting of certain information by both unions and management, but more importantly, it establishes a detailed regulation of the internal affairs of unions, regulates the conduct of union officials, and curtails recognition and organizational picketing.) ▶ *The Landrum-Griffin Act of 1959 allows government to monitor the workings of large labor unions.*

labor market the geographical area within which employers recruit workers and workers seek employment. ▶ *The labor market for this company is very large and demographically diverse.*

labor mobility the ease with which workers are able to change jobs or occupations. ▶ *In rural areas, labor mobility is limited.*

labor organizer a union official whose primary function is to promote the organization of workers into a union. ▶ *Jack, a labor organizer, has just about reached his goal of forming a union at this firm.*

labor pool the source of trained workers from which prospective employees are recruited. ▶ *The labor pool for that specialized occupation is rapidly shrinking.*

labor relations the relationship between an employer and a union, including the negotiation of collective bargaining agreements and the handling of differences arising out of the interpretation and application of the agreements. ▶ *Labor relations can become very tense when discussing wage increases.*

labor theory of value a theory holding that true value is created by labor rather than other factors of production, with the scarcity or abundance of labor required to produce a product determining the product's value. ▶ *The labor theory of value was originated by David Ricardo and later used by Karl Marx.*

labor time ticket a form used to accumulate time spent by labor so that direct labor costs can be charged to production orders. ▶ *With our new automation, the cumulative times on the labor time ticket have decreased.*

labor union AND **trade union** an organized group of workers whose representatives negotiate contracts and other matters with management. ▶ *The labor union has raised the standard of living of the employees.*

lag the time interval between successive, related events. ▶ *Sometimes, there is a lag in the sale of* *an item and the receipt of cash in payment for the sale.*

laissez faire "let one do as one will." (This is a concept popularized by Adam Smith in *The Wealth of Nations*, published in 1776. The phrase implies that government should interfere as little as possible in the regulation and control of business.) ▶ *Under a laissez faire concept, government should maintain a hands-off attitude and let the free interaction of supply and demand forces in the marketplace regulate the business system.*

lame duck an officeholder who has not been reelected but who remains in his legislative position until the newly elected official succeeds him. ▶ *Senator Claxton was defeated in November, he is now a lame duck.*

LAN See *local area network.*

land a tract of ground that may be owned, including anything that grows or is constructed on it. ▶ *In a business sense, land is public or privately owned real estate.*

landlord one who rents real property to another. ▶ *Our landlord is raising our rent!*

landmark a fixed object serving as a boundary mark for a tract of land. ▶ *That enormous rock is a landmark for the corner of my property.*

Landrum-Griffin Act of 1959 See *Labor-Management Reporting and Disclosure Act of 1959.*

lapping the theft of cash received from one customer, made good, and credited to the customer's account by theft from another customer. ▶ *Lapping in various accounts can continue indefinitely*

if the fraud is not discovered.

lapse **1.** the expiration or forfeiture of an insurance policy and its rights and benefits because of nonpayment of premiums. ▶ *The lapse rate for this policy is very high because the premiums are very expensive.* **2.** to expire. ▶ *Because John failed to make payments, the policy lapsed.*

laser printer a computer printing device that uses a laser beam to generate an image and transfer it electrostatically to paper. ▶ *A laser printer produces a high quality grade of printing.*

last in-first out AND **LIFO** a method of inventory identification and valuation that calculates the value of inventory on hand by using the prices of items least recently purchased. (Also used generically for any situation where the first thing in is also the first thing out.) ▶ *Nonperishable goods are not appropriate for the LIFO method.*

latent demand a demand that cannot be satisfied with existing products or services. ▶ *There is a latent demand for medicine having absolutely no side effects.*

lateral transfer the shifting of an employee from one position to another position of equal pay, status, or responsibility. ▶ *Rather than a promotion, Jim changed jobs by receiving a lateral transfer.*

launder money to obscure the source of money obtained in an illegitimate business. ▶ *Max laundered the drug trafficking money by investing in a phony consulting business.*

law the rules, statutes, codes, or

regulations that are enforceable by court action. ▶ *With the passage of the new law, businesses will have more restrictions.*

law of diminishing marginal utility the notion that each succeeding unit of an item consumed will yield less satisfaction than the preceding unit. ▶ *The law of diminishing marginal utility implies that the benefits of consuming additional units increases at a decreasing rate.*

(law of) diminishing returns the notion that the addition of equal amounts of one or two factors of production to the remaining factors will yield successively smaller increases in production. ▶ *Under the idea of the law of diminishing returns, adding more and more people to this assembly line process may cause crowding that will cause diminishing returns from the production process.*

law of the trivial many and the critical few See *Pareto's Law.*

layaway the state of a purchased good being held on the *layaway plan.* ▶ *Tom asked that the suit be placed in layaway until July.*

layaway plan an installment purchase arrangement whereby the vendor retains possession of the merchandise until the buyer has completed making payments on it. ▶ *Our new equipment was purchased on a layaway plan.*

layoff an indefinite separation from the payroll due to factors beyond the employee's control. ▶ *The layoff will not cure all the company's cash flow problems, but it will help reduce costs.*

layout **1.** the arrangement of equipment, storage cabinets, desks, workstations, etc., within a particular factory or office area. ▶ *The new layout in the plant has slightly increased production.* **2.** the rough positioning of an advertisement to show the placement of the items that make up the overall advertisement. ▶ *This layout will have more pictures than words.*

LCL See *less-than-carload.*

lead time the interval between the placing of an order or the initiating of a plan of action and the point in time at which the order is received or actual production is begun. ▶ *This product requires a two-week lead time for production.*

leader a person possessing the ability to persuade others to pursue a course of action. ▶ *General George Patton is considered by many to have been a great leader.*

leadership the ability to persuade others to follow a course of action. ▶ *Based on the disappointing levels of productivity and enthusiasm of our employees, maybe a few hours of leadership training is necessary.*

leading indicators the components of an economic index released by the U.S. Commerce Department's Bureau of Economic Analysis. (*Leading indicators* are thought to predict the future course of the economy.) ▶ *Leading indicators include new orders for consumer goods, stock prices, and vendor performance.*

learning curve a graphic representation of the proposition that the time required to perform a task decreases with regularity until the task has been sufficiently learned. ▶ *Based on the learning curve concept, the time it takes a new employee to complete a task is greater than for an employee who has been doing the task for two weeks.*

lease a contract that grants the use of an object or the use of land or other holdings for a specific period of time in exchange for suitable payment. ▶ *Since we no longer need the equipment, we will not renew our lease.*

leaseback the sale of an asset with a lease of the same asset from the buyer back to the seller. ▶ *To improve our cash flow, we sold the warehouse for $900,000 and arranged for a leaseback for $4,000 a month.*

leased department a merchandise department within a department store that is leased to an outside operator. (Normally, the leasing organization buys all merchandise for the leased department, provides salespersons, and operates the department as a part of the store. The department store supplies space, utilities, credit, and delivery service and in return receives a stipulated percentage of the sales or a fixed sum.) ▶ *Some of the most common leased departments are millinery, shoes, and jewelry.*

leasing the act of participating in a lease agreement. (See also *lease.*) ▶ *Because we could not afford to purchase the computers outright, we are leasing them.*

least squares a statistical technique for fitting a trend line to a given set of data. ▶ *The least squares method is sometimes used in risk analysis for financial management purposes.*

leave of absence time off from work, without pay, allowed to an employee with the right of reinstatement and without the loss of seniority. ▶ *Leave of absence is used sparingly in most companies.*

ledger a book of accounts. ▶ *A ledger may be a bound volume, a loose-leaf binder, a set of punched cards, or a reel of magnetic tape.*

legacy a gift of personal property through a will. ▶ *His legacy will be much appreciated by his children.*

legal entity an individual, a partnership, a corporation, a trust, an association, or other form of organization empowered by law or custom to own property or transact business. ▶ *Individuals who are of age are legal entities.*

legal list a list of firms that are approved by various states for investment by institutions, trusts, fiduciaries, insurance companies, etc. ▶ *Our firm is on the legal list.*

legal monopoly a monopoly created by law. ▶ *Patents and copyrights are examples of legal monopolies.*

legal reserve that portion of a commercial bank's demand and time deposits that the bank is required by law to maintain in the form of cash, readily available balances, or certain eligible securities, for the protection of depositors. (See also *reserve requirement.*) ▶ *Federal Reserve System member banks must keep their legal reserves in cash on deposit with*

Federal Reserve Banks in their districts, but vault cash may be counted as part of the required legal reserve.

legal risk   an uncertainty arising from interpretations of laws, legal relationships, or any instrument pertaining to them. ▶ *The legal risks associated with the passage of the Americans with Disabilities Act may be far-reaching.*

legal tender   money (coin or currency) that is recognized by law as acceptable for the payment of public or private debts, unless the contract between the parties specifically calls for payment in a particular kind of money. ▶ *The U.S. one dollar bill is legal tender in some countries.*

legally competent   the condition of being of legal age, being of sound mind, being under no legal handicaps, and being otherwise able to enter into binding contracts. ▶ *A twelve-year-old child is not legally competent.*

legatee   a person who receives property through a will. ▶ *Johnny, who received a house, a car, and other items from his recently departed father, is a legatee.*

legator   a person who bequeaths property through a will. ▶ *Milton, Johnny's father, is a legator because he left quite a bit of property to Johnny in his will.*

legitimate waste   the unavoidable waste of materials as a result of production. ▶ *Sawdust is legitimate waste in a woodworking plant.*

leisure class   that segment of society that, because of wealth and income, devotes itself primarily to spending money and enjoying leisure and the so-called finer things of life. (First used by the American economist Thorstein B. Veblen.) ▶ *Few people are members of the leisure class, although many would like to be.*

lender of last resort   an entity having the authority and financial capabilities to extend credit to depository institutions in certain instances involving a national or regional emergency, where the inability to obtain credit would have an adverse impact on the economy. ▶ *The Federal Reserve System is the lender of last resort in the United States.*

less-than-carload AND **LCL**   a method of classifying railroad boxcar shipments to determine the rates at which the freight will travel. ▶ *There are several different categories of LCL rates based on volume.*

less-than-truckload AND **LTL**   A method of classifying motor freight shipments to determine the rate at which the freight will travel. ▶ *LTL rates are based on volume or weight.*

lessee   one who leases property from another. ▶ *The lessee negotiated to get her monthly payments lowered.*

lessor   one who leases property to another. ▶ *As a lessor of computers, Steven made quite a bit of money.*

letter of credit   an instrument issued by a bank on another bank or banks, foreign or domestic, to an individual, a partnership, or a corporation by which the bank substitutes its own credit for that of the individual, partnership, or corporation. ▶ *Before we can purchase this machinery, we must get a letter of credit from the bank.*

letter of intent   a preliminary understanding of an intent to take, or not to take, action. ▶ *A letter of intent to proceed with the project was sent to the contractor.*

letter press printing   a type of printing performed by a plate with raised surfaces covered with ink which, when pressed to paper, leaves a printed image. (See also *lithography*.) ▶ *Letter press printing is an old and dependable process.*

letter-quality printer   a device that prints with such a high quality that the print is comparable to that produced by a typewriter. ▶ *A daisy-wheel printer is an example of a letter-quality printer.*

letter stock   that stock not registered with the *Securities and Exchange Commission*, and which cannot be sold to the general public. ▶ *Letter stock gets its name from a notice on the face of the stock certificate.*

leveled time AND **normal time**   the average observed time adjusted by a performance rating factor. ▶ *Leveled time is used in time study analysis.*

leverage   borrowed money used to increase purchasing power and increase profitability of an investment. ▶ *Leverage may increase the financial performance of a company.*

leveraged buyout   **1.** the takeover of another company using borrowed funds. ▶ *The Maynard Company was the target company of a leveraged buyout.* **2.** an action initiated by corporate management to take a public firm private. ▶ *A leveraged buyout is accomplished through debt.*

lex loci   "the law of the place." (Latin.) ▶ *In contracts, lex loci means the law of the place where the contract was made.*

lex non scripta   "unwritten law." (Latin.) ▶ *In our company, it is lex non scripta that we stay until 5:00 P.M.*

liabilities   the claims of creditors on a business or an individual. ▶ *Virtually all businesses have liabilities at some point.*

liability dividend   a notes payable dividend used when a firm is short of cash but has sufficient retained earnings. ▶ *Our company discounted the liability dividend we held before the date of maturity to get some quick cash.*

liability insurance   protection against certain risks furnished by an insurance company, which agrees to cover the insured against all damage claims up to the dollar limit of the policy. ▶ *Over the past few years, the cost for liability insurance has risen at a phenomenal rate.*

libel   a false and malicious written report or publication that tends to injure the reputation of a living person or the memory of a deceased person and to expose the person to public contempt, ridicule, or hatred. (See also *slander*.) ▶ *When the tabloid ran a scandalous story* *about the actress, she sued for libel.*

license 1. a proof of government permission to engage in a particular business or to operate certain equipment, such as an automobile. ▶ *A license usually has the form of a document, a card, a metal plate, etc.* **2.** to grant a *license.* ▶ *The state has the power to license bus drivers.*

licensee one who holds a *license.* ▶ *Joan is a licensee now that she has filed the proper paperwork.*

lien the legal right of one party to satisfy a claim against a second party by holding that party's property as security or by taking possession of it. ▶ *We have a lien on the house.*

life insurance a contract between an insurance company and an individual that provides for the payment of a specified sum of money to a beneficiary upon the death of the insured. ▶ *Our firm makes available life insurance to its employees.*

life-tenant one who holds property for life or for the extent of someone else's life. ▶ *Tom is a life-tenant on the property, and it reverts to the bank upon his death.*

lifestyle a person's pattern of living. ▶ *Tom's lifestyle is quite dull.*

LIFO See *last in-first out.*

limit order See *limit(ed price) order.*

limited AND **Ltd.** a designation which means that shareholders in a corporation have only limited liability for debts incurred by the company. (The limit of their liabili-

ty is in proportion to the extent of their investment. The expression is typical of firms in England and some other English-speaking countries.) ▶ *Since John's investment in the limited corporation is 20 percent, that is also the extent of his liability.*

limited function wholesaler a merchant who takes title to the goods he buys and sells, but who does not perform all of the services performed by a full function wholesaler. ▶ *The principal types of limited function wholesalers are drop shippers, retailer cooperative warehouses, cash-and-carry wholesalers, wagon distributors, rack merchandisers, and assembling wholesalers.*

limited line store a nondepartmentalized store having the bulk of business in a certain broad line of merchandise such as dry goods or groceries. ▶ *Many modern grocery stores have moved away from the limited line store concept, and are now offering many other non-related goods.*

limited partnership an agreement by two or more people to form an enterprise for common gain. (In a *limited partnership*, there is a limit to the liability of at least one of the partners equal to the amount of capital he has invested in the firm.) ▶ *Bill formed a limited partnership with his brother.*

limit(ed price) order an order to buy or sell a security at a stated price or better. ▶ *The broker received a limited price order to buy that security at what would be considered a very low price.*

line executive a high-level manager directly involved in or directly responsible for accomplishing the objectives of an organization. (See also *line officer.*) ▶ *Often, the CEO is a line executive.*

line function an organizational activity directly involved in, or directly responsible for, accomplishing the objectives of the organization. ▶ *The marketing director is responsible for this particular line function.*

line management the administration of activities directly involved in or directly responsible for accomplishing the objectives of the organization. ▶ *As one can guess from the weak financial results, the line management at this company is rather poor.*

line of balance a production control and scheduling technique that graphically illustrates the activities comprising a complex operation. ▶ *Line of balance is used in activities in which time phasing or scheduling is important.*

line of credit a prearranged limit of credit a merchant or bank will give to a customer. ▶ *Our line of credit from that store is $5,000.*

line officer a corporate official directly involved in or directly responsible for accomplishing the objectives of an organization. (See also *line executive.*) ▶ *The person in charge of production is a line officer.*

line printer a device that prints out results from a computer one line at a time—that is to say, very fast. (This is different from a printer that prints a line one character at a time.) ▶ *Our line printer seems to print a little slower than it once did.*

line supervisor one who supervises or oversees production line employees. ▶ *Often, line supervisors are promoted from the employees with whom they formerly worked.*

linear responsibility chart an organizational chart that shows which managers participate, and to what extent, when an activity is planned or a particular decision is made. ▶ *According to the linear responsibility chart, we share almost equally in our participation in company-related activities.*

liquid asset an asset readily convertible into cash. ▶ *A U.S. Treasury bill is a liquid asset.*

liquidation the conversion of assets into cash. ▶ *Generally, liquidation is the compulsory conversion of assets into cash due to an immediate need or at the insistence of creditors; however, liquidation may also occur at the discretion of the owners.*

liquidation value **1.** the price that can be obtained from the sale of assets in liquidation proceedings. ▶ *Unfortunately, the liquidation value of the expensive fur was very low.* **2.** the per share amount to be paid to preferred stockholders upon the liquidation of a corporation. ▶ *The liquidation value of each share is $8.*

liquidity the extent to which a person or a firm has cash or can convert assets into cash quickly. ▶ *A company must have adequate liquidity to operate smoothly on a day-to-day basis.*

liquidity preference   the desire of individuals to hold money or money substitutes versus other forms of assets. ▶ *When interest rates on securities are high, individuals have less desire to hold cash; hence, their liquidity preference for cash is low.*

liquidity ratio   See *acid test ratio.*

lis pendens   "a pending lawsuit." (Latin.) ▶ *Smith v. Jones is lis pendens.*

list price   a published or advertised price subject to trade or cash discounts. ▶ *The list price for this product is $19.95, but I can sell it for $17.95 and still make a good profit.*

listed stock   the stock of a corporation listed for trade on a securities exchange. ▶ *The listed stock for XYZ Company has risen in value.*

lithography   a type of printing performed using a flat surface covered with ink which, when pressed to paper, leaves a printed image. (See also *letter press printing.*) ▶ *Lithography is a common printing process.*

litigant   a party involved in a lawsuit. ▶ *A litigant may be the defendant or the plaintiff.*

litigation   a lawsuit; a legal action. ▶ *Because of the nature of our business, we have been involved in much litigation over the last five years.*

living trust   a trust established by a living person. (See also *voluntary trust.*) ▶ *The living trust established by Alice will benefit the entire family for years.*

living will   a legal document established by a person indicating what steps should be taken with regard to life support systems in the event of a terminal illness or when the individual no longer has control of his or her faculties. ▶ *His living will indicates that if he is in a vegetative state, he does not want life support systems continued past four days.*

Lloyd's of London   an association located in London whose members deal in insurance of various kinds. (Since *Lloyd's of London* is an association and not an insurance company, a Lloyd's policy binds only those members of the association who underwrite the risk on which the insurance is issued.) ▶ *The famous pianist's hands are insured by Lloyd's of London.*

load   the proportion of an investment company's charge for membership, sales commissions, and other costs. ▶ *The ABC Investment Company has a very low load for investors.*

load chart AND **machine loading chart**   a graphic device used in production management for scheduling the activity of a machine. ▶ *The load chart indicates that the T-24 machine will be used 55 hours this week.*

load fund   a mutual fund that is sold for a commission. ▶ *Five percent of the net asset value of the load fund went to the broker as a commission.*

loan shark   an unlicensed moneylender who charges excessive interest. ▶ *A loan shark is viewed as a criminal.*

lobbying the process of attempting to influence legislation. ▶ *Many special interest groups are lobbying legislators to vote for this bill.*

local area network AND **LAN** a series of microcomputers linked within a very limited area. ▶ *In our firm, we are able to send messages to one another through our local area network.*

local rate a rate that applies to transportation moves that are made completely over the line of one carrier without regard to the length of the haul. ▶ *I felt the local rate was priced a little too high.*

lock box system a system whereby a firm's customers mail payments to a post office box, and the payments are then forwarded to the firm. ▶ *A lock box system assumes that payments are credited to accounts in a timely fashion.*

lockout a shutdown of a plant or a place of business by the employer during the course of a labor union dispute, in an attempt to force the union to accept the terms offered by the employer. ▶ *In essence, a lockout is management's version of a strike.*

locus of control place of control; the location of upper management. ▶ *The locus of control is where key decisions are made.*

logo(type) a signature or identifying mark of an enterprise. (It is almost always abbreviated to *logo*. Compare with *brand mark*.) ▶ *A logotype may or may not be trademarked.*

Lombard Street a street in London where the major British financial institutions are located. ▶ *Lombard Street is the British equivalent of Wall Street.*

lonesome pay the compensation paid to individuals who must work extended periods of time alone. ▶ *Forest rangers often receive lonesome pay.*

long having a large holding of a particular security or commodity. ▶ *Because Joy owns three thousand shares, she is long in Hutchins Root Beer.*

long-term debt a debt due after one year or longer. ▶ *All our firm's debts are long-term debts.*

longevity pay a component of salary that is based on length of service with a firm. ▶ *After working here for fifteen years, Paula's longevity pay makes her annual salary $60,000.*

loop a series of instructions performed repeatedly by a computer until a specified condition is satisfied. ▶ *The programmer accidently developed a loop that cannot be exited.*

loophole the ability to circumvent a law or a contractual obligation because of the way the law or the contract is written. ▶ *The potential for a loophole may arise from certain omissions or ambiguities in the law.*

loose standard a period of time in excess of the time required by a qualified worker performing a task with normal skill and effort. ▶ *A loose standard will accommodate workers who may be slightly slower than their coworkers.*

loss **1.** the excess of expenses over income or the excess of cost over profit. ▶ *We have experienced* *a loss in the last three quarters.* **2.** the occurrence of a risk covered by an insurance policy. ▶ *The loss from the hurricane was fully covered by my insurance company.*

loss leader a product offered for sale at a loss in order to attract customers. (The expectation when using a *loss leader* is that once the customers are in the store, they will buy other merchandise in larger quantities, thereby offsetting any loss from the lead item.) ▶ *By using milk as a loss leader, the grocery store hoped to pull customers into the store to buy other items.*

lot a piece of land. ▶ *This lot measures twenty feet by seventy feet.*

lottery a game of chance in which a person pays a small amount of money for an opportunity to win a much larger amount. ▶ *I won $2,000 in the lottery today!*

low balling the pricing of a contract at an extremely low price or cost with the hope of securing the present contract and doing additional or future work. ▶ *Unfortunately, low balling can eat into profits if it is used extensively.*

low end the products or services that are normally priced very low. ▶ *Chewing gum is typical of a low end product.*

low man on the totem pole an individual in an organization who usually has no supervisory responsibilities and little, if any, authority. (Can refer both to men and women.) ▶ *Kelly is always the last to know about new company policies because she is the low man on the totem pole.*

Ltd. See *limited.*

LTL See *less-than-truckload.*

lump-sum payment the settlement of a debt or the receipt of the proceeds of an annuity or insurance policy in one complete payment. ▶ *To end the responsibility of making monthly payments, she made a lump-sum payment to clear her debt.*

luxury good a high-priced, exclusively made good designed to appeal to a customer in the highest income category. ▶ *A fur coat is an example of a luxury good.*

luxury market the consumers in the highest income category. ▶ *A very minute percentage of people make up the luxury market, but they have a lot of money to spend.*

luxury tax a tax on goods and services that are not considered necessities. ▶ *There is a luxury tax on the purchase of jewelry, fur coats, and French perfume.*

M

M1 the basic money supply. ▶ *M1 is made up of demand deposits and circulating currency.*

M2 the money supply equal to *M1* plus time deposits in commercial banks. ▶ *M2 does not include large certificates of deposits.*

M3 the money supply equal to *M2* plus deposits in savings and loan institutions and mutual savings banks. ▶ *M3 does not include certificates of deposits of $100,000 or more.*

Machiavellian manipulative. (Used to characterize a person's management style. Named for Niccolo Machiavelli who postulated that the end justifies the means in politics.) ▶ *John is very deceiving and more interested in getting ahead than in the morality of his methods; he is very Machiavellian.*

machine language a programming language designed for interpretation and use by a computer without translation. ▶ *BASIC and FORTRAN are examples of machine languages.*

machine loading chart See *load chart.*

machine tool a powered device, usually stationary, used in performing work on materials. ▶ *We had to replace the firm's expensive machine tools after the fire.*

macroeconomics the study and analysis of an economic system as a whole. ▶ *Macroeconomics investigates the influence of the demand for and the supply of money on prices, employment, interest, and productive output for a nation as a whole.*

made to order produced to certain specifications. ▶ *This suit I am wearing fits me perfectly; it was made to order.*

Madison Avenue AND **advertising alley** a street in New York where many of the largest and best-known advertising agencies in the United States are located. (The second term is slang.) ▶ *Our company's Madison Avenue ad agency has been a blessing for sales.*

magnaflux method a method for detecting minute defects or flaws in a manufactured part or product of a ferrous nature. ▶ *With the magnaflux method, the product being tested is magnetized and immersed in a solution containing iron filings or a similar material that adheres to the product along any crack or irregularity and interrupts the magnetic field, thus revealing the flaw.*

magnetic disk a data processing storage device on which information is recorded on the magnetizable surface of a circular plate. ▶ *The hard disk in a computer is a type of magnetic disk.*

magnetic ink character recognition AND **MICR** a specially designed group of numbers and symbols printed in magnetic ink in a designated location along the bottom edge of a check or other document. ▶ *Numbers and symbols are electronically sensed by machines designed to process MICR encoded documents.*

magnetic tape a tape or ribbon coated with magnetic material on which data may be recorded magnetically. ▶ *We have the office temperature regulated so as not to harm the magnetic tape.*

mail fraud the illegal deception of consumers through the mail. ▶ *That company committed mail fraud when it asked me to send*

$20.00 to get their product, when, in fact, they simply took my money and moved, without sending the product.

mail order house a firm that sells from catalogs mailed to prospective customers who receive their orders by mail. ▶ *The 1980s saw a boom in mail order houses.*

mailbox rule an acceptance of an offer that occurs when the acceptance is mailed. ▶ *The mailbox rule means that when I send in an order form with a check, an acceptance of the offer has been made as soon as it is in the mail, not when the order is received.*

mailing list a list of organizations or individuals, usually customers or prospective customers, to whom announcements, brochures, advertisements, etc., are mailed. ▶ *A mailing list may be broken down into categories such as age, income, profession, etc.*

mainframe computer a large computer able to handle many computer jobs at once. (Today's minicomputers and some microcomputers can easily handle more work than the early *mainframe computers.*) ▶ *A mainframe computer is larger than a minicomputer or microcomputer.*

main memory the internal memory of a computer. ▶ *The main memory holds more information than a floppy disk.*

maintenance the function of keeping equipment or facilities in good operating condition. (Maintenance is generally divided into two categories: (1) *preventive maintenance,* which is performed on a regularly scheduled basis to prevent or reduce breakdowns during periods of production, and (2) *corrective maintenance,* which places equipment or facilities back in working order after breakdowns or malfunctions have occurred.) ▶ *Our maintenance costs are quite high, but we have few malfunctions.*

maintenance department that department or function within an organization charged with the responsibility of keeping equipment and facilities in good working order. ▶ *The maintenance department has done a superb job of keeping the turret lathes operating.*

maintenance fee a charge by a bank for maintaining an account. ▶ *A maintenance fee may be charged by a bank regardless of the account balance.*

maintenance of membership a clause in a collective bargaining agreement that requires workers who were union members at the time the agreement was signed to remain members for the duration of the contract. ▶ *A maintenance of membership clause usually allows an escape period of fifteen to thirty days for workers to leave a union before the agreement becomes effective.*

major medical a type of insurance covering medical expenses up to a certain dollar figure, usually after a deductible. ▶ *Major medical often pays as much as 80% of medical costs above a predetermined amount.*

majority shareholder a shareholder who controls more than 50 percent of the outstanding shares of a corporation. ▶ *Because Brian owns 51% of the shares, he is a majority shareholder of this firm.*

makeready time the time required to set up and prepare machines and other facilities before starting production. ▶ *The H-155 machine has a makeready time of approximately one hour.*

make-up pay the wages paid to piece rate workers for the difference between actual earnings and minimum wages. ▶ *Make-up pay is a rare form of compensation.*

make work the creating of jobs for the sake of employment. ▶ *Make work involves creating jobs which have no value to an organization.*

maker See *drawer.*

malfeasance the performance of an act that the doer has no right to perform or has contractually agreed not to perform. (See also *misfeasance.*) ▶ *Continuing to operate that part of his business is blatant malfeasance on Howard's part.*

malingerer one who pretends to be ill or disabled in order to continue to receive disability benefits or to get time off from work or from work responsibilities. ▶ *I believe John is a malingerer because, though he is getting disability benefits for his injuries, I saw him moving furniture, jogging, and playing tennis.*

malingering the act of pretending to be ill or disabled in order to continue to receive disability benefits or to get time off from work or from work responsibilities.

Malingering has never been a serious problem with our company's employees.

man-hour   a unit for measuring work done by a single human being. ▶ *A man-hour is equivalent to one employee working at a normal pace for sixty minutes.*

man-machine chart   See *multiple activity chart.*

management   **1.** the art and science of planning, organizing, directing, and controlling the work of others to achieve defined objectives. ▶ *Good management permits a company to be profitable.* **2.** the process of decision making and leadership. ▶ *The management of employees at this company is to be commended.* **3.** that group of people within an organization having decision-making or supervisory responsibilities. ▶ *According to management, everyone will have to work next Saturday.*

management audit   a comprehensive analysis of an organization's structure, plans, policies, procedures, financial controls, methods of operation, and its utilization of human and physical resources and facilities. ▶ *A management audit is necessary before we hire any more employees.*

management by exception   the providing of information to supervisors in which only significant variations from plans are reported or reviewed for corrective action. ▶ *Because Jimmy did not tell his boss during the weekly meeting about the trivial conflicts going on in his department, Jimmy was practicing management by exception.*

management by objectives   the process of setting goals and designing and implementing courses of action in order to reach those goals. ▶ *In a management by objectives system, actual results are compared periodically with expected accomplishments and corrective action taken or new goals set where necessary.*

management by walking around AND **MBWA**   a management technique emphasizing interpersonal contact with employees. ▶ *The owner of a restaurant chain who visits every restaurant in the chain is practicing management by walking around.*

management development   the process of, or techniques for, increasing the skill, competence, and performance of individual managers. ▶ *Some of the best known techniques of management development are job rotation, seminars, conferences, role-playing, and business games.*

management engineer   an individual performing functions similar to an *industrial engineer,* but primarily in an administrative capacity rather than a manufacturing one. ▶ *Management engineers focus on systems and structures involving humans.*

management game   a simulation used to train managers. ▶ *To see how the new managers would react to certain situations, we played a management game.*

management rights   the prerogatives of an employer to take certain action without consulting the union. ▶ *Taking that action was* *within the company's management rights.*

management science the application of the scientific method to problem solving with the goal of providing a quantitative basis for choosing a solution. ▶ *Management science can provide guidance in setting the major policies of a firm.*

management style the approach to leadership that a manager takes. ▶ *Her management style is one that attempts to get input from all employees before decisions are made.*

manager the one who directs or oversees the activities of others. ▶ *The department manager is never late for work.*

managerial accounting an accounting system that uses financial records to help make business decisions. ▶ *Managerial accounting provides information to managers as opposed to financial accounting which provides information to stockholders.*

managerial grid a training method developed by Robert R. Blake and Jane S. Mouton for improving management performance. ▶ *The managerial grid identifies five organizational styles based on two key variables: concern for production and concern for people.*

managerial know-how the ability and knowledge needed to become a manager. ▶ *I don't believe Brian has the managerial know-how to lead his employees effectively.*

mandamus a writ issued by a higher state court to a lesser court, or

peace officer, or corporation, commanding it to perform a certain act. ▶ *A court order to pay back wages is an example of mandamus.*

manifest a shipping document that lists the value, item count, points of origin, designation, and other pertinent information concerning the cargo shipped on a marine vessel—as well as the names of any passengers. ▶ *The manifest will help us determine if the equipment was really on that ship.*

manit a contraction for man-minute—meaning minutes per man. (Refers both to men and women.) ▶ *A manit is equivalent to one employee working at a normal pace for sixty seconds.*

manit system a wage incentive plan that measures work in terms of *manits*. ▶ *In a manit system, incentive pay is awarded for production in excess of a certain number of man-minutes per hour.*

mannequin a life-sized representation of the human body or some part of it used for displaying clothing. ▶ *Modern mannequins are very lifelike.*

manning table a tabular representation of the number of workers by types of positions needed in a work center at various workload volumes. (Refers both to men and women.) ▶ *The manning table indicates we need eight workers to perform a task of this size.*

manpower 1. the available *labor force* in an area. (Refers both to men and women.) ▶ *The manpower in this region is demographically diverse.* 2. all workers, employees as well as managers, in an organization. (Refers both to men and women.) ▶ *Our manpower does not seem as enthusiastic about the firm as last year.*

manpower planning   the process of determining future *manpower* requirements, developing programs to assure a sufficient supply of *manpower,* and utilizing effectively the *manpower* resources of a nation or an organization. (Refers both to men and women.) ▶ *Adequate and effective manpower planning is necessary to run an operation efficiently.*

manpower standard   the number of workers required to process the total workload of a given work center. (Refers both to men and women.) ▶ *For this project, the manpower standard is ten.*

manufacturer's agent   an independent individual who represents one or two manufacturers in a specific marketing area. ▶ *A manufacturer's agent differs from a broker in that the relationship with a manufacturer's agent is continuous rather than intermittent.*

manufacturer's brand   a product brand sponsored by one or more manufacturers. ▶ *A manufacturer's brand product is comparable in quality to a well known brand product.*

manufacturer's representative   See the following entry.

manufacturer's salesperson AND **manufacturer's representative**   a person who is employed by and represents a manufacturer for the purpose of selling goods. ▶ *Because*

Sally sells for ABC Manufacturing, she is a manufacturer's salesperson.

manufacturer's suggested retail price AND **MSRP**   the price at which a manufacturer proposes that a retailer sell a product. ▶ *A manufacturer's suggested retail price is a proposed price because the retailer is not obliged to charge that price.*

manufacturing costs   the expenses incurred in converting materials into finished goods. ▶ *Manufacturing costs increased 25% over last year.*

manufacturing (process)   the system whereby goods are converted from raw materials to goods suitable for sale. ▶ *The manufacturing process in our firm takes two weeks to complete.*

MAPI Capital Expenditure Analysis   a method of evaluating capital expenditures and replacement projects. (This approach, developed by the Machinery and Allied Products Institute, projects into the future such factors as deterioration and obsolescence and considers the impact of the expenditure on revenue and operating costs.) ▶ *MAPI Capital Expenditure Analysis attempts to highlight the future advantages of the expenditure and the rate of return on capital resulting from the investment.*

margin   **1.** gross profit. ▶ *Our margin is shrinking.* **2.** the down payment on securities paid by a purchaser buying on credit. ▶ *In the commodities market, margin is a deposit.*

margin call   a stockbroker's request for more collateral or cash. (If securities are pledged as collateral for a loan and the market value of the securities declines so that *margin requirements* are not met, the financing institution will request more margin from the borrower, who will have to pledge more securities as collateral or pay off part of the loan.) ▶ *Fred got a margin call that took most of his cash.*

margin of profit   See *profit margin.*

margin requirement   the amount of money a bank or broker can lend toward the purchase of stocks or bonds. (The control of the *margin requirement* is in the hands of the *Federal Reserve Board* under authority of the *Securities Exchange Act of 1934.*) ▶ *Low margin requirements promote speculation.*

marginal cost AND **differential cost**   the incremental increase in total cost resulting from the production of one additional unit of output. ▶ *The marginal cost will decline with each successive unit with this new piece of equipment.*

marginal product   the incremental increase in total product resulting from the addition of a single unit of a factor of production. ▶ *The changes did not produce the desired change in marginal product and were therefore revoked.*

marginal productivity   the ability of one additional unit of a factor of production to increase the total product. ▶ *Adding one hour of labor time will increase marginal productivity by one unit.*

marginal revenue AND **incremental revenue**   the incremental increase in total revenue resulting from the sale of one additional unit of output. ▶ *Marginal revenue increased at year end because of seasonal factors.*

marginal utility   the added usefulness supplied by one additional unit of a factor of production. ▶ *The consultant argued against trying to increase the marginal utility of our products during the recession.*

marine insurance   the insurance on property, including vessels and their contents, transported on the high seas. ▶ *Since we will be shipping our products by ship, we'll need marine insurance.*

maritime contract   an agreement that pertains to transportation of goods by sea or to the employment of seamen. ▶ *A maritime contract is necessary for this shipment.*

markdown   a reduction in the price of goods below their normal selling price. ▶ *These goods are out of style so we'll need a markdown to get rid of them.*

markup   the amount added to the cost of goods to determine their selling price. ▶ *A 50% markup on our products means that items we buy for $10, we sell for $15.*

market   **1.** to sell. ▶ *We'll use radio, television, and print media to market our services.* **2.** a place where goods or services are sold; a setting where securities are bought, sold, or traded. ▶ *We'll take the vegetables to the farmer's market to try to make some money.* **3.** the present or potential buyers of goods or services. ▶ *The market for horse-drawn wagons has decreased dramatically.*

market basket a specific group of goods used to determine price changes for consumer goods. ▶ *A market basket is used to calculate the Consumer Price Index.*

market concentration the degree to which present and potential customers are located in a given market area. ▶ *The market concentration for soft drinks is very high in this area.*

market economy an economic system that allows *market forces* to dictate prices and quantities of goods produced. ▶ *Market forces allocate resources in a market economy.*

market forces the factors that drive or propel a market. ▶ *Competition is an example of a market force.*

market index any of several index numbers that measure the trend of prices on the stock market. ▶ *The stock market index has risen sharply this week.*

market order an order to buy or sell shares of a security. ▶ *A market order seeks to get a good price on the security at the time the order is made.*

market penetration a strategy to increase the *market share* of a firm's products in an existing market. ▶ *Market penetration may involve enticing customers to make a switch from a competitor.*

market position the relative rank in the marketplace that a firm has in relation to its competitors. ▶ *Our market position has improved since introducing several new services.*

market potential the total possible sales opportunities for all sellers of a good or service within a given period. ▶ *The market potential for this product appears to be good.*

market power the ability possessed by large corporations in concentrated industries to establish prices and by so doing cause all other firms in the industry to adjust their prices. ▶ *American Airlines exerted its market power when it reduced airfares as a matter of policy.*

market price the current or customary price of a good in the marketplace. ▶ *The market price for our top selling product is $2.00.*

market report a listing of the closing prices of securities that are offered on the stock exchange, or the commodities that are traded on a commodity exchange. ▶ *The market report indicated an overall drop in the prices of securities.*

market research the systematic investigation, analysis, and assessment of the market for an existing or proposed product or service. ▶ *Market research should be conducted before a new product is introduced.*

market segmentation the process of dividing a market into subsets based on factors such as age, income, or sex. ▶ *Market segmentation will help us determine the number of female customers over age 35.*

market share the percentage of sales in a certain market that a product or company has. ▶ *Our market share is growing at a rate of 10% every year.*

market standing a firm's rank, usually according to total sales, among all the firms within a particular industry. ▶ *Our market standing is growing every year.*

marketability the ease with which a security can be converted into cash. ▶ *The marketability of this security is not too good.*

marketable securities stocks and bonds that may readily be converted into cash. ▶ *Government securities and commercial paper are examples of marketable securities.*

marketing the movement and distribution of goods, commodities, or services from the point of production to the point of ultimate consumption. (It encompasses all of the following functions: buying, selling, transporting, storing, standardizing and grading, financing, risk bearing, and the flow of information to and from the marketplace.) ▶ *Marketing is a key factor in the success of a product.*

marketing channel See *distribution channel.*

marketing concept the idea that a business enterprise exists to produce goods and services that will satisfy customers. ▶ *Based on the marketing concept, a firm should carefully study its present and potential customers to determine their wants and needs.*

marketing cooperative an association of producers formed for the purpose of marketing products. ▶ *Marketing cooperatives*

are usually found in agricultural communities.

marketing mix the combination of marketing activities utilized by a firm to promote the sale of its products or services. ▶ *An innovative marketing mix may include advertising, sales promotion, and personal selling.*

marketing plan the overall course of action designed by a firm to advertise, promote, and sell its products or services. ▶ *We have a marketing plan for each of our products and an overall marketing plan for our company.*

marketing research the collecting, recording, classifying, and analyzing of information relative to the sale and transfer of goods and services from producer to consumer. ▶ *Marketing research encompasses research on products and services, research on markets, research on sales and distribution methods, and research on advertising.*

marketing strategy the plan by which a company attempts to achieve its marketing objectives. ▶ *Our marketing strategy consists of spending $3 million on advertising, giving free samples, and offering discounts.*

mass communications See *mass media.*

mass marketing the marketing of a product or service to a large number of people. ▶ *McDonald's and Coca-Cola engage in mass marketing.*

mass media AND **mass communications** a widespread means of communication that reaches the general public, including television, radio, newspapers, and magazines. ▶ *The use of mass media is not an efficient way to reach a small audience.*

mass production a method of quantity production characterized by specialization of equipment and labor, long or continuous production runs, a high degree of planning, and integrated utilization of all production factors. ▶ *Automobiles are manufactured using a mass production process.*

mass storage computer data storage, such as a hard disk that contains data and programs. ▶ *A hard disk is the typical device used in mass storage.*

Master Clerical Data AND **MCD** a system of predetermined time standards designed specifically for office and clerical work. ▶ *Master Clerical Data is based on findings from micromotion analysis.*

Master of Business Administration AND **MBA** a graduate degree in business. ▶ *Now that Steven has completed his undergraduate education, he will seek his MBA.*

material control the systematic regulation of the purchase, storage, flow, and sale of raw materials and finished goods. ▶ *Material control is concerned with maintaining proper inventory levels.*

material standards the regulation of raw materials, production items, and finished goods by various checks and comparisons with previously set criteria. ▶ *According to material standards, these raw materials are unacceptable.*

materiality concept a basic accounting principle stating that ac-

countants or auditors should not unduly concern themselves with trivial or insignificant matters, but should concentrate on items that are significant. ▶ *The materiality concept means that one should weigh the amount of time spent discovering a discrepancy against the amount of the discrepancy.*

materials handling the process of moving materials, such as packing, moving, and storing the materials used in manufacturing. ▶ *We need to improve our materials handling so we can move out finished product faster.*

materials management the grouping under a single manager of all management functions related to the material flow cycle. ▶ *Materials management is responsible for the purchase of raw materials, the internal control of production flow, warehousing, shipping, and the distribution of the finished product.*

materials requisition a request to the stockroom to issue materials. ▶ *To continue with production, we'll need a materials requisition for item #0234.*

maternity leave the time off from work allowed female employees to undergo and recuperate from childbirth. ▶ *With a maternity leave, the employee usually retains her employment rights with no loss of seniority.*

mathematical model a mathematical representation of a process, device, system, or concept. ▶ *According to this mathematical model, the process will take approximately ten minutes to complete once it is* *operational.*

matrix the arrangement of data in tabular form. ▶ *A matrix with its rows and columns can help simplify data.*

maturity the state of an obligation that is due. ▶ *When this note reaches maturity, we will see that the proceeds are given to the right party.*

maturity date AND **date of maturity** the date on which an obligation becomes due. ▶ *The date of maturity is December 31.*

maximin a strategy, in decision making under uncertainty, of selecting the maximum of possible minimum payoffs from alternative solutions. ▶ *Maximin is a pessimistic strategy.*

May Day the date in which fixed minimum brokerage commissions ceased to exist in the United States; May 1, 1975. ▶ *With May Day, discount brokerage houses came into being.*

MB See *megabyte.*

MBA See *Master of Business Administration.*

MBWA See *management by walking around.*

MCD See *Master Clerical Data.*

mean the arithmetic average of a group of values. ▶ *Tom, the accountant, quickly determined the mean of the column of figures.*

measure of central tendency any of several statistical measures designed to reveal the tendency for data in a frequency distribution to group themselves around some middle value in the distribution. ▶ *Examples of measures of central*

tendency are mean, median, and mode.

measured daywork an arrangement whereby a worker is paid a certain amount per day or hour and is expected to meet a certain output quota or efficiency standard. ▶ *In measured daywork, if production exceeds or falls below the established quota or standard, the worker still receives the normal hourly or daily rate of pay.*

mechanic's lien a legal and enforceable claim that a person who has performed work on, or furnished materials for, a given asset is permitted to make against the title to the asset in the event of nonpayment. ▶ *Since Susan could not pay for the work done on her car, a mechanic's lien was enforced by the garage.*

median the value which is found at the middle of a series when a group of values has been arranged in sequence from the smallest to the largest. ▶ *In the set (20, 22, 30, 35, 40, 43, 44) the median is 35.*

mediation See *conciliation.*

medium of exchange a commodity which is readily accepted as payment for goods and services, or in settlement of debts, and is recognized as a standard of value. ▶ *The medium of exchange in most transactions is money.*

megabucks a large sum of money. ▶ *Since Laura's promotion, she has been making megabucks.*

megabyte AND **MB** one million bytes of information. ▶ *One megabyte is actually equal to 1,048,576 storage locations.*

member bank a financial institution affiliated with the *Federal Reserve System.* ▶ *Any federally chartered bank in the United States is required to be a member bank.*

member corporation   an incorporated firm that is a member of the *New York Stock Exchange.* ▶ *Our brokerage firm is a member corporation.*

member firm AND **member organization**   a securities firm that belongs to an established stock exchange. ▶ *Under exchange rules, only an employee can be listed as a member firm, not the firm itself.*

member organization   See the previous entry.

memorandum   an informal, written message sent within an organization. ▶ *Tom's memorandum requests that everyone in our department be present at the next monthly meeting.*

memory   the place where data is stored in a computer. ▶ *Now that we have expanded the memory in this computer, we can run more software.*

memory dump   See *core dump.*

mentor   an individual who guides, counsels, and develops another person within an organization. ▶ *To help Susan adjust to her new supervisory position, Janet is serving as her mentor.*

menu   a list of options on a computer screen. ▶ *According to the menu, I can either format a disk, use a word processing program, or run a spreadsheet program.*

mercantile   concerning the buying or the selling of merchandise. ▶ *In the past, many general stores were known as mercantile stores.*

mercantile credit   See *trade credit.*

mercantilism   an economic policy directed toward increasing a nation's wealth and power by encouraging the exportation of goods in return for gold. ▶ *Mercantilism was prevalent in the seventeenth and eighteenth centuries.*

merchandise   commodities or goods that can be bought or sold, especially on the retail level. ▶ *The store shelves overflow with merchandise at Christmas time.*

merchandise control   the techniques, procedures, methods, and systems used to maintain control over a firm's stocks of merchandise. ▶ *Our merchandise control methods are so effective that we have few merchandise losses.*

merchandising   a function of marketing that covers the selection and buying of merchandise for resale, its pricing, marking, advertising, display, and the actual selling effort. ▶ *Finding a good supplier is just one aspect of merchandising.*

merchant banker   a financial institution engaging in investment counseling, investment banking, negotiating mergers, and other services. ▶ *Merchant bankers are basically European-style banks.*

merchant middleman   See the following entry.

merchant wholesaler AND **merchant middleman**   a marketing middleman who actually takes title to the goods being offered for sale. ▶ *A merchant wholesaler normally handles goods that are to be sold to* *retailers.*

merger the joining of two or more corporations into one through the direct acquisition by one of the corporations. ▶ *A merger differs from consolidation in that no new corporation is created.*

merit increase an increase in pay based on exceptional job performance. ▶ *Based on the results of Tim's performance appraisal, he got a 4% merit increase.*

merit rating a process used to evaluate periodically an employee's performance. ▶ *All employees must receive an annual merit rating.*

metered mail mail stamped by a postage meter. ▶ *Metered mail bears stamps printed in ink rather than adhesive stamps.*

methods analysis AND **work simplification** the process of investigating and/or improving the sequence of body motions, the tools, the equipment, and the workstation used or proposed for use, in performing a given task. ▶ *A methods analysis may indicate that we have been inefficient on our assembly line.*

methods analyst an individual who practices *methods analysis.* ▶ *Our management consultant is also an experienced methods analyst.*

methods engineer an engineer who practices *methods engineering.* ▶ *Charlie, who has a degree in engineering, is training to become a methods engineer.*

methods engineering the process of subjecting a given piece of work to close investigation and analysis in order to eliminate unnecessary steps and develop the most ef-

fective and efficient method of performing each step. ▶ *Methods engineering encompasses the improvement and standardization of methods, equipment, and working conditions, the training of workers, the determination of standard times, and frequently, the development of wage incentive plans.*

Methods-Time Measurement AND **MTM** a system of predetermined motion-time standards in which operations are classified by certain basic human body motions. ▶ *In Methods-Time Measurement, time values are assigned according to the type of motion made, the conditions under which the motion is made, and the distance of movement involved.*

metropolitan area a large city and its surrounding area and communities as designated by the U.S. Census Bureau. ▶ *The Dallas metropolitan area includes many suburbs.*

MICR See *magnetic ink character recognition.*

microcomputer a computer using a microprocessor in the central processing unit. ▶ *A microcomputer is usually a desktop computer.*

microfiche a sheet of microfilm containing multiple images in a grid pattern. ▶ *A standard microfiche sheet is 5 by 6 inches and contains 98 images; however, other sizes are also used.*

microfilm a fine-grain, high-resolution film containing images greatly reduced in size from the original. ▶ *Libraries are now placing many documents on microfilm.*

micromotion analysis the process of classifying manual work into fundamental body motions and analyzing these motions to develop more efficient work methods. ▶ *Micromotion analysis typically requires the filming of work operations.*

microsecond one millionth of a second. ▶ *Microseconds can be used to describe electronic measurements.*

middle management the managers above first-line supervisors but below executive level managers in an organization. ▶ *When a company begins looking for jobs to cut, middle management is often the first to go.*

middle management obsolescence the eroding away of middle management's power and usefulness by the computer. ▶ *Many management scholars believe that widespread use of the computer in organizations will result in recentralization of decision-making authority and responsibility, thus producing middle management obsolescence.*

middleman a purveyor of goods who stands between the producer and the ultimate consumer. (The term is applied to males, females, and corporate entities. The plural is **middlemen**.) ▶ *Wholesalers, jobbers, brokers, agents, and retailers are considered to be middlemen.*

midlife crisis a short period of self-examination occurring in individuals during their late thirties and early forties. ▶ *Joe has plateaued in his company and feels he can no longer contribute to it; he must be going through a midlife crisis.*

migrant worker AND **itinerant worker** an individual who moves from place to place to perform work, usually in agriculture. ▶ *A migrant worker is often poorly skilled and poorly educated.*

milestone a point of significant accomplishment. ▶ *The completion of a task is an example of a milestone.*

Miller-Tydings Act of 1937 a Federal act that legalized *resale price maintenance* agreements between the producer of a product and the retailer of that product. ▶ *The Miller-Tydings Act of 1937 is an amendment to the Sherman Act of 1890.*

millisecond one thousandth of a second. ▶ *Some electronic timing devices are able to measure in milliseconds.*

minicomputer an intermediate-sized computer that is larger than a microcomputer but smaller than a mainframe computer. ▶ *Because of improved technology in microcomputers, the minicomputer is becoming less popular.*

minimax the strategy of minimizing one's expected maximum losses. ▶ *Minimax is a strategy used in all types of planning, not just financial planning.*

minimum rate the lowest rate a carrier will charge for any given amount of freight between two points. ▶ *The minimum rate for shipping this load is $2,000.*

minimum wage the lowest hourly rate allowed by the Federal government. ▶ *For many years, the* *minimum wage in the United States was less than $4 per hour.*

Minnesota Multiphasic Personality Inventory AND **MMPI** a personality test, consisting of 550 statements, that attempts to measure hypochondriasis, depression, hysteria, psychopathic deviation, interest, paranoia, and schizophrenia. ▶ *The MMPI covers most of the problem areas of human personality.*

minority interest that portion of the net worth of a subsidiary company relating to shares not owned by the controlling company or other members of the consolidated group. ▶ *Sally has a minority interest in this firm.*

minute book a book in which the minutes of stockholders' meetings or directors' meetings of a corporation are recorded. ▶ *In small companies, the minutes are kept in one minute book, but in large companies two separate books are generally used.*

MIP See *Monthly Investment Plan.*

misbranding false information on a product label. ▶ *Misbranding involves intentionally labeling a product incorrectly as to its size, weight, contents, etc.*

misdemeanor a minor criminal offense. ▶ *He committed a misdemeanor by stealing that $5.00 item.*

misfeasance performing one's legal duty poorly or incorrectly. (See also *malfeasance.*) ▶ *A fiduciary who sells stock well below its market value may be accused of misfeasance.*

mismanagement the act of poorly managing any activities or operations. ▶ *Mismanagement often leads to higher costs.*

misrepresentation an untrue statement, either unintentional or deliberate. ▶ *Telling us that he had hundreds of clients while he actually had only three, is misrepresentation.*

missionary salesperson a salesperson who does not actually sell a firm's products, but instead assists wholesalers and retailers in their efforts to promote and sell the manufacturer's products. ▶ *A missionary salesperson is usually an employee of a large manufacturing firm.*

mixed economy an economic system characterized by a combination of free enterprise, government regulation, and elements of socialism. ▶ *The United States economy resembles a mixed economy.*

mixed surplus retained earnings and elements of paid-in capital or appreciation surplus, or both. (As found in an owner's equity account.) ▶ *An account containing a mixed surplus can be difficult to audit.*

MMPI See *Minnesota Multiphasic Personality Inventory.*

mnemonic code a programming code in which the names of the operations are abbreviated so that they are easy to remember. ▶ *Examples of mnemonic codes are "mpy" for multiply and "acc" for accumulator.*

mock-up a scale or full-sized model of a building, machine, or other device. ▶ *A mock-up is usu-*

ally built for demonstration or testing purposes.

mode a value in a group of values which occurs with the greatest frequency. ▶ *In this set (4, 4, 3, 4, 8, 9, 4), the number 4 is the mode.*

model a representation of reality. ▶ *The official used a model of the airplane to demonstrate what happened in the crash.*

modem a device for linking computer systems through a telephone line. ▶ *To send this document to Alice faster, we can use our modem to send it directly to her computer.*

modified union shop a workplace that has an arrangement whereby employees who were not members of the union as of the effective date of the union contract are not required to join the union. (See also *union shop.*) ▶ *In a modified union shop, all persons hired after the contract date must join the union.*

modularity the ability to expand a system by adding additional units of hardware or software. ▶ *The modularity of this old computer system is not conducive for enhancements.*

Mom and Pop store a small retail store frequently operated by individuals who are immediate family members. ▶ *Rural areas frequently have Mom and Pop grocery stores.*

momentum a sign of acceleration in an economy or a price. ▶ *Things are looking better; the economy now has momentum.*

mommy track a career track for women that involves fewer hours, less pay, and little opportunity for advancement. ▶ *The mommy track is considered by many to be an example of sex discrimination.*

monetarist an economist who places emphasis on the money supply as a means of making changes in the economy. ▶ *The economist, Milton Friedman, is a monetarist.*

monetary damage a sum of money awarded by a court to a defendant in a case. ▶ *Don received $3 million in monetary damages.*

monetary policy the process whereby the Federal Reserve Bank attempts to influence the economy by controlling the supply of money and credit. ▶ *Regulating the economy is the purpose of monetary policy.*

money any generally accepted medium of exchange and unit of value. ▶ *Rocks, gems, and even animals have been used as money.*

money center bank a bank located in one of the major financial centers of the world. ▶ *Money center banks are located in New York, London, Tokyo, and other major cities.*

money illusion the psychological valuation of money without regard to its purchasing power. ▶ *Money illusion often results in the pursuit of money alone and not the pursuit of other things.*

money market the financial institutions that handle the purchase, sale, and transfer of short-term credit instruments. ▶ *The money market handles such instruments as U.S. Treasury bills and certificates of deposit.*

money market fund a mutual fund which invests in short-term securities. ▶ *A money market fund invests in such things as U.S. Treasury bills, certificates of deposit, and government securities.*

money measurement concept an accounting principle that states that only those tangibles that can be measured in money will be reflected on a firm's books and records. ▶ *The value of hiring an individual with an MBA would not be reflected in a company's records under the money measurement concept.*

money multiplier the numerical factor that shows how great an increase will result in income from each increase in investment spending. ▶ *If investment spending increases by $1 billion and the resultant income produced is $2.25 billion, the money multiplier is 2.25.*

money order an instrument purchased in a bank, a post office, or a retail outlet used to send funds by mail. ▶ *The cost of getting a money order is usually very small.*

money supply the amount of money in circulation. ▶ *The money supply includes deposits in savings and checking accounts.*

monochrome monitor a computer monitor capable of displaying only one color. ▶ *A common color for a monochrome monitor is green.*

monopolistic competition a market situation in which there are a limited number of producers. ▶ *In monopolistic competition, producers will influence price more than consumers.*

monopoly a market situation in which a single seller of goods or services controls the supply of goods or services offered. ▶ *In a monopoly, the supplier is able to regulate the price of what is offered for sale.*

monopsony a market situation in which there is only one buyer for a good or service. ▶ *A monopsony is a very rare market condition.*

monte carlo technique a form of simulation that provides experimental, as opposed to theoretical, answers to problems involving the complex interaction of many random events. ▶ *Computers are very helpful when using the monte carlo technique.*

Monthly Investment Plan AND **MIP** a plan for persons who wish to accumulate stocks over a period of time by investing certain dollar amounts on a monthly or quarterly basis. ▶ *The Monthly Investment Plan was established by member firms of the NYSE in 1954.*

Moody's Investors Service a commercial service that provides various financial information about most large American corporations. ▶ *Probably the most famous and most widely used of the Moody's Investor Service series are the publications that give specific information about corporations, municipalities, railroads, and utilities.*

moonlighting the act of holding down a second job. ▶ *When a person is employed full time at company A, but works nights or weekends on a part-time basis for company B in order to earn additional income, that person is said* *to be moonlighting.*

morale   an ethical, mental, or moral condition with respect to satisfaction, cheerfulness, confidence, etc. ▶ *The morale at this firm went down when we laid off 500 workers.*

mortgage   a lien on fixed or movable property given by a borrower to a lender as security for a loan. ▶ *A mortgage is removed when an obligation is paid in full.*

mortgage bond   a bond secured by a mortgage against specific properties of the insurer. ▶ *A mortgage bond may be secured by real estate.*

mortgage company   a firm that loans money to finance the purchase of real property. ▶ *A mortgage company makes loans on real property based on the appraised value of the property.*

mortgage debt   a financial obligation secured by a mortgage. ▶ *A mortgage debt is basically money owed under a mortgage.*

most favored nation status   a promise extending the best trade privileges to a particular nation. ▶ *Developing countries seek a most favored nation status with the U.S.*

motion analysis   See the following entry.

motion study AND **motion analysis** the analysis of body member movements used in performing an operation or task. ▶ *The purposes of motion study are to identify and eliminate inefficient or wasteful motions and to establish the best possible sequence of motions.*

Motion-Time Analysis AND **MTA** a system of predetermined elemental times used for describing and recording the time spent on the basic motions of a task. ▶ *Motion-Time Analysis is derived from the study of basic human motions.*

motivation   the willingness to exert effort to accomplish something. ▶ *To do this particular task, the employees are going to need a lot of motivation.*

motivation research   the investigation and study of human behavior to determine why individuals behave as they do. ▶ *Motivation research is frequently used by advertisers to find out why people buy certain things.*

Mountain Daylight Time   the adjusted time in the Rocky Mountain region of the United States from early April to late October. ▶ *Mountain Daylight Time is six hours behind Greenwich Time.*

Mountain Standard Time   the time in the Rocky Mountain region of the United States from late October to early April. ▶ *Mountain Standard Time is seven hours behind Greenwich Time.*

mouse   a device with a rolling ball used for inputting information into a computer. ▶ *Typically, a mouse is connected to a keyboard with a wire, but new technology has brought about the wireless mouse.*

moving average   a measure of central tendency in which the arithmetic mean of a consecutive number of values is taken, then the first value is discarded and the next of the remaining values in the series is included. (The *mean* of this new group is taken, and so on, with the number of values in each group always remaining the same.) ▶ *A moving average is often calculated for a security.*

moving expense   the cost incurred in moving a household, office, or manufacturing concern from one location to another. ▶ *The moving expense for relocating our offices from New York to Dallas were very high.*

MSRP   See *manufacturer's suggested retail price.*

MTM   See *Methods-Time Measurement.*

multi-employer bargaining   a form of collective bargaining in which more than one employer participates in negotiations with a union. ▶ *Multi-employer bargaining is frequently used in the construction and clothing manufacturing industries.*

multilateral agreement   an agreement among several parties. ▶ *We reached a multilateral agreement with the other tenants about space usage in the warehouse.*

multimedia   the use of two or more forms of media. ▶ *Marketing promotions often use a multimedia approach consisting of television, radio, and print.*

multinational corporation   a company with facilities in more than one country or which does business in more than one country. ▶ *With production plants in Mexico, England, and the United States, this company is definitely a multinational corporation.*

multiple activity chart AND **man-machine chart**   a graphic representation of operations performed by one worker and one machine, one worker and several machines, several workers and several machines, or several workers. ▶ *As a methods analysis device, the primary purpose of a multiple activity chart is to assist in identifying idle time on the part of a worker or a machine.*

multiple listing   an agreement between real estate brokers to provide information about real estate listings to one another. (All cooperating brokers share the listings and have an equal chance at a sale.) ▶ *With a multiple listing, the listing broker and the selling broker split the commission.*

multiple regression analysis   a statistical technique for measuring the change in one variable caused by changes in two or more related variables. ▶ *Multiple regression analysis involves one dependent variable and two or more independent variables.*

multiplex   the process of transferring data from several storage devices operating at relatively low transfer rates to one storage device operating at a high transfer rate. ▶ *In a multiplex, the high speed device is not obliged to wait for the low speed device.*

multiplier   the ratio of the change in national income to a change in investment. ▶ *The multiplier changes as the economy changes.*

multiprocessing   the simultaneous or interwoven execution of two or more programs or sequences of instruction by a computer or a computer network. ▶ *Multiprocessing* *is often used in airlines and car rental reservation systems.*

multiprogramming   the technique of handling numerous computer routines or programs simultaneously by means of an interweaving process. ▶ *Multiprogramming allows several programs to be stored in one CPU at the same time.*

municipal bond   a bond issued by a state or municipality. ▶ *Municipal bonds carry a lower rate of interest than other bonds.*

Murphy's Law   the notion that if anything can go wrong, it will go wrong. ▶ *Murphy's Law was developed by Ed Murphy, a developmental engineer.*

mutual fund   an investment company that buys and sells its capital stock continuously. ▶ *A mutual fund company provides investment services for its stockholders.*

mutual savings bank   a bank without capital stock, owned by its depositors and managed for them by a self-perpetuating board of trustees. ▶ *Profits from the operation of a mutual savings bank are distributed to the depositors in the form of dividends or are added to the reserve surplus of the bank for greater security of the depositors.*

Muzak   the trade name for soft background music played in offices and stores. ▶ *Muzak often blends in with other background sounds in such a way that many people are unaware that the system is actually in operation.*

mystery shopping AND **phantom shopping**   an activity where individuals are hired to act as customers in order to evaluate quality of service, cleanliness of facility, pricing, etc. ▶ *With mystery shopping, the "secret customers" never identify themselves; the staff never knows the shoppers are there.*

N

naked option AND **uncovered option** an *option sale* in which neither the buyer nor the seller owns the underlying security. ▶ *Writing naked options is a risky way to make money.*

nanosecond one billionth of a second. ▶ *A nanosecond is very difficult for the human mind to comprehend.*

narrow market See *thin market.*

NASD See *National Association of Securities Dealers.*

NASDAQ See *National Association of Securities Dealers Automated Quotations.*

National Association of Securities Dealers AND **NASD** an organization that regulates the over-the-counter markets under the supervision of the *Securities and Exchange Commission.* ▶ *The NASD is a nonprofit organization* formed by the Investment Bankers Conference, Inc. and the Securities and Exchange Commission.

National Association of Securities Dealers Automated Quotations AND **NASDAQ** a system that provides price quotes on over-the-counter securities not listed on the *New York Stock Exchange.* ▶ *NASDAQ is a subsidiary of the National Association of Securities Dealers.*

national bank a banking institution chartered by the United States government to conduct a general commercial banking business. ▶ *A national bank must have the word "national" in its corporate title or the letters "NBA" or "NA" (national banking association or national association) following its name.*

national debt the total indebtedness of a national government. ▶ *The U.S. national debt is increasing every year.*

National Industrial Conference Board a fact-finding organization that conducts research and publishes studies on business, economics, and management. ▶ *Membership in the National Industrial Conference Board is composed of business organizations, trade associations, government agencies, labor unions, colleges and universities, and individuals.*

National Labor Relations Board AND **NLRB** an agency that conducts elections to determine collective bargaining units, and investigates and resolves unfair labor practices, etc. ▶ *The National Labor Relations Board was established under the Wagner Act of 1935 and continued under the Taft-Hartley Act of 1947.*

national savings market the total of all savings and time deposits of individuals, partnerships, or corporations. ▶ *The national savings market includes commercial banks; deposits in mutual savings banks; deposits, shares, and investment certificates in savings and loan associations and credit unions; individual holdings of U.S. savings bonds at current redemption values; and life insurance reserves.*

nationalism the policy of asserting national interests, viewed as separate from the interests of other nations or the world as a whole. ▶ *In times of war, nationalism runs high.*

nationalization the process of a country taking over private industry. ▶ *With nationalization, there is no guarantee that the former owners of the industry will be paid for any assets appropriated.*

natural resources raw materials and wildlife available in nature for human use. ▶ *Minerals, forests, waters, and fish are natural resources.*

NCR paper a type of paper having chemical coating on the reverse side that produces an image on a second piece of paper as the original paper is written or typed on. (*NCR* stands for *no carbon required*.) ▶ *Credit card receipts that do not have carbon paper use NCR paper.*

near money an asset such as a savings account or a government bond that can be converted very quickly into money. ▶ *Near money helps ensure liquidity.*

necessities goods or services essential for the maintenance of life, or which through custom, are considered indispensable for the maintenance of a certain standard of living. ▶ *Food, clothing, and shelter are necessities.*

needs analysis a process of determining what training is necessary for employees or new hires. ▶ *In the needs analysis we conducted, we found that our company should have interpersonal communication training for all employees, including the president.*

negative leadership AND **negative motivation** the direction and motivation of people by means of penalties or threats of penalties. ▶ *Negative leadership does not usually result in high employee morale.*

negative motivation See the previous entry.

negotiable transferable, cashable, or exchangeable by endorsement and delivery or by delivery only. ▶ *The check was not negotiable because it was not endorsed.*

nepotism the practice of granting employment or other favors to members of one's family. ▶ *Because all of the vice presidents are related to the president of this firm, I suspect that a high degree of nepotism is involved here.*

nest egg money or other assets set aside for the future. ▶ *Fred is building a nest egg for his retirement.*

net asset value **1.** in an investment company, the market value of all assets less all liabilities. ▶ *The net asset value is usually divided by the number of shares of stock outstanding to show net asset value per share.* **2.** the excess of book value of assets over liabilities to outsiders. ▶ *Net asset value is net worth.*

net avails the net proceeds of a discounted note. ▶ *The net avails on this $1,000 note are $950.*

net change the difference in value or magnitude of an item from one time period to another. ▶ *The net change in stocks from day to day is often found in the business section of the daily newspaper.*

net income the difference between total revenues and total expenses. ▶ *With our emphasis on reducing expenses, our net income shows signs of improvement.*

net national product the market value of a country's output of goods and services produced within in a given period of time, less the capital consumed in producing those goods and services. ▶ *Net national product is a measure of productivity.*

net operating loss a condition that occurs when allowable deductions are greater than gross income. ▶ *The Internal Revenue Service has specific procedures regarding the reporting of a net operating loss.*

net position the difference between the long and short contracts held by a trader or speculator. ▶ *Net position indicates how much a person will gain or lose by a change in stock value.*

net present value the expected cash flow of an investment. ▶ *An investor can determine if an investment will produce sufficient income by calculating its net present value.*

net proceeds the net amount of money received from a transaction after a deduction of certain expenses. ▶ *The net proceeds from this sale is $200,000.*

net profit the profit remaining after deducting related costs from revenue. ▶ *With the reduction in operating costs, net profit shows signs of improving this quarter.*

net sales the total sales of a business enterprise less returned sales, allowances, and discounts. ▶ *The figure for net sales confirms our suspicion that this company is in trouble.*

net working capital the difference between a firm's current assets and current liabilities. ▶ *If the current assets equal $100,000 and current liabilities equal*

$60,000, then net working capital is $40,000.

net worth   total assets minus total liabilities. (See also *owner's equity*.) ▶ *Joan's income was high but her net worth was low because of all her debts.*

network analysis   a means of recognizing and identifying the relationships between the parts in a system and expressing them in chart form. ▶ *Network analysis is generally concerned with identifying time relationships in a system so that the most effective use of resources can be made in completing a project.*

networking   an attempt to gain extra business through professional contacts. ▶ *Networking is a legitimate way to get new clients or customers.*

neutral monetary system   a system in which money is convertible into commodities at a fixed price. ▶ *A neutral monetary system involves commodities at a nonfluctuating price.*

new hire   a new employee. ▶ *Bob will need a lot of training since he is a new hire.*

new issue   a security that is offered on the market for the first time. ▶ *I'm a little hesitant to purchase this new issue.*

New York Stock Exchange AND **NYSE**   a stock exchange established in 1792 and located in New York City. ▶ *The NYSE is the largest stock exchange in the United States.*

niche   the particular area in a market in which a firm specializes. ▶ *Our niche is consulting only with small businesses having annual sales under $1 million.*

night depository   a small vault located on the inside of a bank but accessible from the outside permitting bank customers to deposit their day's receipts in the bank after regular business hours. ▶ *John opened the door of the night depository and dropped the bag of cash down the chute.*

ninety-day letter   a notice from the *Internal Revenue Service* indicating nonpayment of taxes. ▶ *As the name suggests, a ninety-day letter means within ninety days a taxpayer must either pay the taxes as indicated or challenge the letter in a tax court.*

NLRB   See *National Labor Relations Board.*

no-load fund   a type of mutual fund or investment trust that charges no commission on sales but may charge a management fee. ▶ *I like the hassle-free aspects of a no-load fund.*

no par stock   a stock that has not been assigned a nominal value by the issuing corporation. ▶ *No par stock has no face value.*

no protest AND **NP**   an instruction by one bank to another not to protest an item for nonpayment. (Evidenced by a stamped impression on the face of the item by a qualified endorser, the words "no protest" or the letters "NP" waive notice of nonpayment.) ▶ *With no protest, if an item cannot be collected, the collecting bank will simply return the item without protesting it.*

no-strike clause   a provision in a

collective bargaining contract whereby the union agrees not to strike during the period of the contract, provided the employer meets the terms and conditions stipulated in the contract. ▶ *Without the no-strike clause in the contract, the part of the bargaining process we are in now could be very difficult.*

nolo contendere "I do not want to contend." (Latin. A plea by the accused in a criminal case indicating that the defendant does not wish to contest the case.) ▶ *With a nolo contendere, he implicitly consented to a finding of conviction without expressing any guilt.*

nominal in name only, minimal. ▶ *The court charged the company with a nominal fine: one dollar.*

nominal yield AND **coupon rate** the actual rate of interest of a bond expressed as a percentage of principal amount. ▶ *The nominal yield of the bond was too low.*

nomograph a graphic device for portraying and finding the relationships among several variables. ▶ *The nomograph indicates a direct relationship between the four variables we were concerned about.*

non-current assets assets other than current assets. ▶ *Fixed assets are non-current assets.*

nonforfeiting policy an insurance policy that provides the policyholder with three options if premiums are discontinued: (1) taking the cash value of the policy, (2) purchasing extended term insurance, (3) purchasing a reduced value paid-up policy. ▶ *Under my nonforfeiting policy, I'm taking*

the cash value of the policy.

non-par item a check that cannot be collected at the par or face value when presented to the drawee bank. ▶ *With a non-par item, the drawee bank will deduct an exchange charge from the face value of the item before remitting payment to the collecting bank.*

non-price competition a form of competition between companies who charge identical or very similar prices for their goods or services. ▶ *Companies engaging in non-price competition must usually focus on customer service, cleanliness of facility, etc., in order to influence customers.*

non-programmed decision a decision reached in a nonroutine or unique situation. (The conditions or circumstances surrounding the situation are such that the decision-making process cannot be routinized.) ▶ *Because of our unusual situation, a non-programmed decision was required.*

non-union labor the labor or personnel in a company that is not organized in a union. ▶ *White-collar employees are typically non-union labor.*

non-voting stock a share of stock that is issued by a corporation with no provision to allow the holder of the stock to vote at corporate meetings. ▶ *Unfortunately, I am not allowed to participate in the vote because my stock is non-voting stock.*

nonconforming goods items that do not meet contract specifications or standards. ▶ *I cannot accept this last shipment because all the* *items are nonconforming goods.*

nonconforming use a continuation of a certain use of land that, due to zoning, is no longer permitted. ▶ *Our garage is closer to the property line than it could be if it were built today. It is an example of nonconforming use.*

noncontributory retirement plan a pension plan in which all monetary contributions are made by the employer and none are made by the employee. ▶ *Frank chose that particular firm to work for because they have a noncontributory retirement plan.*

noncumulative preferred stock preferred stock that has no right to unpaid or undeclared dividends of years past, but has only a claim to dividends declared during the current year. ▶ *With noncumulative preferred stock, if a dividend is passed in any year, it does not have to be made up at a later date.*

noncupative will See *nuncupative will.*

nondirective interview a form of interview in which the interviewee is given considerable latitude in determining the topics to be discussed. (Rather than asking direct questions, in a *nondirective interview,* the interviewer attempts to reflect the feelings of the interviewee by restating or repeating key words or phrases, thereby eliciting detailed information concerning the interviewee's emotional reactions, attitudes, and opinions.) ▶ *An interviewer needs special training to conduct a nondirective interview.*

nondurable good a good with a relatively short life span. ▶ *Bread is an example of a nondurable good.*

nonfeasance the failure to perform a required act. ▶ *A fiduciary who does not submit an annual report is committing an act of nonfeasance.*

nonmember bank a state chartered commercial bank that does not belong to the Federal Reserve System. ▶ *A nonmember bank is rare in the United States today.*

nonmember firm a brokerage firm that is not a member of an organized exchange. ▶ *I seem to have better results when working through a nonmember firm.*

nonparticipating policy an insurance policy that does not give the insured the right to receive dividends from company profits. ▶ *The insurance Tom purchased is a nonparticipating policy.*

nonproduction bonus a payment given to workers based on something other than performance or productivity. ▶ *Because our firm made $3 million more than expected, company officials decided to divide $2 million of it up among all of the workers as a nonproduction bonus.*

nonprofit corporation a corporation that is not allowed to earn a profit and does not have stockholders. ▶ *A nonprofit corporation is usually fiduciary in nature and is formed for a specific purpose.*

norm the *mean* or *median* value of a group of values. ▶ *Age 42 is the norm for the employees in the accounting department.*

normal curve AND **bell-shaped**

curve; Gaussian distribution; normal distribution a symmetrical curve around the arithmetic mean resembling a bell. ▶ *The figures plotted out into a normal curve.*

normal distribution See the previous entry.

normal pace a work rate that can easily be maintained day in and day out by a worker without undue physical or mental fatigue. ▶ *Walking three miles per hour over a level plane is considered a normal pace.*

normal price an expected price for a market. ▶ *The normal price of goods can be affected by sudden shortages of raw materials.*

normal profit a profit adequate enough to maintain a firm's existence over the long term. ▶ *The normal profit on this item is $1.*

normal time See *level time.*

Norris-LaGuardia Act of 1932 a Federal act expressly forbidding the enforcement of *yellow-dog contracts* by the courts and the use of the injunction in cases where damage might ensue. ▶ *The Norris-LaGuardia Act of 1932 was overshadowed by the Wagner Act of 1935.*

notary public a person appointed by a state for a stipulated period of time to administer oaths, attest to and certify documents, take affidavits and depositions, and protest negotiable instruments for nonpayment or nonacceptance. ▶ *A notary public usually places a seal on a document and signs the document as a witness.*

note receivable a written promise to pay a specified sum of money, usually on a specified date or at a specified time, and at a specified rate of interest. ▶ *A note receivable is an asset to the party issuing it and a liability to the party that has to pay it.*

notice of dishonor a notice advising all parties to a negotiable instrument that the instrument has been dishonored, and putting all parties on notice that the holder in due course can look to these parties to meet their obligations. ▶ *A notice of dishonor may be oral or written.*

novation an agreement replacing an original party to a contract by a new party. (Such an agreement requires the consent of the original party as well as the new party.) ▶ *Novation transfers both rights and duties, as stipulated in the contract, to the new party.*

NOW account an interest bearing account similar to a checking account. (*NOW* is an acronym for *negotiable order of withdrawal.* See also *super NOW account.*) ▶ *I opened a NOW account in order to earn some interest on my money.*

NP See *no protest.*

null and void not legally enforceable. ▶ *Because he was asking me to do something illegal, I declared the contract null and void.*

numbered account an account in a non-U.S. bank in which the account is known only by a number and not by an individual's or a business's name. ▶ *A numbered account is frequently used when someone wants to hide money.*

numerically controlled machine a machine tool that is operated and

O

obligation a responsibility agreed to or imposed by law, contract, or social relationship. ▶ *He has an obligation to pay me $100, as we agreed.*

obsolescence the state of becoming obsolete, passing out of use, or becoming out of date. ▶ *Phonograph records are in a state of obsolescence.*

occupational hazard a condition in a workplace posing some danger to workers. ▶ *A slippery floor in a meat processing plant is an occupational hazard.*

Occupational Safety and Health Administration AND **OSHA** the organization that maintains safety and health standards in work environments, investigates violations of safety and health regulations, and sets penalties. ▶ *OSHA was established in 1970 under the jurisdiction of the Department of Labor.*

odd lot a transaction of less than the normal unit. ▶ *The ordinary trading unit for actively traded stocks is 100 shares; any trade involving fewer than 100 shares is an odd lot trade under normal circumstances.*

odd lot dealer a stockbroker who buys *round lots* and sells, for an extra fee, stocks in blocks of less than 100 shares. ▶ *I purchased forty-five shares of this stock from an odd lot dealer.*

odd price policy AND **odd pricing** an approach to pricing in which goods are marked for sale in odd amounts. ▶ *Items selling for $99.99, $199.00, or $1.98 are based on an odd price policy.*

odd pricing See the previous entry.

odds and ends an incomplete assortment of something. ▶ *Odds and ends may involve varying sizes, styles, colors, etc., of an item such as shoes.*

off board a trade of shares of stock that is not executed on a national securities exchange. ▶ *The transfer of stock in this case is definitely off board.*

off brand a brand name that is not easily recognized by consumers. ▶ *Off brands are frequently of the same quality as name brands but sell at a lower price.*

off the books an unrecorded transaction. ▶ *Payments which take place off the books are usually not reported to the government for tax purposes.*

offer and acceptance the communication of a proposal by one party to another party followed by the agreement to accept the proposal by the second party. ▶ *You never expect to have offer and acceptance on the same day.*

office management the overseeing and supervising of the adminstrative operations of an organization. ▶ *Office management encompasses the provision of two broad types of services: operating services and control services.*

Office of Management and Budget AND **OMB** an agency of the Federal government that assists the President of the United States to assess the efficiency of the management of the executive branch and to prepare the government's budget. ▶ *The OMB keeps the President informed of work and programs planned and executed by different governmental agencies.*

office romance an intimate relationship between two workers. ▶ *An office romance between Virginia and Tom, her subordinate,* is being construed by many in this office as sexual harassment.

officers the individuals, elected by a board of directors or appointed by an owner, who manage or oversee an organization. ▶ *Officers include presidents, vice presidents, and other high-level executives.*

offset a lithographic printing process that uses a rubber roller to transfer the impression from a plate to the paper. ▶ *Offset printing is a very common process.*

offshore bank a financial institution with headquarters outside the country in which it operates. ▶ *We will run this transaction through our offshore bank in Nassau.*

ogive a curve derived from an array of data or a frequency distribution. ▶ *An ogive resembles a frequency polygon.*

OJT See *on-the-job training.*

Old Age, Survivors, and Disability Insurance AND **Social Security** a Federal program that pays monthly retirement, disability, dependent, and survivor benefits. ▶ *Old Age, Survivors, and Disability Insurance is funded by employer and employee contributions.*

Old Lady of Threadneedle Street the Bank of England. (Colloquial.) ▶ *The Old Lady of Threadneedle Street is one of the world's oldest central banks.*

oligopoly a market situation in which there are few sellers of a particular good or service. ▶ *In an oligopoly, prices are usually higher than in a freely competitive market.*

oligopsony a market situation in

which there are a limited number of buyers of a particular good or service. ▶ *An oligopsony is a rare market situation.*

OMB   See *Office of Management and Budget.*

ombudsman   an individual who investigates complaints or questions about an organization. (Swedish. Originally, an *ombudsman* referred to a government-appointed official who investigated public complaints.) ▶ *I am taking my complaint to the company ombudsman.*

on account AND **on credit**   a partial payment. ▶ *Because I am buying this garment on account, I paid $50 as a down payment.*

on credit   See the previous entry.

on spec(ulation)   work done for a prospect without a contract; the work is purchased only if the prospect is pleased with it. ▶ *Many free-lance writers submit articles to magazines on speculation in the hope that the articles will be purchased for publication.*

on-the-job training AND **OJT**   a method of skill training that utilizes actual work experience. ▶ *On-the-job training is an excellent technique for developing relevant work skills.*

on the money   accurate; exact. (Informal.) ▶ *At the monthly company meeting, William was on the money when he said the reason sales were slumping was due to low morale on the part of the salespeople.*

one cent sale   a sale in which a consumer buys one item for regular price and another of that same item

for one cent. ▶ *The one cent sale advertised one hamburger for $1 and a second hamburger for only a penny.*

one price policy   an approach to pricing whereby similar goods are offered for sale at a given time at one price to all buyers purchasing in comparable quantities. ▶ *We have simplified our pricing by going to a one price policy.*

one price store   **1.** a retail store in which every item is the same price. ▶ *In the United States, there are a lot of $1 stores in which everything is that price.* **2.** an establishment in which the prices of items are not haggled over. ▶ *In a one price store, the price marked on the item is the price that must be paid.*

one stop shopping   a place of business where consumers can buy almost everything they regularly purchase. ▶ *A shopping mall is an example of one stop shopping.*

OPEC   See *Organization of Petroleum Exporting Countries.*

open account   **1.** a type of credit that permits the sale of goods with expected payment at a later date. ▶ *An open account is normally extended on a short-term basis.* **2.** any account that has not been closed out. ▶ *The sales account is an open account until it is closed into the profit and loss account at the end of the month.*

open corporation   a corporation whose stock is widely held. ▶ *The Acme Company, an open corporation, has stockholders around the world.*

open door policy   **1.** a country's

policy of permitting free trade of goods, open flow of information, and unrestricted travel to and from other countries. ▶ *We have an open door policy with many countries.* **2.** the practice of allowing employees access to high-level executives for the purpose of redressing grievances. ▶ *Because our company has an open door policy, I feel I can discuss any problem with upper management at any time.*

open interest the total number of contracts on a commodities futures market that have not been settled by the end of the day. ▶ *When the open interest figure is published, it facilitates investors' evaluation of the market.*

open loop system a system in which control is exercised in terms of outside or predetermined arrangements rather than in terms of the operation. ▶ *Streetlights in an open loop system come on at dusk.*

open market **1.** a market in which trading is not restricted to a particular area or group of people. ▶ *The overall consumer market in the United States is an open market.* **2.** in the stock market, securities traded outside an organized exchange. ▶ *These securities may be bought and sold on the open market.*

open market operations the purchase or sale of government securities, bills of exchange, and bankers' acceptances by the Federal Reserve System. ▶ *Open market operations are performed in order to support the market price of government bonds or to affect member bank reserves and lending policies.*

open order See *good-till-cancelled order.*

open outcry a method of trading on a commodity exchange in which traders must shout out their buy or sell offers. ▶ *In an open outcry, when two traders shout their buy and sell offers at one another, the trade is recorded.*

open policy an insurance policy that does not have an agreed upon value for each item covered. (Compare with *value policy.*) ▶ *John felt that an open policy was the best value for his money.*

open shop a firm where employees do not have to join the union and where the firm does not have to hire union members. ▶ *Our company has an open shop.*

open union a union that does not attempt to restrict its membership through prohibitive initiation fees, excessive dues, severe examinations, or by other means. ▶ *Open unions are much more fair than closed unions.*

operating budget a budget depicting operating revenues and expenses. ▶ *Our operating budget for next year will allow us to market our products more heavily than this year.*

operating expense the amount an organization pays to maintain property. ▶ *Operating expense includes property taxes and utilities.*

operating profit the excess of revenues over expenses, excluding income from sources other than regular activities and nonoperating expenses. ▶ *Our operating profit shows signs of decline.*

operating ratio the relationship of one amount to another derived from comparison of items of income and expense. (See also *financial ratio*.) ▶ *Net profits to gross income is an example of an operating ratio.*

operating revenue that part of a firm's total revenue that is derived from the main manufacturing or service effort of the firm. ▶ *Thanks to our increased productivity, our operating revenue is 10% higher this year than it was last year.*

operating statement See *income statement*.

operating supplies the supplies used in the operation of the business but not in the actual product manufactured by the firm. ▶ *Staples, computer disks, and paper are examples of operating supplies for many firms.*

operations analysis chart a graphic form that lists all important facts affecting the effectiveness of an operation. ▶ *The operations analysis chart is used to identify potential improvements.*

operations management the overseeing of all activities directly related to producing goods or providing services. ▶ *Operations management manages the conversion of inputs to outputs.*

opinion leader one whose ideas and beliefs are models for others. ▶ *Advertisers frequently design ads for opinion leaders in the hope that those people will influence others in a buying decision.*

opinion poll a survey made in an attempt to determine the attitude of the public toward a certain person, idea, or product. ▶ *An opinion poll is frequently used by politicians at election time.*

opportunity cost 1. the cost of a lost opportunity. ▶ *By going to see a movie rather than staying home, making a good grade on this test was an opportunity cost.* 2. the cost of alternative goods or services forgone. ▶ *The opportunity cost of buying Brand A over Brand B is rather high.* 3. the cost of an alternative opportunity for investment. ▶ *An examination of opportunity cost is often used when evaluating a capital investment project.*

optimization the process of choosing the best alternative in a problem situation. ▶ *Because all our options are fairly good, we must attempt to select the one that will allow us to achieve optimization.*

optimum costs the best obtainable costs for a given course of action or level of production. ▶ *By using this new technique we will achieve optimum costs.*

optimum output that rate or level of production that results in the lowest marginal unit cost and the lowest average unit cost. ▶ *We are now operating at optimum output.*

option a legal right to buy or to sell something at a specified price within a specified period of time. ▶ *I have an option on these securities.*

optional dividend a dividend on the stock of a corporation that is authorized for payment in more than one form, according to the desires of the individual stockholders. ▶ *An optional dividend may be taken in cash or in additional shares of stock.*

oral contract an agreement that is spoken rather than written down. ▶ *Most oral contracts are enforceable.*

order 1. a command. ▶ *My boss gave me an order to finish this project before Friday.* 2. a request to buy something. ▶ *We received John's order to buy fifteen copies of our newsletter.*

order bill a negotiable bill of lading. ▶ *The order bill indicates how much we paid for these items.*

order good until a specified time agreement an agreement that allows a broker to act for his client, under previously agreed upon terms, until a certain point in time. ▶ *As his broker, I can make important decisions because we have an order good until a specified time agreement.*

order point system a method of replenishing inventory. ▶ *In an order point system, when the number of units of a particular item reaches a certain predetermined point or level, a fixed number of additional units is ordered.*

ordinary income the income from profits, wages, interest, etc. ▶ *Our ordinary income for this year is $140,000.*

organization 1. structure; a plan of coordination of efforts. ▶ *The organization of this firm leaves a lot to be desired.* 2. a business; an association. ▶ *This organization is comprised of many talented individuals.*

organization chart a graphic representation of an organization showing the relationship between various components and indicating how each of the components are tied together along the lines of authority. ▶ *An organization chart often shows who reports to whom within a company.*

organization file a collection of materials published about or written by an enterprise. ▶ *An organization file includes minutes of meetings, proceedings, promotional material, press clippings, etc.*

organization manual a book containing (1) functional statements for all divisions, departments, or components of an organization, (2) job descriptions for upper and middle management positions, and (3) charts depicting the structure of the organization and its various components. ▶ *An organization manual is useful in formalizing new companies.*

Organization of Petroleum Exporting Countries AND **OPEC** an organization established in 1970 to set global oil prices by coordinating oil production. ▶ *The thirteen member countries of OPEC possess about two-thirds of oil reserves and about one-third of natural gas reserves.*

organization structure the established pattern of relationships among the components or parts of an organization. ▶ *Organization structure is best represented in an organization chart.*

organizational climate a set of properties assumed to be a major force in influencing employee behavior. ▶ *Surveys are often used to assess organizational climate.*

organizer **1.** anyone who engages in the process of organizing. ▶ *Jane is a good organizer; she is very good at putting together groups of people for special projects.* **2.** a person who assists employees in the formation of a collective bargaining unit. ▶ *Because Sam is very much in favor of unions, he is no doubt the organizer at this company.*

organizing the process of bringing together and integrating combinations of workers, machines, materials, and information for the purpose of achieving some goal or series of goals. ▶ *Building a company requires a great amount of organizing effort.*

orientation a type of training designed to acquaint new employees with company policies, procedures, rules, etc., that directly or indirectly affect their employment status with the company. ▶ *All new employees must go through a two-week orientation at this company.*

original entry the first recording of a transaction in a particular ledger or journal. ▶ *A sales journal is a book of original entry because all sales are first recorded there.*

original period that period of time within a time series selected as the base period for the series. ▶ *The original period may not be the first period, but for the time series it is labeled as such.*

OSHA See *Occupational Safety and Health Administration.*

other assets assets of a miscellaneous nature that cannot be classi-fied under other usual asset headings. ▶ *Copyrights and patents are examples of other assets.*

out-of-pocket expenses the minor expenses paid out by an employee or contractor. ▶ *My company considers meals, gas, tips, and phone calls to be out-of-pocket expenses.*

out of the money a call option contract whose *strike price* is higher than the market value of the underlying security. ▶ *Tom writes all his call options out of the money.*

outdoor advertising advertising by means of billboards, posters, signs, and car flyers. ▶ *Outdoor advertising is mainly targeted to automobile drivers.*

outlet store a retail store operated by a manufacturer to sell surplus stock or irregular items. ▶ *We are planning to open an outlet store next year to help move our surplus inventory.*

outplacement the counseling and career-related services provided to individuals who leave a firm involuntarily. ▶ *Workers who are terminated frequently receive outplacement counseling.*

outsource to have another firm—"on the outside"—supply or manufacture a major component. ▶ *Companies that outsource specialized parts often save money in the long run.*

outstanding order a request for goods that has not yet been delivered. ▶ *When Leroy asked where the shipment was, I told him it was still an outstanding order.*

outstanding shares the capital stock of a corporation in the hands of the public. ▶ *Dividends are* based on the number of outstanding shares.

over-the-counter [securities transactions that take place] outside of an organized stock exchange. ▶ *Most new issues of unknown corporations are handled over-the-counter.*

overage too much of something. ▶ *We have an overage in the petty cash account.*

overbought pertaining to a stock issue that has risen very sharply in price; pertaining to a financial market in which the prices have risen faster than value. (The opposite of *oversold.*) ▶ *Overbought securities are very vulnerable to a drop in price.*

overdraft the amount by which the sum total of checks against a demand deposit account exceeds the balance on deposit in the account. ▶ *If a person wrote a check for $3,000, but only had $2,500 in the account, a $500 overdraft would exist.*

overhead the costs of materials and services not directly adding to or identifiable with the product or the service offered by a firm. ▶ *A utility bill is an example of overhead.*

overhead rate the standard rate at which overhead charges are allocated to departments, functions, projects, or products. ▶ *The overhead rate at XYZ Company is 7 percent.*

overproduction the production of more of an item than can be sold at a price in excess of cost. ▶ *This product is no longer selling and we have an overproduction we*

cannot dispose of.

overqualified possessing qualifications beyond that required for a particular job. ▶ *Holding a doctorate degree and ten years of high-level management experience would make one overqualified for an entry-level accounting position.*

override the extra compensation paid to salespeople in addition to their regular commission or salary. ▶ *Frequently, an override refers to the commission paid to a sales manager on the basis of the commissions earned by the sales manager's sales force.*

oversold pertaining to a stock issue that has declined very sharply in price; pertaining to a financial market in which the prices have fallen faster than value. ▶ *This stock must be oversold! It is selling for less than 3% of what it did just three weeks ago.*

oversubscribed a condition that exists when the applications to buy shares of a new issue of stock exceed the amount of stock offered for sale. ▶ *We knew this new issue was going to be very popular, and it has been. It is already oversubscribed.*

overtime the time worked in excess of a worker's regular working time as defined by law or agreement. ▶ *Often pay for overtime is computed at "time-and-a-half" of normal pay.*

overtrading a condition that exists when sales go beyond a level that can be financed with normal working capital. ▶ *Overtrading is a risky process to be involved in.*

overtraining training extending beyond the point at which the trainee has become proficient in carrying out a particular activity or practicing a given trade. ▶ *Overtraining should be considered a waste of time and money.*

overvalued a stock whose high price does not appear justified. ▶ *An overvalued stock will probably drop in price.*

owner's equity AND **stockholder's equity** the total assets of a business enterprise less the total liabilities. (See also *net worth.*) ▶ *Owner's equity is basically an owner's vested interest in a property.*

P

pace rating a method used by a time study analyst to compare the speed or tempo of the worker being studied with the analyst's own concept of normal speed. ▶ *When pace rating is used, the analyst compares times so that any necessary adjustments can be made to the observed time.*

Pacific Daylight Time the adjusted time in the westernmost contiguous part of the United States from early April to late October. ▶ *Please remit your payment today to the Bank of Oxnard by 2:00 P.M. Pacific Daylight Time or incur an additional day's interest charges.*

Pacific Standard Time the standard time in the western United States from late October to early April. ▶ *Pacific Standard Time is eight hours behind Greenwich Time.*

packaging the function of designing a product container and of placing the product within the container. ▶ *While one of the prime purposes of packaging is to protect the product, the package may also be used for advertising purposes or be designed in such a way that it has customer appeal.*

paid holiday any day of exemption, except for illness, from regularly scheduled work for which the employee receives compensation. ▶ *In the United States, Christmas day is normally a paid holiday.*

paid-in capital capital acquired from stockholders. ▶ *Paid-in capital is usually differentiated from that generated from earnings.*

paid-in surplus an increase in the owner's equity account arising from the sale of stock at a price exceeding its par or stated value. ▶ *The sale of stock at a price above par will cause an increase in paid-in surplus.*

paid-up insurance insurance on which all of the required premiums have been paid prior to the maturity of the policy. ▶ *Paid-up insurance refers to a life insurance policy.*

pallet a platform of varying size and design on which materials are placed for hauling or storage. ▶ *A pallet permits the easy movement of materials by a fork-lift truck.*

panic button a state of alarm. ▶ *The panic button was pushed when our biggest customer cancelled his current order and all future orders.*

paper loss See the following entry.

paper profit AND **paper loss** a profit or loss not realized, but which would exist at a given time if a sale and purchase were to take place. ▶ *A paper profit exists only on paper, since until a transaction takes place, it is merely theoretical.* ▶ *A paper loss in a stock price can be erased in another day's trading.*

PAQ See *position analysis questionnaire.*

par (value) the value printed on the face of a stock certificate or bond. ▶ *Par is merely a face value; it is not the actual value of the stock.*

paralegal an individual working in a law firm who is not a member of the bar and who performs routine law office tasks. ▶ *A paralegal does not have to have training as a lawyer to be employed in a law firm.*

parallel processing 1. the operation of a computer so that programs for more than one run are stored simultaneously in its storage and are executed concurrently. ▶ *Parallel processing is useful in pattern recognition applications.* 2. the concurrent operation of two different systems for processing the same data. ▶ *During conversion to a computer system it is normal for an organization to continue to operate its manual or mechanical system alongside the computer system until it has been determined that the computerized system contains no flaws; this is parallel processing.*

paraprofessional an individual who assists a professional. ▶ *A paralegal is a paraprofessional who assists lawyers.*

parent company a company that exercises control over one or more subsidiary enterprises. ▶ *AMR is the parent company of American Airlines.*

Pareto's Law AND **eighty-twenty rule; law of the trivial many and the critical few** the idea that in most business activities a small percentage of the total item count produces the major portion of the work, cost, profit, etc. ▶ *Pareto's Law tries to explain how important small factors are.*

parity 1. the condition of being equivalent. ▶ *Companies are striving for parity between men's and women's salaries in the United States.* 2. a state where the price of a commodity gives the producer of that commodity a certain purchasing power in terms of a base period. (This state is usually achieved by the use of a *support price.*) ▶ *With price supports for U.S. farm-*

ers beginning in the 1930s, the stabilization of farm prices was attempted; the goal was parity.

parity bit a check bit that indicates whether the total number of binary "1" digits in a character or word (excluding the *parity bit*) is odd or even. ▶ *A parity bit is used to force the total number of digits to be either always odd or always even.*

Parkinson's Law the rule that work expands so as to fill the time available for its completion. ▶ *Parkinson's Law was developed by C. Northcote Parkinson, a British writer.*

parliamentary procedure a set of formal rules to be observed when conducting a meeting. ▶ *Parliamentary procedure ensures that a meeting is conducted professionally, fairly, and orderly.*

parsimonious model a representation of reality in which only the most significant variables are included rather than all variables. ▶ *A parsimonious model may be used as a low cost alternative to a model that contains numerous variables.*

partial payment the incomplete discharge of an obligation, either a payment of interest or of principal. ▶ *We received only partial payment for the shipment of September 22; there is a balance of $1,500 due.*

participating preferred stock a type of corporate stock that, in addition to having a fixed dividend rate to which it is entitled, shares with the common stock of the corporation in further distributions of profit under stipulated conditions.

▶ *Participating preferred stock is not commonly used by corporations today.*

participation loan a loan made by one bank, but shared in by other banks. ▶ *A participation loan may be necessary because one bank is not large enough to loan the full amount needed by a borrower.*

partnership See *(general) partnership.*

parts manufactured items that become components of larger manufactured articles. ▶ *Piston rods for automobiles and wheels for trucks are parts.*

party plan selling a marketing technique in which a firm, through its sales force, arranges to have someone give a party at home, at which time the firm's merchandise is demonstrated to the assembled friends of the host or hostess. ▶ *With party plan selling, persons hosting the party normally receive merchandise prizes as payment for their services.*

pass a dividend to miss payment of a dividend. ▶ *The value of the stock plummeted when the company passed a dividend.*

pass through payment a payment made through another person. ▶ *Because Jim gave the money to Janet to give to me, the payment was a pass through payment.*

passbook a book supplied by a bank to a depositor for record purposes. ▶ *A savings account passbook lists all deposits, withdrawals, and interest paid, among other things.*

passbook loan a loan that is secured by pledge of the borrower's savings account as collateral. ▶ *Joy secured a passbook loan from her bank based on the status of her savings account.*

passed dividend a dividend not declared on stock, either common or preferred, at or about the customary dividend date. ▶ *A passed dividend may cause a stock price to drop considerably and remain there for some time.*

passive activity loss a loss caused by inactive investments. ▶ *A passive activity loss may result from investing in a limited partnership.*

past due a delay beyond an agreed upon time for payment. ▶ *Payment for the shipment is now past due.*

patch a section of coding inserted into a computer routine to correct a mistake or to alter the routine in some fashion. ▶ *Considering the awkward way this program processes information, there must be a patch in here somewhere.*

patent the protection granted by the Federal government to inventors giving them the exclusive right to produce and sell their inventions. ▶ *A patent is effective for seventeen years.*

patent pending a statement from the United States Patent Office that a search is being made to ensure that the *patent* is new. ▶ *Even though a patent may be filed with the U.S. Patent Office, it does not mean the invention is patented officially; that is why some products have a statement saying "patent pending."*

paternalism the excessive or exaggerated interest and activities on the part of an employer in providing for the comfort, safety, and general well-being of workers. ▶ *In the U.S., paternalism is thought of in a negative sense, whereas in other countries, paternalism is considered to be something good.*

paternity leave the paid time given to a man whose wife has a child. ▶ *Paternity leave is a relatively new concept in the U.S.*

patron 1. a customer. ▶ *The restaurant patrons were very happy with their dinners.* 2. a sponsor. ▶ *We would like to thank our patron for making it possible to televise this week's opera.*

pattern bargaining an arrangement whereby a union negotiates a contract with the major firm within an industry, and this contract then becomes the pattern for agreements with all other firms in the industry. ▶ *Pattern bargaining involving local unions in a single industry is a vital form of collective bargaining in the United States.*

patterned interview AND **structured interview** a type of employment interview in which the interviewer follows a predetermined plan in order to cover specific areas. ▶ *In a patterned interview, a detailed questionnaire is used to guide the interviewer.*

pay grade the standard rate or range of pay for a particular job. ▶ *All jobs in a single pay grade have a maximum pay rate.*

pay range the distance between the minimum rate of pay and the maximum rate of pay in a particular pay grade. ▶ *A pay range has an upper and a lower limit.*

pay secrecy a policy of not revealing the pay of individuals, jobs, or grades in an organization. ▶ *We do not have pay secrecy at our company; in fact, salary figures of individuals are readily available.*

pay something down to pay a portion of the purchase price, finance the balance, and receive the goods; to pay a portion of the purchase price and pay the balance on taking delivery of the goods. ▶ *I paid $1,000 down on my new car.*

payable to be paid in the future. ▶ *The bill is payable in 30 days.*

payback period the amount of time required for an investment to break even. ▶ *The payback period is important in capital budgeting.*

payee one who is to be paid. ▶ *The payee received half of the money owed to him.*

payer the entity that pays. ▶ *The bank is the payer of the draft.*

payload that part of a cargo that produces revenue. ▶ *Payload is usually expressed in terms of weight.*

paymaster a person in charge of paying wages and salaries. ▶ *The paymaster distributes paychecks every Tuesday.*

payment the act of compensating someone for goods or services that have been or are expected to be received or performed. ▶ *Payment in full was made to the consultant for the work she did on developing a performance appraisal system for the bank.*

payment in kind a payment made with goods or services rather than with money. ▶ *A discount to em-*

ployees is an example of payment in kind.

payoff matrix a table with various courses of action classified by rows or columns against available alternatives similarly classified in columns or rows for the purpose of analyzing the probabilities attaching to each course of action. ▶ *Fred was asked to construct a payoff matrix to help in the budgeting procedure.*

payout period the length of time it takes for an investment to pay for itself. ▶ *The payout period for this investment is one year.*

payroll 1. a list of employees to be paid, with the amounts due each. ▶ *According to the payroll, John made less than anyone else at this company.* 2. the aggregate amount to be paid to all employees. ▶ *Payroll is increasing 10% per year at this firm.*

payroll period the interval of time between scheduled paydays. ▶ *A payroll period may be of any duration such as one week, two weeks, one month, etc.*

PBX See *Private Branch Exchange.*

PC See *personal computer.*

peak load the level of highest volume of activity for a person, machine, or organization. ▶ *Our peak load occurs in the summer.*

peak season the time of the year in which a particular product or service is in high demand. ▶ *The peak season for toys is just before Christmas.*

peaks and valleys the high points and low points of a business cycle.

► *Firms with seasonal sales see frequent peaks and valleys.*

pecuniary relating to money. ► *A pecuniary gain is an addition of money.*

pecuniary benefit a monetary reward associated with some undertaking. ► *I received a pecuniary benefit for the work I did on the XYZ contract.*

pedagogy the art, study, or profession of teaching, especially as it relates to children. ► *Every teacher should have a course in pedagogy.*

pegging the act of fixing a price for a security, commodity, or other item during its initial distribution. ► *Pegging is used for the pricing of gold.*

penetration pricing a method of product pricing in which the initial price for a new product is very low. ► *With penetration pricing, the price of a product will eventually go up as sales increase.*

penny stock a low-priced, speculative stock, ranging in price from a few cents to a few dollars. ► *A penny stock is great for people wanting to be involved in the stock market, but who do not have much money to invest.*

pension a series of payments made to a retired employee. ► *Joan received a pension of $500 per month until her death.*

per capita income the average income per person. ► *Per capita income is calculated by dividing the national income by the total population of a country.*

per diem by the day. ► *Consultants frequently bid projects with* per diem *expenses included in the total bid price.*

percentage order a market or limited price order to buy or sell a given amount of a specified security after a predetermined number of shares of that security have been sold. ► *A percentage order is a type of instruction from a customer to a broker.*

percentile any of the values that divide a frequency distribution into 100 parts, each of which contains 1 percent of the total number of items. ► *On my admission test, I scored in the 92nd percentile.*

perceptual map a graphic representation of customers' perceptions to competing products. ► *A perceptual map assists marketers in deciding what marketing strategy to pursue.*

perfect competition See *pure competition.*

performance appraisal AND **efficiency rating; rating system; service rating** the systematic evaluation of an individual with respect to actual performance in the current position and an assessment of the individual's potential for further development. ► *At this company, we conduct a performance appraisal of each employee once a year.*

performance bond a bond supplied by one party to another party protecting the second party against loss in the event of the first party's failure to complete a contract satisfactorily. ► *A performance bond ensures that a contractor actually performs a job and performs it on time.*

performance index See *utilization index.*

performance rating the process wherein a time study analyst compares the speed or skill and effort of an employee with the analyst's own concept of normal speed or skill and effort, noting the difference between actual and normal so that necessary adjustments can be made to the actual times. ▶ *Performance rating helps to produce a standard time that should be achieved by most employees.*

performance report a report comparing the actual performance of an employee, a group of employees, or a total work center with standard performance. ▶ *A performance report may be prepared on a weekly or a monthly basis.*

period cost an expense that occurs regularly. ▶ *Rent is a period cost.*

periodic inventory AND **physical inventory** the act of physically counting the actual materials, goods, or commodities on hand at specified time intervals. ▶ *A periodic inventory is usually taken on an annual basis.*

periodic ordering system a process in which the number of units in stock of a particular item is reviewed on a fixed periodic basis and additional units are ordered in the quantity needed. ▶ *A periodic ordering system is a method of replenishing inventory.*

peripheral equipment the auxiliary machines that may be placed under the control of the central computer. ▶ *Card readers, card punches, magnetic tape units, and* high-speed printers are peripheral equipment.

perishable item a good that quickly spoils or decays. ▶ *A loaf of bread is a perishable item.*

perk See *perquisite.*

permanent account an account to which other accounts are closed and which is maintained as an item on the balance sheet. ▶ *Cash is a permanent account.*

permanent injunction a court restraint preventing someone from engaging in a particular act. ▶ *A permanent injunction is a legal device that prevents an action of some type.*

perpetual inventory an inventory system in which book inventory is maintained in continuous agreement with actual stock on hand by means of a detailed set of records listing all inventory transactions. ▶ *With perpetual inventory, records are kept in such a way, that at any time, someone may see how many of a particular item is on hand.*

perpetuity an investment providing equal payments forever. ▶ *This investment is great; as a perpetuity, I will get $1,000 per month for the rest of my life!*

perquisite AND **perk** an extra benefit available for certain employees in addition to standard wages and salaries. (Often plural.) ▶ *A company car is a perquisite.*

personal allowance an increment of time added to the normal time for performing a task to permit the worker to attend to personal needs such as getting a drink of water or going to the restroom. ▶ *A* *personal allowance is generally added to normal time in the form of a percentage.*

personal computer AND **PC** a microcomputer. (Typically refers to a *DOS* system.) ▶ *The personal computer has made desktop publishing a reality.*

personal finance company a business enterprise that makes small loans to individuals for personal needs. ▶ *Tom borrowed money from a personal finance company to buy a refrigerator.*

personal identification number AND **PIN** a secret number associated with a credit card or *ATM* card that provides access to a bank account or other accounts. ▶ *Customers who forget their PIN cannot use an ATM and must wait until the bank opens.*

personal property property other than real estate. ▶ *Personal property may be either tangible or intangible.*

personal selling the process of directly and personally assisting and persuading a prospect to purchase a particular item or service, or to act on an idea. ▶ *Some business owners feel that personal selling is still more effective than selling through direct mail.*

personal service a type of contract that commits one party to work for another party at unspecified tasks. ▶ *A personal service agreement is a legally binding contract.*

personality test an instrument designed to assess and measure the personality traits of an individual. ▶ *A personality test is sometimes*

used as a selection tool for employment applicants.

personnel the work force of an organization. ▶ *Overall, I would say the personnel at this company are highly skilled.*

personnel administration See *human resource management.*

personnel department See *human resources department.*

personnel management See *human resource management.*

personnel manual a written document detailing an organization's personnel policies and procedures. ▶ *The manager gave Joan a copy of the personnel manual on her first day on the job.*

Peter Principle the notion that in a hierarchical organization, people tend to rise to their own level of incompetence. ▶ *The Peter Principle was postulated by Lawrence J. Peter.*

petrodollars the money paid to oil-producing countries and deposited in Western banks. ▶ *Petrodollars are in U.S. dollar denominations.*

petty cash See *imprest fund.*

phantom shopping See *mystery shopping.*

Phillips Curve a graphic representation of the proposition that as the rate of unemployment decreases, the rate of inflation rises at a faster rate. ▶ *The Phillips Curve was developed by the economist A.W.H. Phillips.*

phony dividend a dividend paid out of the funds received from the sale of a new issue of stock. ▶ *Phony dividends are illegal.*

physical inventory See *periodic inventory.*

physical life the total potential operating life of a machine, plant, building, etc., as contrasted with the economic life that may be much less because of obsolescence or inadequacy. ▶ *The physical life of this machine is ten years.*

physical verification a personal examination of something. ▶ *We made a physical verification of inventory by actually counting every item in stock.*

pica a unit of type in printing. ▶ *There are six picas to the vertical inch.*

picketing the process of having union members parade in front of the premises of a business enterprise, carrying signs or banners that are directed toward influencing customers not to patronize the firm or to discourage or prevent other employees from reporting for work. ▶ *In the U.S., picketing is legal as long as picketers obey certain guidelines.*

picosecond one trillionth of a second. ▶ *Internal operating speeds of advanced computer systems are sometimes expressed in picoseconds.*

pictograph a pictorial representation of numerical data. ▶ *A pictograph was used in his presentation to illustrate the increase in the number of potential customers in that particular market.*

pie chart a circle chart broken into subdivisions. ▶ *In a pie chart, the size of each division indicates a proportionate part of the whole.*

piece goods goods usually sold by the yard. ▶ *Fabric is an example of a piece good.*

piecework a wage payment plan whereby workers are paid a definite sum of money for each unit they produce. ▶ *In some instances, piecework may be done at home.*

piggyback service a service offered by railroads whereby motor trailers are loaded for overland shipment on railroad cars, unloaded at a railhead near the final destination, and delivered by motor tractor to their destination. (See also *fishyback service.*) ▶ *Since we do not have enough drivers to take these trucks to the West Coast, we may have to use a piggyback service.*

pilot plant a new manufacturing facility that is operated on a trial basis before other such facilities are built and put into operation. ▶ *A pilot plant helps reduce risks associated with large-scale expansion.*

PIN See *personal identification number.*

pin money a small amount of money used for small expenses. ▶ *I only have a little pin money. I don't have enough to buy that book.*

pink-collar job a job that is typically held by a woman who has not attended college. ▶ *My secretary has a pink-collar job.*

pink slip a form used, or an action taken, by an employer to advise an employee that employment is to be terminated as of a certain date. ▶ *John got a pink slip Friday, along with twelve other employees.*

pipeline 1. a conduit for moving fluids or gases overland. ▶ *A* *pipeline is usually found underground.* **2.** an informal information channel that provides confidential information. ▶ *According to the pipeline, Charlie is next in line for a promotion at this company.*

pirating the practice of an employer enticing employees away from other employers by offers of better jobs. ▶ *Our competition is pirating all of our best employees away from us.*

pit AND **ring** the trading area of a stock market or commodity exchange. ▶ *The pit is where traders assemble and make stock offers to one another.*

pitch the number of characters that a typewriter can print in one horizontal inch. ▶ *The pitch of most typewriters is ten or twelve characters.*

Pittsburgh-plus pricing a pricing system, formerly used in the steel industry, in which steel prices were quoted on the basis of the price at Pittsburgh plus additional costs. ▶ *In Pittsburgh-plus pricing, the additional costs added to the Pittsburgh price are based on transportation from Pittsburgh to the point of delivery, regardless of the actual location from which the shipment originated.*

place utility the usefulness or value of goods or services because they are in a particular place where there is a demand for them. ▶ *A gas station located on a long stretch of highway in the desert enjoys place utility.*

placement the process of situating individuals in the type of work or kind of job for which they are suit-

ed. ▶ *Many colleges and universities have placement services to help students find appropriate work in their chosen field.*

planned obsolescence **1.** the design of products so that vital components wear out before other parts. ▶ *With planned obsolescence, companies ensure that consumers will either repair an item or replace it.* **2.** a rapid and continual change in the style, appearance, model, etc., of a product. ▶ *Planned obsolescence creates in the mind of the consumer dissatisfaction with the present version of the product so that the consumer will purchase the new version.*

plant a facility where a company manufactures a product. ▶ *Besides the building itself, a plant includes machinery, equipment, etc., used to manufacture a product.*

plastic (money) a credit card. (Credit cards are made of plastic.) ▶ *The increased use of plastic has fueled the rise in consumer debt.*

pledged asset an asset mortgaged or placed in trust as collateral for a loan or contract. ▶ *A pledged asset is usually some type of personal property.*

plow back the act of reinvesting the profits of a business in the firm. ▶ *New companies frequently plow back profits to finance additional growth.*

plural executive a committee that performs the functions of what is usually one executive position. ▶ *A plural executive is in fact several people, not just one.*

plus tick See *up tick.*

point a unit of measurement of the depth of a unit of type. ▶ *There are seventy-two points to the inch.*

point method a method of job evaluation in which a range of point values is assigned to each compensable factor. ▶ *When using the point method, the rates of pay for specific jobs are determined by comparing the total number of points each job receives with the point values and wage rates of previously selected key jobs.*

point of purchase advertising AND **point of purchase display** advertising appearing at or near the place of purchase of consumer goods. ▶ *Point of purchase advertising is typically located in store windows or near the cash register.*

point of purchase display See the previous entry.

point of sale terminal a cash register connected to a computer that analyzes sales. ▶ *A point of sale terminal can record how many sales have been made by particular salespeople, departments, etc.*

poison pill an issue of new stock offered by a company targeted for a takeover as an attempt to prevent the takeover. ▶ *The purpose of a poison pill is to make a targeted company's stock less attractive.*

poisson distribution a probability distribution that is useful in those instances where there are a large number of variables, each of which has a small, constant probability of contributing to the final outcome. ▶ *The poisson distribution is named after the eighteenth-century mathematician and physicist Simeon Poisson.*

police power the right or duty of a government to impose restrictions on the private rights of its citizens in order to preserve the public order and welfare. ▶ *A zoning law is an example of police power.*

policy 1. a statement, preferably written, that guides or channels subordinates in their thinking or decision making. ▶ *Normally, a policy is said to be a general guide to action.* 2. a contract between an insurer and the insured. ▶ *A policy sets forth the amount of premium to be paid, indicates which risks are or are not covered, specifies the procedures for establishing a claim under the terms of the policy, and indicates other terms and conditions of the insurance contract.*

pool car a railway freight car containing a combination of small shipments. (See also the following entry.) ▶ *See if you can work this small shipment into a pool car and save us some money.*

pool car service a service offered by railroads that permits the combination of a number of small shipments into a single carload or pool car. ▶ *With pool car service, small shipments are charged a lower freight rate than would be charged under less than carload conditions.*

pooling of interests a process whereby two companies, usually of approximately equal financial stature, merge forces. ▶ *When there is a pooling of interests, the merger is usually temporary in nature and is formed to undertake* *a certain project that neither firm wishes to or is capable of undertaking alone.*

population **1.** the number of people who reside within a given geographical area. ▶ *The population of the United States is rising.* **2.** any collection of items or values from which a sample is drawn. (See also *universe.*) ▶ *The sample population consists of 2,500 households.*

population trend changes occurring in the population of a country or region. ▶ *A shift in the average age of the population is an example of a population trend.*

pork barrel a government appropriation for local improvement projects secured on a political patronage basis. ▶ *The senator secured another pork barrel project for his state.*

port of entry the place where goods and people enter a country and where customs offices are located. ▶ *New York City is a famous port of entry.*

portal-to-portal pay the payment given to a worker for the time spent in traveling from the gate of the plant grounds or a mine to the point at which actual work is begun, and from this point back to the gate at the end of the work shift. ▶ *Portal-to-portal pay may be given to workers in those instances where significant time is involved in getting to the actual work site once the worker has entered the company's gate.*

portfolio the entire security holdings of an individual or an institution. ▶ *To reduce risk a portfolio should be diversified.*

portfolio management the administration and control of stocks, bonds, real estate, or any combination of investments held by an individual or an institution. ▶ *Portfolio management is concerned with such issues as investment diversification, liquidity, and rates of return.*

position the tasks and responsibilities performed by one person in an organization. ▶ *In a company, there is a position for every individual.*

position analysis questionnaire AND **PAQ** a structured questionnaire using a checklist approach to identify job elements. ▶ *A position analysis questionnaire is used in job analysis.*

position building the process of buying or selling shares of stock to affect one's financial condition. ▶ *Position building may involve purchasing more of a particular share of stock.*

positioning the act of differentiating oneself from the competition in a particular market. ▶ *Positioning may be achieved through an emphasis on product quality.*

positive leadership AND **positive motivation** the motivation of workers by rewards or promises of rewards as opposed to motivation by fear. ▶ *Positive leadership is far more effective than negative leadership.*

positive motivation See the previous entry.

possession utility the usefulness, value, or satisfaction provided by the actual possession of a particular item of goods or a service. ▶

Possession utility is accomplished by getting products to consumers so that they can use them.

post postscript AND **PPS**   a second additional thought added to the bottom of a letter and appearing after a *postscript*. ▶ *You can't have a post postscript without a postscript appearing before it.*

postage and handling   the additional cost levied to cover postage and handling expenses when purchased items are shipped. ▶ *Her money was refunded, less the charge for postage and handling.*

postage meter   a machine that prints postage amounts on mail or on gummed labels. ▶ *The postage meter saves time when one has a sizeable amount of mail to process.*

postdate   to date a check with a date sometime in the future. ▶ *When someone postdates a check, the check cannot be cashed immediately.*

postdated check   a check dated with a future date. ▶ *A postdated check cannot be paid by the drawee bank until the future date is reached.*

posting   **1.** the process of transferring entries from a document or book of original entry to a ledger. ▶ *Our accountant is busy posting accounts.* **2.** an item posted in a ledger. ▶ *I don't remember this posting. Who entered it?*

postmark   the official United States Postal Service cancellation of postage on an envelope. ▶ *A postmark indicates the date the letter was cancelled and the place of cancellation.*

postscript AND **PS**   an additional thought added to the bottom of a letter. ▶ *A postscript appears after the signature on a letter.*

power of attorney   a legal instrument that authorizes one party to act as another party's agent, either generally or for a specific purpose. ▶ *To be awarded a power of attorney, one does not have to be an attorney.*

PPO   See *preferred provider organization.*

PPS   See *post postscript.*

pre-tax dollars   money that has not yet been taxed; a sum of money yet to be taxed. ▶ *In pre-tax dollars, my salary is quite respectable, but after taxes, I'm almost a pauper!*

precedent   an instance or a case that may serve as an example or model in subsequent instances or cases. ▶ *Many court cases are decided on precedent.*

predatory pricing   the act of pricing goods and services well below the prices of a firm's competitors with the intent of driving the competition out of business. ▶ *Predatory pricing is a risky pricing strategy because competitors may retaliate.*

predetermined elemental time system   a system of elemental time data that has assigned specific time values to various classifications of fundamental body member motions under the premise that the time required for a particular body movement is constant, varying only with the conditions under which the movement is made and the distance of the movement. ▶ *Methods-*

Time Measurement is an example of a predetermined elemental time system.

preemption   the right to purchase something before another party does. ▶ *Preemption gives Tom the right to buy the boat even before anyone else saw it.*

preemptive right   a right protecting stockholders from losing their proportionate interest in a corporation. ▶ *A preemptive right gives stockholders the opportunity to purchase new stock in a percentage amount equal to their present holdings.*

preference bond   See *income bond.*

preference test   a test designed to determine the inherent preference of an individual or individuals for a certain product, package, advertisement, or other new item. ▶ *A preference test is normally used for market research purposes.*

preferential hiring   the practice of giving certain groups or classes of job applicants priority over other groups or classes when filling job vacancies. ▶ *Preferential hiring is a form of discrimination.*

preferred provider organization AND **PPO**   the health care provider an insurance company recommends to its policyholders because the provider has agreed with the insurance company to charge lower prices than other providers. ▶ *When a person gets health insurance, often the insurance company will provide the name and address of a preferred provider organization near the insured.*

preferred stock   a share in the ownership of a corporation having certain designated rights that rank it ahead of *common stock.* ▶ *The most common rights associated with preferred stock are the right to receive dividends before common stockholders and the right to receive a portion of liquidation proceeds before common stockholders.*

premium   **1.** the amount by which the price exceeds its nominal, par, quoted, or usual value. ▶ *There is a $10 premium above the face value of this bond.* **2.** the amount paid for insurance coverage. ▶ *Insurance companies assume the risks of the insured in exchange for a premium.* **3.** an amount paid over and above the usual wage for superior production, excellent workmanship, time worked in excess of normal hours, etc. ▶ *He received a 10% premium for completing the project ahead of schedule.* **4.** a free, additional item given to a consumer for purchasing a particular product. ▶ *Children's cereals frequently contain a premium such as a toy.*

premium pay   compensation in excess of the normal wage rate. ▶ *Premium pay may be given for superior production, excellent workmanship, hazardous work, or hours worked in excess of normal working hours.*

prepaid expenses AND **unexpired costs**   the costs of services or goods purchased in one financial period but not consumed by the time that the financial statement is issued. ▶ *A prepaid expense is shown on the balance sheet as an asset.*

prepay to pay for a good or service before its receipt. ▶ *When ordering something through the mail, it is common to have to prepay the entire order before it will be shipped.*

presentment the exhibiting of a matured note, draft, or bill of exchange to the maker or drawee for payment. ▶ *The note was paid promptly on presentment.*

president the top officer of an organization. ▶ *Typically, vice presidents report to the president.*

presort the process of arranging mail in order of zip codes before it is given to the Post Office. ▶ *Presort reduces costs for the Post Office.*

press kit a package of material for distribution to print or broadcast media. ▶ *A press kit may include statements, names, addresses, phone numbers, photographs, etc.*

pressure group a group that attempts to influence another group in order to obtain support for the position of its own group. ▶ *Normally, a pressure group seeks to influence legislators to pass legislation favorable to the group's interest or to defeat legislation unfavorable to it.*

prestige advertising advertising that attempts to enhance the public's opinion of the company doing the advertising or the public's opinion of its products. ▶ *In many cases, prestige advertising does not show or describe a product, but refers only to the company.*

prestige goods AND **prestige merchandise** goods sought for consumption primarily because the price is high. ▶ *Consumption of*

prestige goods may enhance one's social status or reputation.

prestige merchandise See the previous entry.

prestige pricing a pricing strategy in which goods or services are priced high with the idea that a high price implies high quality or additional value. ▶ *Prestige pricing works best when there is a boom in the economy.*

prevailing wage the level of wage for a certain class of work common to a labor market or an industry. ▶ *The prevailing wage for any class of work can be determined by conducting a compensation survey.*

preventive discipline the steps taken to ensure that workers are aware of company policies and procedures. ▶ *Preventive discipline focuses on avoiding the need for disciplinary action that may arise from violations of a rule.*

preventive maintenance service work on equipment performed to prevent breakdowns or repairs. (See *maintenance*.) ▶ *With adequate preventative maintenance, there should be no need for major overhauls of the firm's truck fleet.*

preventive mediation the actions taken whereby a mediator assists in facilitating negotiations so that an impasse may be avoided. ▶ *Preventive mediation helps keep the bargaining process from becoming stymied.*

price the amount of money asked for goods or services. ▶ *The price for our best-selling product is $2.99.*

price action the fluctuations in the selling price of a stock, bond, commodity, or good. ▸ *The price action of this stock shows many peaks and valleys.*

price break   a discount on the selling price of an item. ▸ *Because this product has not been selling well, the manufacturer gave us a price break to pass on to the consumer.*

price change   a reduction or increase in a price. ▸ *The price change in this product is prominently displayed in our newspaper ads.*

price code   a symbol representing a particular price. ▸ *According to the price code, items marked with a red dot are half price and those marked with a blue dot are 75% off the regular price.*

price control   the government regulation of the prices of goods and services, usually imposed to impede inflation. ▸ *A price control is usually effective for only a short period of time.*

price cutter   a business that attempts to outsell competitors through lower prices. ▸ *Many new small businesses feel that they must be a price cutter in order to compete with other more established firms.*

price discrimination   the act of charging different prices to different buyers of the same goods. ▸ *Many consultants commit a form of price discrimination by charging not-for-profit companies a different price than for-profit companies are charged.*

price earnings ratio   the market price of a share of stock divided by the annual earnings per share. ▸ *A company in a high growth indus-*

try usually has a high price earnings ratio.

price fixing   **1.** a collusion between two or more competing firms designed to avoid price competition by charging identical prices or by raising and lowering prices at the same time. ▸ *Price fixing is illegal in most countries.* **2.** the government regulation of the prices of goods and services. ▸ *Price fixing by the government usually occurs during a national crisis.*

price index   a device used to show the relative change in the price of a good between a given year and a base year. ▸ *The often-used CPI is an example of a price index.*

price lining   the practice of offering several categories of merchandise each of which has a different price. ▸ *Price lining reflects differences in quality, design, or other characteristics.*

price rigidity   the tendency for the price of goods to remain fixed despite changes in the demand for them. ▸ *Price rigidity frequently, but not always, is the result of a lack of competition.*

price scanner   a device that reads printed bar codes on merchandise and relates the information to a computer. ▸ *A price scanner is computer-based.*

price support   an action taken by the Federal government to maintain a certain minimum price for particular goods or commodities. ▸ *With a price support, the government makes up the difference between the stipulated minimum price and the actual market price.*

price variance the difference between standard cost and actual cost resulting from a change in the price of materials or labor. ▶ *Now that the minimum wage has increased, we have a price variance of one dollar per item at this company.*

price war severe price reductions on the part of one seller followed by additional price cuts by other sellers. (This is repeated through several rounds of price cutting.) ▶ *If a price war persists for any length of time, some sellers will be forced out of the market.*

pricing policy the guidelines used by a business enterprise to set the prices for its goods or services, to revise those prices periodically, and to provide for discounts from established prices. ▶ *We evaluate our pricing policy every year at this company.*

prima facie "at first appearance." (Latin.) ▶ *There is strong prima facie evidence to support Ellen's discrimination case.*

primary boycott a situation wherein the group conducting a boycott, refrains from dealing with the offending firm and attempts to persuade the firm's customers to do likewise. ▶ *A primary boycott is normally conducted by a union.*

primary data original information. ▶ *Primary data is gathered by means of original research, formal investigations, surveys, observations, or experiments, but not from published data or previous research done by someone else.*

prime rate the rate of interest charged by banks to business borrowers with the highest credit ratings. ▶ *The prime rate is the lowest advertised rate of interest charged by a bank.*

prime time in radio and television broadcasting, that period during the evening hours when the greatest potential audience is available. ▶ *Prime time covers a three-hour period, from 8:00 P.M. to 11:00 P.M. in the Eastern Time zone, and from 7:00 P.M. to 10:00 P.M. in the Central Standard Time zone.*

principal 1. the person represented by a broker in a transaction. ▶ *A principal is the client of a broker.* 2. the face amount of a bond or note. ▶ *The principal on this note is $100.* 3. an officer in a firm. ▶ *As CFO, Don is a principal in the firm of ABC Consulting.*

principle a fundamental or general truth upon which other truths or propositions depend. ▶ *The principle upon which this invention is based is really very simple.*

printer 1. a device for printing computer-generated data onto paper. ▶ *At this firm, we have both a dot-matrix and a laser printer.* 2. one who prints. ▶ *Our printer only charged us half price because he did not print our sales piece with the right color ink.*

printout the output from a computer printed on paper. ▶ *Please send the printout to the marketing department as soon as it is ready.*

priority a right or claim that precedes other rights or claims in terms of importance or time. ▶ *This project has priority over the one I gave you last week.*

private bank an unincorporated banking institution, chartered by the state in which it operates, which is owned and operated by an individual or a partnership and consequently has no capital stock. ▶ *The private bank concept was popular in 19th-century England.*

Private Branch Exchange AND **PBX** a telephone switchboard located on a subscriber's premises in which both central office trunk lines and station lines are terminated for the organization's telephone use. ▶ *The Private Branch Exchange is becoming obsolete in the United States.*

private brand AND **house brand; private label** a product whose identification or brand is that of the wholesaler or retailer selling the product. ▶ *A private brand product is typically of the same quality as a brand name product.*

private carrier a situation in which a firm or an individual owns its own transportation methods. ▶ *A private carrier carries only its own goods.*

private company See the following entry.

private corporation AND **private company** a company whose stock is held by the officers or employees of the company rather than the general public. ▶ *It is sometimes difficult to get information about a private company.*

private enterprise system an economic system based on private rather than public ownership of the means of production. ▶ *The private enterprise system is the basis of American economic structure.*

private label See *private brand.*

private placement the process whereby capital is raised by selling corporate securities directly to large investing institutions such as insurance companies, endowment funds, etc. ▶ *Private placement is generally offered only to a small group of investors.*

private property the real and personal property owned by individuals and business enterprises. ▶ *In the U.S., virtually everything in one's home is private property.*

private sale a sale advertised only to a select group of customers. ▶ *The bookstore held a private sale for its best charge account customers.*

private sector the companies operating within the context of free enterprise. ▶ *A government agency is not part of the private sector.*

private warehouse a building owned by a firm, typically for its own use, for the storage of goods for further distribution. ▶ *A private warehouse gives our company more control over inventory and order processing.*

privatization the process of making a company or something else private. ▶ *A company that used to issue stock but wishes to buy it all back so that it is no longer a public company, is engaged in privatization.*

pro bono "for good." (Latin. Describes work done at no charge to the customer, especially in the legal field with reference to performing services for the poor.) ▶ *Lawyers and consultants frequently perform pro bono work for* *charitable organizations.*

pro forma balance sheet See *pro forma statement.*

pro forma income statement See the following entry.

pro forma statement AND **pro forma balance sheet; pro forma income statement** an accounting, financial, or other type of statement containing, at least in part, hypothetical amounts. ▶ *A pro forma statement provides "what if" scenarios.*

pro rata proportionately; in proportion to. ▶ *The money was distributed pro rata.*

pro tem "for the time"; temporarily. ▶ *A mayor pro tem for a city fills in for the mayor when the mayor is out of town.*

proactive pertaining to actions taken to foresee problems or events and deal effectively with them before they become troublesome. ▶ *Proactive management anticipates problems.*

probabilistic model a representation of reality that attempts to predict the outcome of events by assigning risk factors to unknown or unpredictable quantities in the model. ▶ *One benefit of a probabilistic model is that it requires an assessment of risk.*

probability a measurement of the likelihood of an event occurring. ▶ *The range of probability is between 0 and 1.*

probate the legal act of submitting a will before a court of law to establish official proof that the instrument presented is the last will and testament of a decedent. ▶ *Probate*

determines the validity of a will.

probationary employee a new employee who is going through a trial period. ▶ *At the end of a trial period, usually one to three months, the probationary employee who proves satisfactory becomes a regular employee.*

procedure a guide to action that outlines a specific work sequence. ▶ *A procedure depicts the exact steps to follow in performing a given task or accomplishing a certain activity.*

procedure flowchart a graphic representation of a procedure depicting the steps or work flows within and between departments. ▶ *A procedure flowchart frequently uses symbols for particular steps.*

procedures analysis the process of investigating the steps used in carrying out a procedure in order to eliminate wasteful steps and develop the most effective and efficient sequence of steps. ▶ *Procedures analysis includes the preparation, issuance, and periodic updating of written procedural instructions.*

procedures analyst an individual who practices *procedures analysis.* ▶ *John was too impractical to become a procedures analyst.*

procedures manual a book containing written statements of all formalized procedures for accomplishing work within an organization. ▶ *Consult the procedures manual before you begin the task.*

proceeds the amount of cash, property, or other services received after the sale or disposition of property, from a loan, or from the sale or issuance of securities. ▶ *The proceeds from the sale were $10,000.*

process **1.** an arrangement of various operations that systematically produce a product or products. ▶ *The manufacturing process used at this plant is very complex.* **2.** a writ ordering a defendant to appear in court. (See also *summons; subpoena.*) ▶ *The process was served on the defendant during her lunch hour.*

process costing a method of cost accounting whereby costs are assigned or allocated to processes or operations and averaged over the total number of units produced. ▶ *Process costing is used primarily in continuous production operations such as refineries, chemical plants, and canneries.*

process layout the arrangement or grouping together of similar equipment. (See also *group by product.*) ▶ *With a proper process layout, all lathes would be located together, all milling machines would be located together, etc.*

procurement an acquisition of goods or services to operate an enterprise. ▶ *The procurement of raw materials will help us get back to work.*

producer one who brings something into existence. ▶ *General Motors is a producer of automobiles.*

producer's cooperative an association of producers for the purpose of marketing as a group the goods produced by each member of the association. ▶ *Our producer's cooperative does a better job at*

marketing than any of us could alone.

producer's goods items purchased and used in the production of a product. ▶ *Examples of producer's goods include machinery, raw materials, and equipment.*

producer's risk the calculated probability that, under a given sampling plan, certain goods of acceptable quality will be rejected under the plan. ▶ *Producer's risk is computed in statistical quality control analysis.*

product costs the charge or expenses attributable to the manufacture of a product. ▶ *The product costs for this item total $4.50 for each one produced.*

product differentiation a marketing technique that focuses on or attempts to create differences between products. ▶ *Product differentiation may be based on real or perceived differences in products.*

product layout the grouping together of all equipment required to make a certain product. ▶ *Product layout results in a heterogeneous grouping of machines.*

product liability the responsibility manufacturers, sellers, etc., have to compensate consumers for harm caused by defective products. ▶ *Businesses should purchase insurance to protect against potentially high liability claims.*

product life cycle the period of time that a product will have willing buyers. (In the *product life cycle,* a product is developed and establishes a market, which then grows, matures, fades, and finally ceases to be.) ▶ *The product life* *cycle of fad clothing is only a few months.*

product mix the composite variety of items manufactured or distributed by a producer or sold by a wholesaler or retail firm. ▶ *Businesses desire a product mix that gives the highest profits possible.*

production capacity the total productive potential. ▶ *Production capacity at this plant is 3,000 units per day.*

production control the process of planning, routing, scheduling, dispatching, and expediting the flow of materials, parts, etc., within a plant from raw material to finished product. ▶ *Production control assists in assuring efficient use of materials, processes, workers, etc.*

production flow the systematic movement of items from one stage in the manufacturing process to the next. ▶ *We need to examine the production flow of this operation to eliminate wasted time.*

production line AND **assembly line** a method of manufacturing in which machinery and equipment are arranged in the sequence in which they are used in the production or assembly process. ▶ *Automobiles are assembled on a production line.*

production management that portion of the field of management concerned with the process of planning and controlling all phases of manufacturing. ▶ *Among the activities involved in production management are planning and controlling of production processes, production quantity, produc-*

tion quality, and all production-servicing activities such as purchasing and maintenance.

production planning AND **production scheduling** the process of systematically scheduling workers, materials, and machines in order to produce products efficiently and economically and meet desired delivery dates. ▶ *The basic concern of production planning is efficient scheduling.*

production (process) the activities involved in manufacturing a good. ▶ *Production includes purchasing raw materials, using those raw materials in specific processes, and packaging and storing finished goods.*

production scheduling See *production planning.*

production worker an employee of a firm who is directly involved in the manufacturing or processing of goods. ▶ *A production worker is usually paid an hourly wage.*

productivity the ratio of the quantity of output to the quantity of input. ▶ *A new machine should increase productivity substantially.*

profession a vocation requiring knowledge of some department of learning or science. ▶ *Medicine is an example of a profession.*

professional association an organization for individuals in a certain profession. ▶ *In the U.S., there is a professional association for virtually every profession.*

professionalism the act of conducting oneself in ways that exemplify professional character, spirit, or methods. ▶ *In light of several specific instances occurring in the* *last two months, I would say the professionalism of this law firm has slipped somewhat.*

proficiency the skill or experience in some subject, area of endeavor, or task. ▶ *After just one month of practice, many individuals show a proficiency in typing.*

profile chart a graphic representation that summarizes the employment test scores of a job applicant when more than one test is used. ▶ *The profile chart indicates the pattern of abilities and aptitudes of an applicant as determined by various tests.*

profit 1. the excess of revenue, proceeds, or selling price over related costs. ▶ *For May, we show a $700,000 profit.* 2. that which remains after all factors of production have been compensated. ▶ *Profit is a return on capital investment.*

profit and loss statement See *income statement.*

profit center a component of an organization that is expected to produce a profit. ▶ *Our publishing division has become a profit center under the reorganization plans.*

profit margin AND **margin of profit** the difference between revenue and cost. ▶ *The profit margin on milk and eggs is not very great.*

profit sharing plan a system for distributing to employees a predetermined share of a firm's profits for a specified period. ▶ *Distributions in a profit sharing plan are in addition to wages or normal compensation received by employees.*

profit taking the sudden selling of stock by speculators to realize the profits they have made on stock holdings. ▶ *Profit taking tends to cause prices to fall.*

profit-volume graph See *break-even chart.*

profitgraph See *break-even chart.*

program 1. a series of actions and steps to be taken to accomplish specified objectives. ▶ *The program we have in mind for this firm will require several major decisions about financing, marketing, and operating the business.* 2. a sequence of instructions that will cause a computer to perform a series of predetermined and prescribed data processing operations. ▶ *We just purchased a new accounting program for our computer.* 3. to write a sequence of instructions for a computer to perform. ▶ *Fred was unable to program his new computer because he lost the instruction manual.*

program trading the computerized trading of stocks. ▶ *Program trading is designed to buy and sell certain stocks at predetermined price levels.*

programmed decision a decision of a routine nature occurring with some frequency or regularity. ▶ *Because of its routineness or regularity, rules for making a programmed decision in this area can be formulated easily.*

programmed instruction a self-instructional teaching method in which the material to be learned has been broken into small, meaningful units that can be presented to the student one unit at a time. ▶ *Programmed instruction allows learners to proceed at their own pace while at the same time actively involving them in the instruction process.*

progress payment a sum of money paid periodically for contract work performed. ▶ *A progress payment is frequently used in the construction, consulting, and defense industries.*

progression schedule a formal plan for automatically upgrading and increasing workers' wages at stated intervals. ▶ *Our progression schedule states that we will examine workers' wages every six months.*

progressive discipline a disciplinary method in which a more severe punishment is assessed against an employee for each successive infraction. ▶ *Our progressive discipline involves giving first a verbal warning to an employee, then a written warning, a second written warning, then time off from work without pay for a few days, and finally, termination.*

progressive tax a tax system in which the higher an individual's income is, the more that person pays in taxes. ▶ *A progressive tax places the greatest tax burden on those who earn the most money.*

promise an expression of intent; a pledge. ▶ *A promise may be written or expressed verbally.*

promissory note a written promise to pay another a specified sum of money on or before a certain date. ▶ *A promissory note evidences a loan from a bank.*

promo See *promo(tional item)*.

promotion 1. all those activities that supplement personal selling and advertising. ▶ *Displays, trade shows, exhibits, and demonstrations are examples of promotion.* 2. an advancement to a position of greater responsibility. ▶ *A promotion usually brings with it increased compensation.*

promo(tional item) the merchandise given without charge to a customer or used as a means of encouraging the use or purchase of a product or service. ▶ *A pen with a company name printed on it that is distributed to a customer is an example of a promotional item.*

promotional salary increase an increase in pay resulting from advancement to a higher salary grade. ▶ *When Ann got her promotion to Vice President of Human Resources, she received a $5,000 promotional salary increase.*

proof a preliminary transcript of printed matter, submitted for correction before the final printing. ▶ *I received a proof of the article to check for mistakes before it appears in the January issue of the magazine.*

proof of loss a document submitted by the insured to the insurer in support of a claim. ▶ *With a proof of loss, the insurer determines the validity of the claim on the basis of the data submitted.*

propaganda the systematic dissemination of information in which the intent is to cause people to accept or believe the information. ▶

Government propaganda is frequently used in times of war. ▶ *My grandfather always said that the newspaper was nothing but propoganda.*

propensity the inclination or tendency to do something. ▶ *The propensity to save money is very low in the United States compared with some other countries.*

property material goods and rights that can be owned and transferred. ▶ *There are two forms of property: real and personal.*

property dividend a corporate dividend paid in property rather than cash. ▶ *We received a property dividend from the Mendoza Corporation.*

property insurance a type of insurance coverage that pays for actual loss or damage to the insured's property due to fire, rain, lightning, etc. ▶ *Property insurance often specifies a maximum amount of money that will be paid for any one instance of loss.*

proprietary advantage a condition that exists when a firm has a potentially superior market position with a certain product or products. ▶ *A proprietary advantage is usually reinforced through a patent, copyright, or trademark.*

proprietorship See *(sole) proprietorship.*

prospectus a written offer to sell securities. ▶ *A prospectus outlines the financial condition of a corporation and provides details concerning the new security issue.*

protective tariff a tariff on imports that is high enough to protect domestic producers from effective competition by foreign producers. ▶ *A protective tariff is just one tool used in a policy of protectionism.*

protest a written statement under seal, giving formal notice to parties secondarily liable, that an instrument has been dishonored by refusal to accept it or by refusal to make payment on it. ▶ *A protest can be used on a promissory note.*

proxy a written statement authorizing one person to act for another. ▶ *A proxy was drafted so I could vote in the stockholders' meeting in place of John.*

proxy fight a takeover technique in which the acquiring company seeks the approval of the stockholders. ▶ *In a proxy fight, the acquiring company tries to convince stockholders that the current top management is incompetent and should be replaced.*

proxy statement a document accompanying the solicitation of a stockholder's proxy by a corporation. ▶ *Our files indicate that you were not given a proxy statement.*

prudent man rule a principle that guides a trustee in the handling of trust investments. (This can be used in reference to both men and women.) ▶ *The prudent man rule states that when money is left in a trust without specific instructions for its investment, the trustee's own judgement can be used in making investments as long as the trustee acts in a judicious manner.*

PS See *postscript.*

psychic income the noneconomic rewards received by a person for work in certain jobs or occupations. ▶ *Psychic income includes such things as prestige, recognition, pleasant work surroundings, social value of the work, etc.*

psychometrics the use of statistical techniques in psychological measurements. ▶ *Psychological norms are established through psychometrics.*

public company See the following entry.

public corporation AND **public company** a company whose stock is held by the general public rather than by officers or employees of the company. ▶ *The stock price for a particularly large public company can be found in the financial section of many newspapers.*

public debt the total indebtedness of local, state, and national governments of a country. ▶ *The public debt for a country includes the national debt.*

public domain 1. that land that is owned and controlled by the state or Federal government. ▶ *We are now walking on land in the public domain.* 2. the situation that exists when patents or copyrights expire or were never obtained, and the ideas or inventions formerly protected may be used by anyone who desires to do so. ▶ *There are a lot of software programs in the public domain that can be used without fear of copyright infringement.*

public offering the sale of a new issue of corporate securities to the general public rather than to financial institutions. (See also *initial public offering.*) ▶ *They had hoped to make a public offering this month, but market conditions were not right.*

public property the goods or real estate owned by local, state, or Federal governments. ▶ *A state park is an example of public property.*

public relations the efforts of a business firm that are directed toward creating and maintaining a favorable impression on the part of the public toward the firm. ▶ *The XYZ company launched an effort in public relations to counteract bad publicity about its new product.*

public sale a sale by auction in which the general public is invited to bid. ▶ *A public sale will be held for the downtown office building seized by the Federal government.*

public sector the companies and activities operated by a governmental entity. ▶ *Social services are in the public sector.*

public utility a business enterprise afforded monopoly status by the local, state, or Federal government. ▶ *A telephone company is an example of a public utility.*

public warehouse a warehouse that rents storage spaces to the public. ▶ *When we move, we need to be sure to remove the items in the public warehouse.*

publication 1. to make public. ▶ *The publication of the opening of our new store was a real boost.* 2. a journal, newspaper, book, etc. ▶ *According to this publication, stock prices will fall next month.*

publicity a nonpaid form of nonpersonal presentation of goods, services, or ideas to a group. ▶

Today, publicity sometimes includes paid advertising.

puff [for a salesperson] to exaggerate the qualities, characteristics, or capabilities of particular goods or services. (Slang or colloquial.) ▶ *When the salesman told me the dishwasher also served as a great clothes washer and dryer, I knew he was puffing the product.*

pull a degree of influence. ▶ *Ronnie, Vice President of Operations, has the pull necessary to get me a promotion.*

pump priming the infusion of money into the economy by means of large-scale government expenditures for public works or other activities. ▶ *Normally used during periods of depression, pump priming is designed to increase purchasing power and employment as well as to raise the general level of economic activity.*

punch card See *Hollerith card.*

punched paper tape a strip of special paper on which data are recorded by means of a series of holes punched into the paper. ▶ *The width of punched paper tape varies according to the number of holes that may be punched across it.*

punitive damages a monetary award given by a court in excess of actual damages. ▶ *Joy received $2 million in punitive damages from her lawsuit.*

purchase book a special *book of original entry* used to record the purchase of goods or materials. ▶ *We begin a new purchase book every fiscal year.*

purchase discounts account a ledger that records the discounts taken on purchases because the invoices were paid promptly. ▶ *The purchase discounts account shows a total of $1,000 in discounts this year.*

purchase invoice a document describing the details of a sale prepared by the seller of merchandise and sent to the buyer. ▶ *The retailer forgot to send us a purchase invoice for the order we sent them.*

purchase limit the budgeted amount for purchases for a department. ▶ *The purchase limit on office supplies for this department is $750 per month.*

purchase returns and allowances account an account used to record the return of merchandise to the vendor or deductions from the purchase price of damaged or defective goods kept by the purchaser. ▶ *The purchase returns and allowances account is found in the general ledger.*

purchases account a ledger account used to record the purchase of goods or materials. ▶ *Our purchases account indicates we spent over $100,000 last year on supplies.*

purchasing the act of buying goods or services for money. ▶ *We are purchasing a new computer to replace this outdated one.*

purchasing agent an independent middleman who arranges purchases for buyers. ▶ *Our purchasing agent enabled us to get a bargain price on the last shipment of goods.*

purchasing power the ability to buy goods and services. ▶ *What is the current purchasing power of the dollar?*

pure competition AND **perfect**

competition a market condition in which (1) there are many buyers and sellers, (2) buyers are indifferent as to the seller from whom they purchase, (3) there is no product differentiation, (4) there is no collusion among sellers, (5) all buyers are well informed about market conditions, and (6) the buyers and sellers seek to serve their own interests. ▶ *With pure competition, there are no individual buyers or sellers large enough to influence the market.*

purposive sampling See *judgment sampling.*

push money the additional compensation paid to retail sales personnel for exerting extra effort in persuading customers to purchase particular goods or brands of merchandise. ▶ *In our store, we receive $100 in push money for every 300 of these items we sell.*

put (option) a transferable option to deliver a given number of shares of stock at a stipulated price at any time during a given period of time, usually not exceeding three months. ▶ *A put is a contractual agreement.*

p/v graph See *break-even chart.*

pyramid the hierarchy of an organization. ▶ *In a hierarchical organization, the president is at the apex of the pyramid.*

pyramiding a trading technique used by stock market speculators whereby the additional equity that arises in a margin account when the price of a stock increases is used to support additional stock purchases without further cash investment. ▶ *Pyramiding is a technique requiring leveraging.*

Q

Q-rating a determination of the popularity of an individual or product. ▶ *A Q-rating provides information as to whether a product is recognized and whether or not it is liked.*

qualified the possession of the necessary credentials or requirements. ▶ *The qualified candidate for the job will have a graduate degree and ten years' related experience.*

qualitative analysis an evaluation that examines factors not easily measured. ▶ *A qualitative analysis is appropriate when assessing the morale level within an organization.*

quality 1. the essential character of something. ▶ *The quality that is most important to some consumers is low cost.* 2. a property or characteristic. ▶ *This product does not meet our quality expectations.*

quality circle a small group of employees who meet regularly to discuss methods, techniques, procedures, etc., for improving the quality of work in an organization. ▶ *Our quality circle meets on the first Monday of every month.*

quality control the procedure of establishing acceptable limits of variation in size, weight, finish, etc., for products and services. ▶ *Quality control methods help maintain a finished product or service within specified limits.*

quality of work life the extent to which an employee's personal needs are met through experiences within the organization. ▶ *One way to achieve a high degree of quality of work life is to have a participatory or democratic management style.*

quantitative analysis an evaluation that examines factors that are readily measurable. ▶ *Quantitative analysis uses information such as* *sales data, production rates, manufacturing costs, etc., in conducting an assessment.*

quantity discount an allowance given by a seller of goods to a purchaser because of the large size of the individual purchase. ▶ *A quantity discount of 20% was given on our order of 3,000 units of item X34.*

quantity theory of money AND **crude quantity theory (of money)** the theory that the general price level in an economy is determined by the quantity of money in circulation. ▶ *The quantity theory of money is concerned with the velocity with which the quantity of money circulates.*

quantum leap a major change. ▶ *We made a quantum leap in thinking around this company when we decided to focus on customer service rather than on the bottom line.*

quasi contract an obligation imposed by law for the purpose of preventing an injustice in situations where there is no contract between the parties involved. ▶ *On grounds of a quasi contract, funds paid to an individual by mistake can be recovered.*

quasi-public company a corporation privately owned and operated, but for purposes in which the public at large has some interest. ▶ *A charitable corporation is a quasi-public corporation.*

quenching a process used to produce a desired degree of hardness in a metal. ▶ *With quenching, the more rapidly a metal is cooled, the harder it will be.*

questionnaire an orderly series of questions used to gather *primary data.* ▶ *We used a questionnaire to see how companies felt about the quality of service they were providing to their customers.*

queuing theory a mathematical technique for solving waiting-line problems. ▶ *By applying queuing theory, many banks have lessened the amount of time a customer waits for a teller.*

quick assets assets that can be converted into cash very rapidly. ▶ *Marketable securities are quick assets.*

quick cycle manufacturing a production or processing operation characterized by rapid completion. ▶ *Quick cycle manufacturing is usually expressed in terms of minutes or hours.*

quick ratio See *acid test ratio.*

quickie strike See *wildcat strike.*

quid pro quo "something for something"; "this for that." (Latin.) ▶ *In a legal sense, quid pro quo means consideration—that is, a payment.*

quitclaim deed a written instrument that releases a right or interest in land, but does not include any remedy or warranty. ▶ *A warranty deed is preferable to a quitclaim deed.*

quorum the minimum number of officers, directors, or members of an organization who must be present at a meeting in order to proceed with the purpose of the meeting. (The bylaws of the organization determine the minimum number.) ▶ *Unfortunately, we cannot conduct the meeting because we do not yet* *have a quorum.*

quota a predetermined standard amount. ▶ *Our quota on defects is not to allow more than one per one hundred items produced.*

quota bonus a bonus provided to salespersons for meeting or exceeding a *quota*. ▶ *I received a quota bonus of $500 for exceeding the sales goal of 250 units.*

quota sampling a research sampling procedure that selects a limited number of observations from a population by separating the population into groups on the basis of known attributes or characteristics and drawing a certain number of cases from each group. ▶ *Quota sampling makes it possible to get useful results from a small sampling.*

quotation AND **quote** **1.** the current selling or asking price of any security or commodity. ▶ *The broker gave me a quotation on this stock.* **2.** the price submitted by a supplier to a purchaser. ▶ *Please provide me with a quotation on the products listed below.*

quote See the previous entry.

R

rack jobber AND **rack merchandiser** a type of full service wholesaler that installs company-owned display racks in retail outlets in order to display the company's merchandise. ▶ *A rack jobber is very common in the grocery business.*

rack merchandiser See the previous entry.

Racketeer Influenced and Corrupt Organizations Act AND **RICO** a Federal act designed to convict companies and individuals of insider trading. ▶ *The Racketeer Influenced and Corrupt Organizations Act was used, some have felt, too excessively in the late 1980s.*

raider an individual or a corporation that attempts to takeover another firm by buying a large block of stock. ▶ *A raider may need to buy only 10% of a corporation's stock to have enough for a takeover.*

raiding 1. the process of taking over another corporation. ▶ *The investor is raiding another firm.* 2. the process of enticing employees of another firm to one's own company. ▶ *Our competition is raiding us of all our best employees.*

raincheck a note given to customers when advertised products are currently out of stock, entitling them to purchase the products at the advertised price when the stock is replenished. ▶ *I am sorry we are out of stock on this particular item, sir. Would you like to take a raincheck on it?*

rally a rise in the price of a security or market after a period of decline. ▶ *It is predicted that the market will rally soon.*

RAM See the following entry.

random access memory AND **RAM** primary storage in a computer in which data can be randomly stored and accessed. ▶ *The size of* *a computer's RAM indicates the computer's overall capacity.*

random number table a set of numbers, formed at random, arranged in tabular form. ▸ *Don used a random number table to pick his six numbers for the lottery drawing.*

random sample a selection of a limited number of observations drawn entirely by chance from a population. ▸ *In a true random sample, each item in the population has the same probability of being selected.*

range the difference between the largest and the smallest value in a group of data. ▸ *The range of a sample simply indicates the two extremes; it is of little usefulness in assessing the dispersion of data.*

rank and file everyday; general; common. (Refers to the average worker.) ▸ *When the rank and file employees hear about this, they will be angry.*

rank correlation a method of measuring the relationship between the rankings of two series of statistical data. ▸ *Rank correlation can be used when conventional correlation is not suitable.*

ranking method a technique for evaluating jobs in which the jobs are listed in rank order from the highest level job in the organization to the lowest level job. ▸ *The ranking method is a simple approach to the determination of salary scales.*

ratchet effect sharp irregularities in the product life cycle, especially during the decline phase. ▸ *It was easy to recognize that the product life cycle was coming to an end because of the ratchet effect.*

rate buster a worker whose production exceeds the rate of production informally established by the work group. ▸ *A rate buster is not looked upon favorably by other employees.*

rate cutting the act of reducing the time standard for a production operation or reducing the amount of money paid for the operation. ▸ *Rate cutting is considered particularly negative when the reduction is thought by the workers to be unjustified in terms of changes in product design, quality requirements, production methods, etc.*

rate of change the relative or percentage change in a statistical series from one period to the next, or from a base period to the present period. ▸ *The rate of change for this series is 25 from last year.*

rate of exchange See *exchange rate.*

rate of return See *yield.*

rate setting the establishing of production standards through the use of work measurement techniques. ▸ *Once rate setting is complete we can compute incentive compensation for production above the rate.*

rating a method or process used to evaluate employee performance periodically. ▸ *The human resource manager is setting dates for rating performance.*

rating scale a graduated series of criteria or reference points that are used as a standard for measuring, evaluating, or classifying. ▶ *A rating scale is frequently used in job evaluation and performance appraisal.*

rating system See *performance appraisal.*

ratio the relationship of one number to another. ▶ *The ratio of profit dollars to sales dollars at our firm is 1 to 2.*

ratio analysis a technique that examines the ratios of balance sheet items to other balance sheet items or the ratios derived from comparisons of income and expense items. ▶ *Ratio analysis is frequently used in financial analysis to ascertain a company's performance.*

raw material something that will be converted or transformed into a finished product. ▶ *Steel is a raw material in the automobile industry.*

reacquired shares the corporate shares that have been returned to the firm, usually through repurchase by the company. ▶ *All reacquired shares go into the company treasury.*

read only memory AND **ROM** the storage created by a computer in which data and/or instructions can be read only. ▶ *Nothing can be written into ROM memory.*

Reaganomics the economic policies developed by former U.S. president, Ronald Reagan. ▶ *Reaganomics is characterized by conservatism and free market economic policies.*

real estate land or anything permanently attached to the land. ▶ *A building is also part of real estate.*

real estate agent an independent third party who brings buyers and sellers of real estate together so that transactions may be consummated. ▶ *The real estate agent found an office building that met our specifications and was priced below what we were willing to pay!*

real estate investment trust a mutual fund in which investors buy shares in a trust invested in real estate. ▶ *A real estate investment trust must have widely dispersed ownership.*

real estate mortgage a mortgage on real property. ▶ *We obtained a real estate mortgage on our farm.*

real income AND **real wages** the purchasing power of monetary income. ▶ *Real income determines the quantity of goods that can be purchased with the money a person earns.*

real interest rate the current interest rate less the inflation rate. (The interest eaten up by inflation has no purchasing power.) ▶ *The current interest rate is 6% but inflation is 2% so the real interest rate is 4%.*

real rate of return the current rate of return less the inflation rate. (See also the previous entry.) ▶ *Real rate of return on an investment is expressed in terms of purchasing power.*

real time the feedback of information from a system within such a short period of time that any necessary corrections in the operation of the system can be made before the output of the system is finalized. ▶ *Real time computing is* *particularly useful in ongoing kinds of processes.*

real wages See *real income.*

realization concept a basic accounting principle that states that revenue is considered as being earned on the date at which it is realized or the date when goods or services are furnished to the customer. ▶ *The realization concept determines the dates on which payments or income is recorded.*

realized made real; completed. ▶ *The transaction was realized when the product was delivered.*

rebate **1.** the act of refunding some part of the charge made for goods or services. ▶ *The manufacturer will rebate $1.00 for every purchase made.* **2.** the part of the charge made for a good or a service that is refunded to the purchaser. ▶ *A $5.00 rebate was given to every customer.*

recall **1.** the process whereby a firm calls in the securities that it has issued by paying the current owners an agreed upon price. ▶ *The corporation will recall the issued securities.* **2.** the act of a manufacturer who requests that defective goods be returned for repair or replacement. ▶ *Usually, there is no charge to consumers for a recall initiated by a manufacturer.* **3.** the act of rehiring employees from a layoff. ▶ *After a two-month layoff period, the company will finally recall the employees.*

recall campaign an advertising campaign conducted by a manufacturer for the purposes of a recall of defective goods. ▶ *The company* initiated a recall campaign in the newspaper to alert consumers to the need to return the defective toy.

recapitalization the voluntary exchange of one corporate security for another. ▶ *An example of a recapitalization is the exchange of debentures for mortgage bonds.*

receipt written evidence of payment; written evidence of receiving something. ▶ *The clerk gave Tom a receipt after he paid for the groceries.* ▶ *The jeweler gave Alice a receipt for the watch that she left for repair.*

receipts earnings; money taken in. ▶ *Business was very good this month and our receipts are up by 30 percent.*

recession a moderate or temporary decline in economic activity. ▶ *A recession is characterized by increased unemployment and slightly reduced consumption.*

reciprocal buying an arrangement whereby the seller of a good or service buys a good or service from the customer. ▶ *Reciprocal buying helps establish a good buyer-seller relationship.*

reclamation a restoration to productive use. ▶ *The reclamation of this land includes building a public park on it.*

reclassification of stock an alteration of the capital structure of a corporation. ▶ *Reclassification of stock may involve issuing preferred stock when a company currently has only common stock.*

recognition **1.** the formal acknowledgement by an employer that a specific union is authorized to represent those employees that are within a designated collective bargaining unit. ▶ *The management team made an official recognition of the union.* **2.** an acknowledgement of an employee's good behavior, action, or deed. ▶ *The manager gave recognition of Tom's exceptional sales record by giving Tom a plaque.*

record date the date on which the records of stockholders will be established for the payment of dividends. (All stockholders shown on the books as owners on the *record date* are entitled to receive dividends. Since shares are traded frequently, this determines who will get the dividend when it is paid.) ▶ *The board of directors set July 1 as the record date for the payment of the annual dividend.*

records management AND **information management** a system for collecting, maintaining, and disposing of an organization's stored information. ▶ *Records management will require a specialized department in a large firm.*

(records) retention schedule a chart or listing of documents or records maintained in the files of an organization. ▶ *A records retention schedule shows the period of time each document or record should be accessible in its original form, the period of time each should be retained in inactive storage, and the point in time at which each should be destroyed.*

recourse the right of a holder in due course of a negotiable instrument to force prior endorsers of the instrument to meet their legal obligations by making good the

payment of the instrument if dishonored by the maker or acceptor. ▶ *Recourse is negated when the endorser signs the instrument with "no recourse."*

recovery the period following a depression or recession in which the economy begins to improve. (A *recovery* is characterized by a slight increase in employment and consumption.) ▶ *The recovery was accompanied by an increase in consumer spending.*

recruitment attracting and hiring personnel. ▶ *Recruitment is an ongoing activity in a large firm.*

recruitment bonus an extra financial sum given to a person for locating potential employees. ▶ *A recruitment bonus is usually given only for locating applicants for uncommon or highly specialized jobs.*

recycling the reprocessing of used materials into new goods. ▶ *Recycling is commonly used for glass, plastic, and paper.*

red circle rate a salary currently being paid to an employee that falls outside the pay range established for a job class. ▶ *A red circle rate is a common problem with salaries of existing employees when a new compensation system goes into effect.*

red ink loss; debt. (When bookkeeping was done manually, black ink was used to indicate credits and *red ink* for debits. The opposite of *black ink*.) ▶ *We would hate to see red ink on the bottom line next quarter.*

red tape overly burdensome, elaborate, complex, or unnecessary rules, regulations, policies, or procedures. (*Red tape* makes things more difficult or time consuming than is necessary.) ▶ *This red tape created by the personnel department is preventing us from taking corrective action.*

redemption the retirement of stocks or bonds by the issuing corporation through repurchase. ▶ *Redemption usually occurs at a price previously agreed upon.*

redemption fund See *sinking fund.*

redemption price the price at which a corporation will repurchase its stocks or bonds in order to retire them. ▶ *The redemption price is typically set well in advance of redemption.*

redemption value the worth of a bond, note, or any instrument, or evidence of debt, at a stated time or at maturity. ▶ *Redemption value is usually par value plus a premium.*

rediscount rate the rate of interest charged for discounting commercial notes and drafts. (See also *discount rate.*) ▶ *The rediscount rate varies in time.*

reduction in force AND **RIF** a layoff. ▶ *A reduction in force may be the only way to trim personnel costs quickly.*

reference check the contacting of the personal or business references given by a prospective employee in order to gather information about the applicant's background, personality, etc. ▶ *A reference check allows verification of the information supplied by an employment applicant.*

referendum the act of submitting measures, already approved by a legislative body, to the vote of the electorate to ascertain their opinion. ▶ *The results of a referendum are not normally binding on a legislative body.*

refinancing the retirement of existing debt by the issue of new securities; the replacement of old debt with new, usually less costly, debt. ▶ *The object of refinancing may be to extend the maturity date of a loan, reduce the interest rate, or a combination of the two.*

refrigerator car a boxcar equipped with refrigeration coils and capable of keeping the contents of the railroad car in a chilled state. ▶ *A refrigerator car is especially useful for perishable items.*

refund **1.** to return cash or a check. ▶ *The store will refund our money for this defective item.* **2.** a return of cash or a check. ▶ *I received a full refund for the money I paid in light of the poor service I got.*

regional bank a bank operating in a small geographic location. ▶ *A regional bank is smaller than a money center bank.*

registered bond a bond whose owner's name is listed on the books of the issuing firm. ▶ *In order to affect transfer of ownership, a registered bond must be endorsed by the owner.*

registered representative a full-time employee of a member stock brokerage firm who has met the requirements stipulated by a stock exchange. ▶ *A registered representative is usually referred to as a broker.*

registered trademark a legally protected logo, design, or motto used to differentiate a product from other similar products. ▶ *A registered trademark appears on packaging and written information about a brand name and is identified by the symbol, ®.*

registered trader a member of a stock exchange who holds a financial interest in and trades in particular stocks. ▶ *Margaret, a member of the New York Stock Exchange, is a registered trader.*

registrar a bank or trust company appointed by a corporation to account for the original and all subsequent issues of the company's capital stock, the cancellation of certificates presented for transfer, and their reissue. ▶ *All of the certificates were turned over to the registrar for processing.*

registration the process of qualifying stocks or bonds for sale to the public. (*Registration* involves filing various documents with state commissions or with the *Securities and Exchange Commission.*) ▶ *The registration of the stock is now complete and they can be sold as planned.*

registration statement a requirement of the Federal Securities Act of 1933, which provides that a company issuing new securities must file a statement of pertinent financial facts about itself. ▶ *A registration statement must contain complete details about the firm and the security issue involved.*

regression analysis the development and study of average relationships between variables by means of the *least squares* method of correlation. ▶ *Regression analysis describes how one variable is related to another.*

regressive tax a tax whose burden falls more heavily on those with lower incomes than it does on those with higher incomes. ▶ *A sales tax is a regressive tax because those with lower incomes pay a larger percentage of their incomes in sales taxes than those with higher incomes.*

regulated industry an industry that is heavily regulated by the government. ▶ *The electric utility industry is an example of a regulated industry.*

Regulation A a regulation of the *Securities and Exchange Commission* that exempts certain classes of domestic and Canadian securities from registration. ▶ *Regulation A provides for simplification of registration procedures.*

Regulation E a regulation of the *Securities and Exchange Commission* that exempts from registration certain small business investment companies. ▶ *Regulation E gives exemption to certain businesses licensed under the Small Business Investment Act of 1958.*

Regulation Q a Federal banking regulation that limits the rates banks can pay on time deposits. ▶ *Regulation Q was first instituted under the Banking Act of 1933 and has been amended several times since then.*

Regulation S-X a *Securities and Exchange Commission* regulation that defines the form and content of financial statements. ▶ *The statement was flawed in that it was not as prescribed by Regulation S-X.*

Regulation T a Federal regulation that controls the amount of credit that may be extended by members of national securities exchanges and brokers doing business through them for the purchase of securities. ▶ *Regulation T sets up initial margin requirements.*

Regulation U a Federal regulation that controls the amount of credit that may be extended by banks for the purchase of securities. ▶ *The bank ran into trouble with Regulation Q and had to produce a mass of paperwork to resolve it.*

Regulation Z a Federal regulation that requires that creditors provide full disclosure of the terms of a loan. ▶ *Regulation Z forces disclosure of the annual percentage rate of a loan.*

reinsurance the practice of one insurance company purchasing insurance from another. ▶ *Reinsurance is a method by which insurance companies help lessen their risk.*

reliability the consistency with which a given test yields the same results. ▶ *A test should have a reasonable degree of reliability before it is used as a selection tool.*

remedy a legal means of correcting or preventing a wrong or of enforcing a right. ▶ *Joe sought remedy for the injuries caused by the defective product.*

remit to transfer, transmit, or send money to another person or organization. ▶ *Please remit $20 for full payment of your order.*

remittance the money transferred, transmitted, or sent to another person or organization. ▶ *The remittance of $20 has been mailed.*

remuneration a payment of money for work done, services performed, a loss, an expense, etc. ▶ *Contestants on the game show received a remuneration from the sponsor.*

renewal the liquidation of an existing loan on or before its maturity by permitting the borrower to execute and to substitute a new note with a different date, for the old note. ▶ *A renewal creates a new obligation and extends the term of credit.*

rent an amount paid for the use of land or the improvements thereon, or for the use of capital goods. ▶ *We pay $1,000 per month in rent for this office space.*

reorder to place another order for the same product, service, etc. ▶ *We will reorder twelve of item number 345AB.*

reorder point the point at which additional quantities of an item will be ordered. ▶ *The reorder point may be based on quantity levels, time, or other factors.*

reorganization the voluntary readjustment of a corporation's debt and capital stock or a readjustment of debt and capital stock as ordered by a court of law. ▶ *A reorganization may take place if a company declares bankruptcy.*

replacement the act of replacing an employee or a piece of equipment with another. ▶ *A replace-*

ment for the defective machine should be purchased immediately.

replacement price the current market price of a good. ▶ *The replacement price of an item of merchandise is sometimes higher than the original purchase price, especially in times of inflation.*

reporting pay See *call pay.*

reporting period that period of time encompassed by or reflected on a given report. ▶ *Our reporting period is one year.*

repossession the retaking of an article of personal property sold under a credit arrangement due to failure to meet payments. ▶ *The repossession of the truck occurred because the contractor had missed 3 payments.*

reprimand an oral or written reproof by a person in authority. ▶ *Tom's reprimand was worse because it was made in front of his coworkers.*

reprivatization the turning over to the private sector of functions previously performed by the government. ▶ *Allowing private firms to provide fire protection and ambulance services are examples of reprivatization.*

repudiation the refusal to perform in whole or in part a contractual obligation. ▶ *Repudiation is generally a legal right.*

request for bid AND **RFB; request for quotation; request for proposal; RFP** a formal invitation by a potential purchaser to suppliers to submit price proposals on specific goods or services. ▶ *The city issued a request for bid to various contractors for proposals on con-*

structing a new school building.

request for proposal See the previous entry.

request for quotation See *request for bid.*

requisition to request the acquisition of goods or services. ▶ *We must requisition more paper for the office copier.*

resale price maintenance a practice in which the manufacturer fixes the minimum price at which particular goods may be sold to the ultimate consumer. ▶ *With resale price maintenance, the manufacturer imposes sanctions on price cutting by the retailer.*

rescission cancellation. ▶ *When rescission of a contract occurs, parties return to the same position they were in before the contract was made.*

research a systematic, scholarly, or scientific investigation or an inquiry into some topic of interest. ▶ *Their research included a survey of current customers to assess their satisfaction with the company's products.*

research and development that function of a firm charged with inventing, designing, or otherwise creating and developing new products or ideas. ▶ *The Research and Development Department is responsible for three new products this year.*

reserve fund that portion of a firm's profits not paid out in dividends but retained to meet exceptional demands or opportunities. ▶ *The board agreed to use the reserve fund to purchase the land adjacent to the factory.*

reserve requirement a legal requirement that commercial banks maintain an amount of cash or cash equivalents on hand. (See also *legal reserve.*) ► *A lot of banking activity is concerned with meeting the reserve requirement.*

reserve stock goods that are not necessarily in view for the customer, but are available for sale if necessary. ► *We don't have any more of these items on the shelf, but let me check to see if there are some more in reserve stock.*

resident buyer a buying organization located in a central wholesale market and serving clients who are too small or too geographically removed to have their own buyers in the market at all times. ► *As a resident buyer, Joan kept her clients informed of market conditions and sources of supply.*

residual value See *salvage value.*

resistance to change a behavioral attitude that reflects the reluctance or unwillingness of people to accept new or different ways of doing things. ► *Coping with resistance to change by employees is one of the toughest parts of a manager's job.*

resolution an action or a proposal for action. ► *The resolution made by the board of directors of the corporation will go into effect immediately.*

responsibility an obligation to execute assigned duties. ► *In order to be effective, responsibility must be accompanied by sufficient authority to perform the duties.*

responsible bidder a company bidding on a request for bid that is financially sound, honest, and competent to perform the work requested. ► *A bankrupt company bidding on a project is not a responsible bidder.*

rest allowance See *fatigue allowance.*

restitution the compensation or its equivalent given for loss, damage, or injury caused by another. ► *Restitution may simply involve giving certain property back to an individual.*

restraint of trade any action that tends to hinder the free exchange of goods or services or to lessen competition. ► *Restraint of trade may include price fixing, creation of a monopoly, or any other similar action.*

restricted security a stock or bond that is traded even though the trade is not registered with the *Securities and Exchange Commission.* ► *A registered security is sometimes traded in a private sale.*

restrictive endorsement an endorsement of a negotiable instrument that limits any further negotiation. ► *An example of a restrictive endorsement is "for deposit only" written on the back of a check over the depositor's signature.*

retail the business of selling directly to the consumer. ► *The retail industry generally sells goods in small quantities rather than in bulk.*

retail bank a commercial bank that deals primarily with small customers. ► *A retail bank offers a wide variety of consumer services.*

retail investor See *small investor.*

retail sale a sale of goods or services in which the buyer is an ultimate consumer, not a business or institution. ▶ *The customer's motive in a retail sale is usually personal or family satisfaction.*

retail store a place of business, open to the public, in which sales are made primarily to ultimate consumers. ▶ *A retail store sells in small quantities from stocks of merchandise displayed and stored on the premises.*

retailer a merchant who sells primarily to ultimate consumers. (While a *retailer* may sell to businesses or institutions, the bulk of sales are to individuals, and are usually in small quantities.) ▶ *Joan found it rough going as a retailer of children's clothing.*

retailing the activities involved in selling goods or services to ultimate consumers who purchase them for personal or household use. ▶ *Retailing focuses on the needs and wants of ultimate consumers.*

retained earnings the residue of net earnings after the distribution of dividends to the stockholders. ▶ *Retained earnings are cumulative from year to year and become part of the owner's equity account.*

retainer a fee paid to a lawyer, consultant, or other professional for professional services, as needed, over a period of time. ▶ *The consultant was given a one-year retainer of $40,000 by the company.*

retardation a period of sluggish economic activity. ▶ *Retardation may signal the onset of a depression.*

retention schedule See *(records) retention schedule.*

retired bond a bond that has been redeemed by its issuing company. ▶ *A retired bond is no longer in circulation.*

retirement the permanent withdrawal from gainful work by an employee, usually with a pension or a retirement allowance. ▶ *Retirement may be a result of old age, disability, or illness.*

retirement plan a program established to provide income for workers when they retire from employment. ▶ *A retirement plan may be established by self-employed individuals.*

retrenchment the process of reducing organizational expenses or cutting back on personnel. ▶ *Retrenchment is usually an attempt to save money.*

retroactive pertaining to something that extends back to a previous date. ▶ *Retroactive pay is wages for work performed at an earlier date or since an earlier date.*

return See *yield.*

return on capital See the following entry.

return on investment AND **return on capital** profit produced by any type of investment. ▶ *Return on investment is usually expressed as a percentage of the total investment.*

revaluation the upward adjustment of a country's fixed exchange rate. (See also *devaluation.*) ▶ *The* *pound is undergoing revaluation against the dollar at the present time.*

revenue 1. the cash received from the sale of products or services, or from earnings. ▶ *Revenue is cash received from interest, dividends, rents, and wages.* 2. the gross receipts of a governmental unit as derived from taxes, duties, fees, etc. ▶ *Revenue is governmental income.*

revenue sharing a split of revenue between partners in a business or between governmental entities. ▶ *Revenue sharing is common in limited partnerships.*

reverse stock split the issuance of one share of corporate stock in exchange for more than one share of stock currently outstanding. ▶ *A reverse stock split decreases the number of shares outstanding without affecting the total value of all the stock.*

revocable trust a trust that may be terminated by its creator. ▶ *A revocable trust has certain advantageous tax implications.*

revocation a withdrawal, annulment, cancellation, destruction, or reversal. ▶ *The revocation of the contract was inevitable.*

revolving credit an arrangement that permits a consumer to purchase goods up to a given amount and allows a certain length of time to pay for them. ▶ *Revolving credit is a form of installment buying.*

revolving letter of credit a letter of credit issued for a specific amount that renews itself for the same amount over a given period of time. ▶ *A revolving letter of*

credit is a written document.

RFB See *request for bid.*

RFP See *request for bid.*

rhochrematics the science of managing material flow. ▶ *Within a business organization, rhochrematics would encompass producing, marketing, transporting, processing, handling, storing, and distributing goods.*

RICO See *Racketeer Influenced and Corrupt Organizations Act.*

rider a clause that has been added to an original contract, bill, or insurance policy. ▶ *The purpose of a rider is to add some special idea, thought, or coverage not included in the body of the original document.*

RIF See *reduction in force.*

rigging the market the act of making a number of bids for stocks to artificially drive up the price of the stocks. ▶ *Rigging the market gives the appearance of high demand for a particular stock.*

right- and left-hand chart a methods analysis chart on which the motions made by one hand in relation to those of the other hand are recorded and classified. ▶ *The right- and left-hand chart is the basic methods analysis tool.*

right of survivorship the right one person has to joint property when one of the owners dies. ▶ *Based on her right of survivorship, she is entitled to this property now that her husband has deceased.*

right of way the right to pass over land owned by another. ▶ *Frequently, right of way is obtained* *by a government exercising the right of eminent domain.*

right-sizing   action taken by a company to reduce work force or shed excessive units. ▶ *The purpose of right-sizing is to reduce an organization's size to one that will likely be more efficient and effective.*

right to work law   a state statute forbidding union shop agreements under which an employee must join a union after entering the employ of a firm that has a union. ▶ *Right to work laws are often opposed by organized labor.*

ring   See *pit.*

riot selling   the selling of merchandise at greatly reduced prices. ▶ *The riot selling of children's clothes drew a large crowd even before the store opened.*

risk   the possibility of suffering harm or loss from any means. (See also *consumer's risk; credit risk; financial risk; legal risk; producer's risk.*) ▶ *Risk is the element of uncertainty that occurs when any task is undertaken.*

risk analysis AND **risk management**   a methodical study of an investment or a course of action to determine the probability of its success or failure. ▶ *According to the risk analysis we conducted, this venture represents a sound investment.*

risk arbitrage   *arbitrage* that involves risk. ▶ *Entities with vast financial resources sometimes engage in risk arbitrage.*

risk management   See *risk analysis.*

Robinson-Patman Act of 1938   a Federal act prohibiting firms engaged in interstate commerce from granting or receiving discounts or service concessions where the effect of such concessions will tend to substantially lessen competition. ▶ *Discounts for quantity purchases are allowed under the Robinson-Patman Act of 1938 if the vendor can justify them in terms of cost, with the burden of proof resting upon the vendor.*

robot   a machine operated by a computer, which performs certain tasks. ▶ *A robot is particularly useful in performing repetitive tasks.*

robotics   the science of robots. ▶ *Robotics attempts to improve the efficiency and productivity of robots.*

role conflict   a condition occurring when an individual must attempt to achieve opposing goals in an organization. ▶ *Role conflict is common when someone has two or more supervisors.*

role congruence   a situation where the expected role and the actual role are essentially the same. ▶ *Role congruence reduces organizational conflict.*

role perception   the role one thinks or believes that one plays in an organization. ▶ *My role perception does not match my job description.*

role-playing   a training technique wherein the trainees assume the attitudes and behavior of, as well as act out the roles of, the individuals involved in a particular situation. ▶ *Role-playing is a very effective* *technique for training managers in situations requiring interpersonal communication.*

role prescription the role an organization specifies that a person play. (Compare with *job description*.) ▶ *A role prescription is concerned more with goals than with procedures.*

role theory the study of social roles and how they interact. ▶ *Role theory studies such things as role conflict, role congruence, role perception, and role prescription.*

rolling stock the wheeled vehicles owned by a railroad or a trucking company. ▶ *Rolling stock includes boxcars, trucks, locomotives, etc.*

ROM See *read only memory.*

Rorschach Test a projective form of psychological personality testing consisting of a series of cards containing ink blots. (The person taking the *Rorschach Test* describes what is seen in the ink blots, thereby, according to psychologists, revealing certain personality traits.) ▶ *Fred thought that most of the cards in the Rorschach Test represented ink blots!*

rotating shift the practice of having all workers change their work periods at certain intervals. ▶ *With a rotating shift, each worker in turn may work on the first shift, second shift, or third shift.*

roughneck an oil field worker. ▶ *A roughneck may perform several different jobs on a drilling rig.*

round lot AND **even lot** a unit of trading on one of the financial exchanges. (Generally, a *round lot* is 100 shares of stock or $1,000 par value in the case of bonds, except

in special instances.) ▶ *Joan always buys stock in even lots.*

route selling the selling of goods in a predetermined geographical sequence. ▶ *A milkman or newspaper deliverer are examples of people who do route selling.*

routine a computer program or a part of a program. ▶ *The computer is taking a long time to finish that routine.*

routing the specification of the route or path that any work or product is to follow. ▶ *Usually, routing involves specifying operations in proper sequence and naming specific departments, equipment, and personnel involved in the production process.*

royalty compensation paid for the use of property, especially a patent or copyright. ▶ *A royalty is usually a percentage of the total income produced from the use of the property.*

résumé a summary of a person's educational background, work experience, accomplishments, etc. ▶ *A résumé is usually submitted before one is interviewed for a job opening.*

rubber check a check that is no good. (Slang or colloquial. A *rubber check* "bounces.") ▶ *He got in trouble for trying to cash a rubber check.*

Rule of 72 the amount of time it takes money to double when compounded interest is being earned. (Divide the interest rate into 72 to get the approximate number of years until the original sum has doubled.) ▶ *At 6 percent, the Rule of 72 indicates that it will take* *approximately 12 years for the original sum to double.*

Rule of 78s   a technique for determining unearned interest on a prepaid loan contract. ▶ *The Rule of 78s uses fractions in the calculation of interest with 78 being the denominator and one through twelve, the numerators.*

rumor   a story or statement that cannot be confirmed with certainty as to its truthfulness. ▶ *A rumor is going through the plant that 100 employees will be laid off.*

rumor mill   a person or group of persons who frequently originate or spread rumors. ▶ *The rumor mill is responsible for the idea that 100 employees will be laid off at this plant.*

Rust Belt   the area of the United States (primarily, the Ohio Valley), formerly known as the *Steel Belt,* where steel was once a major industry. ▶ *The Rust Belt gets its name because the Steel Belt is no longer producing at the capacity it once was, hence plants are closed and the equipment is rusting.*

S

safe harbor a legal position adopted when trying to comply with a law. ▶ *A safe harbor is used when a law or statute is very vague.*

safety engineer a person who has been trained or who has specialized in the field of industrial accident prevention. ▶ *The safety engineer prepared a 14-point program for reducing accidents at our plant.*

safety stock AND **buffer stock** extra inventory that is carried as a protection against running out of stock. ▶ *We had to fall back on our buffer stock last month.*

salariat the [salaried] working class. ▶ *The salariat is made up of those individuals who work.*

salary the fixed compensation paid to an employee weekly, monthly, etc. ▶ *Unlike wages, salary does not depend directly upon the number of hours worked.*

salary supplement an employer's contribution to the private pension funds, health and welfare funds, payment of insurance premiums, etc., received by salaried employees. ▶ *Benefits are a salary supplement.*

sale and leaseback an arrangement in which one firm sells equipment to another entity for cash and then leases the equipment back for a period of time. ▶ *The purpose of a sale and leaseback is to take advantage of certain tax breaks.*

sales analysis the systematic study of the sales made by a business enterprise. ▶ *A sales analysis is conducted with regard to product, territory, salesperson, period, etc.*

sales book a book in which a retail salesperson keeps record of sales. ▶ *Often, a sales book is provided with one or two carbon copies, one of which is given to the customer as a receipt.*

sales budget an estimate of the total expected sales and selling expenses. ▶ *A sales budget is classified by product, territory, or salesperson, for a specified period.*

sales engineer a salesperson who sells industrial equipment of a complex nature. ▶ *The sales engineer is trying to sell us a numerically controlled machine.*

sales forecast an estimate of sales for a specified future period. ▶ *According to our sales forecast, sales next year will be approximately $500 million.*

sales management the planning, organizing, supervising, and controlling of the selling functions of a business enterprise. (*Sales management* encompasses research into markets, products, and distribution methods; recruiting, training, and overseeing salespersons; establishment and control of sales territories; control of selling expenses; development of compensation plans; and sales promotion.) ▶ *The techniques and practices of good sales management can make the difference between a successful company and a failure.*

sales plan a statement of expected sales for a specified period. ▶ *The sales plan is based on the sales forecast.*

sales potential the estimated total market for any class of product or service. ▶ *The sales potential for iced coffee is probably limited in the United States.*

sales presentation the actual formal contact a salesperson has with prospective customers. ▶ *In a classic sales presentation, the sales-person outlines the benefits of the product or service, answers questions, meets and counters objections of the customer, and finally closes the sale.*

sales promotion activities that supplement or improve the sales function. ▶ *Sales promotion includes sales aids, brochures, displays, technical assistance, and trade shows.*

sales quota a sales goal set for an individual salesperson, a group of salespeople, or a specific organizational unit. ▶ *A sales quota is usually expressed in dollars.*

sales resistance a negative attitude on the part of a buyer or prospective buyer toward the purchase of a good or service. ▶ *Sales resistance is usually directed toward the salesperson or the item being sold.*

sales return a good returned to the seller. ▶ *Our company has a no-questions-asked sales return policy.*

sales tax a percentage tax imposed on goods sold. ▶ *A sales tax is paid by the purchaser to the seller, who then remits that amount to the government.*

sales territory a geographic area assigned to a salesperson or sales department. ▶ *Her sales territory encompasses all of the eastern states of the United States.*

salesperson an individual who sells something. ▶ *In some instances, a salesperson must be licensed, as in real estate.*

Sallie Mae See *Student Loan Marketing Association.*

salvage the things of value remaining from a fire, an accident, or the scrapping of an asset. ▶ *The salvage from the fire included a file cabinet, a metal desk, and a few odds and ends.*

salvage value AND **residual value** the amount that can be realized from an asset at the time it is sold or otherwise disposed of at the end of its useful life. ▶ *The salvage value of an item is determined after it has been depreciated.*

sample **1.** that portion of a population selected in order to ascertain the characteristics of the total population. ▶ *A sample is typically used in statistical applications because the population is too large to work with.* **2.** a product distributed free of charge to consumers or prospective consumers. ▶ *For a free sample of our newsletter, send your request to our headquarters.*

sampling the act of selecting a small portion of a larger population in order to ascertain the characteristics of the total population. ▶ *The sampling method we are using is random.*

sampling error the difference between the true value of a population and the value of that population as estimated from a sample. ▶ *Sampling error arises from the fact of sampling; that is, examining only a portion of the whole rather than the whole.*

SASE See *self-addressed stamped envelope.*

satellite banking an arrangement whereby one bank (the satellite) has a close affiliation with another bank and makes extensive use of the various facilities or services provided by that bank. ▶ *In satellite banking, the satellite bank is normally a small institution located in the outlying trade area of its larger affiliate.*

satisficing behavior the process of finding satisfactory solutions rather than optimal solutions in a problem situation. ▶ *Satisficing behavior is appropriate when the optimal solution is too expensive or simply not feasible.*

saturation a condition occurring when a market has been fully penetrated. ▶ *Now that we have saturation, we can reduce the ad campaign.*

savings the excess of income over expenditures during a given period. ▶ *Savings is money that has not been spent.*

savings account a deposit account with a commercial bank or a savings institution that earns interest and does not include check writing. ▶ *A savings account generally draws interest at a lower rate than other investments.*

savings and loan association a mutual, cooperative financial institution that is (1) chartered by a state or the Federal government, (2) quasi-public in nature, (3) owned by individuals, and (4) privately managed by its members for their mutual benefit and financial advantage. ▶ *A savings and loan association receives the savings of its members and uses these savings to finance long-term loans.*

savings bank a corporation chartered by a state to receive savings deposits. ▶ *A savings bank may be* a stock organization or it may be mutually owned by its depositors.

savings bond a bond designed to appeal to individual savers, issued by the Treasury Department of the United States government. ▶ *A savings bond, which is designed to encourage thrift, may be purchased by the public in post offices, banks, or in the personnel offices of most business firms.*

Say's Law of Markets an economic theory that postulates that supply creates its own demand. ▶ *Formulated by a French economist, Jean Baptiste Say, Say's Law of Markets states that general overproduction cannot occur because every supply generates a demand for that supply.*

SBA See *Small Business Administration.*

scab a strikebreaker; someone who accepts employment in a firm that is being struck. (Slang and derogatory.) ▶ *The owners hired a bunch of scabs to do our work.*

scale order an order to buy or to sell a given number of securities with specifications as to how many are to be sold at stipulated price variations. ▶ *A scale order attempts to average the price of securities bought or sold.*

scalper a person who sells tickets to a sold-out event for the highest price obtainable. ▶ *A scalper may sell tickets for as much as two times the normal price or more.*

Scanlon Plan a group incentive arrangement whereby employees and employer agree to a standard per unit labor cost. ▶ *In a Scanlon Plan, any savings resulting from*

reductions in cost are shared equally between the workers and the company.

scanner a device that copies an image from paper and transmits it to another location. ▶ *A FAX machine is a type of scanner.*

scarcity a condition in which the supply of certain goods or services is insufficient to meet the demand. ▶ *Scarcity is a result of limited resources.*

scatter diagram a graphic depiction of bivariate data. ▶ *In a scatter diagram, each observation is shown as a point on a graph, with each of the variables represented on one of the graph's axes.*

schedule a supporting, explanatory, or supplementary analysis that accompanies an accounting statement. ▶ *A list of items attached to a financial statement is a schedule.*

scheduling the establishing of times at which to begin and complete each step in a procedure. ▶ *The prescribing of when each step required in manufacturing a product is to be performed is an example of scheduling.*

scientific management AND **Taylorism** the philosophy, principles, and methods of efficient management. (*Scientific management* is a school of thought developed by Frederick W. Taylor and is concerned with the ways and means of increasing worker productivity.) ▶ *This company could use a little scientific management to improve its efficiency.*

scientific method a logical approach to problem solving. ▶ *The* *scientific method includes (1) defining the problem, (2) collecting data, (3) analyzing the data, (4) developing a hypothesis, and (5) testing the hypothesis.*

scientific wages wages or rates of compensation that have been determined through the use of scientific approaches and techniques. ▶ *Scientific wages are based on such things as work measurement and job evaluation.*

scrambled merchandise various types of merchandise lines carried by retail stores. ▶ *Food stores, particularly supermarkets, now carry many drug items, toilet goods, housewares, and other goods that are not traditional food store items.*

scrap the refuse of industrial production. ▶ *Scrap may or may not be salable.*

screening the process whereby applicants who do not fill the requirements for a particular job are eliminated from further consideration for that job. ▶ *Screening may be done on the basis of an interview with the applicant or on the basis of a careful examination of the applicant's employment application or résumé.*

scrip a written claim indicating that the bearer is entitled to receive something of value. (From *script.*) ▶ *A corporation may issue scrip to its stockholders instead of cash dividends with the scrip being redeemable at a future date.*

scrip dividend a corporate dividend paid in the form of *scrip.* (Often used to represent fractional shares of stock.) ▶ *A scrip divi-*

dend is not paid in cash or shares of stock.

sealed bid a price quotation submitted to a purchaser in a sealed envelope. ▶ *In a sealed bid situation, all bids submitted are opened simultaneously, thereby preventing a competitor from gaining knowledge of another competitor's bid until all bids have been announced.*

seasonal discount a special discount given typically to retailers by manufacturers or to consumers by retailers based on the season. ▶ *A seasonal discount is typically given when goods are out of season.*

seasonal employment the hiring of workers during peak seasons. ▶ *In the United States, seasonal employment is most common during the Christmas season.*

seasonal fluctuation the variation of some business activity due to the influence of a particular time of the year. ▶ *The frozen yogurt and ice cream industry has a seasonal fluctuation in which demand is greatest during summer months.*

seat a membership in an organized exchange. ▶ *The price of a seat is very expensive today.*

SEC See *Securities and Exchange Commission.*

second See *(factory) second.*

second mortgage a mortgage on real property already encumbered with a first mortgage. ▶ *A second mortgage typically has a higher interest rate than a first mortgage.*

second shift AND **swing shift**   an eight-hour work shift beginning at approximately four o'clock in the afternoon and ending around midnight. ▶ *I had to work second shift and I hated it.*

secondary boycott   the act of picketing directed against a company with which a union has no dispute in order to force that company not to handle the products of another firm with which the union does have a dispute. ▶ *The secondary boycott is illegal under provisions of the Taft-Hartley Act of 1947.*

secondary distribution AND **secondary offering**   the sale of a block of securities by an investment banker as an *off board* transaction to other dealers or stock exchange members. ▶ *Secondary distribution is a sale of previously issued securities.*

secondary offering   See the previous entry.

second   See *(factory) second.*

secretary   **1.** a corporate official responsible for maintaining minutes of meetings, safeguarding the corporate seal, preparing corporate reports, handling public relations, etc. ▶ *The company secretary is present at all board meetings.* **2.** an individual who assists a manager or official in an organization. ▶ *Tom hired a new secretary.*

secular bull market   a long-term market of rising prices. ▶ *The analyst believes that we are in a secular bull market that has at least another two years to run.*

secular trend   a sustained long-term trend. ▶ *A secular trend ex-* amines the long-term movement of economic data.

secured loan   a loan that is backed by the pledge of marketable securities or other marketable valuables as collateral. ▶ *A secured loan safeguards the lender in the event of nonrepayment.*

Securities Act of 1934   a Federal statute providing for the regulation of securities exchanges and over-the-counter trading by the *Securities and Exchange Commission.* ▶ *The Securities Act of 1934 requires the publication of financial information by corporations listed on an exchange.*

Securities and Exchange Commission AND **SEC**   a Federal agency that regulates the selling of securities. ▶ *The Securities and Exchange Commission was created in 1934.*

security   written evidence of the ownership of or the rights to property. ▶ *A certificate of stock ownership is a security.*

seed money   finances provided by an investor for the start-up of a new business or other venture. ▶ *Seed money is sometimes in the form of a loan.*

segmentation   a marketing strategy in which a market is divided into portions. ▶ *Segmentation categorizes a market by geographical location or by the type of buyer.*

selective strike   a strike against one or a few firms in an industry. ▶ *A selective strike serves as a threat to other firms in the industry experiencing the selective strike.*

self-actualization   the need to be creative, expressive, and achieve one's highest potential. ▶ *Self-actu-alization is the highest priority of human needs postulated in Abraham H. Maslow's hierarchy of needs theory of motivation.*

self-addressed stamped envelope AND **SASE** an envelope—to be given or sent to someone—that has one's own address on it along with the correct postage. ▶ *For a reply, be sure to enclose a SASE.*

self-employed individuals who establish and own their own businesses. ▶ *The self-employed assume all the risks of running a business.*

self-fulfilling prophecy causing an event to happen simply by believing it will happen. ▶ *Convinced that his company was going to fail within five years, Tom's actions were not concerned with making his business profitable. Therefore, it was a self-fulfilling prophecy that his business did fail within just a few years.*

self-insurance an insurance plan in which an individual or firm uses money set aside to cover a loss, instead of purchasing a policy from an insurance company. ▶ *Self-insurance is ideal in situations where losses rarely occur and when they do occur are relatively minor ones.*

self-liquidating loan a short-term commercial loan that is paid off from the proceeds realized from the sale of the product or commodity. ▶ *A self-liquidating loan is normally supported by a lien on a given product or commodity.*

self-service retailer a retailer who offers little or no sales assistance to customers. ▶ *A self-service retailer builds business on low prices and convenience.*

sell short to sell borrowed securities in hopes of buying the security back later at a lower price, pocketing the difference, and returning the cheaper security to the owner from whom it was borrowed. ▶ *It is risky to sell short in a rising market.*

seller one who provides a buyer with a good or service in return for cash or its equivalent. ▶ *A seller needs a buyer to be in business.*

seller's market a situation in which demand is greater than supply. ▶ *In a seller's market, prices tend to be high.*

seller's option a seller's right to select the time and place of the delivery of a commodity. ▶ *In a seller's option, the seller even has the right to determine the quality of the commodity within the terms stipulated in the contract.*

selling agent an independent middleman who continuously represents his or her principal and has complete responsibility for selling the entire output of goods produced by the principal. ▶ *A selling agent has wide latitude as to selling prices.*

selling costs the expenses incurred in selling or marketing goods or services. ▶ *The salaries of salespeople and the costs of advertising, credit, and collection are selling costs.*

sellout a sale of all goods on the premises. ▶ *A sellout may be the result of a firm going out of business.*

semantic differential degrees of difference in the intensity of meaning expressed on a continuum from one extreme to another with degrees being represented by different, related words. ▶ *A semantic differential is used in marketing studies where the researcher wishes to determine the degree to which the respondent likes or dislikes a product.*

semantics the study of words and their meanings; the meanings of words and the changes in those meanings. ▶ *Semantics is often given as the reason that people do not understand each other's statements.*

semi-finished good a good that has been subjected to certain manufacturing processes but has not yet been converted into a salable item. ▶ *A semi-finished good, at some point, will be a finished good.*

semi-manufactured good a partially processed good. ▶ *A semi-manufactured good is sold to other manufacturers for further processing.*

semi-monthly twice per month. ▶ *Paychecks at this company are distributed semi-monthly.*

semi-skilled worker an individual who has not yet attained, or is currently attaining, the necessary education and training required to be a skilled worker. ▶ *An equipment operator is usually a semi-skilled worker.*

semi-variable cost a cost that remains fixed until a certain point in production has been reached, at which time the cost becomes variable as production increases. ▶ *Electricity is a semi-variable cost.*

senior issue a corporate security issue that has preference in the event of the liquidation of the corporation, over another security issue. ▶ *Preferred stock is a senior issue.*

seniority an employee's length of service with a given organization. ▶ *When determining which employees are to be laid off, seniority is usually the deciding factor.*

sensitivity training a technique for increasing human relations understanding and skills. ▶ *Sensitivity training is used for increasing self-understanding and the reactions of others to oneself by means of interactions within the framework of small group meetings.*

separation the parting of an employer and an employee. (A euphemism for an act of dismissal, retirement, or resignation. See also *termination*.) ▶ *I was owed two weeks' vacation pay at the time of separation.*

separation pay AND **severance pay** the compensation for time not worked given to a worker whose employment with a firm has been terminated. ▶ *Separation pay is not usually paid to workers who are discharged for just cause.*

sequestered account a commercial banking deposit account that has been impounded under due process of law. ▶ *Disbursement from a sequestered account is subject to court action.*

serial bond an issue of a bond that is redeemable in installments. ▶ *A serial bond is typically issued by a municipality.*

serial work subdivision the arrangement of work into a series of small jobs. (See also *production line*.) ▶ *With serial work subdivision, each item moves progressively from job to job until it is completed.*

service **1.** work not resulting in a salable product, performed for pay. ▶ *A service is intangible, whereas a product is tangible.* **2.** assistance provided to a purchaser. ▶ *Many companies pride themselves on their high levels of service to the customer.*

service charge AND **service fee** an additional cost added to the price of an item to cover the costs of processing a transaction. ▶ *To make this transaction, a service charge is required.*

service club a service organization dedicated to the community. ▶ *The Kiwanis Club is an example of a service club.*

service department that department which repairs and otherwise services products sold by a store. ▶ *The service department can assist you with your complaint.*

service fee See *service charge.*

service life the useful period of time an asset is expected to perform. ▶ *The service life of this equipment is 10 years.*

service rating See *performance appraisal.*

set-up time the time required to change a machine or a method of production from one product or production plan to another. ▶ *The set-up time for this machine is approximately half an hour.*

settle **1.** to pay. ▶ *You can settle your bill with our accountant.* **2.**

to end legal proceedings by mutual consent. ▶ *The newspapers report that the two parties will settle out of court for an undisclosed amount.*

settlement day the date on which a security is delivered and paid for—usually a few days after the transaction. ▶ *I hope I have enough money in the account by settlement day to pay for the stock.*

severance benefit any monetary benefit that a worker receives upon termination of employment with a firm. ▶ *Separation pay is an example of a severance benefit.*

severance pay See *separation pay.*

severance tax a tax on natural resources that are removed from the ground. ▶ *A severance tax is levied on oil.*

sex discrimination any disparate or unfair treatment in employment situations based on the sex of an individual. ▶ *Sex discrimination is prohibited by Title VII of the Civil Rights Act of 1964.*

sex-plus discrimination discrimination based on the sex of an individual and some other factor. ▶ *Not hiring a female applicant because she has small children is an example of sex-plus discrimination.*

sexual harassment any unwelcome sexual advances or the creation of a hostile working environment. ▶ *Sexual harassment is illegal.*

shakeout a market condition in which weaker companies are forced from the market by stronger ones. ▶ *Companies which have a poor financial condition are usually the* *first to go in a shakeout.*

share   a proportional unit of ownership of a corporation. ▶ *A stock is a share of ownership.*

share draft   a checking account instrument offered to its members by credit unions. ▶ *A share draft is tantamount to a check, but it is still technically a draft.*

shareholder   See *stockholder.*

shareholder's right AND **stockholder's right**   any one of several privileges attached to the ownership of stock. ▶ *One shareholder's right is to vote for directors of a corporation.*

shark   a predatory businessperson, particularly one who tries to take over a business against the will of the business's owners. ▶ *The company hired consultants to devise a plan to protect it from sharks.*

shark repellent   the actions taken by the target of a *shark* to prohibit a takeover from occurring. ▶ *A shark repellent might be the requirement that 90 percent of current stockholders approve of any takeover.*

shelf life   the length of time a good remains in useful condition and can be sold in a store. ▶ *The shelf life for meats, for instance, is very short.*

shelf space   the amount of space available for a particular kind or brand of product on the shelves of a retailer store. (*Shelf space* is typically measured in inches.) ▶ *The competition for grocery store shelf space is usually fierce.*

Sherman Antitrust Act of 1890   a Federal statute prohibiting contracts or acts in restraint of trade or tending to create a monopoly. ▶ *The Sherman Antitrust Act of 1890 was enacted to prevent the growth of monopolies and to restore free competition.*

shift   a work period of a predetermined length. ▶ *There are normally three, eight-hour shifts in a day.*

shipper   one who ships goods from one place to another. ▶ *We are contracting with a shipper to send our products overseas.*

shipping   the movement of goods from one place to another. ▶ *We are shipping five tons of grain to a buyer in South America.*

shipping and handling   the additional cost levied when purchased items are mailed, to cover the expenses of mailing and packaging the goods. ▶ *Shipping and handling on all orders from our company is $4.95.*

shop steward   a labor union official who represents employees and handles union affairs within an area or department of a firm. ▶ *A shop steward is elected to that position.*

shoplifting   the act of stealing goods from a retail establishment. ▶ *It is estimated that shoplifting accounts for as much as 10% of the retail price of goods.*

shopping center   a concentration of retail outlets and service facilities located in a suburban area. ▶ *A mall is an example of a shopping center.*

shopping good   a good that is usually purchased only after careful consideration and comparison by the customer. ▶ *A shopping good typically has a relatively high price.*

short See *short sale.*

short circuit to bypass the prescribed route in favor of the most direct route. (In business, this would involve avoiding one's immediate supervisor and taking a grievance, complaint, or suggestion directly to a higher level supervisor.) ▶ *Because of the communication problems Bill has with his supervisor, he will often short circuit him.*

short covering the purchase of a security by a trader who has earlier gone short, that is, sold a security at an agreed-upon price for future delivery. ▶ *Short covering is an effort to take profits or accept loss in order to prevent further loss.*

short interval scheduling AND **SIS** an approach to work measurement in which time is expressed in terms of batches of work that can be completed in a short period of time. ▶ *A short period of time in short interval scheduling is normally one hour.*

short position a condition in which stock has been sold short and has not been covered as of a particular date. (See *short sale.*) ▶ *An investor holding a short position, hopes to buy the stock back at a later date and at a lower price.*

short run a period of time not longer than one year. ▶ *The short run is easier to predict than the long run.*

short sale AND **short** the sale of borrowed securities, such as stocks, bonds, commodities, currencies, etc., in hopes of buying the security back later at a lower price, pocketing the difference, and then returning the cheaper security to the owner from whom it was borrowed. ▶ *The market went up and I had to make a short sale to cover my shorts.*

short shipment a condition occurring when a vendor is not able to completely fill a customer's order and ships only a part of that order. ▶ *According to the notice we received, this is a short shipment, and the remainder will be shipped at a later date.*

short-term credit credit extended for a period of time ranging up to one year. ▶ *Short-term credit usually has lower rates than long-term credit.*

short-term financing capital that has been obtained for a short period of time. ▶ *Short-term financing is usually for less than a year.*

shortfall an insufficiency of cash or revenue; less cash or revenue than predicted. ▶ *The budget shortfall caused more borrowing.*

shrinkage a loss. ▶ *A shrinkage of goods is a loss due simply to depletion.*

shut-down point the point in a production run or process where the continued operation will result in a loss to the firm. ▶ *The shut-down point of an operation should always be determined in advance.*

shyster a professional who resorts to trickery or unethical or illegal practices in order to enrich himself or herself and take advantage of clients. ▶ *He is a shyster lawyer.*

SIC Number See *Standard Industrial Classification Number.*

sick leave the time off from work allowed an employee due to illness. ▶ *Sick leave may or may not be paid time off.*

sidewalk sale a sale conducted by a store in front of the establishment, typically on the sidewalk. ▶ *It never fails to rain when Joan wants to conduct a sidewalk sale.*

sight bill a bill of exchange that is payable when received or "seen." (Compare with *time bill.*) ▶ *All the bills we get from companies with cash flow problems are sight bills.*

sight draft a draft payable upon presentation and delivery to the drawee. ▶ *A sight draft is simply a bill payable on demand.*

silent partner a member of a partnership who does not actively participate in the management of the firm but does share in the distribution of the profits. ▶ *Unless a silent partner is qualified as a limited partner, the silent partner has the same liability as an active partner.*

simo chart a graphic representation of an operation in which the basic motions used by the right hand and left hand are plotted in relation to each other. ▶ *A simo chart provides the information needed to improve worker efficiency.*

simple average See *arithmetic mean.*

simple interest interest that is computed on the original period. ▶ *A rate of 10% simple interest is less than a 10% compound interest rate.*

simplex method a form of linear programming that makes solutions possible in algebraic equations where there are more unknowns than equations. ▶ *The simplex method is useful in solving large-scale manufacturing problems.*

simulation the duplication of real-world conditions or situations in the form of a model. ▶ *Simulation is used to test alternative solutions, decision rules, or systems.*

sinecure a position requiring little or no work but providing relatively high pay. ▶ *I believe Steve has a sinecure because he makes a lot of money, but yet has time to play golf, go camping, and engage in other leisure activities.*

single liability the situation in which a stockholder is liable for a corporation's losses. ▶ *In single liability, the stockholder is liable for losses only to the extent of the stockholder's investment in the corporation.*

single-line store a business establishment that carries only a single line of merchandise. ▶ *A store that carries only dry goods is an example of a single-line store.*

single-name paper AND **straight paper** a note for which only one legal entity, the maker, is obligated to make payment at maturity. ▶ *Many securities are either straight paper or single-name paper.*

single-price policy a retail pricing approach whereby all items, or all items of a given kind, within a store are marked at one price. ▶ *Because all of our goods are* *marked at one dollar, we have a single-price policy.*

sinking fund AND **redemption fund** the cash or other assets set aside for the retirement of a debt, the redemption of stock, or the protection of an investment. ▶ *A sinking fund is basically money set aside for an obligation.*

SIS See *short interval scheduling.*

sit-down strike a work stoppage in which employees cease work and refuse to leave the company's premises. ▶ *A sit-down strike is a rare form of work stoppage today, but it was very common in the 1930s.*

site a plot of land. ▶ *This looks like a good site for our headquarters.*

situational leadership an approach to leadership in which the leader examines the situation or circumstances before applying a particular leadership style. ▶ *With situational leadership, one must understand the intricacies of human behavior.*

situs the position, location, or "seat" of something or someone. (Latin.) ▶ *John's situs is his permanent legal residence.*

sixty-day notice a sixty-day period in which strikes and lockouts are prohibited. ▶ *A sixty-day notice is given at the time of labor contract negotiations.*

skewness the degree to which a frequency curve lacks symmetry. ▶ *Skewness occurs when the mean, median, and mode of a frequency distribution are not identical in value.*

skill the ability to use one's knowl-

edge or proficiency in devising an efficient method of accomplishing a given objective. ▶ *A skill may be mental or manual.*

skill and effort rating AND **Westinghouse leveling system** an approach to performance rating in which the time study analyst measures skill, effort, conditions, and consistency. ▶ *A skill and effort rating is an important tool in achieving a high level of efficiency.*

skilled labor work that requires some type of training or apprenticeship before a person can successfully pursue that line of work. ▶ *Operating a turret lathe is an example of skilled labor.*

skills inventory a collection of information maintained on nonmanagerial employees as to their availability and preparedness to move into lateral or higher level positions. ▶ *Information contained in a skills inventory includes education, experience, work skills, certifications, performance appraisals, etc.*

skimming the taking or concealing of money ▶ *Skimming from a business is illegal.*

SKU See *stockkeeping unit.*

slander oral defamation, rather than written defamation. (Compare with *libel.*) ▶ *The entire speech was nothing but slander! I'll sue!*

slave driver an employer, manager, or supervisor who has employees work at an excessively high pitch or for extended periods of time. ▶ *My boss is a real slave driver who expects his people to work every weekend.*

sleeper something with high potential that is not easily recognized. ▶ *A corporation labeled as a sleeper may have stock that will soon rise dramatically in value.*

sleeping beauty a firm that has not been approached by an acquirer but has the characteristics or features an acquirer might desire. ▶ *This little company is a sleeping beauty just waiting for some big players to take it over.*

slow cycle manufacturing that production or processing characterized by lengthy completion time. ▶ *Slow cycle manufacturing involves several hours or longer.*

slow-down a deliberate and purposeful reduction in the output of product. ▶ *The employees participated in a slow-down to show their disapproval of the new personnel policies.*

slump a temporary decline in the volume of general business activity. ▶ *A slump may refer to the decline in the volume of business done by a specific industry, company, or product line.*

slush fund a pool of money set aside for unusual circumstances or situations. ▶ *A slush fund may or may not be illegal.*

small business a business characterized by few employees and relatively small sales. ▶ *Many major firms have started out as small businesses.*

Small Business Administration AND **SBA** a permanent agency of the United States government established to assist small business enterprises. ▶ *The Small Business Administration was established*

by the Small Business Act of 1953.

small investor AND **retail investor** an investor who buys only in small quantities. ▶ *A small investor tends to come into the market at market peaks.*

smart money investors who are considered knowledgeable. ▶ *The smart money thinks IBM stock will double next year.*

snowballing growing at an increasing rate. ▶ *The financial reports indicate that our business is snowballing.*

social audit an examination of the effects a company or industry has on society. ▶ *A social audit analyzes such things as what society's expectations for a company are.*

social Darwinism the notion that the most resourceful, capable, and hardworking people will rise to positions of importance or prominence in any society. ▶ *The notion of social Darwinism is inspired by Charles Darwin's biological observation that, among animals, the fittest survive.*

social responsibility the responsibility a person or firm has in meeting the expectations of society. ▶ *Ensuring against, or attempting to reduce, pollution is an example of the social responsibility many industries have.*

Social Security See *Old Age, Survivors, and Disability Insurance.*

socialism an economic system under which the means of production and distribution are owned by the people. ▶ *Under socialism,* *production is for the good of the people rather than for profit.*

sociometry that field of study or endeavor concerned with measuring attitudes of social acceptance or rejection. ▶ *Sociometry examines attitudes through the expressed preferences of members of a social group.*

soft currency national money that is subject to unusual fluctuations in value; any money with no stability in purchasing power. (Compare with *hard currency.*) ▶ *Soft currency may be subject to wild fluctuations either domestically or in international trade.*

soft good a nondurable consumer good. ▶ *Vegetables are a soft good.*

soft market a condition that exists when the supply of a product or products is greater than the demand. ▶ *In a soft market, prices tend to be low.*

soft money an undependable source of money. ▶ *The university got a lot of soft money in government grants that dried up when the economy got worse.*

soft sell a sales approach relying on unobtrusive methods to sell a good or service. (Compare with *hard sell.*) ▶ *The product is so desirable that a soft sell was all it took.*

software the programs and routines that give instructions to computers. (Compare with *hardware.*) ▶ *I had to buy updates to my favorite software program in order to take advantage of the latest new features.*

sole bargaining right the right of a particular union to bargain collec-tively for all workers within a designated bargaining unit. ▶ *The sole bargaining right encompasses workers who may not even be a member of the union.*

(sole) proprietorship AND **individual proprietorship** a business enterprise owned and operated by a single person. ▶ *In a sole proprietorship, the owner receives all the profits and takes all the risks.*

solvency the ability of a firm or an individual to meet financial obligations as they become due. ▶ *Solvency refers to the financial status of a company or person.*

source document the original document from which data is prepared in a form acceptable to a computer or other data processing machine. ▶ *A source document, a purchase order, was illegible.*

source program a computer program written in a programming language. ▶ *The computer translates the source program into instructions the machine can "understand."*

span of control AND **span of management** the number of subordinates a single manager can supervise effectively. ▶ *Span of control is typically limited to no more than twenty employees.*

span of management See the previous entry.

special assessment bond a municipal bond that is issued for public improvements. ▶ *A special assessment bond is paid for by special taxes levied against the properties benefiting from the improvements.*

special bid an order for a large block of stock. ▶ *With a special bid, the bidder will pay a special commission to his or her broker, while the seller pays no commission.*

specialist 1. an individual possessing extensive knowledge and experience in one particular area. ▶ *Maynard is a specialist in sales training.* 2. a member of a stock exchange who handles orders for other brokers as well for the specialist's own account. ▶ *A specialist deals in one or just a few issues.*

specialist block purchase the purchase of a large block of stock outside the regular market by a *specialist,* usually for the *specialist's* own account. ▶ *A large number of specialist block purchases crossed the tape just as the market closed.*

specialist block sale the sale of a large block of stock outside the regular market by a *specialist,* usually for the *specialist's* own account. ▶ *In a specialist block sale, the specialist sells at a price near the prevailing market price.*

specialized capital goods capital equipment that can only be used for certain purposes. ▶ *Equipment used for the manufacture of rubber tires is an example of specialized capital goods.*

specialty good a good for which the consumer is willing to pay more. ▶ *A specialty good tends to be relatively expensive.*

specialty store a retail establishment that handles a restricted class of goods for which the consumer is willing to pay more. ▶ *A shop that sells only fine chocolates is an example of a specialty store.*

specie metallic money. ▶ *A gold coin is specie.*

speculation AND **speculative buying** willingly assuming above-average risks in the hope of gaining above-average returns on a business or financial transaction. ▶ *In a speculation, the investor hopes to gain a large profit or a quick profit.*

speculative buying See the previous entry.

speculator one who is willing to assume above average risks in the hope of gaining above average returns on a business or financial transaction. ▶ *A speculator must be prepared to lose money in many instances.*

spin-off the transfer by a corporation of a portion of its assets to a newly formed corporation in exchange for capital stock in the new corporation. ▶ *Spin-off is a form of divestiture.*

splintered authority decision-making power split among a number of people. ▶ *The policy of having splintered authority forced Fred to join with other managers to make the decision.*

splintered ownership widespread ownership of a company with little concentration of control. ▶ *In splintered ownership, there are no stockholders owning a substantial percentage of the company's stock.*

split See *(stock) split.*

split-halves method a method of

determining the reliability of a test. ▶ *In the split-halves method, one divides the results of a test into two parts and then examines the correlation of the results of the two parts.*

split order an order for a large amount of securities that is divided into smaller portions and involves many transactions. ▶ *The purpose of a split order is to avoid causing wild fluctuations in the market price of a security.*

split shift a work period in which there is a break in the working hours. ▶ *Restaurant workers frequently have a split shift in which they work several hours around the noon lunch period, take most of the afternoon off, and return to work around the evening dinner period.*

split ticket a price tag on a good that is perforated so that a section of it can be kept by the merchant. ▶ *The portion of a split ticket retained by a merchant is for stock control purposes.*

spoilage the ruin of goods owing to rot or decay. ▶ *The spoilage occurred when the fruit was exposed to freezing temperatures.*

sponsor an individual or organization that places and pays for advertising. ▶ *The sponsor of the television program objected to the script.*

spot delivery a delivery that can be made immediately. ▶ *We need two tons of crushed granite for spot delivery.*

spot good a good that is available for immediate delivery. ▶ *Because this item is a spot good, it is always in stock.*

spot market a *cash market* in commodities; a market in which commodities are traded for immediate delivery. ▶ *In a spot market, commodities are frequently purchased for cash.*

spot price the current price at which a commodity can be immediately delivered. (See also *cash price.*) ▶ *Spot prices can change rapidly.*

spread the difference between the price offered and the price bid on a security. ▶ *There is a $3 spread on this security.*

spreadsheet a form used for calculations consisting of rows and columns. ▶ *Spreadsheets are easily manipulated on a computer.*

squeeze out an attempt by majority stockholders to force out minority stockholders. ▶ *A squeeze out may be the result of a power play by some directors.*

stability index the ratio of the number of workers employed in an average month in a given year to the number of workers employed in the highest employment month of the year. ▶ *The stability index is a measure of seasonal fluctuation or stability of employment.*

stabilization the process of fixing and maintaining a set price for a security during its initial offering to the public. ▶ *Stabilization ends when the issue has been selling for a period of time.*

staff **1.** the work force of an organization. ▶ *Our staff is very dedicated to the goals of this company.* **2.** to secure employees and managers for an organization. ▶ *We* *must staff this firm with more qualified individuals.*

staffing that portion of human resource management concerned with recruiting, selecting, and situating employees and managers. ▶ *Staffing requires a great understanding of the total human resource management function.*

stagflation a condition in which there is high unemployment, slow growth, and rising prices. ▶ *Before the 1970s, stagflation was unprecedented.*

stale check a check dated 90 days to 180 days prior to presentation for payment. ▶ *A stale check is marked as such and returned unpaid to the bank or customer from which it was received.*

standard a specified output goal. ▶ *A standard is expressed in terms of quantity, quality, cost, or time.*

Standard and Poor's Composite Index an index of the prices of 500 listed industrial, transportation, and utility stocks. ▶ *The Standard and Poor's Composite Index is used as a measure of the overall trend of stock prices.*

standard data a compilation of elemental time values used for setting standards on work similar to that from which the data were developed. ▶ *Standard data may be developed from a predetermined elemental time system such as Methods-Time Measurement or from a firm's own time study data.*

standard deviation a measure of the dispersion of a frequency distribution. ▶ *Standard deviation is a measure of variability.*

standard hour an hour of time during which a specific quantity of work of acceptable quality is performed. ▶ *A standard hour specifies both quantity and quality of work that must be performed by a worker.*

Standard Industrial Classification Number AND **SIC Number** a system of classifying economic activities by the use of four-digit numbers. ▶ *The SIC Number was established under the supervision of the Bureau of the Budget for the purposes of gathering, tabulating, and analyzing data on the manufacturing and non-manufacturing areas of economic endeavor.*

standard mileage rate the rate for deductions for business travel allowed by the *Internal Revenue Service.* ▶ *The standard mileage rate is expressed in so-many-cents per mile.*

standard of living the composite quantities and qualities of goods and services that a person, group, or nation considers essential for its well-being. ▶ *Standard of living is basically a measure of affluence.*

standard output that quantity of output established as a norm for some given period of time. ▶ *Standard output is usually determined through an industrial engineering study.*

standard time AND **work standard** the time required by a qualified worker to produce one unit of output or to accomplish a single set of tasks. ▶ *Standard time assumes* *that a worker is working at a normal rate of speed under uniform conditions, and is experiencing normal fatigue and delays.*

standard wage rate a uniform or single wage rate for each kind of job or occupation. ▶ *The standard wage rate is simply the base pay for a job or occupation.*

standards department that organizational unit charged with the responsibility of developing and maintaining standards relative to production rates or times. ▶ *A standards department is common in manufacturing plants.*

standing plan a plan designed to deal with recurring situations or problems. ▶ *An attendance policy is an example of a standing plan.*

staple a good that is bought regularly. ▶ *Food is a staple.*

starch test a method of determining the effect of a printed advertisement on a potential consumer. ▶ *In a starch test, the marketing researcher tests the amount of recall a consumer has of a particular advertisement.*

start-up something new. ▶ *A start-up business is a new business.*

state bank a bank chartered under the banking laws of a state and authorized to receive deposits and make loans. ▶ *A state bank is subject to examination and regulation by the chartering state.*

state-of-the-art the most up-to-date. ▶ *Our company's computers are state-of-the-art equipment.*

statistical inference the process of generalizing about the characteristics of a large population from a limited quantity of observed data. ▶ *When making a statistical inference, there is potential for error in making generalizations.*

statistical quality control a method for establishing and controlling product quality levels. ▶ *Statistical quality control uses mathematical, statistical, and probability techniques.*

statistics that field of study involving the collection, classification, and analysis of facts based upon numbers of occurrences or observations. ▶ *Statistics is computational by its nature.*

status one's social rank or standing within a group. ▶ *In a company, the president has the highest status.*

status quo the situation as it is now. ▶ *Maintaining the status quo means keeping things as they are now.*

status quo ante the situation as it was before. ▶ *It is believed that in the Korean War, status quo ante was the best outcome that could be achieved.*

status symbol a visible denotation of one's social rank or standing within a group. ▶ *A status symbol may be a reserved parking space, a private office, or wall-to-wall carpeting.*

statute a law enacted by a legislative body. ▶ *A number of new statutes are passed each time the legislature meets.*

statute of limitations a law that renders certain rights legally unenforceable after the passage of a certain period of time. ▶ *A* *statute of limitations exists for most situations.*

statutory voting the voting procedures in a corporation where every share equals one vote. ▶ *Statutory voting concentrates power in the hands of those who own the most shares.*

Steel Belt the area of the country, primarily the Ohio Valley, where steel was once the major industry. (See also *Rust Belt*.) ▶ *The Steel Belt was once prosperous.*

steward a worker who represents union coworkers in negotiations or other contacts with the employer. ▶ *A steward is typically elected by fellow workers under the terms of a union agreement.*

stipend a salary. ▶ *My stipend at the university is rather modest.*

stipulation a condition. ▶ *A stipulation for paying off the debt was included in the contract.*

stochastic model a model in which some important variables are not under control, and the outcome of any action is subject to random variations. ▶ *A stochastic model is a representation of reality wherein random outcomes are recognized.*

stock 1. one or more shares in a corporation. ▶ *Stock is usually bought from a stockbroker.* 2. inventory. ▶ *Stock includes raw materials, semi-finished goods, or goods ready for sale.*

stock certificate evidence of the ownership of one or more shares of the capital stock of a corporation. ▶ *A stock certificate is a written instrument.*

stock corporation a firm whose ownership is divided into shares evidenced by transferable certificates. ▶ *A stock corporation issues stock.*

stock dividend the distribution of authorized but unissued shares to the corporation's stockholders as a dividend. ▶ *A stock dividend is given in the form of stock rather than in the form of cash.*

stock dividend payable a dividend in stock that has been declared by a corporation but has not yet been paid. ▶ *A stock dividend payable appears on the corporation's books as a liability.*

stock jobbing the illegal selling of worthless securities. ▶ *Walter was accused of stock jobbing and was banned from the securities business.*

stock on hand See under *inventory*.

stock option a right to purchase shares of stock in a corporation under certain conditions. ▶ *Part of her year-end bonus was in stock options in the company.*

stock power a power of attorney to handle stock transactions. ▶ *Stock power permits a party, other than the owner of stock, to legally transfer the title of ownership to a third party.*

stock purchase plan an arrangement whereby a corporation permits its employees to buy stock in the corporation. ▶ *In a stock purchase plan, employees may have an opportunity to buy stock below market price.*

(stock purchase) warrant a certificate that gives its holder the right or option of buying stock at a stated price. ▶ *While there is usually a time limit on a warrant, it can be for an indefinite time period.*

stock right AND **subscription right** a right issued to present stockholders to purchase shares of new stock on a pro rata basis. ▶ *Tom's broker notified him of the stock rights associated with shares in XYZ company.*

(stock) split the division of the shares of a corporation into a larger number of shares. ▶ *A stock split is usually done to reduce the market price per share and thereby broaden the trading appeal of the stock.*

stock turnover See *inventory turnover.*

stockbroker a registered agent who buys and sells stocks, bonds, and commodities. ▶ *Stockbrokers are connected to the world of securities trading by computer.*

stockholder AND **shareholder** one who owns stock in a corporation. ▶ *A stockholder may possess preferred or common stock.*

stockholder of record an owner of shares in a corporation. ▶ *Stockholders of record have their names on the books of the corporation.*

stockholder's equity See *owner's equity.*

stockholder's right See *shareholder's right.*

stockkeeping unit AND **SKU** a system using numbers to identify products. ▶ *Every variation of each product is assigned a stockkeeping unit.*

stockout a condition existing when an order or a requisition for goods cannot be filled because the quantity of the good in inventory has been depleted. ▶ *A company can lose business if a stockout occurs regularly.*

stop loss order a customer's order to a broker to sell a customer's stock if the shares decline in value to a certain point. ▶ *A stop loss order is designed to minimize losses.*

stop order an order suspending trading in a security. ▶ *The Securities and Exchange Commission will occasionally issue a stop order for a particular security.*

stop payment order an order issued by a depositor instructing the bank to refuse payment of a specific check drawn by the depositor. ▶ *A depositor has up to six months to issue a stop payment order as long as the check has not been cashed.*

storage dump See *core dump.*

store a place where merchandise is offered for sale. ▶ *A store is typically a retail establishment.*

store brand a product that has the store's name on the label rather than a manufacturer's name. ▶ *A store brand tends to be priced lower than name brand goods.*

straddle the option of either buying or selling a specified amount of stock within a stated period of time. ▶ *A straddle consists of an equal number of call options and put options.*

straight commission compensation paid as a percentage based on the dollar amount of goods sold. ▶

Straight commission is often paid to salespersons in order to eliminate the need for base pay.

straight line depreciation a method of depreciation in which an asset's total cost is divided into equal amounts and expensed for that amount each year. ▶ *Straight line depreciation takes into account an asset's useful life.*

straight line production a form of production carried out in which parts are manufactured, assembled, or altered along a straight production line. ▶ *The assembly line is an example of straight line production.*

straight loan AND **unsecured loan** a loan granted to an individual or a legal entity, with no collateral, where the basis for granting the loan is the ability of the borrower to repay. ▶ *The young man was unable to get a straight loan and had to find someone to co-sign the papers.*

straight paper See *single-name paper.*

straight time the standard rate of pay per hour received by an employee. ▶ *Straight time is the base rate for a job.*

strategic business unit an autonomous division of a business responsible for all aspects of developing, marketing, and selling a specific product or line of products. ▶ *The purpose of defining a strategic business unit is to assign the unit strategic planning responsibilities.*

strategic management the formulation, implementation, and evaluation of an organization's ob-jectives. ▶ *The basic key to strategic management is evaluation.*

strategy a general means for accomplishing something. ▶ *A strategy is a broad plan, which gives guidance to a business.*

stratified sample a sample drawn from relatively homogeneous subgroups of a population. ▶ *A stratified sample uses the characteristics of the universe in the selection of a sample.*

Street See *Wall Street.*

street name a broker's name rather than the name of the customer. (The *street* refers to *Wall Street,* where the *New York Stock Exchange* is located.) ▶ *A street name is used at the request of the customer or when the securities have been purchased on margin.*

stress the body's reaction to any demand made on it. ▶ *Techniques to manage stress are essential in modern business.*

stress interview a type of interview in which the interviewer assumes a role of hostility toward the interviewee. ▶ *John was given a stress interview in a deliberate attempt to annoy, embarrass, or frustrate him in order to determine his ability to control himself under stress.*

strict liability the legal responsibility one has even if one is not at fault. ▶ *An example of strict liability is when a manufacturer is held liable for injury due to improper use of the product by the consumer.*

strike a concerted withholding of the labor supply in order to force an employer to grant the demands of the employees or the union. ► *In a strike, employees carry signs and may yell complaints against the company they are striking.*

strike authorization authorization given to a union leader to call a strike. ► *With strike authorization, the union leader does not have to consult with union members to call a strike.*

strike benefits payments given by the union to employees on strike. ► *Strike benefits are given to strikers because while on strike they are not earning money from the company.*

strikebreaker an employee hired by an organization during a period of time in which a strike is in progress. ► *The reason for hiring strikebreakers is to end the strike by hiring new employees to do the work.*

strike duty the responsibility or tasks assigned by union leaders to strikers. ► *Manning a picket line is a strike duty.*

strike fund the money set aside by a union for use during a strike. ► *A strike fund covers such things as strike benefits.*

strike price AND **exercise price** the price at which a stock option to buy or sell becomes an order to buy or sell. ► *The exercise price is $40, and when the price of the stock reached that amount, it was sold.*

stringent money market a period in which corporate borrowers experience difficulty in obtaining loans. ► *In recent years, corporations have faced a stringent money market.*

strip shopping center an accumulation of stores joined together and sharing a common parking lot. ► *A strip shopping center differs from a mall in that a mall is an enclosed structure.*

Strong Vocational Interest Blank a test used to measure a person's suitability for forty-five occupations and professions. ► *The Strong Vocational Interest Blank compares a person's interests and prejudices with those of people already in the different occupations.*

structural unemployment that unemployment caused by a change in technology. ► *To prevent structural unemployment, workers should receive continuous training in new areas of technology.*

structured interview See *patterned interview.*

Student Loan Marketing Association AND **Sallie Mae** a corporation established in 1972 formed to guarantee student loans for college and university students. ► *The Student Loan Marketing Association has enabled many students to receive college loans.*

SUB See *supplemental unemployment benefit.*

subassembly two or more parts joined together to form a unit that is only part of a complete part. ► *This particular subassembly will be used in the manufacture of our atomic weather vanes.*

Subchapter S Corporation a corporation formed by an individual or individuals who report income on their personal tax returns. ► *A Sub-*

chapter S Corporation is usually formed by a small business.

subcontract a contract by which one party who has agreed to perform work for a second party arranges with a third party for the actual performance of all or part of the work. ▶ *In a subcontract, the first party still remains liable to the second party for performance of the contract.*

sublease AND **sublet** [for a person who has leased property from the owner] to lease the property to another person. ▶ *Frank will sublease his office to Tony for only $200 per month.*

sublet See the previous entry.

subliminal advertising a form of advertising designed in such a way that the person to whom the advertising message is directed is not consciously aware of having seen or heard the message. ▶ *Advertisers are struggling with the ethical considerations involved in subliminal advertising.*

suboptimization the process of choosing the best alternative for a subsystem in terms of the objectives of the larger system, of which the subsystem is a part. ▶ *In some instances suboptimization refers to the act of not working to one's fullest potential.*

subordinate rating a performance appraisal carried out on someone of higher rank by one of lower rank. ▶ *There is a question as to the reliability of a subordinate rating.*

subordinated debenture a debt that has been declared junior, or of lower rank, to another debt issue. ▶

A subordinated debenture is paid after all other higher ranked debts are paid.

subordination the placement of something in a lower rank or order. ▶ *Subordination is the state of a second mortgage.*

subpoena a *summons* to appear in court. (See also *process.*) ▶ *A subpoena is issued by a judicial authority and requires a person to be present at a certain place and time, or face a penalty.*

subrogation the substitution of one creditor or claimant for another. ▶ *In a subrogation, the substitute is known as the* subrogee.

subrogee an entity entitled to collect the debt due another entity. (See also *subrogation*) ▶ *Fidelity Insurance is the subrogee in the Smith claim.*

subroutine a part of a computer program that performs a specific portion of the function of the program. ▶ *Subroutines handle parts of the program that are repeated often.*

subscribed capital AND **subscribed shares** that portion of the capital stock of a corporation that has been contracted for, but has not yet been paid for. ▶ *When subscribed capital is paid for, it becomes paid-in capital.*

subscribed shares See the previous entry.

subscriber one who agrees to receive and pay for a product or a service for a certain period of time. ▶ *The most common example of a subscriber is one who pays a price to receive a magazine for a* *certain time period.*

subscription the act of subscribing. ▶ *We received a one-year subscription to* Forbes.

subscription price **1.** the price at which new shares of stock issued by a firm are sold to current stockholders. ▶ *The subscription price of the initial issue is $10.* **2.** the price at which an item of goods or a service is bought. ▶ *The annual subscription price for this magazine is $18.*

subscription right See *stock right.*

subsidiary a company owned or controlled by another company. ▶ *A very large company may have many subsidiaries.*

subsidy a financial grant given to a business or individual by the government. ▶ *The purpose of a subsidy is to get a business established or to provide financial assistance to one in need.*

subsistence allowance the money available to employees to pay for the basics of company travel. ▶ *A subsistence allowance covers such things as travel costs, meals, lodging, etc.*

succession the transfer of rights. ▶ *Usually, succession refers to property rights.*

suggested retail price a price that is recommended by the manufacturer for a particular product. ▶ *The suggested retail price is not binding on the retailer.*

suggestion box a receptacle for customers' or employees' improvement ideas submitted under a *suggestion system.* ▶ *Suggestion boxes are usually placed in convenient locations throughout the company.*

suggestion system a formalized plan established by an employer to encourage employees to submit ideas to improve the firm. ▶ *In a suggestion system, employees may receive monetary rewards for accepted suggestions.*

suit to quiet title a legal procedure instituted to clear up claims of ownership to real property. ▶ *We are going to have to file a suit to quiet title to clear up the dispute regarding the Smith holdings.*

sum-of-the-years-digits a method used to accelerate the depreciation of capital goods. ▶ *In the sum-of-the-years-digits method, the sum of the years over which the item is to be depreciated is used as the denominator, while the numerator for any given year is the number of years remaining in the period of depreciation.*

summons a written notice calling a person to court. (The *summons* is delivered to the person who is to go to court. See also *process; subpoena.*) ▶ *He received a summons at noon for a 2:00 P.M. court appearance.*

Sun Belt the states in the southern tier of the United States. ▶ *In the last two decades, business opportunities have been better in the Sun Belt.*

sunk cost a previous cost that is not recoverable in a given situation. ▶ *With a sunk cost, no current or future action will affect the outlay.*

sunrise industry an emerging industry with a great impact on the economy. ▶ *The computer industry is a sunrise industry.*

sunset industry a very mature industry. ▶ *The automobile industry is a sunset industry in the United States.*

super NOW account a deposit account that has a higher interest rate than the typical *NOW account.* ▶ *A super NOW account still does not bear as much interest as more risky investments.*

supermarket a large, self-service retail food and household merchandise store. ▶ *A supermarket is typically found in a suburb.*

superstore a large store. ▶ *A superstore is often a very large specialty store.*

supervision the process of guiding and overseeing subordinates. ▶ *All managers practice supervision of some type.*

supervisor one who oversees and directs the activities of others. ▶ *A supervisor is typically a first-line manager who directs the activities of the employees.*

supplemental compensation compensation paid in addition to standard pay, which is based on seniority, productivity, percentage of profits, etc. ▶ *Supplemental compensation may be in financial or nonfinancial form.*

supplemental unemployment benefit AND **SUB; supplemental unemployment compensation** a payment from private unemployment insurance plans given to laid-off workers. ▶ *A supplemental unemployment benefit is given in addition to state unemployment insurance compensation.*

supplemental unemployment compensation See the previous entry.

supplies goods, products, or materials used in the operation of a business but not directly in the product that the firm makes. ▶ *Pencils, paper clips, and typing paper are supplies of a food processing firm.*

supply the quantity of an item of goods or a service that is available for sale in the market. ▶ *Supply has a strong correlation to demand.*

supply curve a graphic representation of variations in the quantity of a product that will be offered at different prices. ▶ *The supply curve usually says that the more you buy, the cheaper the price.*

supply side economics AND **trickle-down economics** an economic theory contending that cuts in the tax rate will stimulate the economy. ▶ *Supply side economics was proposed by Arthur Laffer.*

support price a price of a commodity set to insure that the producer receives payment that is equal in purchasing power to that of the same amount in a previous period. (See also *parity.*) ▶ *The government threatened to remove all the support prices.*

surcharge an extra charge or cost. ▶ *There is a surcharge on rental cars that are driven only one way rather than round-trip.*

surety someone who guarantees the performance of another. ▶ *Tom refused to act as surety on his brother's performance.*

surety bond a guarantee by a third party to insure that a contractual agreement between two other parties is carried out under penalty of forfeiture of the bond. ▶ *The names of the three parties involved in a surety bond are principal, surety, and obligee.*

surplus the excess of assets over liabilities and the stated or par value of capital stock. (See also *earned surplus.*) ▶ *The company hasn't generated any surplus in years.*

surrender value the money given to an insured individual by an insurance company on a life insurance policy that has been cancelled before its maturity date. ▶ *The surrender value of this policy is $10,000.*

surtax an additional tax that is added to another tax already in effect. (See also *surcharge.*) ▶ *A surtax is based on the amount of the basic tax.*

suspended trading a temporary halt in the trading of a security. ▶ *Suspended trading usually occurs because of a pending news release on the status of a company.*

suspense account a temporary account in which receipts or disbursements are carried until they can be properly identified and disposed of. ▶ *Our accountant set up a suspense account for cash receipts from customers who could not be immediately identified.*

suspension a disciplinary action in which an employee is not allowed to report for work for a specified period of time. ▶ *Jack's suspension for fighting lasted one week.*

swap arrangement an agreement whereby two or more individuals or institutions exchange something. ▶ *A swap arrangement may involve the exchange of goods, buildings, land, or other property.*

sweatshop a business enterprise that subjects its employees to long hours, low pay, and often, harsh supervision. ▶ *I got tired of working for that sweatshop and quit.*

sweep account an account, such as a money market account attached to a brokerage account, to receive, periodically and automatically, interest, dividends, and revenue from the sale of securities. ▶ *Any funds left in the account are put into my sweep account each Friday.*

sweepstakes a sales promotion in which customers enter a contest to win prizes. ▶ *In a sweepstakes, entrants typically write their name, address, and phone number to have a chance at winning, and there is usually no obligation to buy something to enter.*

sweetheart contract a collective bargaining agreement that is favorable to the employer and the union officials, but not to the rank and file membership of the union. ▶ *A sweetheart contract is sometimes established with a bribe.*

swing shift See *second shift.*

symbolic logic the technique of substituting symbols for statements, propositions, numbers, classes of things, or functional systems. ▶ *An algebraic formula is an example of symbolic logic.*

symbolic model a representation of reality in which symbols are used to illustrate the relationships involved. ▶ *A-L=P is a symbolic model of the balance sheet for a business in which A=assets, L=liabilities, and P=proprietorship of owner's equity.*

sympathy strike a strike in which a union that has no direct dispute with the company but simply wishes to show support for the demands of another union with workers at the same company. ▶ *A sympathy strike provides indirect pressure on an employer.*

syndicate a combination of individuals formed to achieve a common business objective. ▶ *A typical syndicate would be a group of investment bankers acting together to underwrite and distribute a new issue of securities.*

synergy the idea that the whole is greater than the sum of its parts. ▶ *Synergy in business recognizes the importance of individuals to the operation of the business.*

synthetic process AND **synthetic production** a manufacturing process whereby several raw materials are combined to form new products. ▶ *Rayon is created through a synthetic process.*

synthetic production See the previous entry.

system a series of interrelated or interdependent parts operating sequentially according to a predetermined plan toward the accomplishment of some goal or series of goals. ▶ *We had to expand the mail system in our plant.*

systemic discrimination the use of employment practices that unintentionally discriminate against protected classes. ▶ *A require-ment that a worker be able to lift 60 pounds may be systematic discrimination against members of protected classes who cannot do so.*

systems analysis an approach to analyzing and solving problems through a systematic examination of alternatives. ▶ *Systems analysis is conducted on the basis of resource cost and the benefit associated with each alternative.*

T

10-K a report prepared annually by companies issuing stock. ▶ *A 10-K is required by the Securities and Exchange Commission.*

t account a form of account used to demonstrate the effect of an accounting transaction or a series of transactions, or for solving accounting problems. ▶ *In a t account, the name of the account appears across the top with the debits on the left side and the credits on the right side.*

t/t See *tank truck.*

Taft-Hartley Act of 1947 a Federal act that established a balance of power between unions and employers. ▶ *The Taft-Hartley Act of 1947 is an amendment to the Wagner Act of 1935.*

take-home pay the actual amount of wages or salary a worker receives after all deductions have been made for items such as taxes, FICA, insurance, etc. ▶ *Jill's take-home pay is about $30,000 per year.*

takeover the acquisition of one business enterprise by another. ▶ *A takeover is carried out through purchase, exchange of capital, or other similar means.*

tally to record, compute, or score. ▶ *Frank will tally the accounts payable.*

tangible something that is real and can be physically touched. ▶ *Equipment, desks, and computers are all tangible.*

tangible asset AND **tangibles** a capital asset having physical existence. ▶ *A building is a tangible asset.*

tangible premise a fact taken into consideration in the managerial planning process that can be expressed as a quantity or specific value. ▶ *Plant capacity is a tangible premise.*

tangibles See *tangible asset.*

tank truck AND **t/t** a motor vehicle that has been constructed to carry fluids such as oil, gasoline, or acid. ▶ *The volume of a tank truck usually runs from 4,000 to 8,000 gallons.*

tanker 1. a very large oceangoing vessel that has been constructed to carry fluids. ▶ *The most common tanker is an oil tanker.* 2. a motor vehicle that has been constructed to carry fluids. ▶ *Tanker is another name for tank truck.*

tape librarian a worker who maintains control over the reels of magnetic tape used by computers. ▶ *A tape librarian issues magnetic tape to the computer operator, returns it to storage when the operator is finished with it, and otherwise sees that the tape is taken care of.*

tare the weight of a container, and any packing material, exclusive of its contents. ▶ *Tare may apply to the weight of a transportation vehicle, exclusive of its contents.*

target company a company that has been chosen by a *raider* as a possible company to take over. ▶ *The ABC Company seems to be a target company of the XYZ Company.*

target market that part of the market possessing the characteristics of typical customers. ▶ *A target market for a certain sports car may be males between the ages of 25 and 45 who earn between $40,000 and $70,000 annually.*

target rate of return the desired rate of return on an investment. ▶ *The target rate of return on the Smith investment is 23%.*

tariff a duty imposed by a government on imported or exported goods. ▶ *A tariff is sometimes used to raise revenue or to protect domestic firms from foreign competition.*

task a definite amount of work assigned to a worker. ▶ *A task is simply a unit of work.*

task list a detailed enumeration of the individual tasks comprising an operation. ▶ *A task list is used frequently in industrial engineering studies.*

task team a group of people assembled to accomplish a particular organizational objective. ▶ *A task team is temporary in nature and is disbanded when its work is accomplished.*

tax an assessment levied by a government. ▶ *A tax is assessed on individuals and businesses to raise money for the government.*

tax accounting that branch of accounting dealing with taxes and tax laws. ▶ *Tax accounting includes the preparation of tax returns.*

tax avoidance a legal method of avoiding the payment of a tax. ▶ *Tax avoidance means taking full advantage of all possible deductions and exemptions.*

tax base the valuation or unit to which a tax rate is applied to determine the amount of tax payable. ▶ *An individual's income is an example of a tax base.*

tax burden the amount of taxes that must be paid by an individual or organization. ▶ *The tax burden on this year's income will be $1,250,000.*

tax credit   a direct reduction in the amount of taxes owed. ▶ *A tax credit is given for child and dependent care expenses.*

tax evasion   an illegal effort to avoid the payment of taxes. (See also *tax fraud.*) ▶ *Failure to report taxable income is tax evasion.*

tax exempt   not subject to taxes. ▶ *Property which belongs to a church is tax exempt.*

tax exempt bond   a security of a state, city, and certain other public authorities whose interest payments are excluded by Federal law from the payment of income taxes. ▶ *With a tax exempt bond, the bondholder pays no taxes on income received from the bond.*

tax fraud   the crime of paying less taxes than owed. (See also *tax evasion.*) ▶ *She spent two years in jail for tax fraud.*

tax lien   a claim made by a taxing agency against a person or firm for nonpayment of taxes. ▶ *A tax lien is imposed for nonpayment of school taxes.*

tax loophole   an omission, a discrepancy, or a discriminatory provision in the tax laws that permits a taxpayer to legally avoid the payment of taxes or to pay less taxes than if the loophole had not existed. ▶ *If you discover a tax loophole, you should use it.*

tax sharing   the practice of a tax being levied and collected in one political entity and shared with another political entity. ▶ *The Federal government practices tax sharing when it makes grants to states and cities.*

tax shield   a method of legally avoiding taxes on earned income. ▶ *A tax shield is usually created through the establishment of a trust or endowment fund.*

taxable income   the gross income less deductions and exemptions. ▶ *For individuals, taxable income is adjusted gross income less certain allowable deductions and exemptions.*

Taylorism   See *scientific management.*

team building   a managerial technique that seeks to improve the performance of a work group. ▶ *Team building emphasizes the use of goals and goal setting by the team.*

Teamsters Union   See *International Brotherhood of Teamsters.*

teaser ad   an advertisement that reveals little, if anything, about the product being promoted or the manufacturer or seller. ▶ *A teaser ad is designed to arouse curiosity.*

technical analysis   an analysis of securities that bases buy or sell decisions on past performance of the securities. ▶ *Computers are very useful for a technical analysis.*

technological forecasting   the process of predicting advancements and changes in technology. ▶ *Technological forecasting is part guessing and part research.*

technological unemployment   the unemployment caused by any change in the methods of production. ▶ *Typically, technological unemployment refers to unemployment resulting from the replacement of workers by machines.*

teleconferencing   the use of computers or television for the purpose of conducting meetings involving persons in different geographical locations. ▶ *Teleconferencing provides convenience and can result in substantial cost savings.*

telefacsimile See *facsimile (transmission).*

telemarketing the use of the telephone in promoting, and selling products or services, as well as performing all customer service functions. ▶ *Telemarketing usually refers to selling products or services over the telephone.*

teleprocessing a central computer system processing data from remote locations connected to the central computer by telephone lines. (*Teleprocessing* is a term registered by the International Business Machines Corporation.) ▶ *Our company has just enlarged the teleprocessing center.*

telex an international telecommunications service. ▶ *Telex is Western Union's telecommunications service.*

teller a bank employee who receives or distributes money. ▶ *A teller has direct contact with a bank's customers.*

template a pattern or guide used to make something. (This can be a metal or wood pattern or an electronically stored pattern that is part of a computer program.) ▶ *A computer template saves time for a user.*

tenant one who leases land or a building. ▶ *We have a problem with one particular tenant who is always late with his monthly payment.*

tender an offer of payment in discharge of an obligation. ▶ *Joseph will tender the final payment of his debt today.*

tender offer an offer made to stockholders to buy a specific amount of stock at a specific price and by a specific date. ▶ *A tender offer is usually made publicly.*

term insurance a life insurance policy with no cash surrender value, which covers a fixed period of time instead of a person's entire life. ▶ *Term insurance may be for five years, ten years, or some other period.*

termination the discharging of an employee. (See also *separation.*) ▶ *Termination of 3,000 employees will be necessary to curb costs.*

test market a market area used in evaluating consumer reaction to a new product. ▶ *A test market is used to evaluate acceptance and estimate total sales potential before committing large amounts of resources to the marketing of the product.*

testamentary trust a *trust* established through a will. ▶ *A testamentary trust protects the estate left by a deceased individual.*

testator a person who makes a will. ▶ *The testator willed all his property to her oldest son.*

testimonial a statement by a respected individual promoting the value of a product, service, or company. ▶ *A testimonial gives credibility to a product, service, or company.*

testing bureau a service used by retail establishments for the purpose of checking products before making volume purchases. ▶ *A* *testing bureau helps alleviate risk in buying certain unknown products.*

The Street See *Wall Street.*

Thematic Apperception Test a projective form of personality test in which the person being tested interprets a series of illustrations. ▶ *The Thematic Apperception Test was developed in the late 1930s by Henry Murray, an American psychologist.*

Theory X a view that the average person has an inherent dislike of work, lacks ambition, wishes to avoid responsibility, and must be coerced and controlled in order to accomplish organizational goals. ▶ *Theory X is the traditional view of human behavior and motivation as described by Douglas McGregor.*

Theory Y a view that physical and mental effort are natural, that people will seek out responsibility under proper conditions, that ingenuity and creativity are widely distributed qualities, and that under present industrial conditions, human potential is only partially utilized. ▶ *Theory Y is a more flattering view of humans than Theory X.*

Theory Z a Japanese view of management, human behavior, and motivation emphasizing participative management, trust, tradition, shared values, etc. ▶ *Theory Z was described by William Ouchi.*

therblig a basic work element. (The term was coined by Frank B. Gilbreth to refer to any of the seventeen elementary subdivisions that he identified in a cycle of work

motions. *Therblig* is Gilbreth spelled backward.) ▶ *How many therbligs does it take to pick up a telephone receiver?*

thin market AND **narrow market** a market condition in which there are relatively few bids to buy or offers to sell. ▶ *A thin market may be for a single item or may refer to an entire market.*

think tank a research department or firm. (Informal or colloquial.) ▶ *A think tank may be the research department or unit in any organization.*

third market transaction a security transaction that takes place off the stock exchange premises. (Said of the purchase and sale of securities between two or more institutional buyers.) ▶ *Most company takeovers are third market transactions.*

third party a person affected by an action but not directly involved. ▶ *A third party has no legal interest in a particular transaction.*

third shift AND **graveyard shift** an eight-hour work shift beginning at approximately midnight. ▶ *The third shift has a lot of night owls on it.*

Third World the underdeveloped countries with growing economies. ▶ *The Third World consists of certain countries in Asia, Africa, and Latin America.*

thrift institution a savings bank or a savings and loan association. ▶ *A thrift institution typically makes loans on residential property.*

thrift shop a retail store selling used goods. ▶ *A thrift shop is usually established by charitable* *organizations to raise money.*

throughput the middle step in data processing. ▶ *Throughput occurs between input and output.*

throughput time the productivity of a machine or system. ▶ *Throughput time is measured in terms of output per unit of time.*

throw the number of lines per vertical inch that can be printed by a typewriter. ▶ *The most common throw is six.*

Thurstone Temperament Schedule a personality test that attempts to measure seven personality traits. ▶ *The Thurstone Temperament Schedule is useful in matching employees to jobs.*

ticker (tape) the system that prints prices and volumes of securities trades that take place on an exchange. ▶ *The ticker ran many hours late on the day of the crash.*

tickler a device, such as notes on a calendar or a special computer program, that provides a reminder that something needs to be done. ▶ *A tickler serves as a reminder and a follow-up file.*

tight money an economic condition in which the money supply is limited and interest rates are increasing. ▶ *Changes in monetary policies can cause tight money.*

time bill a bill of exchange that is payable at a fixed or determinable future date rather than immediately. (Compare with *sight bill.*) ▶ *All of the time bills are paid at the last possible minute.*

time deposit a bank deposit that normally bears interest. (Check writing is not permitted in a *time deposit.*) ▶ *In a time deposit, the funds are deposited under terms of an agreement whereby the bank may require the depositor to give advance notice of intention to withdraw all or part of the funds.*

time loan a loan payable at some specified future date. ▶ *A time loan cannot be terminated by either the borrower or lender before the specified date.*

time log a record maintained by a worker on which the worker lists each activity performed, the amount of time spent, and the number of items processed. ▶ *A time log is usually maintained on a daily basis.*

time management the process of allocating time devoted to daily activities in such a way that maximum productivity is achieved. ▶ *Time management attempts to eliminate wasted time.*

time measurement unit AND **TMU** a unit of time in the *Methods-Time Measurement* system of predetermined elemental time data. ▶ *A TMU is equal to 0.00001 hour or 0.00006 minute.*

time series a sequence of values corresponding to successive time points or periods. ▶ *A time series deals with historical data.*

time sharing the use of a computer for two or more purposes or by two or more people during the same overall time period. ▶ *Time sharing is accomplished by interspersing component actions in very short time periods.*

time study a procedure whereby the time for performing an operation or any part thereof is determined through actual observation and timing of the work being performed. ▶ *A stopwatch is the basis for virtually any time study.*

time utility the usefulness or value of a product because of its availability at the time it is needed. ▶ *Time utility refers to having a product available when the customer desires it most.*

tip 1. inside information. ▶ *A tip in the stock market refers to insider trading.* 2. an extra financial compensation for performing a job well. ▶ *The waiter in the restaurant received a $10 tip from the patron who was pleased with the service.*

title a document that shows evidence of ownership. ▶ *When Harry bought the car, he immediately received the title.*

title block the section of a blueprint, drawing, set of specifications, etc., which carries the title of the item, its creator, company name, scale of the drawing, and the effective date of the drawing. ▶ *A title block usually appears in the lower right-hand corner of a drawing.*

title insurance insurance protecting the rights of ownership of a person who has received the title to the ownership of property. ▶ *Title insurance is a form of contract that protects owners against other claims of ownership.*

title retaining note a time purchase in which the owner retains title to the property in question until such time as the property is paid for. ▶ *A title retaining note is*

common when an automobile is purchased.

TMU See *time measurement unit.*

tolerance the limits within which the measurements of a machined item will be considered acceptable. ▶ *These precision parts are manufactured with very high tolerance.*

tombstone ad a newspaper advertisement announcing a new issue of securities. ▶ *A tombstone ad is not necessarily an offer to buy or sell.*

ton-mile a unit of measurement used in the transportation industry. ▶ *A ton-mile is the equivalent of transporting one ton a distance of one mile.*

tool control that function that controls the distribution and use of tools employed in the production or maintenance operations of a firm. ▶ *With tool control, tools are usually issued for use from a tool warehouse to an individual for the performance of a certain job or for a given period of time.*

tort an injury to a person, property, or right of another not arising from contract. ▶ *A tort is a civil wrong.*

total quality management AND **TQM** a philosophy emphasizing quality of goods or services which includes strategies for seeking continuous improvement in quality. ▶ *Total quality management typically takes a top-down approach, but must have company-wide support to be truly successful.*

TQM See the previous entry.

trade 1. a swap of one item for another. ▶ *A trade is usually an* *even exchange.* **2.** a profession. ▶ *To make himself more employable, Wilbur is learning a new trade.*

trade acceptance a draft drawn by the seller of goods on the buyer and accepted by the buyer. ▶ *In a trade acceptance, the buyer becomes the acceptor.*

trade advertising the process of placing advertisements for consumer products in certain trade publications. ▶ *The purpose of trade advertising is to encourage retailers to buy particular products.*

trade agreement an agreement between countries that affects trade. ▶ *A trade agreement may stimulate or restrict trade.*

trade association an organization of business firms in a particular trade or field of work. ▶ *A trade association provides for the interchange of information, the establishment of standards, and other activities of interest and benefit to its members.*

trade barrier any regulation or restriction that interferes with the free exchange of goods and services between different political jurisdictions. ▶ *A tariff is a trade barrier.*

trade credit AND **mercantile credit** the credit extended by one businessperson to another when goods are sold for resale or commercial use, but payment is postponed. ▶ *A trade credit creates an account receivable.*

trade deficit the excess of imports over exports. ▶ *Trade barriers can help turn around a trade deficit.*

trade discount a deduction from list price of an article. ▶ *A trade discount is normally expressed as a percentage.*

trade-in the used merchandise accepted as partial payment for some new item purchased. ▶ *A trade-in is frequently accepted when buying a new car.*

trade magazine a publication targeted to a particular trade, industry, or profession. ▶ *A trade magazine exists for just about every industry in the United States.*

trade name the name under which a product is sold or marketed. ▶ *In the U.S., it is not illegal for a company to mention the trade name of a competitor in advertisements.*

trade off the giving up of one thing for another. ▶ *Paula made a trade off when she decided to enlist in the military for four years in order to receive substantial college benefits after the four years.*

trade secret a formula or method known only to a certain firm, which gives that firm an advantage over its competitors. ▶ *In some instances, a trade secret is technically a monopoly.*

trade show an exhibition of goods and services targeted to members of a particular trade association. ▶ *A trade show in the restaurant industry includes samples of food products that attendees can taste to see if the products would be appropriate for their restaurants.*

trade surplus the excess of exports over imports. ▶ *Many countries would enjoy seeing a trade surplus year after year.*

trade term a condition under which goods are sold or purchased. ▶ *A common trade term is 1-10, net 30, which means that the purchaser is entitled to take a 1 percent discount if he pays in ten days; otherwise, the net amount of the invoice is payable in thirty days.*

trade union See *labor union.*

trademark a distinctive identification of a manufactured product or of a service. ▶ *A trademark may take the form of a name, a sign, a motto, or an emblem.*

trader one who buys and sells something. ▶ *In the United States, a trader is typically one who buys and sells securities.*

trading area the geographic area from which consumers are drawn to a retail store or a retail shopping district, or the area from which retailers are drawn to a wholesale firm or wholesale center. ▶ *The trading area of our store is the easternmost part of Dallas County in Texas.*

(trading) floor the trading area where stocks and bonds are bought and sold on a stock exchange. ▶ *The floor of the New York Stock Exchange is a noisy, busy, exciting place to be.*

trading post a location on the floor of a stock exchange where stocks are traded in multiples of ten rather than in *round lots.* ▶ *We need to make sure we have a broker at the trading post throughout the day.*

trading stamp a coupon, offered by a retailer to a purchaser, in return for spending a certain amount of money. ▶ *Once a customer has accumulated a significant number of trading stamps, the customer can redeem them for a wide variety of products.*

traffic **1.** trade between different businesses or countries. ▶ *Traffic between the two countries has come to a halt until an agreement can be reached.* **2.** the number of people entering or passing by a given establishment. ▶ *Traffic has been particularly good today, just look at our receipts.*

traffic management that function of a firm charged with the responsibility of planning, organizing, directing, and controlling the firm's transportation requirements. ▶ *According to traffic management, we will need to purchase three more trucks.*

traffic manager a person who is charged with the management of the transportation function of a firm. ▶ *The traffic manager has developed a more efficient means of transporting our goods.*

trailer the part of a motor vehicle that carries the actual cargo. ▶ *The trailer itself is pulled by a motorized vehicle.*

transaction account an account with a financial institution with withdrawals by negotiable instruments. ▶ *An example of a transaction account is a NOW account.*

transaction cost the cost of buying or selling an investment. ▶ *The cost of billing is a transaction cost.*

transfer the passage of property from one party to another. ▶ *Transfer usually includes the title* *to the property being traded.*

transfer agent an agent appointed by a corporation to make legal transfers in the ownership of its common stock. ▶ *A transfer agent is sometimes responsible for maintaining a current list of stockholders and distributing dividends.*

transfer tax a tax levied on the transfer of stock. ▶ *The Federal government and some states levy a transfer tax on the sale or other transfer of ownership of shares of stock.*

transportation the shipping of goods or the moving of people. ▶ *Transportation involves significant coordination to ensure that shipments arrive at the appropriate time and in sufficient quantities.*

travel agent a person or firm who handles travel arrangements and hotel accommodations for the general public. ▶ *A travel agent can be helpful in finding the lowest airfare.*

traveler's check a special check issued by banks and other institutions, usually for a fee, for use by travelers. ▶ *The use of a traveler's check protects the purchaser from the loss that might occur if currency were stolen or inadvertently lost.*

traveler's letter of credit a letter of credit addressed by a bank to its correspondent bank authorizing the person named in the letter to draw drafts on the issuing bank to the extent of the credit specified. ▶ *A traveler's letter of credit is usually paid for in advance.*

treasurer the corporate officer responsible for the receipt, custody, and disbursement of corporate funds. ▶ *In some instances, the treasurer of a firm is also the controller.*

treasuries negotiable instruments sold by the U.S. government. ▶ *Treasuries is a shortened name for treasury securities.*

treasury a location where valuables are kept or an account where records of cash are kept. ▶ *Our treasury is in dismal shape.*

Treasury bill an obligation of the United States Treasury, maturing in less than one year. ▶ *A Treasury bill bears no interest but is sold at a discount from face value.*

Treasury bond 1. a bond issued by the United States Treasury. ▶ *A Treasury bond has a maturity of ten years or longer.* 2. a corporate bond that has been reacquired from the holder. ▶ *A Treasury bond is sometimes kept in the corporate treasury.*

treasury department a department of a government that receives and disburses public money. ▶ *The treasury department of a country is usually responsible for minting coins.*

treasury stock the stock that has been issued by a corporation but has been returned to the control of the corporation. ▶ *Treasury stock is returned to a corporation through purchase or as a gift.*

Treasury Tax and Loan Account a demand deposit account containing funds of the United States Treasury. ▶ *A Treasury Tax and Loan Account is maintained in a* *commercial bank in the name of the Federal Reserve Bank of the district.*

trend   a general inclination or direction of movement. ▶ *The trend in American business is to focus on customer service rather than on the bottom line.*

trend line   a line that describes the relationship between two or more variables over time. ▶ *A trend line is useful in statistical applications.*

trial balance   a list of all debit and credit balances in a ledger to verify their equality. ▶ *A trial balance is usually prepared at the end of the fiscal year.*

trial offer   a promotional offer given to customers to try a new product or service for a specified period of time before making a buying decision. ▶ *As a trial offer, try our magazine for three months for $19.99 instead of the regular price of $29.99.*

trial size product   a very small package of a product given away free or sold for a nominal fee. ▶ *The purpose of a trial size product is to gain consumer acceptance of the product so that the consumer will purchase a larger size.*

trickle-down economics   See *supply side economics.*

troubleshooting   the process of discovering and solving problems. ▶ *Finding out why the computer is not working will require extensive troubleshooting.*

truck wholesaler   See *wagon distributor.*

truckload   a rate classification for moving goods by motor vehicle. ▶

The truckload rate is usually the lowest motor freight rate available and varies from state to state.

truncate   to eliminate or cut off a portion of something. ▶ *In computer programming, to truncate means to round off numbers to the nearest whole number.*

truncated account   an account in which the customer does not receive cancelled checks. ▶ *The reason a customer may want a truncated account is because it is a cheaper account.*

trust   a fiduciary arrangement in which property is held and administered by one party for the benefit of another party. ▶ *A person managing a trust is known as the trustee.*

trust company   an institution that engages in the business of settling estates, administering trusts, administering guardianships, and performing other related services for individuals and business organizations. ▶ *A trust company is usually chartered by the state.*

trust indenture   a written document containing the terms and conditions of a trust. ▶ *A trust indenture normally contains a description of all property placed in the trust.*

trust officer   the individual who manages the trust department in a bank. ▶ *In some cases, the trust officer is also on the board of directors.*

trust receipt   a document acknowledging the responsibility for property held in trust for a specified party. ▶ *A trust receipt is used in securing a debt.*

trustee an individual who holds money or property for another. ▶ *A trustee holds legal title to property.*

Truth in Lending Act See *Consumer Credit Protection Act of 1968.*

tummies frozen pork bellies, the source of bacon. (Slang.) ▶ *The price of tummies plummeted early in the session.*

turnaround time the time required to perform, complete, and present or deliver a job or project. ▶ *The turnaround time on the repair of this computer is about four weeks.*

turnkey pertaining to a project or system that can be used immediately without further purchases or elaborate setup. (Refers to an automobile where you simply turn the key and drive off.) ▶ *XYZ Company makes the most cost efficient turnkey system for library circulation management.*

turnover **1.** the number of times during a given period that the inventory of a firm is sold. ▶ *Turnover is usually examined once a year.* **2.** the number of employees who voluntarily or involuntarily terminate their employment with a firm during a given period. ▶ *The high turnover is adversely impacting our production efficiency.*

turnover cost the expense involved in terminating or discharging employees and in recruiting, selecting, and training other employees to fill the vacancies created. ▶ *The turnover cost for each employee who is terminated at this company is about $10,000.*

two-bin system an approach to

inventory control in which every item in stock is stored in two bins. ▶ *In a two-bin system, items in the first bin constitute the working stock and items in the second bin constitute the reserve stock.*

two-dollar broker an independent stockbroker who executes orders for other brokers. (Slang. The term refers to charging a flat two dollars per hundred-dollar value for executing orders.) ▶ *Sam worked for years as a two-dollar broker, and retired at the age of 55.*

two-fer (one) a promotional technique in which something is sold in quantities of two for the price of only one. ▶ *A two-fer sale is on for computer disks; we can get two disks but pay for only one!*

two-name paper AND **double-name paper** a note for which two persons or entities are liable for payment at maturity. ▶ *The trust held a lot of two-name paper, much of which would never be worth anything.*

two-tier wage system a pay structure that bases pay for the same job on the date of hire. ▶ *Typically in a two-tier wage system, workers who have higher seniority receive higher wages than recent hires.*

tying agreement See the following entry.

tying contract AND **tying agreement** an arrangement whereby a seller sells or leases a particular product or line of products only on condition that the buyer also purchase or lease another product or line of products, or that the buyer refrain from buying or leasing similar products from other sellers. ▶ *Under Section 3 of the Clayton Act of 1914, in some instances a tying contract is illegal.*

typeface the printing surface of type. ▶ *This sentence is in an italic typeface.*

type font an assortment of type of one style and size. ▶ *Times Roman is a type font.*

type I error the probability of rejecting a hypothesis that is true. ▶ *A type I error is represented by α, the Greek letter alpha.*

type II error the probability of accepting a hypothesis that is not true. ▶ *A type II error is represented by β, the Greek letter beta.*

U

ultimate consumer a person who purchases goods or services for personal or family use, or for household consumption. ► *An ultimate consumer plans to use the products or services purchased and not resell them.*

ultra vires "beyond the power." (Latin. Refers to an act of a corporation that is outside the purposes and ordinary business of a corporation. Such acts are not legal.) ► *Ultra vires acts are treated differently by the laws of the various states.*

unadjusted rate of return a method of estimating rate of return. ► *Unadjusted rate of return is calculated by dividing income by average investment for a certain period of time.*

unavoidable delay allowance a delay that is beyond the control of the worker and prevents the worker from doing productive work. ► *An example of an unavoidable delay allowance is a delay provided for a possible machine breakdown.*

uncollected funds the checks in a bank deposit that have not been collected by the depository bank. ► *A bank customer may not withdraw money represented by uncollected funds.*

uncollectible account See *bad debt.*

uncovered option See *naked option.*

under the table an unethical or illegal agreement or arrangement. ► *The congressman received money under the table for his help in defeating the bill.*

undercapitalized a condition that exists when a business has insufficient amounts of ownership funds to support the size of an operation. ► *From our financial statements,*

I don't see how we can begin this new project because we are simply undercapitalized.

underemployed   a condition that exists when a person works at a job that does not fully utilize the person's capacity or ability. ▶ *A nuclear scientist employed as an elevator operator is underemployed.*

underground economy   that portion of the economy in which transactions are not reported for taxation purposes, such as cash sums paid to workers and all illegal money transactions. ▶ *The underground economy does not necessarily include only illegal acts.*

underinsured   a person or company that does not have sufficient insurance to cover all losses. ▶ *When it comes to medical insurance, many people in the U.S. are underinsured.*

understudy training   a form of training in which a person is being developed to assume, at a future time, the full duties and responsibilities of the position currently held by the person's immediate superior. ▶ *The concept of understudy training is borrowed from the theatrical arts.*

underwrite   1. to insure. ▶ *The insurance company agreed to underwrite our policy.* 2. to agree to buy any unsold shares of a security. ▶ *To make the offering more attractive, the investment banker agreed to underwrite the securities.*

underwriter   1. a person or firm that assumes an insurance risk in return for compensation. ▶ *Every insurance company is an underwriter.* 2. an investment banker or

investment banking syndicate that agrees to buy any unsold shares of a security. ▶ *An underwriter agrees to guarantee the sale of a security and use diligent efforts to market the issue.*

underwriting syndicate   a joint venture by two or more investment bankers to purchase an issue of securities from a corporation and re-sell them to the public. ▶ *An underwriting syndicate assists in the marketing of securities.*

unearned income AND **unearned revenue**   funds that have been paid in advance for goods or services to be provided in the future. ▶ *The money we received this month as payment for next month's rent is unearned income.*

unearned revenue   See the previous entry.

unemployable   individuals who cannot be employed because they lack skills, training, education, etc. ▶ *I don't know why she applied for this position; she is unemployable.*

unemployment   the condition in which people who are willing and able to work cannot find gainful employment. ▶ *Unemployment is a frustrating experience for many.*

unemployment compensation   the payments from the government to unemployed workers who meet the requirements and qualifications established by state laws. ▶ *In general, to be eligible for unemployment compensation, a worker must be unemployed involuntarily, be willing and able to take offered work, have previously worked in a position covered by* *unemployment compensation, and have completed a specific waiting period.*

unemployment insurance a type of insurance designed to protect a worker from financial loss as a result of involuntary loss of employment and the inability to secure other gainful work. ▶ *Premiums for unemployment insurance are collected by the Federal and state governments in the form of a payroll tax.*

unenforceable contract a contract that may not be enforced by legal action, although it may create an obligation. ▶ *An example of an unenforceable contract is a verbal agreement that is required to be in writing, but isn't.*

unexpired costs See *prepaid expenses.*

unfair competition an imitation or the blatant copying of another's advertising or product; any other unethical or illegal practices designed to secure a seller a larger share of the market. ▶ *Unfair competition includes misleading advertising, infringement on a trademark, discriminatory pricing, dumping, selling below cost, use of tying contracts.*

unfair trade practice a business practice designed to force a competitor out of business, to deceive consumers, to create a monopoly, or to substantially lessen competition. ▶ *Examples of unfair trade practices are false or misleading advertising, inaccurate product labeling, and price cutting.*

Uniform Guidelines on Employee Selection Procedures a set of procedures and regulations developed by the Federal government to regulate hiring practices. ▶ *The Uniform Guidelines on Employee Selection Procedures assists employers in assuring that they do not discriminate on the basis of race, color, sex, religion, or national origin.*

unincorporated not incorporated; not formed into a legal entity. ▶ *If an unincorporated company possesses the characteristics of an incorporated one, it will be taxed as an incorporated entity.*

union an organization of workers created for the purposes of securing higher wages, shorter hours, improved working conditions, greater benefits, etc., from an employer. ▶ *Management usually deals with a union rather than individual workers.*

union contract AND **labor agreement** the formal collective bargaining agreement between a union and a firm. ▶ *After many hours of negotiating, a union contract was finally signed.*

union dues the fees paid for the privilege of membership in a union. ▶ *Next year, union dues will increase by 10%.*

union label a label on a product that identifies the product as one made by *union labor.* ▶ *Some union members will purchase a product only if it has a union label on it.*

union labor workers who are organized in a union as opposed to those who are not. ▶ *Union labor costs more per hour than nonunion labor.*

union made goods manufactured or produced by union labor. (The words "*Union made*" frequently appear on labels of consumer goods and inform purchasers that the goods were produced by union workers.) ▶ *My shoes are union made.*

union security the right of a union to exist within a particular company. ▶ *Provisions for union security are usually made in collective bargaining agreements.*

union shop an arrangement whereby all employees within a collective bargaining unit are required to join the union and to maintain membership as a condition of employment. (See also *modified union shop*.) ▶ *A union shop is permissible only where state law allows it.*

union steward a worker in a given department or work unit who represents the union. ▶ *A union steward collects dues, solicits new members, posts union announcements, and represents workers in certain contacts with management.*

unissued stock the shares of stock in a corporation that have been authorized but have not been made available for sale. ▶ *Unissued stock differs from treasury stock in that treasury stock has been issued, sold, and reacquired by the corporation in some manner.*

unit bank a single, independent bank that conducts all of its operations at one office. ▶ *John prefers to put his money in a unit bank because he feels the customer service is much better there.*

unit time standard the amount of time required by a qualified worker, performing at a normal rate of speed under uniform conditions and experiencing normal fatigue and delay, to produce one unit of output. ▶ *A unit time standard is the most common type of work measurement standard.*

United States Department of Agriculture AND **USDA** a Federal department formed in 1862 to improve farms, conserve natural resources, and inspect and grade the quality of food products. ▶ *The inspector from the United States Department of Agriculture made a careful examination of the grain storage area.*

United States Employment Service an agency that supervises a nationwide system of state operated and administered public employment offices. ▶ *The United States Employment Service is an agency of the U.S. Department of Labor.*

unity of command the idea that a subordinate should receive orders from only one superior. ▶ *Because I have to report to three supervisors, there is no unity of command in my department.*

univariate analysis the analysis of values of a single variable. ▶ *Univariate analysis is used in the determination of the standard deviation.*

universal product code AND **UPC** a bar code number used to identify products. ▶ *A universal product code is read by a scanner.*

universe a collection of items or values from which a sample is drawn. ▶ *The sample was too small to tell us anything about the universe we were examining.*

unlimited liability   the right of creditors to claim any and all assets of a debtor in satisfaction of claims held against the business establishment of the debtor. ▶ *Unlimited liability is a characteristic of the sole proprietorship and partnership forms of business enterprise.*

unlisted trading privilege   a condition that occurs when a member of an exchange is allowed to trade a stock although the company has not made application to the exchange for its stock to be listed on the exchange. ▶ *An unlisted trading privilege transaction must have the approval of the Securities and Exchange Commission.*

unpaid dividend   **1.** a dividend that has been declared, but not yet paid. ▶ *An unpaid dividend is a liability.* **2.** a passed [skipped] dividend on cumulative preferred stock. ▶ *The unpaid dividend will be paid next quarter.*

unsecured loan   See *straight loan.*

unskilled labor   **1.** any work that requires little or no training. ▶ *Operating a lever all day is an example of unskilled labor.* **2.** those workers who perform work requiring little or no training. ▶ *Unskilled labor is a smaller percentage of the work force today than it was in the past.*

unsubscribed shares   the shares of stock not sold when a firm issues new stock and offers those shares to current shareholders. ▶ *We had an unusually large number of unsubscribed shares in this offering.*

unwritten law   See *common law.*

up tick AND **plus tick**   a market transaction made at a price higher than the sale immediately preceding it. ▶ *Each up tick is an increase in the price of a security.*

UPC   See *universal product code.*

upgrade   an improvement. ▶ *We made an upgrade in our computer by adding more memory.*

upkeep   the care and maintenance required to maintain equipment, a company, an area, a department, a house, etc. ▶ *The upkeep on this office is getting very expensive.*

upswing   a positive change or acceleration in something. ▶ *The economy is experiencing an upswing.*

upward mobility   the ability to move to a higher socioeconomic status. ▶ *Upward mobility is characterized by flashy cars, high salaries, expensive homes, etc.*

USDA   See *United States Department of Agriculture.*

useful life   the normal operating life of an asset. ▶ *The useful life of something is evaluated in terms of its utility to the owner.*

user friendly   pertaining to computer software or hardware that is easy to use. ▶ *The new accounting program we purchased is very user friendly.*

usury   the lending of money at a rate of interest higher than that allowed by statute. ▶ *Charging someone 50% interest on a loan is definitely usury!*

utility 1. the ability of a product or a service to satisfy human needs or wants. ▶ *The utility of any item depends on how close it comes to an individual's ideal of that item.* **2.** a public service corporation. ▶ *An electric, a gas, a water, or a telephone company are all examples of utilities.*

utilization index AND **efficiency ratio; performance index** a measure of the efficiency of a work center, a group of workers, or an individual worker. ▶ *The utilization index is determined by dividing the total hours worked at standard by the net available hours multiplied by 100.*

V

vacancy rate   the percentage of space that is unoccupied. ▶ *The vacancy rate in this office building is 23%.*

validity   the degree to which a given test measures what it purports to measure. (This is a special use of the term in statistics.) ▶ *Validity is usually expressed as a coefficient of correlation.*

valuation   the assessment of the value or the price of something. ▶ *The valuation of our assets was much lower than I expected it to be.*

value   the worth of an asset. ▶ *Value is usually expressed in terms of money.*

value added retailer AND **VAR**   a seller of goods who combines the goods with additional products or services before offering the goods to consumers. ▶ *A VAR can charge higher prices because of the higher perceived value of the product.*

value added tax AND **VAT**   a tax levied on a product at each step of its manufacture or distribution. ▶ *A value added tax is levied in proportion to the value added to the product by each processing stage.*

value analysis AND **value engineering**   a means of systematically analyzing every component and every operation in the manufacture or processing of a product, and then examining the function and usefulness of each component and operation in relation to cost. ▶ *Value analysis examines not only processing steps but also the material used to make a product.*

value engineering   See the previous entry.

value policy   an insurance policy that establishes an agreed upon value for each item covered in the event of total loss. ▶ *The Smiths' value policy covered fully all the* *art and china they had accumulated in their travels.*

VAR   See *value added retailer.*

variable annuity   an annuity contract providing for the investment of a sum of money in a choice of investment instruments as protection against inflation and erosion of the value of the dollar. ▶ *With a variable annuity, the size of periodic payments to the annuitant will vary from time to time as the underlying values of the securities fluctuate.*

variable cost   a cost that tends to vary with changes in the level of activity. ▶ *Prime examples of variable cost are raw materials costs and direct labor costs.*

variable deduction   an item of a fluctuating nature that is withheld from a worker's payroll check. ▶ *Federal income tax withheld, since it is computed on the basis of gross earnings that may change from one pay period to the next, is an example of a variable deduction.*

variable pricing   a pricing strategy that involves charging customers different prices. ▶ *Variable pricing is common for companies who charge a lower price to not-for-profit firms than they do to for-profit firms.*

variable rate mortgage   a home mortgage in which the interest rate is adjustable over time. ▶ *With a variable rate mortgage, the interest rate charged will fluctuate periodically.*

variance   **1.** the difference between actual profit, expenses, sales, etc., and budgeted profit, expenses, sales, etc., for a given pe-riod. ▶ *Variance from budget may be positive or negative.* **2.** the square of the standard deviation. ▶ *Variance is used to measure the dispersion of a distribution.*

variety store AND **dime store; five and ten cent store**   a retail store that carries a large selection of low cost merchandise. (Although there are few products that can be sold for as little as 5 or 10 cents, the use of the term persists, especially with older people.) ▶ *The variety store used to be known as a dime store or a five and ten cent store.*

VAT   See *value added tax.*

VDT   See *video display terminal.*

velocity of money   the number of times that an average dollar is spent during a given period. ▶ *Velocity of money is usually computed for a period of one year.*

vendee   a purchaser of goods or services. ▶ *A vendee is a buyer.*

vending machine   a machine that dispenses items upon the deposit of a coin in a slot. ▶ *Common items purchased from a vending machine include cigarettes, candy, and coffee.*

vendor   a seller of goods. ▶ *A new vendor has opened a store on the same street as our business.*

vendor's lien   the right of a seller to hold title to property until the purchase price has been recovered. ▶ *A vendor's lien is usually implied rather than expressed in writing.*

venture   an undertaking that is usually daring and of doubtful outcome. ▶ *A new venture is often associated with entrepreneurs.*

venture capital   a sum of capital subject to considerable risk. ▶ *The franchisee secured venture capital to open a new unit.*

venture capitalist   an investor willing to undertake great financial risk in hopes of earning a great profit. ▶ *Many new ideas become successful products because of investment by venture capitalists.*

venue   the geographical area over which a court exercises its jurisdiction. ▶ *A Federal District Court has a very large venue.*

verbatim   word for word. ▶ *A verbatim transcript contains every word that was said.*

vertical combination   the common ownership of two or more firms or manufacturing concerns engaged in different stages of the production and marketing of goods. ▶ *A vertical combination, if used effectively, will help cut operating costs.*

vertical cooperative advertising   a form of advertising in which the manufacturer of a product pays for an agreed-upon percentage of the advertising placed by a retailer. ▶ *Vertical cooperative advertising saves advertising dollars for retailers and at the same time gives greater geographical exposure to a manufacturer's product.*

vertical market   a market characterized by one product used by one or a very few industry groups. ▶ *The market for machinery designed to make shoes is a vertical market.*

vested   a right of immediate or future enjoyment that cannot be altered without the express consent

of the party possessing the right. ▶ *When my profit sharing plan is fully vested I will be assured an income sufficient to live on when I retire.*

vested interest   an established claim to real or personal property or to the status quo. ▶ *I have a vested interest in seeing the company grow because I am a stockholder in it.*

vestibule training   a training approach in which an attempt is made to duplicate in the training center, as closely as possible, the material, equipment, and conditions that will be found in the actual workplace. ▶ *Vestibule training is a very effective, though sometimes costly, method of training.*

vicarious liability   the liability one person has for the actions of another. ▶ *Vicarious liability is commonly used in the trucking or delivery industries wherein employers have a legal responsibility for the drivers of the vehicles.*

vice president   a corporate official, normally one level below president. ▶ *When the president dies, Oliver, who is vice president of operations, is expected to take her place.*

video display terminal AND **VDT**   the monitor and keyboard used with a computer. ▶ *The VDT generates a lot of heat.*

videoconferencing   a system whereby several people located in different places geographically, can see and speak to one another. ▶ *Videoconferencing is often used for seminars in which hundreds or even thousands of people can* *watch a seminar without the expense of traveling and actually attending the event.*

vocational training training designed for a specific trade or vocation. ▶ *Nursing, welding, and auto repair are occupations that usually require vocational training.*

voice mail a telephone system in which messages are recorded, stored, and retrieved. ▶ *I left a message on Barry's voice mail.*

void without legal force or not legally binding. ▶ *Because I forgot to sign the check, it is void.*

voidable capable of being rendered void at some time. ▶ *Even though something is voidable, such as a contract, it is still binding until one party wishes to be released.*

voluntary chain an association of retailers who agree to buy exclusively from a certain wholesaler; independent stores forming a buying cooperative. (See also *chain store.*) ▶ *In a voluntary chain, in return for buying from one wholesaler, each retailer obtains a discount, advice on merchandising and retail prices, and the benefit of group advertising and promotion.*

voluntary trust a trust established by a deed of transfer of property made willingly by an individual or other legal entity to a trustee for a specified purpose. ▶ *A voluntary trust may become effective before the donor dies.*

voting right the right of a stockholder to vote at a corporate stockholders' meeting. ▶ *A stockholder's voting right is outlined in the*

corporate charter and in company policies.

voting stock the shares of corporate stock that give the owner the right to vote at corporate stockholders' meetings. ▶ *Common stock is usually voting stock.*

voting trust a trust in which stockholders place their collective shares in the hands of a trustee. ▶ *A voting trust agreement means that the trustee may vote on behalf of the stockholders.*

voucher check a check that shows the particulars of a payment. ▶ *A voucher check usually shows all the accounting details of a payment on a detachable stub.*

voucher system a system whereby invoices and other evidences of liability are collected, audited, recorded, and settled by means of vouchers, voucher checks, and a voucher register. ▶ *A voucher system usually records invoices in chronological order.*

W

wage a payment made to an employee by the employer for work performed. ▶ *A wage is usually expressed in terms of money per hour.*

wage and salary administration that function of personnel management concerned with the development and implementation of sound policies and programs of employee compensation. ▶ *Wage and salary administration encompasses job evaluation, development of wage structures, wage surveys, wage incentives, wage adjustments, supplementary payments, profit sharing, and other pay-related areas.*

wage ceiling the top wage per hour that may be paid to a given class of workers. ▶ *We had to institute a wage ceiling since seniority had pushed up so many salaries.*

wage contour the wage structure of a group of companies linked together by a common product market or labor market. ▶ *A wage contour has occupational, geographic, and industrial dimensions to it.*

wage curve a graphic representation of the relationship between jobs, job classes, and job evaluations and their corresponding wage rates. ▶ *A wage curve is sometimes linear rather than curvilinear.*

wage differential the difference in rates of pay between two jobs. ▶ *If job A pays $6.00 per hour and job B pays $5.50 per hour, the wage differential is $.50.*

wage floor the bottom wage per hour that may be paid to a given class of workers. ▶ *A wage floor is a lower limit on pay.*

wage-price spiral the interaction between wage increases and price increases. ▶ *In a wage-price spiral, an increase in prices leads to* *an increase in wages that leads to further increases in prices.*

wage structure the established levels or ranges of compensation within a labor market, an industry, or a plant. ► *Generally, a wage structure consists of pay grades having a wage spread that goes from a minimum rate of pay to a maximum rate for each pay grade.*

wage survey a study conducted to determine the wage rates paid by other firms in an industry or in a geographical area for identical classifications of work. ► *One can usually get a copy of the results of a current wage survey from certain government agencies or from trade associations.*

Wagner Act of 1935 a Federal statute that gives employees collective bargaining rights, requires employers to bargain in good faith, establishes procedures for conducting elections for union representation, and defines unfair labor practices on the part of the employer. ► *The Wagner Act of 1935 established the National Labor Relations Board.*

wagon distributor AND **truck wholesaler; wagon jobber** a form of merchant middleman who services small retailers from the stock of items carried in the wagon distributor's truck. ► *A wagon distributor must travel widely to reach many customers.*

wagon jobber See the previous entry.

waiver the intentional relinquishing of a known right. ► *A waiver is simply the giving up of a right voluntarily.*

walkout a form of strike in which workers leave work they have begun. ► *One reason for a walkout is to send a message to management that working conditions need to be improved.*

Wall Street AND **The Street; Street** the street in New York where many major financial institutions are located. ► *Wall Street had a negative reaction to the President's proposals.*

Walsh-Healey Act of 1936 a Federal statute stipulating that workers on government contracts in excess of a stated amount must be paid at least the prevailing minimum wage, with time-and-one-half for work in excess of eight hours per day or forty hours per week. ► *The Walsh-Healey Act of 1936 prohibits the employment of males under sixteen years of age and females under eighteen.*

want ads See *classified advertising.*

ward a minor or an incompetent person who is under the control of a guardian. ► *In the U.S., a contract signed by a ward is difficult to enforce.*

warehouse a place where merchandise is stored. ► *With the increase in production, we will need a new warehouse within the next two years.*

warehouse receipt an instrument given by a warehouse manager as evidence of receiving goods or merchandise for storage in the warehouse. ► *A warehouse receipt has printed on it the date goods were placed into storage.*

warehousing the act of storing

goods or merchandise in a warehouse. ▶ *The Acme Company is warehousing all its products in facilities all over the country.*

warrant See *(stock purchase) warrant.*

warranty an assurance by a seller, usually given in writing, that goods or property sold will perform as represented for a specified period of time. ▶ *The warranty states that this radio will be free from defects for 12 months.*

warranty deed an instrument by which a selling party claims to hold good title to the property being sold and is personally liable for any defects in the title that may arise in the future. ▶ *Liens or encumbrances are noted on the warranty deed.*

wash sale the selling of something and then buying an identical number of the same thing again. (The term is used in reference to Federal income taxes. If an investor sells a stock at a large loss and purchases the same stock 30 days before or after the sale, the sale is a *wash sale* and the capital loss cannot be deducted from Federal income taxes.) ▶ *Losses resulting from a wash sale are not tax deductible.*

wasting asset an asset, usually a natural resource, which is consumed in its use. ▶ *A mineral deposit is an example of a wasting asset.*

watered stock the shares of stock issued in excess of the fair value of the assets contributed in exchange for the stock. ▶ *If investors do their homework, they are unlikely to end up purchasing watered stock or other shares of questionable value.*

WATS See *Wide Area Telephone Service.*

waybill a transportation document used to facilitate the movement of freight. ▶ *A waybill is prepared by an agent at the point of origin and contains information such as point of origin, destination, routing, car number and initials, consignor, consignee, description of the goods, weight, and freight charges.*

weak market a market characterized by more sellers than buyers and a decline in prices. ▶ *A weak market is not good for business growth.*

wear and tear that portion of depreciation caused by ordinary use, disuse, passage of time, or action of the elements. ▶ *The wear and tear on the machinery is reflected in our new financial statements.*

weighted application blank an application for employment in which the various items or questions on the form are assigned different values or weights on the basis of the employer's past experience as to which are most important. ▶ *College education would be given little or no weight on a weighted application blank for a carpenter, but would be accorded considerable weight for an accountant.*

weighted average an arithmetic average in which the numbers being averaged are assigned proportional values, or weights, so as to reflect the significance of each number. ▶ *A weighted average is frequently used as a means of attaching importance to the values* *of different stocks that are being averaged. The stock prices of larger companies are given greater weight than those of the smaller companies.*

wellness program a company-sponsored program focusing primarily on the prevention of illness. (Common areas covered in a *wellness program* are alcohol and drug abuse, physical fitness, stress management, job burnout, and AIDS awareness.) ▶ *Since the company introduced its wellness program, absenteeism has been dropping.*

Westinghouse leveling system See *skill and effort rating.*

wheel and deal to negotiate. ▶ *During lunch, we plan to wheel and deal over the proposed contract.*

Wheeler-Lea Act of 1938 a Federal act that broadened the definition of unfair acts or practices in commerce and declared unlawful false or misleading advertising of foods, drugs, cosmetics, and therapeutic devices used in the diagnosis, treatment, or prevention of disease. ▶ *The Wheeler-Lea Act of 1938 amended the Federal Trade Commission Act of 1914.*

when issued the trading of securities on some new basis as soon as the new basis is authorized, but before issuance of the new shares actually takes place. ▶ *When issued occurs in the case of stock splits.*

whipsawed the result of making a wrong buy-sell decision during periods of high price fluctuations. ▶ *Sellers are whipsawed if they sell something at one price and imme-*

diately following the sale, the price goes up.

whistleblower a person who reveals corruption, illegal acts, or other wrongdoings in an organization. ▶ *The whistleblower told her story to the news media.*

white collar crime a nonviolent criminal act committed by businesses or businesspeople—mostly *insider trading, fraud,* and *bribery.* ▶ *The exposure of white collar crime generally leads to a scandal.*

white collar union a labor union comprised primarily of office and professional workers. ▶ *The American Federation of Government Employees is a white collar union.*

white-collar worker a professional or technical practitioner, manager, official, non-farm proprietor, or clerical worker whose job is essentially nonmanual. (Compare with *blue-collar worker.*) ▶ *A white-collar worker usually makes more money than a blue-collar worker.*

white elephant sale a sale held by a business that will soon cease operations. ▶ *Great bargains can be found at a white elephant sale.*

white knight a corporation sought by the target company of a hostile takeover, to save the target company from the acquiring company. (Slang.) ▶ *The tactic of a white knight is usually to offer a much higher price for a target company than the hostile takeover company.*

whole dollar accounting an accounting procedure in which cents are dispensed with and transactions are recorded in terms of dollars only. ▶ *With whole dollar* *accounting, $10.05 would be recorded as $10.00.*

whole life insurance an insurance policy that furnishes protection for a person's entire life rather than for a stipulated period. ▶ *Whole life insurance is usually paid for in annual premiums.*

wholesale the process of selling to customers who buy for resale to others. ▶ *To buy wholesale, one must usually purchase goods in bulk.*

wholesale bank a commercial bank that deals primarily with large business enterprises and other banks. ▶ *A wholesale bank is very different from a retail bank.*

Wholesale Price Index a measure of the monthly changes in wholesale prices compiled by the U.S. Bureau of Labor Statistics. ▶ *A representative group of about 2,000 commodities is included in the Wholesale Price Index.*

wholesale sale a sale of goods to a person or firm that buys primarily for resale to others. ▶ *Anytime goods are purchased for resale the transaction is considered to be a wholesale sale.*

wholesaler a person or firm selling goods to customers who buy primarily for resale. ▶ *A wholesaler is a middleman in the channel of distribution.*

Wide Area Telephone Service AND **WATS** an arrangement whereby a telephone subscriber, for a flat monthly fee, may make or receive an unlimited number of long-distance calls within certain specified large areas. ▶ *The amount of the monthly charge for a WATS line*

depends upon the extent of the calling area.

wildcat strike AND **quickie strike** an illegal work stoppage that has not been called or approved by union leadership. ▶ *Union leaders were furious with members who participated in the wildcat strike.*

will the legal instrument whereby a person disposes of property at death. ▶ *In Julia's will, the house was left to her only daughter.*

windfall profit an unforeseen gain due to a change in the price of an item of goods or a security. ▶ *From the sale of this new product, we received a windfall profit of $100,000!*

window 1. a specified period of time. ▶ *The services are to be scheduled during a narrow window this month.* 2. a portion of a computer screen. ▶ *In order to make the graph, I need to open another window to see the data that goes into the graph.*

window dressing 1. something added to a report or presentation because of its eye appeal. ▶ *The window dressing on the annual report included brightly colored borders, photographs, and several illustrations.* 2. artificially changing items in accounting statements by executing transactions shortly before the end of an accounting period. ▶ *Window dressing is a financial cover-up.*

window envelope a mailing envelope with a transparent or cutout panel that permits the address on the enclosure to serve as the mailing address. ▶ *A window envelope eliminates the need and cost of* *having someone address each envelope separately.*

wire fate an instruction accompanying checks or other items sent for collection to out-of-town banks, requesting that the sending bank be notified by wire whether the item is paid or not. (This is the equivalent of "Please wire me the fate of this transaction." See also *advise fate.*) ▶ *The wire fate instruction was not honored and John lost valuable time waiting for the money.*

wire house a member of a stock exchange that maintains a permanent communications network. ▶ *A wire house maintains its communications network within either its own company, among other correspondent firms, or a combination of the two.*

wire transfer an instruction to a bank to pay or credit a sum of money to a designated payee. ▶ *A wire transfer is known as such because it is sent by telephone, telegraph, or cable.*

withdrawal an act of removing money from a banking institution, credit union, or similar institution. ▶ *He made a withdrawal of $40 from his bank.*

withholding a portion of an employee's income that is withheld by an employer. ▶ *Withholding is used to pay taxes, pensions, insurance, etc.*

withholding tax a tax deducted from a worker's paycheck. ▶ *A withholding tax allows a worker to pay taxes on income as it is earned rather than delaying payment until the end of the year.*

without recourse a statement made by an endorser of an instrument which means that if payment on the instrument is refused, the endorser is not liable. ▶ *Without recourse is typically used on negotiable instruments such as checks.*

without reserve a notice to bidders in an auction that no minimum bid is required on an item. ▶ *In an auction without reserve, a person could, theoretically buy something for one dollar even though the value of the item may be a hundred or even a thousand times that.*

Wonderlic Personnel Test a commonly used test of general intelligence. ▶ *The Wonderlic Personnel Test contains a set of fifty items and requires only twelve minutes to administer.*

word an ordered set of binary code that occupies one storage location and is treated by the computer circuits as a unit and transferred as such. ▶ *Ordinarily, a word is treated by the control unit as an instruction and by the arithmetic unit as a quantity.*

word processing a method of creating and editing text on a computer. ▶ *Word processing has revolutionized the way mass mail is created and sent.*

words per minute AND **WPM** the number of words a person can type within sixty seconds. ▶ *When calculating words per minute, typographical mistakes are subtracted from the total number of words typed.*

work center a distinct portion of an organization, under the direction of a single supervisor, which performs homogeneous work, utilizing similar machines, processes, procedures, methods, etc. ▶ *Normally, a work center is the smallest functional component in an organization.*

work cycle the entire sequence of operations in a task or job. ▶ *The work cycle for this task is actually very short and is comprised of few steps.*

work distribution chart a device used for studying work assignments and job content within a work group. ▶ *A work distribution chart classifies major activities and shows the amount of time each worker, as well as the total work group, spends on each activity.*

work experience the experience gained through employment. ▶ *As you can see from my résumé, I have had a varied and interesting work experience.*

Work Factor system a predetermined elemental time system in which time is proportional to specific factors involved in the work. ▶ *Factors involved in a Work Factor system are body member, distance, direction, weight, control, etc.*

work-in-process AND **goods-in-process** manufactured items in various stages of completion in a factory. ▶ *All work-in-process must be covered with dust cloths overnight.*

work measurement a means of establishing an equitable relationship between the volume of work performed and the amount of manpower utilized in performing that volume. ▶ *The basic purpose*

of work measurement is to specify the amount of time it should take to perform a given amount of activity.

work measurement analyst an individual who, having the necessary training, experience, and personal characteristics, practices *work measurement.* ▶ *The work measurement analyst we hired has done a lot to improve operations here.*

work order a written authorization to perform a specified job or operation. ▶ *A work order is used in production management to initiate the manufacture of a good.*

work sampling a quantitative technique for analyzing the activity times of workers and machines. ▶ *Work sampling, based on the laws of probability, operates under the premise that a random sample drawn from a large group will tend to resemble the group from which it is drawn.*

work sheet a columnar sheet employed by an accountant to record data in a neat and orderly manner. ▶ *The work sheet used to be in a paper and pencil format, but computers have changed that.*

work simplification See *methods analysis.*

work standard See *standard time.*

work unit the basic identification of work accomplished or services performed. ▶ *A work unit is simply the unit count of an activity.*

workaholic a person who works excessively. ▶ *A workaholic usually has health problems or interpersonal problems.*

worker's compensation the cash, medical care, or other similar benefit given to employees who are injured on the job. ▶ *Sometimes, worker's compensation provides money to survivors of an employee who is killed while working.*

worker's compensation insurance a type of insurance that protects employers against liability for accidents sustained in the workplace. ▶ *With worker's compensation insurance, injured employees are paid an amount specified by the laws of each state.*

worker's compensation laws statutes designed to compel employers to assume financial liability for accidents sustained in the workplace by employees. ▶ *The establishment of worker's compensation laws led to improved safety in the workplace.*

working asset an asset, other than a capital asset, used in a firm. ▶ *The raw material used in the manufacture of a product is an example of a working asset.*

working capital the excess of current assets over current liabilities. ▶ *Working capital is a measurement of how well a firm can meet its obligations.*

working class that portion of the total population which works, especially those of lower socioeconomic status. ▶ *In some instances, working class does not include managerial personnel.*

working conditions factors that affect or influence the environment in which employees work. ▶ *Since the early 1900s, working conditions have greatly improved.*

working control sufficient ownership of a company to direct the policies of the company. ▶ *To have working control, one needs to own or control the largest block of shares.*

working papers the schedules, forms, and other papers used by an accountant to prepare balance sheets, income statements, and other financial reports. ▶ *Working papers are used in the collecting, classifying, correcting, and summarizing of information.*

working poor employees who work full time, but not at a rate sufficient enough to improve their standard of living. ▶ *The working poor remain below the poverty level even though they are fully employed.*

workstation that portion of an office or a manufacturing work center where a worker carries out assigned tasks. (Usually not as large as an office.) ▶ *A workstation includes the space required for a machine, desk, file cabinet, auxiliary equipment, etc., used by the worker.*

WPM See *words per minute.*

writ a written formal order of a court. ▶ *A writ contains instructions that have the force of law.*

write-down a decrease in the book value of an asset without a corresponding outlay of cash or property or an inflow of capital. ▶ *We took a write-down on most of the machine tools when we automated.*

write-off the elimination of an asset from a firm's books. ▶ *The firm took a write-off on the*

Springfield facility. It was a total failure.

write-up   the increase in book value of an asset without a corresponding outlay of cash or property or an inflow of capital. ▶ *The installation of a small part allowed us to take a write-up on most of the trucks in our fleet.*

XYZ

X(D)   ex-dividend. (A symbol indicating that stocks are trading without a dividend.) ► *The symbol, XD, is often found in financial newspapers.* ► *The X at the top of the column means ex-dividend.*

yellow-dog contract   a contract of employment under which a worker, as a condition of employment, agrees not to join a union. ► *Under Federal legislation, a yellow-dog contract is illegal.*

yield AND **rate of return; return**   the actual rate of monetary gain on an investment. ► *A yield consists of the dividends, interest, or profit provided by an investment.*

yield to maturity AND **YTM**   the internal rate of return on a bond when it is held to the time of maturity. ► *In computing yield to maturity, interest on the bond must also be included.*

yo-yo   a stock with frequent fluctuations in price. ► *A yo-yo is a risky stock to own.*

youth market   that portion of the market for goods or services represented by people under the age of twenty-five. ► *The youth market is somewhat unpredictable in its buying behavior.*

YTM   See *yield to maturity.*

yuppie   "young urban professional." (Slang acronym. A young, career-oriented person with a high income and education.) ► *Do all yuppies drive those little German cars?*

zero-based budgeting   a method of budgeting in which each item in the proposed budget must be justified. ► *In zero-based budgeting, budgets are created without regard to last year's expenses; in other words, one starts from zero.*

zero coupon bond   a bond that does not pay any interest, but is discounted deeply from its face value when offered for sale. ▶ *The buyer of a zero coupon bond receives the full face value of the bond at the time of maturity.*

zero defects a program designed to improve production quality and encourage error-free performance. ▶ *A method for getting a zero defects program to appeal to employees is to emphasize the employees' pride of workmanship.*

zero growth a condition in which growth is not occurring. ▶ *We are in a state of zero growth—sales have stabilized and we have garnered no new customers.*

zero sum game a game in which the algebraic sum of all gains and losses is zero. ▶ *In a zero sum game, for every gain by the winner, there is an equal loss for the loser.*

zip + four a method of addressing mailing labels with four additional numbers added to the standard five-digit zip code to improve efficiency. ▶ *In zip + four, the four additional digits are connected to the Zip Code with a hyphen.*

zip code a five-digit code developed by the United States Postal Service to simplify the sorting and delivering of mail. ▶ *With the advent of the zip code, mail delivery was made more efficient.*

zipper clause a statement in a collective bargaining agreement that indicates that anything not appearing in the agreement is not agreed upon. ▶ *A zipper clause is good for the duration of the contract.*

zone pricing a pricing system whereby all buyers located within a certain geographical area pay the same delivered price for goods. ▶ *With zone pricing, each region has its own price for a particular good or shipment.*

zoning ordinance a measure passed by a municipal government to control the types of businesses or buildings that are permitted in a given area. ▶ *Our proposed zoning ordinance attempts to prevent retail stores and other entities from being built in the middle of a housing development or neighborhood.*